D0554338

RETOOLING
FOR GROWTH

RETOOLING
FOR GROWTH

*Building a 21st Century Economy
in America's Older Industrial Areas*

RICHARD M. MCGAHEY
JENNIFER S. VEY
editors

*Published in association with The American Assembly
Columbia University*

BROOKINGS INSTITUTION PRESS
Washington, D.C.

Library of Congress Cataloging-in-Publication data
Retooling for growth : building a 21st century economy in America's older industrial areas / Richard M. McGahey and Jennifer S. Vey, editors.
        p.   cm.
"Published in association with The American Assembly, Columbia University."
Summary: "Offers achievable strategies for revitalizing industrial areas and building upon the potential of overlooked resources of economic, physical, and cultural significance. Addresses such challenges as fostering entrepreneurship, reducing poverty and inequality, and augmenting the number of skilled professionals. Provides analysis of healthy economic development practices for public and private sectors"—Provided by publisher.
    Includes bibliographical references and index.
    ISBN 978-0-8157-5556-2 (cloth : alk. paper) 1. Industrial policy—United States. 2. Entrepreneurship—United States. 3. United States—Economic conditions—2001— Regional disparities. I. McGahey, Richard. II. Vey, Jennifer S.

HD3616.U47R47 2008
338.973—dc22   2007051331

9 8 7 6 5 4 3 2 1

The paper used in this publication meets minimum requirements of the American National Standard for Information Sciences—Permanence of Paper for Printed Library Materials: ANSI Z39.48-1992.

Typeset in Adobe Garamond

Composition by Circle Graphics, Inc.

Printed by R. R. Donnelley
Harrisonburg, Virginia.

Contents

v

Foreword

America is a nation of cities and towns: 80 percent of Americans live in or around cities. The past 15 years have been good ones for most of America's cities. Population is growing, crime is down, and livability is up. But many of the nation's cities are struggling to find their place in the new global economy. Most are communities that thrived during the Industrial Revolution in the late 19th century and the first half of the 20th century—Pittsburgh, the former steel capital of the world; Detroit, the former Motor City; Cleveland, once an industrial giant; and dozens of others. These communities are challenged to find viable economic development strategies for the 21st century.

Concentrated mainly in the Northeast and Midwest, these cities are grappling with a series of challenges, including slow job growth, declining home values, a diminishing tax base, and concentrated poverty. These issues undermine their ability to attract and retain the growth industries and skilled workers needed to create a better economic future.

The world economy is going through a major transition that is benefiting some cities and regions and leaving others behind. The growth of global supply chains, the entry of emerging economies into the global workforce, and the mobility of capital are all changing the rules of engagement in the world economy.

The challenge is clear. The future health of our older industrial cities will be determined by their ability to adapt to these changes, reshaping local, state, and federal policies and harnessing the power of private investment to boost global competitiveness.

These cities need policies, practices, and techniques designed to help them overcome their challenges and leverage their assets. Strategies for the future may be radically different from those that worked in the past. We believe that older industrial cities must capitalize on their current economic strengths and grow new economic capacity.

Helping these cities find new ways to grow and thrive is in our national interest. By 2050 demographers estimate that the U.S. population will grow from today's 300 million to 420 million, an increase of 40 percent. Successfully managing this rapid growth requires that we work to help the nation's older industrial cities and regions become healthy, competitive communities where all residents have economic opportunity and a good quality of life.

There are many reasons this work is critical for our nation. We'd like to focus on two.

First, revitalizing and repopulating America's older industrial areas are vital to achieving sustainable economic growth. Both of us have led our institutions in helping to create regional growth that fosters jobs and economic development while respecting the natural environment. To this end, we've worked with business, government, community, and environmental representatives to protect open space and ecologically valuable lands, and invest in the redevelopment of the cities and older suburbs left behind as jobs and people have moved outward.

Second, strengthening older industrial areas simply makes good economic sense. We already have made billions of dollars in infrastructure investments in our older industrial areas. These areas are home to a substantial portion of several states' population—almost 40 percent of the population of Pennsylvania, 30 percent of the population of Michigan, and more than a third of the population of Ohio—representing an enormous economic base. Stronger, more competitive cities mean more jobs, rising incomes, reduced sprawl, and a more efficient, fiscally prudent use of public funds and existing infrastructure.

Finding the best approaches to help these cities become successful competitors in the world economy is a major challenge in itself. Rick McGahey and Jennifer Vey have provided a book that invigorates the discussion in a dramatic way. This is a book of thought-provoking and stimulating essays about how the nation's leaders need to rethink economic development strategies in these older industrial areas. The book is part of a larger project that The American Assembly is conducting to revitalize older industrial cities in America. We are honored to be co-chairs of that effort.

One of us governs a state with many older cities and towns. The other leads the largest bank in the nation, providing banking and other financial services to customers in many of America's older industrial cities. Our contacts with these constituents and customers tell us that while the economies of these areas may be challenged, the spirit of the people living in them is undaunted. Their commitment to building a strong future for their communities is one of our nation's greatest assets.

We look forward to working with The American Assembly, and all Americans, to help our older industrial cities meet the challenges of the global economy in the 21st century.

Hon. Edward G. Rendell
Governor
Commonwealth of Pennsylvania

Kenneth D. Lewis
Chairman and CEO
Bank of America

December 2007

Preface

The United States was not primarily an urban nation just half a century ago. Now our population predominantly lives in metropolitan areas, and our economic future is dependent on their health. The largest 100 metropolitan areas contain 65 percent of America's population and generate 75 percent of the gross domestic product. The economies in most of these metropolitan areas and their cities are thriving, and many of these central cities are the core location for shifts to the knowledge-based global economy of the 21st century.

Though metropolitan areas will be increasingly important, some of the nation's older industrial metropolitan areas are having difficulty finding their niche in today's global marketplace. The economic stagnation of these metropolitan areas, many of which are clustered in the Northeast and Midwest, has many complex causes, including a decline in manufacturing as a share of national employment that rendered older plants obsolete, a movement of people and jobs to low labor-cost areas, residential shifts to other regions, social and racial segregation, and inappropriate government policies.

It has been said that a nation cannot be great if it squanders its legacy cities, and renewed economic health in these areas will add to the nation's prosperity. These areas have many significant assets—including land; infrastructure; business opportunities; underutilized labor; and many of the nation's major medical, educational, and research institutions—all critical building blocks for our nation's future competitiveness. Restoring competitiveness to these places also conserves our environment, as new growth can occur within them without endangering our country's open spaces.

Using the underutilized assets in the nation's older industrial metropolitan areas is important to our national well-being, and America needs to renew its investment and its commitment to these areas. A shift in the current economic calculus and changes in behavior by all stakeholders will be required to attain this goal. A realignment to revive prosperity can succeed, but only if it is part of a new national compact, which includes the full engagement of all sectors.

This volume of readings was commissioned as part of a project sponsored by The American Assembly, a national nonpartisan public policy forum affiliated with Columbia University. Since its founding in 1950, The American Assembly has often explored aspects of the nation's urban policy with innovative projects including "Community Capitalism," "The Cities and the Nation," "The Farm and the City," among others, and the examination of older industrial metropolitan areas continues the legacy of The Assembly's founder Dwight D. Eisenhower and his mandate to The Assembly "to illuminate issues of national policy."

Chairman and CEO of Bank of America Kenneth D. Lewis and Pennsylvania Governor Edward G. Rendell served as this American Assembly project's co-chairs. It was directed by Paul C. Brophy, president, Brophy & Reilly LLC, who has been a recognized urban policy expert for more than twenty-five years and has led or been involved with almost all of The Assembly's projects in this field. The success of "Retooling for Growth" is in large part due to his vision and efforts. The project was ably assisted by a steering committee, whose names are listed in the appendix. The project set out to identify a broad framework of actions that, if implemented, can help these older industrial areas create 21st century economies with robust growth and shared prosperity.

The chapters in this volume were first used as background for the 106th American Assembly held at The Hotel Hershey, Hershey, Pennsylvania, on November 8–11, 2007. A distinguished group of authorities and representatives of government, business, law, labor, academia, nonprofit organizations, and the media convened to examine policies, approaches, and development strategies aimed at meeting the needs of older industrial metropolitan areas seeking to find their place in the changing global economy. The participants' names, affiliations, and their report of the findings and recommendations are included in the appendix of this volume. We are deeply grateful to the book's editors,

Richard M. McGahey and Jennifer Vey, for their contributions and to the excellent production team at the Brookings Institution Press.

We gratefully acknowledge the generous support of Bank of America, the Ford Foundation, the Rockefeller Foundation, the Surdna Foundation, the William Penn Foundation, the Kresge Foundation, and JPMorgan Chase & Co. and their active and continued involvement in the issues surrounding older industrial metropolitan areas.

In 1993 The Assembly produced a report entitled "Interwoven Destinies: Cities and the Nation" that helped launch a wave of new thinking and a slew of new metropolitan organizing activities, much of it noting that suburbs were only as strong as the cities with which they were linked. It is the expectation of The American Assembly and the project leadership of "Retooling for Growth" that this volume and the accompanying Assembly report will serve similarly as impetus for America's older industrial metropolitan areas to undertake examinations of their own situations and develop policy recommendations to renew their core urban areas. Strengthening our cities strengthens our nation, and while America's cities may have different legacies and different challenges, the nation faces a common set of global challenges and shares a common national future.

The supporters of this project as well as The American Assembly take no position on the subject presented herein for public discussion.

DAVID H. MORTIMER
The American Assembly

PART ONE

Frameworks

1

Regional Economic Development in Theory and Practice

Richard M. McGahey

A lthough the American economy has entered the sixth year of the current expansion, job growth during the current recovery is significantly slower than in the past. On a peak-to-peak basis, most indicators for the current recovery lag behind the postwar average—GDP growth is 2.6 percent, compared to a postwar average 3.3 percent gain; wages and salaries are 1.2 percent higher, compared to a postwar average of 2.8 percent; and employment is up only 0.6 percent, compared to a postwar average of 1.7 percent.[1] And there is a marked slowdown since 2003. Between 2003 and the first half of 2007, real median hourly wages have actually declined by 1.1 percent, and even for the top 20 percent of wage earners, hourly wages have risen by only 0.5 percent. Incomes also are growing significantly slower than productivity during this recovery. Since 2000, overall productivity is up by 19.8 percent, while real weekly earnings rose by 3.5 percent for women and actually declined by one percentage point for men.[2] So although the American economy continues to grow, it is producing jobs at a slower rate than in typical recoveries, and many of those jobs are actually paying declining real wages.

Richard McGahey is a program officer at the Ford Foundation. The views expressed in this chapter are his.

Not surprisingly, economic problems are disproportionately concentrated in older metropolitan regions, especially those where traditional manufacturing and related sectors continue a long-term structural decline. In 2006, on an annual basis, of the forty-nine largest cities in the United States, unemployment was the worst in Detroit, but also very high in Milwaukee (forty-seventh), Oakland (forty-sixth), St. Louis (forty-fifth), Baltimore (forty-third), and Philadelphia (fortieth).[3] Although many cities are showing signs of life in terms of growing downtown real estate markets and other indicators, they continue to show overall higher levels of economic distress than the nation, distress that also affects their surrounding regional economies.

According to a variety of analyses, the problems facing low-income workers and regions are essentially determined by larger national or global economic forces. The increase in globalization has meant that jobs, especially lower-skilled jobs, can be more easily moved out of the country. A corollary argument is that higher-skilled jobs are those most likely to stay in the United States, placing an ever-higher premium on skills and education, which disadvantages lower-skilled workers. Declining unionization and continuing racial and gender discrimination and exclusion also contribute to the problem. And increasing numbers of poor, lower-skilled immigrant workers have been entering the United States, leading some analysts to argue that this creates increased competition with native-born lower-skilled workers. This claim is disputed by others, who assert that immigration has no major impacts.[4]

Of course, national policy factors such as trade, immigration, federal taxation and regulation, and macroeconomic policy are beyond the control of any one region. But in contrast to these broad macroeconomic analyses of the causes of lagging economic performance, there is a renewed interest in what cities, regions, and states can do to improve their economies. For a multitude of other policy factors are under greater state and local control. Zoning, land use, and nonfederal fiscal and taxation policy are relatively free of federal direction. Education and workforce development policies and finance, along with some labor regulation, are largely state and local responsibilities. Environmental laws and regulations vary considerably among jurisdictions, both in formal law and in actual application and enforcement. Many states and localities provide or support financial, technological, and technical assistance to businesses. State and local procurement is locally controlled, and transportation policy is largely directed by states and localities, although supported through federal taxes.

This chapter reviews regional efforts in economic development, with special attention to the problems facing older industrial cities and regions. Paradoxically, in a time where the impact of global economic forces is increasing, strategies to increase prosperity and economic growth increasingly are focused at the regional level.

Economic Development Subsidies and Their Critics

In the twentieth century, regional economic development policy in the United States became focused on using tax and other incentives and subsidies to encourage companies to relocate to other states. During the Depression, Mississippi pioneered the use of Industrial Development Bonds (IDBs) to finance facilities for companies moving from the North.[5] IDBs and other policy inducements spread, with cities also offering a variety of location incentives to firms. The practice of attracting firms across state lines, often with a variety of financial inducements, is known derisively as "smokestack chasing" or, more recently—as relocation efforts expanded beyond industrial firms—as "buffalo hunting."

The use of incentives to induce business relocation became very widespread, and there now is a somewhat dizzying range of incentives offered to firms. Peter Fisher identifies three broad classes of incentives—discretionary, entitlement, and tax cuts—and the picture is further complicated by programs that focus on specific industries (manufacturing, high technology), specific locations (economically distressed regions, urban "blight" areas, rural communities), differing uses of funds (plant and equipment, firm-specific job training, research and development, infrastructure), in-state versus out-of-state firms ("retention" versus "attraction"), different sections of the tax code (corporate income, property, payroll), and different public agencies (cities, states, quasi-public development corporations, special-purpose tax districts, public authorities). In part because of this wide-ranging array of options, many of them not subject to public disclosure or scrutiny, it is difficult to know how much is being spent, and with what impact. Two independent estimates valued state and local incentive spending at approximately $50 billion nationally in 1996, although both studies cautioned that the estimate was very likely too low, given imprecise valuation and the lack of transparency, and a diverse range of incentives.[6]

Incentive-based approaches to economic development have long been under fire on a number of fronts. One line of criticism is rooted in mainstream economic theory and the distinction between public and private goods. In this view, governments should compete for business on the basis of their general economic and policy climate, including factors such as overall tax rates, regulation, and educational quality, but should not use taxes and spending to compete for individual businesses. The use of scarce public revenue to induce changes in location by private firms means that less money is available to spend on appropriate public goods, and private firms receive a windfall for economic activity that they likely would have carried out anyway.[7]

A second critique of subsidies was developed by the Corporation for Enterprise Development (CfED), a nonprofit that advocates policies that look at the full range of factors supporting a healthy economy—not just tax rates and regulation, but education and workforce skills, environmental quality, and infrastructure. CfED's principal means of communicating this approach has been the "Development Report Card for the States," first issued in 1987, which created broad indexes of activities and outcomes deemed vital to economic growth and shared prosperity. When first issued, the report card was positioned against conventional cost indexes of economic development or "business climate," especially the one issued by a consulting firm, Grant Thornton, which primarily measured costs and taxes for manufacturing firms and ranked locations accordingly—lower costs and taxes were largely equivalent to a high ranking.

Indexes like Grant Thornton's viewed all public expenditures as costs facing individual firms, even if those costs were taxes and public spending to support infrastructure and education, two factors that are essential to economic growth. Further, higher wage costs in these indexes were viewed as a negative from the firm's point of view, but these costs can also be viewed as an indicator of greater prosperity, and therefore as an indicator of economic success.[8]

In contrast, CfED's approach looked at broad factors associated with outcomes such as high per capita income, job creation, business expansion, small business start-ups, education, research and development, and infrastructure. The various subcomponents of the analysis have changed somewhat during the past twenty years, but the overall logic remains the same. The report card now focuses on three broad domains, composed of sixty-seven specific measures: *performance* (including economic, quality of life, and environmental data); *business vitality* (including business start-ups and closings, and industrial diversity); and *development capacity* (ranging from educational expenditures and performance to infrastructure quality and investment).

This perspective leads to very different policy recommendations than a pure cost-reduction approach. Rather than tax reduction and firm subsidies, CfED's perspective emphasizes investment in infrastructure, education, and training; attention to the needs of existing businesses in the region; and support of new business formation and innovation through increased access to capital, improved technology transfer, and education and training programs aimed at entrepreneurs and small-business owners.[9] Although this approach shares the critique of firm-specific subsidies that microeconomic theory puts forward, it is also generally critical of competition based purely on lowering costs and overall tax rates, something that the pure microeconomic approach endorses.

CfED's work was instrumental in introducing a new perspective into economic development policy debates, one that focused on economic outcomes for states and their whole population, especially low-income people. It criticized policies and programs that focused on specific firms, and put forward a much broader view of what it takes for successful, sustained economic development. The report card has functioned in significant part as a way to advocate for this approach to development, as opposed to a strategy dominated by cost reduction or subsidies to specific companies.

The multifaceted approach to economic development, reflected in the comprehensive nature of CfED's report card, is based on a rich vision of economic development, but, ironically, that very complexity and range also made it less useful for economic development agencies and policymakers. Individual governments or public agencies do not control many of the factors cited by CfED (education, infrastructure, environmental quality), and many also do not have staff or personnel trained or oriented in those directions.

Instead, another approach that also is critical of purely cost-driven strategies aimed at individual firms has achieved a good deal of popularity in recent years. Associated with Michael Porter of the Harvard Business School, this approach advocates policies oriented around "clusters" of economic activity: region-specific concentrations of firms, industries, workforce skills, and potential growth opportunities.

On the basis of his work on competitive strategy for firms, Porter already was one of the world's most prominent business scholars and consultants when he turned his attention to regional and national economic development. In his 1990 book, *The Competitive Advantage of Nations,* Porter argued that economic success, properly defined, focused on producing "a high and rising standard of living for its citizens," that high and rising productivity was the key to that goal, and that different groups of firms in different nations specialized to achieve that end.[10]

Porter's analysis was based on the now-famous "diamond" diagram outlining four sets of factors that together formed competitive advantage for firms, and by extension, for groups of firms: *factor conditions,* available to all firms, such as physical and human resources, infrastructure, and capital; *demand conditions* for products or services (Porter emphasized the quality rather than the quantity of demand, with more demanding and sophisticated customers seen as a critical source of pressure for firm and industry innovation); *related and supporting industries* in the region; and *firm strategy, structure, and rivalry.*[11]

Although Porter's work has been used extensively to advocate for and analyze regional clusters within the United States, it is striking that the analysis in his 1990 book is based almost entirely on analyses of nations, not regions within them. Porter and his research team had conducted very detailed case studies of ten advanced national economies, and those studies undergirded his analysis. He did say, almost in passing, that the analysis "can be readily applied to political or geographic units smaller than a nation," noting the geographic concentration of successful firms in regions within the United States. Later in the book Porter says that the combined forces of the "diamond" caused "*clustering* of a nation's competitive industries."[12] Porter viewed the geographic clustering of industries as actually spurring healthy competition among firms and exposing inefficiencies in business practices that could be exploited by rivals.

Despite the fact that Porter's book was based on analysis of national economies, the regional application of his framework was very rapidly taken up by state governments and others. The Connecticut Economic Conference Board had Porter brief state legislators on state policy in 1991, and an industry-focused report on the competitive position of Massachusetts was presented in the same year. Within two years, five states had begun some economic development based on regional clusters, and the practice has continued to grow.

There are basic economic arguments in favor of a regional focus. Regions have specific concentrations of industries, occupations, workers, and businesses that do not respond uniformly in the same way to aggregate national economic conditions, and labor markets for many nonprofessional and low-wage workers are specific to their regions.[13] Economic theory, since the work of the nineteenth-century economist Alfred Marshall, contains a rich literature on how regions can gain economic advantage from spillovers of technology, industry concentration, and labor-force development. Marshall's famous description of why industrial districts persist bears repeating:

> When an industry has thus chosen a locality for itself, it is likely to stay there long. . . . The mysteries of the trade become no mysteries; but are as it were in the air. . . . Good work is rightly appreciated, inventions and improvement in machinery, in processes and the general organization of the business have their merits promptly discussed: if one man starts a new idea it is taken up by others and combined with suggestions of their own; and thus it becomes the source of further new ideas. And presently subsidiary trades grow up in the neighbourhood, supplying it with implements and materials, organizing its traffic, and in many ways conducing to the economy of its material.[14]

Porter's framework had, and continues to have, broad appeal because of his prior work on business strategy for firms, his reputation as a leading business scholar and consultant, and the style of his presentation, which is "couched in the more accessible verbal language of business competitiveness rather than the mathematically refined vernacular of urban and regional economics."[15] The emphasis on clusters also fit well with growing policy attention to retaining and expanding existing firms, rather than focusing on attracting new ones. The appeal to state and local economic development officials rested in part on the claim that regions can prosper even without controlling macroeconomic forces such as taxation, fiscal policy, or trade. Porter's work appeared at a time when many states had been concentrating on encouraging high-technology investment, and many of the early examples in this literature are based on high-technology sectors, especially Silicon Valley in California, Route 128 in Boston, and the Research Triangle in North Carolina.[16]

Porter's work was not without its critics, especially on the question of economic inclusion and the role of cluster policies in helping low-income people and communities. Bennett Harrison and Amy Glasmier criticized Porter's application of cluster and competition theory to low-income urban neighborhoods and cities, arguing that he had failed to appreciate the need for stronger involvement by government and community development organizations. But even these critics gave Porter credit for his work and advocacy on behalf of low-income neighborhoods, saying that he had "almost single-handedly rejuvenated and legitimated—even if he has not exactly invented—such approaches."[17]

Although all approaches to regional economic development, and cluster approaches in particular, concentrate on economic growth, there is little attention to inclusive growth or social equity in a region as part of economic development. Joseph Cortright's review of cluster literature found that "relatively few studies . . . have examined the relation between clustering and wages" and virtually none have looked at poverty alleviation in relation to cluster strategies.[18] Some recent work has focused on rural areas and clusters, with explicit attention to rural poverty, but the metropolitan economic development literature has not been focused on poverty or equity.[19]

This deficiency was documented in a 2002 report by Rural Technology Strategies, "Just Clusters," which reported on a 2001 conference on cluster strategies and equity. The conference focused on knowledge- and skill-intensive clusters, and concluded:

Clusters are, by their nature, demand driven, with companies acting in their own best interests. Many rural and urban areas—which generally have lower levels of education and income—are thus caught between a rock and a hard place. They can match neither the still-lower incomes of offshore regions to compete for labor-intensive clusters nor the amenities and talent of America's high tech and cultural centers to attract knowledge intensive clusters.[20]

However, the conferees concluded that cluster approaches held promise for increasing economic opportunity for poor cities, regions, and workers, if policymakers and businesses could realign existing practices and programs. Clusters, if linked to strong workforce development programs, business assistance programs for small and minority-owned businesses, and support for a variety of intermediary organizations could "intentionally forge a pathway leading to higher incomes and stronger economies."[21] This vision moves back in the direction of the broader policy recommendations embedded in CfED's critique of subsidy policy, but like that approach, would require sophisticated coordination and implementation across a wide variety of often-uncoordinated institutions and organizations.

The Persistence of Subsidies

Cluster strategies are now ubiquitous in economic development. A cursory scan of state and regional economic development plans and policies will find work on clusters firmly embedded in strategic plans, policy initiatives, and regional visions of economic growth as expressed by governors and mayors, but also business organizations and universities. The Economic Development Administration of the U.S. Department of Commerce has promoted cluster strategies for several years, commissioning a detailed series of research reports and providing technical assistance to economic development agencies that want to use cluster analyses and practices.[22] The National Governors Association (NGA), in cooperation with the Council on Competitiveness, has issued a major report, *Cluster-Based Strategies for Growing State Economies,* authored by Stuart Rosenfeld, one of the nation's leading scholars and practitioners on clusters. The NGA also offers workshops on cluster strategies for state officials and economic development staff.[23] A wide range of consultants and academics conduct highly detailed cluster analyses, and a recent survey of economic development organizations found that more than half had commissioned one or more industry cluster studies.[24]

The explicit critique of economic development subsidies, and legislative efforts to rein them in or limit them, also have grown. A widely shared critique of subsidies as ineffective and wasteful ranges across the political spectrum, with more conservative groups seeing subsidies as market distortions and wasteful public spending, and more liberal groups seeing them as undeserved giveaways to companies that do not need them, taking revenue away from critical public needs. On the legislative front, according to Good Jobs First, the leading public interest organization in the nation that tracks and critiques economic development subsidies, ten states have enacted disclosure laws, twenty states have some type of "clawback" provision that allows recapture of subsidies if promised development targets are not met, and over forty states have some type of job quality standards attached to the receipt of subsidies. (At the same time, there is a good deal of skepticism about how aggressively such provisions are enforced.)[25]

A related critique focuses on urban and suburban sprawl. This analysis sees a combination of powerfully interlinked forces in finance, governmental organization, transportation policy, housing construction, and class and racial division fostering ever-sprawling development that degrades the environment and moves jobs and opportunity farther from poor people.

So firm-specific, subsidy-driven "buffalo hunting" approaches to development have come under sustained attack from a diverse group of critics. The critics range from conservative free-market advocates who want an end to all public subsidies to business-oriented consultants and organizations who want to shift resources to cluster-based approaches to groups who want to redirect subsidies to other pressing economic and social needs such as infrastructure, education, and health care. In contrast to most research in the field, one recent study claims measurable benefits from competing for industrial plants among jurisdictions, but it has been criticized on a variety of grounds, especially because the authors did not include data on the size of incentives, so they did not assess whether the benefits of the incentives under study outweighed the costs.[26]

It comes as somewhat of a surprise, given the breadth of the critique, that states and localities continue to make substantial use of "buffalo hunting" approaches. These subsidy policies are tracked and criticized by groups such as Good Jobs First, and some of the state-level groups that are part of the State Fiscal Analysis Initiative (SFAI) or the Economic Analysis and Research Network (EARN),[27] but the persistence of subsidies in practice even as their analytic support has eroded is one of the major paradoxes in this field.

Examples of large subsidy-driven deals abound. Critics of attraction deals point to the $320 million in subsidies provided to United Airlines to develop an aircraft maintenance facility in Indianapolis. The center was projected to employ a staff of more than five thousand, at high wages. The deal was made during the recession of the early 1990s, and over ninety cities bid for it. The city and state put $320 million into the deal, and United pledged another $500 million for expansion. At its peak, United employed close to twenty-five hundred mechanics at the facility, but then United, and the airline industry, hit hard times. United's investment topped out at $229 million, and the facility closed in 2003. The city and state struggled to find other tenants, while public sector costs rose to around $40 million annually in bond payments and maintenance costs. The center's space was slowly filled by a variety of tenants, capped off by Wellpoint, Inc., with a call center and specialty drug distribution center employing nine hundred, described by the Indianapolis Mayor's office as "high-tech" jobs. (Wellpoint received an additional subsidy of up to $10.1 million in forgivable loans, tax credits, and rent credits.)[28]

Even though some public decisionmakers recognized that the deal might be wasting public resources, they felt subsidies were necessary in order to compete with other jurisdictions. Governor Joseph Kernan of Indiana, in a statement that could be echoed by a myriad of public officials, said, "I understand the argument that taking jobs away from Boston and putting them here is nationally a zero-sum game. But Indiana, like virtually every other state, is not going to unilaterally disarm."[29]

The inability or unwillingness of governments to end a policy that many recognize may be wasteful and ineffective has led some critics to despair of reform and instead to call for federal intervention to end subsidies. This culminated in the recent *DaimlerChrysler* v. *Cuno* litigation, in which an Ohio federal appeals court held that state investment tax credits to attract a manufacturing plant violated the Constitution's Commerce Clause, which gives Congress the authority to manage trade between states.[30] The decision was overturned by the U.S. Supreme Court, which held that the plaintiffs did not have standing to sue. While the case was in litigation, it sparked efforts in Congress to ratify the right of states to use subsidies. The case underscored the complexity of the politics of subsidies, with state governments, business organizations, and labor unions advocating subsidies, while a combination of liberal organizations such as the Center on Budget and Policy Priorities and conservative advocacy organizations who favor a sharply limited role for government lined up against them.

In addition to classic "buffalo hunting" subsidies aimed at attracting firms from outside a state, many jurisdictions now provide incentives to firms to prevent them from moving—"retention" subsidies. In New York City, recent subsidies to construct new headquarters for financial firms have resulted in more than $650 million to Goldman Sachs and at least $240 million to JPMorgan Chase. The Chase subsidies were justified in part because of a supposed counteroffer from Stamford, Connecticut, but Stamford officials later confirmed that there had been no discussions with Chase.[31] Subsidies also are routinely used by local governments within metropolitan areas to compete with each other for businesses. In 2005, the

Applebee's restaurant chain negotiated with several suburbs in the Kansas City region for a new headquarters; the project eventually went to the neighboring city of Lenexa for $12.5 million in local benefits (on top of $14 million from the state to keep them on the Kansas side of the border). The new site is ten miles from the old headquarters.[32]

The Applebee's case illustrates one reason for the persistence of subsidies and highlights a major barrier to more effective regional development approaches— the fragmentation of and competition among governments in regions. The economic boundaries of a region spill across multiple jurisdictions, and sometimes state lines, encompassing a very large number of separate jurisdictions and economic development actors.[33] But there are relatively few incentives or mechanisms for these jurisdictions to cooperate with each other, even if they recognize that such cooperation is in their mutual interests.

In fact, proliferation of governmental units—new jurisdictions as the metropolitan area grows, along with special-purpose districts and various types of public or quasi-public authorities—often is advocated as a way to increase economic development. Although some of this growth in jurisdictions can be attributed to advocacy from relatively narrow real estate development interests, the growth of special units with bonding or taxing authority also is linked to efforts to get around mandated debt limits on existing government. Although debt for various projects can be raised in this way, the new units do not necessarily increase the region's overall revenue-generating ability, leading to longer-term problems in repaying debt and declining ratings from finance agencies.[34]

Recent analyses find that governmental fragmentation harms overall regional economic development. In one comprehensive study, Jerry Paytas compared 285 metropolitan areas, from 1973 to 1997, focusing on a measure of metropolitan competitiveness based on a dynamic shift-share analysis incorporating employment levels, industry mix, income, and regional economic performance. The study found a "strong and negative influence" from metropolitan governmental fragmentation on economic competitiveness. Fragmentation was highest in the Northeast and the Midwest was second—two regions with large concentrations of older industrial cities.[35]

But Paytas also found that simply centralizing functions at the state level did not resolve the fragmentation problem—in fact, it further decreased metropolitan competitiveness, with particularly harmful effects on smaller metropolitan areas, the "worst-case scenario" being "a fragmented metropolitan area within a centralized state." The largest contributor to metropolitan fragmentation, with a consequent negative impact on economic competitiveness, was creation of new governmental units in the region—not only new political jurisdictions, but also new units within existing governments. Paytas concluded that "the proliferation strategy is a trap for the long-term health of local governments."[36]

Varying electoral cycles and diverse and contradictory incentives for the multiple jurisdictions in a regional economy, and the persistence of unproductive or contradictory economic development policies within regions, suggest that the problem of intraregional competition cannot be effectively solved solely by the public sector, which often does not have the capacity for longer-term economic development planning, and where political leaders' time horizon is often short. The policies are driven by the need for quick results that conform to electoral cycles; the differing needs and views of legislative and executive branch stakeholders, including legislators who want to reward their own district; and the skills and orientation of traditional economic development agency staff, who work closely with real estate developers and are not rewarded for other, less tangible outcomes than specific relocation of a single firm or facility.

These pressures are much more pronounced in declining economies and older industrial regions. But state governments are not a magical solution to this problem; although there is an important role for states, they need to be flexible in relation to the long-term competitive needs of particular regions. And the problem is compounded by the lack of a broader range of interested stakeholders who support longer-term programs that may have relatively slow payoffs.[37]

Engaging Other Stakeholders—Business, Workforce, and Philanthropy

The difficulty of changing economic development practice through government actions alone means that other nongovernmental stakeholders need to be involved on a sustained basis. In recent years, regional efforts have been carried out by business groups and philanthropy, and also have used workforce development as an entry point into regional economic development efforts.

Business

There is a long history of business organizations being involved with economic development. Much of that work, especially by broad membership organizations at the state or national level, traditionally has focused on reducing the costs to companies through changes in the tax code, reducing regulatory burdens, and seeking other ways to reduce costs. Although advocacy for cost reduction remains an important feature for many regional business organizations, the focus on making cities and regions economically competitive in a broader sense than just low costs has been picked up by several business-led organizations.

In 2003, FutureWorks and the Alliance for Regional Stewardship conducted a detailed study of twenty-nine regional business-civic organizations, to analyze innovative practices and to see "what contributions do business-civic organizations make to the health of major metropolitan regions." The researchers interviewed sixty-three executives from business organizations, analyzed the results of a web-based survey, and talked with a wide range of stakeholders in these regions.

They concluded that these organizations were shifting priorities from a focus on a traditional, purely cost-reduction perspective to a focus on broader regional competitiveness. A smaller number also were directly concentrating on economic inequality in their regions. But moving to a regional perspective confronted them with substantial organizational and funding challenges, and many found that adopting a regional perspective required changes in their own organizational practices and structures.[38]

It sometimes is not apparent to other regional stakeholders that business organizations are largely membership driven, and must provide useful services for their members. Like other sectors, there is competition among business organizations for members, and firms can be variously organized by geography, cluster, size, ethnicity or gender of owners, and other factors. Changing practices and adopting a new focus run the risk of losing a sometimes fragile membership base. Also, many organizations report that a continuing wave of corporate mergers and more rapid turnover of high-level business personnel in their regions make it harder to engage senior leaders of major firms on a sustained basis. And there are substantial barriers and a legacy of misunderstanding between business-led groups and community organizations, especially in poor cities and neighborhoods.

Nevertheless, there is an emerging generation of regional business leaders, often strongly influenced by Michael Porter's work, which accepts the need to focus on the regional economy. But remember that Porter's analytic work is most supportive of business organizations that support clusters of similar industries in a region, not a broad organization across industries. Linking diverse business sectors, and competing for support from firms and industry groups, remain a substantial challenge for these regional business organizations.[39]

These challenges will not be easy to overcome. In the Detroit metropolitan region, the continuing rapid decline of the major American automobile companies, coupled with years of racial polarization and distrust between the city and suburbs, has created a very difficult climate for regional economic development. Detroit Renaissance, a business-led civic organization that historically had concentrated on the city of Detroit, has now joined with other regional organizations, both business and nonprofit, to launch "One D: Transforming Regional Detroit," a collaborative that seeks to strengthen a regional economic perspective through specific development projects. The collaborative has carried out a detailed economic analysis of the region and is concentrating on six target areas, focusing initially on the mobility and logistics sectors, but also on entrepreneurial, creative, and educational strategies. The project also is working in conjunction with other organizations to address regional political fragmentation and race relations.[40]

In the central New York region around Syracuse, the business-led Metropolitan Development Association has long been one of the key organizations in a business relocation and attraction strategy. Although the region, like many economically declining metropolises, continues to emphasize attraction strategies, it also has broadened its approach to include expansion of existing enterprises and now is working to develop linkages among technology-based firms in the region, collaborating with the region's universities to retain new graduates, and creating a stronger sense of regional economic identity that spans twelve counties in the Syracuse area.[41]

Other efforts are under way, sometimes in explicit cooperation with government. In Oakland, California, the Oakland Metropolitan Chamber of Commerce has taken the lead in forming the "Oakland Partnership," which has the explicit goal of fostering "sustainable, equitable economic growth." McKinsey and Company conducted a study of Oakland's economic situation, the results of which are being rolled out in cooperation with a series of economic development task forces created by Mayor Ron Dellums.[42]

Workforce and Human Capital

Regions also are the most important locus for workforce development and human capital. Many labor markets, especially those for low-income workers, are local or regional in nature. Key institutions such as community colleges run through different governance systems, and face different institutional incentives and management. Programs in welfare reform, training for dislocated workers, English as a second language, community colleges, and others all are governed primarily at the state and local levels. Industry clusters such as health care, infrastructure and construction, transportation and logistics, and hospitality and retail also all operate at the regional level in terms of most of the decisions that affect low-income workers.

Innovative workforce development programs also are focusing more intently on the needs of industries in their regions. Much of the emphasis in economic development policy, whether on subsidizing individual firms or on supporting clusters, emphasizes working with companies in areas such as site development, technology transfer, and business management assistance. But in the past several years, some efforts in regional economic revitalization have emphasized, instead, the skills and education of the regional workforce. There are two principal approaches here: one that trains and aligns workforce resources with clusters or sectors, and another that emphasizes the development, attraction, and retention of highly educated and creative people, without much regard to specific business sectors. Although these two approaches sometimes are lumped together in a broad emphasis on "talent," they differ in their origins, focus, and implications for policy.

Just as with economic development resources, workforce resources are scattered and uncoordinated in most regions. In 2002, The Reinvestment Fund identified over $1.2 billion in Pennsylvania for workforce development funding, broadly defined, but showed that the funding was fragmented in forty-nine separate funding streams, administered by literally hundreds of entities, without common performance standards, reporting systems, links to other regional economic resources, or accountability procedures. A similar picture would result from an analysis of workforce development funding in almost any state and region.[43]

For years, efforts in reforming workforce development policy concentrated on governance issues about the composition of workforce boards, and the allocation of spending by different formulas among competing organizations. In contrast, during the 1990s the main innovations in workforce development have grown out of sectoral workforce development programs that were launched by local organizations and stimulated by support from foundations. Building on the observed success of innovative local projects such as Project QUEST in San Antonio and the Center for Employment Training (CET) in San Jose, and with support from the Charles Stewart Mott, Ford, Annie E. Casey, and Rockefeller foundations, sectoral efforts were linked in networks. Evaluations showed promising results in a climate where many are skeptical about the potential effectiveness of workforce programs.[44]

Sectoral programs have a natural affinity with cluster-based economic development strategies. When they focus on specific sectors, employer demand can be aggregated, education and training providers can target specialized training, and potential career ladders can be developed. The quality of the local workforce is seen in cluster theory as a critical variable in regional success, further reinforcing the linkage. The sectoral work supported by foundations has been explicitly focused on advancement for the poor, which has led many of these programs to concentrate on sectors employing a large number of low-income workers, such as health care.

States also have aligned training along sectoral lines with less regard to equity issues as part of cluster strategies. In some cases, such as the state of Connecticut's metal manufacturing cluster and the Northeast Oklahoma Manufacturers Council, broad cluster projects have grown out of sectoral training programs.

The community college has emerged as the key institution in this type of cluster-focused training. Community and technical colleges have long embraced a mission of assisting local business, but they often operated in a reactive mode, rather than defining their mission in relation to specific industry concentrations and needs. That is changing rapidly, and community colleges now play an increasingly important role in aligning education and training with economic development.[45] There are many examples of individual community colleges that work effectively with employers, and some that focus on clusters and concentrations of industry in their region. But these efforts are more characteristic of individual community colleges, often tied to leadership at the particular institution, and are less a function of broader system efforts.[46]

The state of Washington has perhaps the most extensive effort to link post–high school training with cluster strategies in economic development. The state has designated eleven "Centers of Excellence" in community colleges, in such sectors as construction, process manufacturing, and health technology. The centers are resources for community colleges to work with employer associations and assist in developing appropriate curricula and career pathways for students and workers who need further education and training.[47]

Although cluster-focused workforce strategies often show less commitment to the goal of building career ladders for low-income workers, several analysts have noted the alignment of sectoral workforce development programs with cluster strategies and concluded that workforce development could play an important role in bridging the equity gap between lower-skilled workers and higher-skilled jobs in knowledge-based clusters. In the late 1990s, a group of foundations invested in pilot programs in six cities to explore the role of funder collaboratives and sectoral workforce approaches for low-income workers. Most of these pilot programs ended up focusing on clusters in their respective regions, and the promising results have led to a new national effort to expand these approaches.

In the fall of 2007, a consortium of foundations and the U.S. Department of Labor launched the new National Fund for Workforce Solutions, which aims at raising up to $50 million and leveraging another $200 million for regional efforts to link education and training more closely to business needs, and also make public policy more effective in assisting low-income workers and the businesses that employ them. Initial sites in the fund program are focusing on training in a variety of sectors: biotechnology (Bay Area), health care and building services (Boston), health care and aviation (New York City), and health care, biotechnology, and construction (Baltimore). The fund announced four new sites in September 2007 and plans to provide support to forty metropolitan and rural sites over the next few years, while pulling together lessons from the work and engaging in public education and policy development.

All of the regional projects have close links with public economic and workforce development efforts, but at the same time are independent of the public system. For example, in New York City, the Workforce Development Funders Group conducts aligned program funding in collaboration with the city's Department of Small Business Services. The Boston program, SkillWorks, works closely with the city of Boston and surrounding jurisdictions and the state of Massachusetts, and has become a voice for increased levels of funding and more effective workforce programs, with successful outcomes ranging from more effective use of Food Stamp funds for training to increased state funding for training and support services, following the SkillWorks model.[48]

The most ambitious program aligned with the new fund is Pennsylvania's Industry Partnership Project. As part of a broader effort to make workforce development more effective in economic development, coupled with a focus on troubled regional economies and sectors, the state has allocated $15 million annually to training in high-priority occupations, with an additional $5 million to support the intermediary organizations necessary to have effective regional partnerships. The partnerships are regionally based and concentrate on a specific set of industry clusters. In a competitive process, funds are awarded to multiemployer partnerships of business, labor, education and training, and community organizations. The project requires ongoing evaluation and results-oriented targets, and provides information and peer-learning opportunities to the various regional programs. To date, the program has provided training to over 24,000 workers from over 5,700 companies.[49]

A second prominent approach to regional development that emphasizes human capital encourages regions to focus on improving the quality of life for higher-income professionals, including both improvement of public education and also amenities such as arts and culture. The theory, based on the work of Richard Florida and others, is that attracting and holding young, mobile, college-educated professionals will give a region an economic advantage.[50] Critics have questioned the causality—whether the movement of professionals is a cause or an effect of growth in certain sectors—but the approach is widely discussed and increasingly is being applied in development circles.[51]

The emphasis on attracting and retaining creative, highly educated talent has led to a wave of efforts in cities to make themselves more attractive to this cohort. Several cities—Philadelphia, Memphis, Portland, Providence, Tampa, and Richmond—have commissioned studies that position them in relation to the demographic trends in other regions and the nation as a whole. In a series with the clever title, "The Young and the Restless," these six studies provide very detailed demographic information on each city, along with generic advice about how to attract and retain younger educated people. In some cases, such as that of Philadelphia, the generic advice about attracting people is linked to a regional strategy focused on high technology and innovation-based businesses, but for other cities, recommendations for attracting young people are exactly the same and are not tailored to the specific city or region or set of industry clusters.[52]

There is one major national policy effort to bring cluster-based analysis together with an emphasis on attracting and developing talent—the U.S. Department of Labor's WIRED program, standing for "Workforce Innovation in Regional Economic Development," which was begun in 2005. There have been three rounds of grant awards for regional proposals, with three years of funding in each round. Total projected federal spending for the thirty-nine current WIRED regions is $325 million, with significant required matches from states and regions.

WIRED uses the work of the Council on Competitiveness that advocates the development and capture of leading technology sectors as a regional growth strategy. According to the Labor Department, WIRED "is designed to support the development of a regional, integrated approach to workforce and economic development and education." The WIRED regions range from rural to urban and include both older industrial regions and newer, faster-growing ones.[53] The development of WIRED drew heavily on work carried out by the Council on Competitiveness, whose regional innovation project focused on clusters, with research support from Michael Porter.[54] Porter coordinated a detailed cluster study of technology- and innovation-based sectors in five U.S. regions, and those case studies formed the basis for the council's report. This work is the most explicit linking of cluster analysis to a focus on higher-educated talent, in comparison with the broader non-sector-specific approaches that are found in the work of Richard Florida and the "Young and the Restless" series.

Philanthropy

The examples in workforce development are part of a larger engagement by philanthropic institutions in regional economic development activity. As part of the WIRED process, the Charles Stewart Mott Foundation organized a successful regional application for a thirteen-county region in central Michigan, centering on older industrial cities such as Flint, Lansing, and Saginaw. Drawing on Mott's extensive knowledge and leadership in workforce development and its role as a neutral partner in an economically declining region, the region organized the "Mid-Michigan Innovation Team." Enjoying strong participation from Michigan State University and other universities, regional community colleges, civic organizations, and the nonprofit Center for Automotive Research, the mid-Michigan program targets clusters in advanced transportation and manufacturing, alternative fuels and energy, health care, and construction, along with a parallel program to promote and develop entrepreneurship.

The mid-Michigan strategy emphasizes "talent," but defined broadly to include not only next-generation leaders and highly educated people but also the current regional workforce, with a focus both on current workers and students in the K-to-16 system. A central goal of the strategy is collaboration with the various government agencies and programs in the region, and the strategy outlines in detail the array of programs to engage. But the WIRED grant and the program are run through the Prima Civitas Foundation, a collaboration led initially by Michigan State, with support from a nonprofit organization, the Corporation for a Skilled Workforce, directed by a steering committee with representatives from foundations, higher education, business and economic development organizations, and other civic leaders.[75] It is a striking example of a broad regional collaborative that focuses both on clusters and on broad and inclusive regional prosperity, with strong leadership from anchor institutions, especially in higher education and philanthropy.

Another philanthropically led effort has focused more on higher technology and innovation in its region. In the Pittsburgh region, the Heinz Endowments have led these efforts through their Innovation Economy Program, which emphasizes three main goals: stimulating innovation-based businesses and clusters; developing career paths, especially for low-income and underrepresented groups; and supporting public policy and regional planning to assist the development and success of regional business clusters.

The Pittsburgh efforts started with, and have maintained, a strong cluster and regional focus and have deepened their work with the labor force, especially low-income groups. The strategy builds on one potential strength of philanthropy—its ability to take risks and be flexible. Grants have gone to a wide range of organizations, including joint economic development efforts among the major research universities, smart growth and sustainable development organizations, community colleges, and regional loan funds. The Heinz Endowments' new strategic plan emphasizes a regional perspective, reflecting its view that the region is at a "tipping point" that can start to reverse years of "slow job and population growth, racial and gender inequities, fragmented government, and a negative self-image."[56]

This effort, which has drawn on work at the Metropolitan Policy Program of the Brookings Institution, again links an emphasis on clusters and innovation with creating employment opportunities, developing and articulating a regional perspective, and engaging with public policy and government as a collegial but independent voice.

A third philanthropic effort, which helps to coordinate over one hundred foundations, organizations, and individual donors in northeast Ohio, is the Fund for Our Economic Future. Formed in 2004, the fund is a collaborative that makes grants to regional organizations, supports research emphasizing current economic conditions and the region's position relative to others, and funds civic engagement activities to educate the region's population and decisionmakers and to help build regional identity.

The fund has brought together sixteen counties in the region, centered on Cleveland and surrounding cities, and also has supported broad public involvement in the development of regional strategy. In the initial phase of work, the fund supported a process that resulted in "Advance Northeast Ohio," an initiative with four main strategic goals: business growth and attraction, workforce preparation, growth through racial and economic inclusion, and government collaboration and efficiency. They funded an elaborate regional process involving leaders from the sixteen counties and over 21,000 residents, to better understand people's views of the economy and priorities for the future. The fund tracks public opinion on the region's economy through an "NEO [Northeast Ohio] Barometer," which is made widely available.[57]

Each of the four strategy areas works on a continuing set of specific goals and outcomes, and the fund is committed to measuring and reporting on the strategy's progress. The fund also tracks the region's overall economy, through an innovative regional "dashboard" that shows the region's relative economic performance on eight broad growth factors, with a number of specific subcomponents. The region is then assessed in relation to over 130 U.S. metropolitan areas on the same broad set of indicators, and also tracked over time on its own performance.[58]

Other foundations have focused on specific aspects of economic development processes, such as the Kauffman Foundation's support of entrepreneurs and new businesses, the Annie E. Casey Foundation's focus on how economic and workforce development affects the well-being of children and families, the Surdna Foundation's new work on "weak-market" cities, and the Charles Stewart Mott

Foundation's interest in sectoral workforce and economic development strategies. The MacArthur Foundation is supporting a research network on "Building Resilient Regions." Increasingly, foundations are supporting economic development efforts in their respective cities and regions, although their strategies are still in formation in several cases.[59]

Challenges for the Future

This is an exciting time for regional economic development efforts. In part because of a lack of attention from federal policy and in part because a variety of analyses suggest that regions can and must play a larger role in their own economic destiny, a wide variety of initiatives either are under way or are being considered. In this chapter I have discussed efforts that make use of clusters and sectors, workforce development, and talent attraction, but other analyses and initiatives are grounded on anchor institutions such as universities and medical systems, new approaches to technology transfer, linkages to smart growth, and entrepreneurial development.

These ideas have particular resonance in older industrial cities, where many specific examples of these types of work can be found. Most analysts now accept that the employment base for manufacturing and industrial work will continue to shrink, and that regions must find new ways to thrive economically. That will include continuing to work with manufacturing, which is too deeply embedded in these regions to simply be abandoned, and, where there are a variety of new initiatives focused on that sector, to draw on innovations in cluster approaches, technology transfer, and workforce development.[60]

This interest and innovation in regional development needs to be encouraged and supported, even though the current complicated and not always well-connected set of new ideas creates both opportunities and threats. The opportunity is to build more cohesive regional economic development policy and practice in older cities. The threat is another round of fractured policy and programs that are not linked into an overall, sustained vision for regional economic prosperity shared equitably by all residents and communities in a region.

This suggests some guideposts for moving forward in regional development, along with some unanswered questions and challenges for the next phase of work.

Improve Government Economic Development Policy

The persistence of subsidies and the challenges facing elected officials to "do something" about economic decline mean that subsidy policies are likely to persist.

Especially in weak-market cities and regions, there will be continuing political pressure to halt economic decline, and the challenge to policy is to craft as intelligent and comprehensive a policy as possible. If that is not done, other ideas and approaches will take center stage and use valuable and limited public resources. Although the particular mix of policies and programs will vary depending on a region's economic makeup, there are some good practices that all regions should use.

Increase transparency. There is a wide range of economic development subsidies in use, and only some of them, in some jurisdictions, are open to public view. Making these policies more transparent is essential to making more intelligent use of them. Good Jobs First keeps track of various transparency measures and the successes and difficulties involved in using them.[61]

Tie subsidies to specific, measurable benefits. Although there is a concern in weak markets that negotiating with developers and the private sector will cause a loss of investment, there also is a concern that development subsidies may not produce tangible benefits for poor residents. Over 120 cities and counties have passed "living wage" agreements that require government contractors to pay wages and provide benefits that will provide higher standards of living for poor workers and their families. Many cities are enacting "community benefit agreements" (CBAs) that require companies that receive public development assistance to provide concrete benefits in the form of job quality, use of minority contractors, employment of local residents, construction of low-income housing, and other benefits, an approach pioneered by organizations such as the Los Angeles Alliance for a New Economy.[62]

Align economic and workforce development programs with the regional economy, not with governmental boundaries. In all regions, the architecture of programs follows governmental lines, not the contours of the regional economy. The higher the degree of fragmentation, the more waste and duplications of resources there are, and the harder it is for private sector firms and organizations to work with the public sector. There is an important role for state government here to realign programs and change the incentive for regional cooperation, as local governments have too many negative incentives to compete with each other.

Work with groups of firms, not individual businesses, whenever possible. One of the broad points of agreement among all critics of ineffective subsidies is that making deals with individual firms is wasteful and counterproductive. Whenever possible, economic and workforce development programs should work with groups of firms. Cluster approaches take this one step further and look to align programs with groups of firms that share needs and interact and cooperate with each other.

Groups of firms also can be aligned geographically, which allows working with the wide variety of public resources that target neighborhoods and communities.

Role of Civic, Business, and Nongovernmental Stakeholders

Civic, business, and nongovernmental stakeholders must play a sustained and independent role in regional strategy. The many incentives for governments to engage in short-term competition with each other, or simply not to coordinate their economic, infrastructure, and workforce policies within a single economic region, mean that change will need other engaged stakeholders.

Regions need effective business organizations that engage with other stakeholders on regional policy. Cluster approaches to economic development policy rest implicitly on the idea that there are strong, functioning private sector organizations to work with in key industry concentrations in regions. But the reality is far from that, and work needs to be done to build effective, engaged business organizations both within clusters and across regions.

Strategies must engage and work with, but not be captured by, government. Regions need a strong, long-term focus that is not grounded exclusively in government agencies. Of course, there cannot be successful regional strategies without government involvement. Too many critical factors—infrastructure, education, taxation, and regulation—are the responsibility of the public sector. At the same time, governments face very significant challenges in conducting successful strategies on their own. Limited time horizons stemming from electoral cycles and short-term budgeting, fragmentation and competition among governments in regions, and a difficulty in sustaining a long-term focus due to the fiscal and political pressures in older regions, all mean that nongovernmental institutions must have a central, friendly, but independent role in regional strategies.

Philanthropy can play a key role. Foundations are especially well suited to play an important role in convening regional stakeholders, and supporting work on a long-term vision with accountable results. But foundations will need to engage more closely with public policy if regional success is ever to reach scale. There are public resources that are ill-used and misaligned, and sometimes working in ways that are counterproductive to regional success. Nongovernmental groups need an independent voice to point that out and offer ideas for improvement. Practices like intraregional tax and subsidy competition for relocating existing firms within a region need to be criticized and challenged, and alternative visions of regional prosperity and identity need to be articulated and sustained.

Different institutions can take the lead. There are examples of regional efforts led by business and civic organizations, philanthropies, higher educational institutions, and government entities. There isn't a single formula for who should convene and lead these efforts. Visionary political leaders should welcome strong organizations of nongovernmental stakeholders as an important voice in confronting the political challenges to regional success. These stakeholder organizations can be convened and led by business, higher education, or philanthropy, but cannot be successful unless they branch out to include other sectors.

Building a Common Regional Identity

Regions need to develop and implement strategies and build a common identity. Far too often, relationships between core cities and smaller regional cities and suburbs are hostile and unproductive, even though they all are part of the same regional economy. Issues of politics, taxation, and race, along with the presence of incentives that encourage suburban sprawl, all contribute to the inability of separate locales to see a common regional economic destiny. Changing these views and building a regional identity are critical for success.

Map the economy, measure its progress, and inform the region. Information is critical for regional strategy and for building a sense of regional identity. Detailed information on existing and emerging business clusters can be amassed and made available to business organizations, workforce development providers, opinion leaders, and the public, to help them understand the challenges the region faces and the opportunities and assets it possesses. There also needs to be ongoing data analysis on the region's progress, presented in easily accessible formats to the public. One excellent example is the Fund for Our Economic Future, in the Cleveland region; it produces an ongoing set of "dashboard" indicators that are based on a detailed analysis of the region's economy and social conditions, and can be used to compare the region to other metropolitan areas around the country. These indicators are updated on an easily accessible website.

Encourage regional cooperation and limit intraregional competition. A combination of government and nongovernmental stakeholders will be needed to build regional cooperation and limit destructive intraregional competition. Governors have an important role here. For example, the federal WIRED program requires that regional players put a proposal together but that it be submitted by the state's governor. This gives governments and regional organizations incentives to cooperate, but also forces states and governors to think strategically about which proposals they would submit and to encourage and direct regional actors to increase their cooperation.

There is no single "best" starting point, but strategies must constantly build out. Regions have started work with a focus on high-technology business development, attracting and retaining highly educated young people, workforce development, smart growth, clusters, and building regional identity. There is no single "best" way to start, but all of the best efforts recognize that the network, and focal points, need to keep expanding. Older industrial regions face a multitude of problems, and a successful strategy in one arena can be undermined or neutralized by negative forces elsewhere.

At the same time, strategies must stay focused. Given the scope of problems in older industrial regions, taking on everything in depth at once will likely lead to little or no impact. Successful strategies recognize the breadth and interconnectedness of their region's problems but choose to dig in and make an impact on specific issues.

Equity and inclusion are critical for success, but are not well developed or integrated into many strategies. The goal of regional prosperity has to include having a positive impact for all residents, or the region will continue to suffer, and political support for scaling up the work will be hard to obtain. Strategies that rely solely on reducing costs, wages, and benefits can impoverish a region, making it difficult to create and sustain prosperity. A low-skilled, poorly housed, and socially disrupted labor force cannot provide the skills and productivity needed for strong economic growth. Moreover, regions that are poor economic performers do not generate the revenues necessary to invest in education, infrastructure, environmental quality, and other public goods necessary for sustained prosperity. At the same time, traditional community development organizations need to broaden their horizons and see that their community and neighborhood are part of a larger regional economy and that adopting this perspective can have tangible benefits for their residents and communities.[63]

As this discussion underscores, there are enormous challenges for economically troubled regions in putting a comprehensive strategy together. Coordinating economic or workforce policy in any single dimension is difficult enough; to ask governments and other stakeholders to work simultaneously across the multiple dimensions outlined here, and in this volume's other chapters, may seem especially difficult in an economically challenged region that faces a daily set of crises and fiscal difficulties.

But it is precisely the depth and interrelated complexity of the necessary elements facing older industrial cities and regions that require such ambitious and comprehensive efforts. And there are promising examples of work emerging on a number of fronts, which take a realistic view of the problems facing a region but also are building new, inclusive efforts that assess the region's current place in the economy, map regional challenges and assets, bring diverse stakeholders together, and take concrete actions to make real progress, building on and amplifying positive economic and social trends for urban regions. Fostering this work in older industrial regions while supporting and learning from existing and emerging efforts can help not only these regions but also the nation's economy, creating prosperity for all Americans and meeting the challenges of global economic change.

Notes

1. Alvira-Aron Dine, Chad Stone, and Richard Kogan, "How Robust Is the Current Economic Expansion?" report (Washington, D.C.: Center on Budget and Policy Priorities, June 28, 2007).
2. Jared Bernstein and Lawrence Mishel, "Economy's Gains Fail to Reach Most Workers' Paychecks," Briefing Paper 195 (Washington: Economic Policy Institute, September 3, 2007).
3. U.S. Bureau of Labor Statistics, "Unemployment Rates for the Fifty Largest Cities," available at http://www.bls.gov/lau/lacilg06.htm.
4. Compare George Borjas, "Increasing the Supply of Labor through Immigration: Measuring the Impact on Native-Born Workers" (Washington: Center for Immigration Studies, May 2004), and David Card, "Is the New Immigration Really So Bad?" *Economic Journal* 115, no. 507: 300–23.
5. Critics of economic development subsidies note that Real Silk Hosiery, which moved to Durant, Mississippi, and is widely considered to be the first company in the country to move because of these types of incentives, received a twenty-five-year lease on the newly constructed factory for five dollars per year, along with other benefits and support from subsequent bond issues. But prior to the final payoff of the initial bond, Real Silk closed all of its factories in Durant and became an investment company. See Donald L. Bartlett and James B. Steele, "States at War," *Time,* November 9, 1998.
6. On classifying incentives, see Peter Fisher, "The Fiscal Consequences of Competition for Capital," in *Reining in the Competition for Capital,* edited by Ann Markusen (Kalamazoo, Mich.: W. E. Upjohn Institute for Employment Research, 2007), pp. 57–85. Estimates of the total cost of incentives are found in Kenneth Thomas, *Competing for Capital: Europe and North America in a Global Era* (Georgetown University Press, 2000), and in Peter Fisher and Alan Peters, "The Failure of Economic Development Incentives," *Journal of the American Planning Association* 70, no. 1: 27–37.
7. The classic version of this argument is found in Charles M. Tiebout, "A Pure Theory of Local Expenditures," *Journal of Political Economy* 64, no. 5 (October 1956): 416–24. An excellent application in terms of development subsidies is Melvin L. Burstein and Arthur J. Rolnick, "Congress Should End the Economic War among the States," *Annual Report* (Federal Reserve Bank of Minneapolis, 1994).
8. Business climate rankings are discussed and critiqued in Peter Fisher, *Grading Places: What Do the Business Climate Rankings Really Tell Us?* (Washington: Economic Policy Institute, 2005).
9. CfED also has increased its attention to asset development policies for families as an important element in economic development strategy.
10. Michael Porter, *The Competitive Advantage of Nations* (New York: Free Press, 1990), p. 6.
11. Ibid., pp. 71–124; emphasis in original.

12. Ibid., pp. 29 and 148; emphasis in original.

13. The market for seasonal migrant agricultural workers is one exception.

14. Alfred Marshall, *Principles of Economics* (London: Macmillan, 1890), book 4, chapter 10, p. 332. The theoretical and applied literature on clusters has grown dramatically since Porter's book was published. For an excellent discussion of the economic theory and practical issues relating to clusters, see Joseph Cortright, "Making Sense of Clusters: Regional Competitiveness and Economic Development," discussion paper (Brookings Institution, Metropolitan Policy Program, 2006).

15. Edward Feser and Michael Luger, "Cluster Analysis as a Mode of Inquiry: Its Use in Science and Technology Policymaking in North Carolina," *European Planning Studies* 11, no. 1: 14.

16. Stuart Rosenfeld notes that the term *cluster* came into economic development practice in SRI International reports on organizing economic development in Florida, published in 1989–90.

17. Bennett Harrison and Amy Glasmier, "Why Business Alone Won't Redevelop the Inner City," *Economic Development Quarterly* 11, no. 1 (February 1997): 31.

18. Cortright, "Making Sense of Clusters," pp. 42–43. Cortright reports that a 2005 search of abstracts on scholarly articles using the search terms *industry cluster* and *poverty* did not turn up any citations.

19. Center for Regional Development, Purdue University, and Indiana Business Research Center, Kelley School of Business, Indiana University, *Unlocking Rural Competitiveness: The Role of Regional Clusters* (U.S. Economic Development Administration, January 2007).

20. Stuart A. Rosenfeld, *Just Clusters: Economic Development Strategies That Reach More People and Places* (Carrboro, N.C.: Regional Technology Strategies, September 2002), p. 8.

21. Ibid., p. 50.

22. See the materials at http://www.eda.gov/Research/ClusterBased.xml.

23. National Governors Association and the Council on Competitiveness, *Cluster-Based Strategies for Growing State Economies* (2006). Information on NGA workshops can be found at http://preview.nga.org.

24. Western Carolina University, Institute for the Economy and the Future, and University of Illinois, Regional Economics Applications Laboratory, *Regionalism and Clusters for Local Development: Needs Assessment Results* (U.S. Economic Development Administration, 2007), p. 15.

25. For further information on Good Jobs First, see their website, www.goodjobsfirst.org/accountable_development/overview.cfm.

26. Michael Greenstone and Enrico Moretti, "Bidding for Industrial Plants: Does Winning a 'Million Dollar Plant' Increase Welfare?" Working Paper 04-39 (Cambridge, Mass.: National Bureau of Economic Research, November 2004). Also see William Hoyt, Christopher Jepsen, and Kenneth R. Troske, "An Examination of Incentives to Attract and Retain Businesses in Kentucky" (University of Kentucky, Center for Business and Economic Research, January 2007).

27. For example, the Mountain Association for Community Economic Development (MACED) has produced a "unified economic development budget" for Kentucky, which details the full range of state spending for economic development, providing a useful tool for activists and those who seek greater accountability for public spending, which can include business groups.

28. Louis Uchitelle, "States Pay for Jobs, but It Doesn't Always Pay Off," *New York Times*, November 10, 2003; Office of the Mayor, City of Indianapolis, "Indianapolis Lands More Than 900 New Life Sciences Jobs," press release, December 4, 2006.

29. In Uchitelle, "States Pay for Jobs."

30. *DaimlerChrysler Corporation et al.* v. *Charlotte Cuno et al.,* 547 U.S. Part 2 (2006).

31. Charles V. Bagli, "As Lower Manhattan Recovers, Many Question Use of Subsidies," *New York Times,* June 16, 2007.

32. The headquarters move, and the associated tax breaks, are now up in the air, as Applebee's was recently acquired by IHOP. See "Tax Break for Applebee's Now Uncertain," *Kansas City Star,* July 16, 2007.

33. Counting not only general-purpose city, town, and county governments, but special-purpose districts, school districts, and others, revealed a very large number of governments in older industrial areas. For example, in 2002, the Pittsburgh, Pennsylvania, Metropolitan Statistical Area contained 905 distinct governments.

34. Alberta Sbragia, *Debt Wish: Entrepreneurial Cities, U.S. Federalism, and Economic Development* (University of Pittsburgh Press, 1996).

35. Jerry Paytas, "Does Governance Matter? The Dynamics of Metropolitan Governance and Competitiveness," Carnegie-Mellon University, Center for Economic Development, December 2001, p. 15.

36. Ibid., p. 24.

37. See Margaret Dewar, "Why State and Local Economic Development Programs Cause So Little Economic Development," *Economic Development Quarterly* 12, no. 1 (February 1998): 68–87.

38. FutureWorks, "Minding Their Civic Business: A Look at the New Ways Regional Business-Civic Organizations Are Making a Difference in Metropolitan North America," report (Watertown, Mass., September 2004).

39. For a detailed discussion of current challenges and specific organizational examples, see chapter 5 of this volume, by Stephen Moret, Mick Fleming, and Pauline Hovey.

40. New Economy Strategies, *Road to Renaissance: A Collaborative Strategy for Regional Economic Growth* (Washington, November 2006).

41. Metropolitan Development Association of Syracuse and Central New York, *2006 Annual Report* (Syracuse, 2007).

42. Oakland Metropolitan Chamber of Commerce, *Taking Stock of Oakland's Economy* (Oakland, April 2007).

43. David Jason Fischer and others, *Seeking a Workforce System: A Graphical Guide to Employment and Training Services in New York* (New York: Center for an Urban Future, December 2003).

44. This history is detailed in Richard McGahey, "Workforce Intermediaries: Recent Experience and Implications for Workforce Development," in *Workforce Intermediaries for the Twenty-First Century,* edited by Robert P. Giloth (Temple University Press, 2004).

45. See Stuart Rosenfeld, Jim Jacobs, and Cynthia Liston, "Cluster-Based Workforce Development: A Community College Approach," White Paper (Carrboro, N.C.: Regional Technology Strategies, April 2003).

46. Individual cases and a typology are presented in Robert Harmon and Keith MacAllum, *Documented Characteristics of Labor Market–Responsive Community Colleges and a Review of Supporting Literature* (U.S. Department of Education, Office of Adult and Vocational Education, 2003).

47. Katherine L. Hughes and Melinda Mechur Karp, *Strengthening Transitions by Encouraging Career Pathways: A Look at State Policies and Practices* (Washington: American Association of Community Colleges, 2006).

48. Descriptions of the pilot sites and the new fund, along with reports on such topics as forming funder collaboratives, public policy advocacy, and industry-specific training approaches that build career opportunities, can be found at the National Fund's new website, www.nfwsolutions.org.

49. See, among other documents, Center for Workforce Information and Analysis, *Pennsylvania's Targeted Industry Clusters* (Harrisburg: Pennsylvania Department of Labor and Industry, 2006).

50. The best-known proponent of this view is Richard Florida, whose book, *The Rise of the Creative Class* (New York: Perseus, 2002), has attracted a great deal of attention and attempts to enact policies based on the analysis. Florida, like Michael Porter, has formed a consulting firm to work with cities and regions.

51. Porter had noted, briefly, that "geographic concentration of an industry acts as a strong magnet to attract talented people and other factors to it." But attracting talent in his analysis was only one "determinant" of regional clusters of competitive firms. Porter, *Competitive Advantage of Nations,* p. 157.

52. See the series of reports for the six cities at The Young and the Restless, a website created by Joseph Cortright and Impresa Consulting, www.restlessyoung.com/yar.

53. The older industrial regions include three in Michigan, centered around Grand Rapids, Flint, and Detroit. Other regions with older cities at their core include Philadelphia, Newark, Wilkes-Barre–Scranton, Rochester, and Milwaukee. On WIRED's overall strategy, see Emily Stover DeRocco, "WIRED Town Hall Remarks" (U.S. Department of Labor, February 22, 2006), available at www.dol.gov/_sec/media/speeches/20060222_wired.htm.

54. Michael Porter, Monitor Group, ontheFRONTIER, and Council on Competitiveness, *Clusters of Innovation: Regional Foundations of U.S. Competitiveness* (Washington: Council on Competitiveness, 2001).

55. See Mid-Michigan Innovation Team, *Regional Implementation Plan* (East Kalamazoo, October 2006).

56. Grant Oliphant, "Drafting the Plan," *h Magazine,* winter 2007, p. 9.

57. See www.neobarometer.org.

58. Randall Eberts, George Erickcek, and Jack Kleinhenz, "Dashboard Indicators for the Northeast Ohio Economy: Prepared for the Fund for Our Economic Future," Working Paper 06-05 (Federal Reserve Bank of Cleveland, April 2006).

59. The Community Foundation of Southeastern Michigan is assembling the largest philanthropic fund in the nation to date, $100 million, for their New Economy Initiative in the Detroit metropolitan region. See Sherri Begin, "$100m Fund for Detroit Coming?" *Crain's Detroit Business,* April 1, 2007.

60. See chapter 9, by Daniel Luria and Joel Rogers, in this volume.

61. Greg LeRoy, *The Great American Jobs Scam: Corporate Tax Dodging and the Myth of Job Creation* (San Francisco: Berrett-Koehler, 2005) for a disheartening catalogue of bad economic development deals, but also encouraging examples of the various efforts to increase transparency and accountability.

62. Julian Gross, Greg LeRoy, and Madeline Janis-Aparicio, *Community Benefits Agreements: Making Development Projects Accountable* (Los Angeles: Good Jobs First and the California Partnership for Working Families, 2005).

63. See chapter 4, by Manuel Pastor and Chris Benner, and chapter 13, by Angela Glover Blackwell and Radhika Fox, in this volume.

2

Revitalizing America's Older Industrial Cities: A State Agenda for Change

Jennifer S. Vey

Take a walk around any number of U.S. central cities, and you'll have a keen sense that the nation is in the midst of an urban renaissance. Employment is up, populations are growing, and many urban real estate markets are hotter than ever, with increasing numbers of young adults, immigrants, and empty-nesters reenergizing downtowns and neighborhoods that had long been in decline.[1]

Unfortunately, not all cities are fully participating in this resurgence. Throughout the country—and particularly in the Northeast and Midwest—a large number of older industrial communities are still struggling to make a successful transition from an economy based on routine manufacturing to one based on more knowledge-oriented activities. (See Chapter 6 in this volume for more information on the methodology employed to identify these cities.) Typically labeled as "distressed," "declining," or "weak," for the past several decades, the pervasive image of these cities—think Cleveland and Buffalo, Flint and Scranton—has been one of empty downtowns, deteriorating neighborhoods, and struggling families. Still grappling to overcome the painful legacy of severe industrial decline and population loss, these cities—and, for most, their surrounding regions—simply haven't seen the widespread economic revitalization now being enjoyed by so many other urban areas around the nation.

These cities weren't always in such troubled economic circumstances. To the contrary, they were once the economic, political, and cultural hubs of their respective regions, and the engines of the nation's economic growth. They were vibrant communities where new ideas and industries were conceived and cultivated, where world-class universities educated generations of leaders, where great architecture and parks became public goods, and where glistening downtowns grew up within blocks of walkable, tree-lined neighborhoods where the middle-class swelled and thrived. They were, in short, physical testaments to the innovation and spirit that shaped the nation and its citizens.

And so they can be again. Despite their challenges, older industrial cities remain a vital, if undervalued, part of the economy, particularly in states where they are heavily concentrated, such as Ohio and Pennsylvania. They also have a range of other physical, economic, and cultural attributes that, if fully leveraged, can serve as a platform for their renewal. In fact, major demographic and economic trends are presenting these cities with their best chance for a comeback in decades, with changing household structures, globalization, and technological advances causing a revaluation of the density and diversity that set urban areas apart from newer suburban communities.

Many older industrial cities are already experiencing some of the benefits of these changes, as new residents, new buildings, and new firms bring about real estate appreciation and revitalization to select streets and neighborhoods. But these pockets of recovery aren't enough to overcome widespread economic malaise, evidenced by these cities' continued struggle to overcome slow (or no) employment and business growth, low incomes, high unemployment, diminishing tax bases, and concentrated poverty. Good things are happening—but they need to happen more, and more extensively, in order to truly turn these cities around.

Public policy is crucial to this process—but it can't take the same old tack. If older industrial cities are to fully capitalize on the positive trends now at hand, government leaders—working in partnership with a range of for-profit and non-profit stakeholders—need to design and implement a new urban agenda, one aimed not at managing these cities' economic decline but at stimulating their economic revival. Cities, to be sure, must necessarily take the lead in developing their own goals for long-term revitalization, and a strategy by which to achieve them. But states can and should be powerful allies in helping cities carry that strategy out. Unfortunately, it's a role they have largely abdicated, to the detriment of the millions of people who call these communities home, of the wider economic regions of which they are part, and, ultimately, of all those who live, work, do business, and pay taxes in states that are themselves striving and struggling to remain competitive in the new economy.

This chapter focuses on how to reinvigorate America's older industrial cities. It begins by describing the challenges facing these communities, discussing some of the economic, demographic, and policy "drivers" behind their current condition. It then makes a case for why the moment is ripe for advancing urban reform, offers a five-part agenda for how states can help cities get there, and explains why anyone should care that they do. Finally, it lays out how local, regional, and state government, business, and civic leaders should organize themselves to move such an agenda forward—and ultimately ensure that America's older industrial cities are again innovative, vibrant, high-quality communities where their residents have the choices and opportunities needed to thrive.

The Origins and Challenges of America's Older Industrial Cities

Once upon a time, America's older industrial cities were thriving centers of business and commerce, the loci of the country's growth and prosperity. Although they were certainly not without their troubles, their relevance and function in the economy were understood and unquestioned.

But over the past five decades, globalization and rapid technological change have created a new economic paradigm in which the role of many central cities has become uncertain at best, downright precarious at worst. The seeming inability of the most distressed of the nation's cities to adapt to new economic realities can largely be explained by three interrelated economic, demographic, and political forces—and choices—that together have trapped them in a self-reinforcing cycle of decline.

The shift from a manufacturing economy to a knowledge-based one has left many older industrial cities still grappling to find their economic niche.

From the mid-nineteenth century until the mid-twentieth, the industrial revolution allowed cities—particularly those in the Northeast and Midwest—to grow and flourish as the new centers of the country's economic activity.

By the middle part of the twentieth century, however, changes in the global economy, coupled with technological advances and geopolitical shifts, began to diminish the importance of the geographical attributes upon which America's great industrial towns were built. First, other—cheaper—places to set up and maintain shop emerged, enabling the inexorable movement of manufacturing firms from cities to suburbs, from the North to the South, and from the United States to countries abroad. This physical redistribution of manufacturing was later coupled with advances in automation that sparked increases in productivity and a reduction in companies' overall employment needs.

Together, this "double whammy" rocked the economies of what had once been the nation's industrial powerhouses, evidenced by continued employment losses, slow income growth, and high poverty, among other indicators. The decline of manufacturing isn't in and of itself the reason for these cities' poor economic condition, however. Rather, it is the long-term legacy costs of deindustrialization that continue to hamper their recovery.

The first of these costs is these cities' failure to replace the large numbers of well-paying industrial jobs they've lost with high-paying jobs in other, rapid-growth sectors. Douglas E. Booth's research on industrial life cycles in the Northeast and Midwest demonstrates, for example, that a dominance of older established industries can actually thwart entrepreneurship and new business creation, and that employment destruction in old industries can overpower employment creation in new industries for a very long period of time.[2] Today's more successful cities, in fact, are generally either those that were not so heavily dominated by manufacturing, or those that were better able to navigate the transition from a manufacturing economy to one that is more diverse.

Lagging numbers of college-educated residents are a second legacy cost, representing a lingering vestige from a time when a high school education was all that was needed to attain the vast majority of good jobs. Today that is no longer the case, as jobs in most high-paying occupations demand a higher degree.[3] Not surprisingly, this lack of education is hampering these cities' economic development: for example, the analysis of 302 cities described in chapter 6 reveals that even a 1 percentage point increase in the percentage of the city population with at least some college in 1990 was associated with a 0.41 percentage point increase in employment growth over the next ten years. Meanwhile, low educational levels are also contributing to older industrial cities' lower income levels: according to a recent report by the Institute for Higher Education Policy, in 2004 the average total personal income of workers nationwide with only a high school diploma was $25,053, over $23,000 less that those with a bachelor's degree.[4]

Finally, deindustrialization has left a tremendous environmental legacy, manifested in the large numbers of contaminated parcels that scar older industrial cities' waterfronts and urban cores. A ride through any older industrial city reveals the trap of deterioration these sites are caught in, as they continue to be stigmatized by significant regulatory and financial constraints to redevelopment. This in turn has a ripple effect on proximate sites, suppressing values, discouraging investment, and devaluing cities' shorelines and historic neighborhoods—the very assets on which their future growth depends.

Extreme economic and residential decentralization has left the poor and minorities isolated in the urban core, spatially "cut off" from education and employment opportunities.

Decades of population loss during the latter half of the twentieth century exacerbated older industrial cities' deteriorating economic condition.

The first major exodus from urban cores began as early as the late nineteenth century, enabled first by rail, then by streetcar, and, within a few decades, accelerated substantially by the automobile. Although this movement was slow at first, as the twentieth century wore on, new highways, cheap mortgages, and racial prejudice lured millions of predominantly white upper- and middle-class Americans to the ever-expanding urban fringe, leading to rising levels of what was already entrenched urban black-white segregation, particularly in the large industrial areas of the Northeast and Midwest.[5]

By 1970, years of middle-class flight coupled with a declining industrial base had left many American cities hypersegregated, increasingly poor, and fiscally strapped—trends that would largely continue to worsen over the ensuing two decades.[6] During this period, cities were generally seen as grim places ravaged by poverty and unemployment, crime, and crack—views, not wholly unwarranted, that were reflected in the media and movies of the day.

By the 1990s, however, the tide had begun to turn for many cities. The crack epidemic receded, crime rates fell, and populations grew, resulting in the turnaround of many cities—from Chicago to Chattanooga—that had more or less been left for dead. But even as domestic and foreign immigration has since contributed to the rise of American city populations writ large, older industrial cities continue to struggle to attract and retain middle-income residents.

The economic impact of these patterns has been twofold. First, they have had a terrible effect on the families left behind in deteriorating neighborhoods with limited access to employment opportunities and good schools. Second, they have continued to undermine older industrial cities' economic prosperity and perpetuate the cycle of economic isolation. Population loss and high concentrations of poverty contribute to lower tax bases, higher crime rates, and greater demands for social services, undercutting cities' overall fiscal health and amplifying the gaps between cities and suburbs. Perhaps even more important, such conditions undermine cities' ability to cultivate a skilled workforce and frustrate their efforts to grow and attract the firms so essential to building and sustaining a strong economy.

Sixty-plus years of federal, state, and local policies have largely stacked the deck against cities, undermining their ability to attract and retain businesses and residents.

Both broad economic trends and the locational preferences of individuals and families have been the primary forces behind urban decline, but public policy and practice at all levels have in many ways exacerbated the problem. Through their substantial investments in infrastructure, economic development, social programs, and education, as well as through outmoded or cumbersome laws and regulations, federal, state, and local governments have—often unwittingly, sometimes not—facilitated the migration of people and jobs (and the tax base they provide) toward an expanding metropolitan fringe, while reinforcing the concentration of poverty and economic decline in older established areas.

For example, major federal policies on tax, trade, transportation, and immigration have a significant impact on the vitality of city economies and influence the shape of metropolitan growth. Meanwhile, federal policies on education, job training, wages, financial services, health care, and housing have a profound effect on the life opportunities of low- and moderate-income city residents. Many of these policies tend not to be spatially neutral. For instance, beginning with the construction of the interstate highway system, federal transportation spending has facilitated outward growth; today it continues to leave many older communities without the resources needed to build and maintain their aging roads and transit systems.[7] Federal housing and home ownership policies have tended to favor wealthier suburbs over urban neighborhoods.[8] And from Urban Renewal to more recent initiatives such as Urban Empowerment Zones, urban "redevelopment" programs have yielded a mixed bag of isolated successes, dismal failures, and many unanswered questions over what types of policies and incentive programs are most effective in improving distressed city neighborhoods.

States, particularly, have a huge role to play in shaping the form and function of localities. Through an array of policies and an enormous amount of investment, states determine the geography of governance, the fiscal playing field for municipalities and school districts, and the location and quality, in part, of regional economic growth. States also help shape the opportunities available for low- and middle-income families. Unfortunately, over the past half century state policies and practices have generally not been favorable to urban areas. At best, these communities have been treated with benign neglect, with state programs and investments focused predominantly on managing urban decline, as opposed to stimulating economic recovery. At worst, state policies and spending habits—

in transportation, housing, and economic development, among other areas—have actually worked against cities, encouraging growth in newer communities at the expense of cities and their residents.

Finally, although local governments have certainly had to grapple with economic and political forces larger than themselves, they are not simply hapless victims. Bloated government structures, poor service delivery, outmoded and unpredictable redevelopment processes and procedures, and economic development policies focused on fads are just a few ways in which cities repel new businesses and residents from locating in the city, diminish the opportunities available to existing families, and ultimately undermine their ability to overcome the real challenges associated with fueling economic growth that is robust, sustainable, and inclusive. It is these challenges that, together with their state and federal counterparts, older cities must find new and innovative ways to overcome.

Seizing the Moment for Change

Despite the economic challenges they face, the moment is ripe for the revival of older industrial urban economies. Older industrial cities possess a unique set of characteristics and resources that, if fully leveraged, could be converted into vital competitive assets. These include distinctive physical features, such as waterfronts, walkable urban grids, public transit, and historic architecture; important economic attributes, such as dense employment centers, universities, medical facilities, and, for some cities, proximity to more economically robust metropolitan areas; and rich social and cultural amenities, such as public art, theater, sports, and museums. Moreover, older industrial cities are still important centers of regional identity, inspiring a sense of pride and place, which, while often abstract, can be the first seed from which to nurture the momentum for change.

After decades of painful economic restructuring, the time is now for these cities to seize upon new trends and attitudes that have begun to revalue their special qualities. The 1990s brought a sea change in how urban areas are viewed—as places in which to invest, conduct business, live, and visit. The result has been a return of the market in many cities—or at least substantial parts of cities—that the private sector had once abandoned, and then ignored.

Unfortunately, most older industrial cities as yet have received only a small taste of the benefits of recovery. Although the potential is clearly there, many of the attributes just described are still largely underleveraged by state and local leaders, and undervalued by the marketplace. The moment to turn the tide is now.

Table 2-1. *Physical, Economic, and Cultural Assets of Older Industrial Cities*[a]

State and cities	Historic properties	Four-year colleges and universities	Community colleges	Hospitals and medical facilities	Museums	Major-league sports teams
Connecticut						
Bridgeport	54	1	2	3	1	0
Hartford	131	2	1	4	3	0
New Haven	60	3	1	3	3	0
Illinois						
Decatur	8	1	1	2	0	0
Indiana						
Muncie	37	1	3	1	3	0
Terre Haute	41	2	2	4	1	0
Massachusetts						
Fall River	104	0	1	3	1	0
New Bedford	32	0	0	1	2	0
Springfield	81	3	1	4	2	0
Maryland						
Baltimore	9	13	3	22	18	2
Michigan						
Detroit	227	4	2	14	4	5
Flint	19	5	1	3	2	0
Kalamazoo	40	2	1	4	2	0
Saginaw	29	0	0	5	2	0
Missouri						
St. Louis	7	15	5	23	15	3
New Jersey						
Newark	73	3	1	6	4	0
Trenton	40	1	0	5	5	0
New York						
Albany	57	6	4	5	7	0
Binghamton	20	1	1	3	2	0
Buffalo	66	6	3	11	7	2
Rochester	111	6	4	5	8	0
Schenectady	19	2	2	4	2	0
Syracuse	70	4	5	7	6	0
Utica	22	2	3	3	1	0
Ohio						
Canton	38	1	2	3	3	0
Cincinnati	242	7	10	16	6	3
Cleveland	216	8	4	14	9	3
Dayton	98	2	6	8	5	0

Table 2-1. *Physical, Economic, and Cultural Assets of Older Industrial Cities*[a] *(continued)*

State and cities	Historic properties	Four-year colleges and universities	Community colleges	Hospitals and medical facilities	Museums	Major-league sports teams
Mansfield	48	2	1	2	0	0
Springfield	29	1	1	2	3	0
Warren	9	0	2	3	0	0
Youngstown	48	1	1	5	3	0
Pennsylvania						
Allentown	17	2	2	4	2	0
Altoona	14	1	0	4	3	0
Erie	28	3	4	7	1	0
Harrisburg	35	2	3	3	2	0
Lancaster	78	2	3	3	8	0
Philadelphia	517	18	8	29	28	4
Pittsburgh	149	9	14	19	9	3
Reading	30	3	2	2	2	0
Scranton	26	2	2	4	3	0
Rhode Island						
Providence	155	5	0	6	4	0
Wisconsin						
Milwaukee	162	11	1	17	5	2
West Virginia						
Huntington	27	1	3	7	1	0
Total:	3,323	164	116	303	198	27

Source: Author's compilation, based on National Register of Historic Places, 2007; U.S. Department of Education, National Center for Education Statistics, 2007; American Hospital Association annual survey database, FY 2005; American Association of Museums, 2007; NFL, NBA, NHL, MLB, WNBA, MLS.

a. The analysis by Wolman and others of 302 U.S. central cities revealed that 65 are economically distressed when compared with their peers (see chapter 6, of this volume). Over two-thirds of these 65 cities (44) are located in the northeastern and midwestern states of Connecticut, Illinois, Indiana, Massachusetts, Maryland, Michigan, Missouri, New Jersey, New York, Ohio, Pennsylvania, Rhode Island, West Virginia, and Wisconsin, though cities in these fourteen states make up only 29 percent of cities in the complete dataset.

A series of demographic trends are having a profound influence on how and where people choose to live and could significantly benefit older industrial cities.

First, the nation is growing. Every state in the union experienced some growth during the 1990s, as did 93 percent of the nation's metropolitan areas, and the country's population is expected to rise by at least another 67 million people by 2025.[9] Not only do older industrial cities have a chance to capture a portion of the population growth taking place in their own metropolitan areas—even if such growth is relatively slow—but some also have an chance to take advantage of economic and demographic trends in proximate metros experiencing robust growth. For example, the "Live Baltimore" campaign has been promoting its comparatively affordable housing and convenient transit access to Washingtonians who want easy access to the nation's capital without the high costs. The potential is much the same in cities such as Providence, Springfield, New Bedford, and Fall River (near Boston) and Scranton, Allentown, Trenton, and New Haven (near New York), which are also experiencing similar "overflow" effects.

Much of this growth is being fueled by immigrants. Twelve percent of the country's current population was born outside the United States—the highest share since 1930, and one that, if existing trends continue, is likely to grow.[10] Increasing numbers of immigrants could be a boon to slow- or no-growth cities. Urban areas have always been, and continue to be, major gateways for foreign newcomers, and many cities that grew in the 1990s would not have grown at all— or would have shrunk even more—but for these groups. Despite the fact that the integration of foreign immigrants can bring about its own set of trials, over the long term these newcomers can bring new businesses, new markets, and new life to city neighborhoods.[11]

Meanwhile, our domestic population is aging. In 2000, residents over sixty-five accounted for almost 13 percent of the total population, a share that will continue to rise as the baby boomers move into "senior" status.[12] Older industrial cities have an excellent opportunity to sell themselves to this group, many of whom may be looking to give up their suburban homes in favor of environments that provide walkable access to shopping, services, and medical facilities. There are already signs that growing numbers of middle-aged "empty-nesters" are exploring city lifestyles: for example, the number of married couples without children living in a sample of the nation's downtowns, a group that includes those whose children have grown, as well as other childless couples, grew 17 percent during the 1990s, after having dropped in the previous two decades.[13] Further, recent research shows that, though the growing numbers of seniors and baby boomer "pre-seniors" will continue, on balance, to live in suburban areas, those migrating into cities in recent years have higher incomes than those leaving cities for the suburbs.[14]

Finally, the nation's family structure is changing. Over the past several decades, men and women have been delaying marriage and having fewer children, which, together with the aging population, are causing households to become smaller and more numerous, and the demand for housing units to increase.[15] These changing household structures already appear to be fueling a demand for more urban environments: in 2000, those in the twenty-five-to-thirty-four-year-old age group— the group Joseph Cortright calls "the young and restless"—were about 33 percent more likely than other Americans to live in a close-in metropolitan neighborhood, up from 12 percent in 1990.[16] Several older industrial cities are already magnets for this cohort: as of 2000, young adults made up over 30 percent of Philadelphia's downtown, for example, and nearly 27 percent of Milwaukee's.[17] If these trends persist, cities will have a strong upper hand in the increasingly competitive race to replace increasing numbers of retiring workers.

Although economic changes have undoubtedly contributed to the decline of cities reliant on "old-economy" industries, moving forward, they also have the potential to give them back their competitive edge.

The nation's shift from an economy based on the production of commodities to one dominated by the design, marketing, and delivery of goods, services, and ideas may provide advantages for urban areas. In the first place, service firms and new economy industries (including some types of advanced manufacturing) are generally more flexible in their demand for space than heavy manufacturing, allowing cities to better compete with their surrounding suburbs. In addition, firms' increasing penchant for disaggregating their physical locations by function has provided cities with new opportunities to attract "command-and-control" functions (for example, headquarters, marketing), research and development facilities, and consumer servicing operations that may benefit from denser, more urban locations.[18]

These economic shifts also demand greater numbers of highly educated, highly skilled workers, now the single biggest driver of economic growth across metropolitan areas.[19] This could be advantageous for cities. Although the average share of residents with a bachelor's degree is lower, on average, in older industrial cities than in their metropolitan areas, the reverse is actually true for most other cities—demonstrating the attractiveness of urban environments for many talented workers. Meanwhile, the number of downtown residents with a college degree has skyrocketed, even in economically struggling communities: research on downtown trends in forty-four cities revealed that the downtowns of Philadelphia (66.7 percent), Milwaukee (46.2 percent), and Baltimore (45.7 percent) were each among the top ten based on their share of residents with a bachelor's degrees.[20] Considering that, nationally, just over 24 percent of residents held a higher degree in 2000, these numbers can be a major selling point for cities in their quest to attract new firms.

Meanwhile, the role and function of colleges and universities, medical research institutions, and other institutions of higher learning in economic development and community revitalization are growing and changing. With so many of these institutions located within their borders, nearly all older industrial cities have an unprecedented chance to leverage the myriad economic benefits they provide. Beyond their role as educators, these institutions are increasingly vital to many local and regional economies, as trainers of the future workforce, as incubators of new knowledge-economy firms, and as employers, purchasers, and real estate developers. They are also major drivers of economic growth and revitalization, helping breathe life into faltering downtowns as in Cleveland; influencing neighborhood planning and development as in Philadelphia; and stimulating new local enterprises as in Pittsburgh. Perhaps most significantly, these schools are growing their roles as civic leaders, actively participating in decision-making about improving the health and vitality of their surrounding cities and regions.[21]

Finally, density may matter as never before. A variety of new urban scholars has begun to suggest that denser labor markets and more vibrant urban centers can actually improve economic performance, giving cities a clear advantage over many of their suburban counterparts. These scholars start from the premise, foreshadowed over one hundred years ago by Alfred Marshall, that density is a primary purpose of cities, and that clusterings of talented people are a prime driver of economic growth. Cities, and other dense agglomerations of economic activity, facilitate firms' ability to access workers and suppliers and foster the "knowledge spillovers" essential to spurring the innovations that increasingly drive economic competitiveness.[22] Density also matters on the labor side of the equation. The large number of employers within an urban area allows workers to change jobs more easily, giving them both greater flexibility and stability than employees in nonurban locales.

Cities have an opportunity to take advantage of a profound political and constituency moment.

As these demographic and economic trends unfold, public sector and nonprofit leaders are becoming increasingly aware that strong urban economies are key to building family security, healthy neighborhoods, and sustainable, prosperous regions, and they're shifting their policies and investment practices as a result.

To begin with, there are clear signs that some state leaders are recognizing and acting upon the link between city revitalization and competitive regional growth. For example, over the past several years, current or former leaders of Massachusetts, Michigan, and Pennsylvania have variously pursued strategies and policies focused on encouraging smarter land-use practices, brownfields remediation, open space preservation, and urban redevelopment. New governors in states with large concentrations of older industrial cities are also beginning to speak of the importance of urban revitalization, providing a unique chance to advance an agenda specifically aimed at these cities' interests.

Many philanthropic, civic, and community development organizations—including such groups as the Urban League, the Heinz Endowments, and Policy-Link, as well as numerous local and regional organizations—are also beginning to advance a new form of urban revitalization that focuses on market revival. These groups are now integrating poverty and housing initiatives with better schools, parks, transit, and public safety, and are launching programs focused on entrepreneurship and wealth building. They are also getting involved in initiatives to increase economic competitiveness and encourage innovation and the creation of quality jobs.

Finally, environmental and smart-growth leaders are increasingly focusing on the critical role that cities play in curbing sprawl, conserving open space, reducing pollution, and enhancing the nation's energy efficiency. For example, Smart Growth America is now an active partner in helping to organize statewide networks to advance state and local agendas for renewing older industrial cities. At a more regional level, PennFuture has added the Next Great City Initiative, dedicated to increasing the economic competitiveness and environmental health of Philadelphia, to its list of environmental protection programs. These groups and others like them will be vital partners in efforts to restore the economic health of cities as a means of protecting the nation's environmental health.

New attitudes and practices regarding density and development patterns are certainly still evolving. Yet efforts to date demonstrate that older industrial cities have an unprecedented opportunity to build broad-based coalitions around market-oriented approaches to urban revitalization, network building that will be crucial to their ability to seize upon the demographic and economic moments now at hand.

A State Policy Agenda for Revitalizing Older Industrial Cities

Certainly there appears to be no better time in recent history for reinventing and reinvigorating older industrial city economies. But to capitalize on positive trends, these communities need a new strategy for change, one that moves beyond policies and programs aimed at managing urban decline and instead includes a set of integrated policies and practices that together aim to improve citywide market performance. Such a strategy must start with local leaders, who must take the lead in establishing a vision for their future and a plan for implementing it. But they can't go it alone.

States are critical partners in any plans for older cities' revitalization, a point possibly belied by the fact that discussions of urban policy tend to focus on local action and federal programs. Some states are already taking a more active, if still limited, role in reinvigorating their urban areas. That's surely a good thing. But to truly catalyze older industrial cities' recovery, states need to develop a comprehensive urban agenda—one that both redresses state policies and practices that undermine urban prosperity and also advances pro-active, innovative ideas for change. Such an agenda needs to cut across what are typically separate and siloed policy areas, and should have five primary objectives:

Fix the Basics

To help older industrial cities create a strong climate for investment, states need to do their part to help them address the fundamentals. Even the best efforts at urban revitalization will have little chance of succeeding if the educational system is broken, residents and visitors feel unsafe, and the fiscal climate for businesses and residents simply "prices them out" of locating in the city. It is therefore vital that states help their cities "fix the basics": improve K–12 schools, curb crime, and create a cost climate competitive with cities' surrounding jurisdictions.

Transform neighborhood schools. Already substantial funders of local districts, states need to undertake a series of reforms to ensure that failing local districts have adequate resources, quality teachers, and modern facilities located in stable neighborhoods. First, states need to examine and update their funding formulas such that their investments are being fairly distributed across jurisdictions on a stable and predictable basis. Recent analysis by the Education Trust found that after adjusting for local costs of providing education, over 50 percent of states actually provide less funding per pupil to high-poverty, high-minority school districts than to low-poverty, low-minority districts.[23] Second, states should invest additional resources to help attract good teachers to schools in distressed urban areas and other challenging environments. This means not only ensuring that their base salaries, working conditions, and training opportunities are competitive with those in wealthier suburban districts but also providing bonuses (as North Carolina has done) for attracting, and keeping, highly qualified instructors in hard-to-staff schools. Third, states should follow the lead of Massachusetts by funding longer school days in struggling districts. The state is currently expending about $1,300 a day per student to lengthen the traditional school day in nineteen pilot schools, an effort that Governor Deval Patrick is planning to expand.[24] Finally, states need to help cities improve the environment in which students learn each day by targeting major investments toward capital improvements in aging inner-city schools. States should require that such funding be part of long-term local plans to make surrounding neighborhoods safe and stable for the children and families who live there.

Make the streets safe. Although safety typically is thought of as a purely local responsibility, states can in several ways serve as valuable funders, partners, and catalysts for more effective crime-control strategies in cities. Governors can help improve coordination of criminal-justice resources and serve as leaders in the effort to bring the many players in the criminal-justice system to the table to maximize coordination in efforts to reduce crime. In Michigan, in 2004, Governor Jennifer M. Granholm convened a Task Force on Jail and Prison Overcrowding to bring state and county governments together to ensure that limited resources for incarceration were being focused on incarcerating the most violent offenders.[25] States can also help local police departments improve the effectiveness of policing by funding state-of-the-art data systems, such as New York's well-known Comp-Stat system, to measure crime and manage police resources. Finally, and perhaps most significantly, states can play a powerful role in reducing the number of criminals who keep cycling through the system. States should work with local governments to design programs to help released offenders find housing and employment and get the substance abuse and mental health support they need in order to become healthy, productive urban residents. For instance, under Washington State's Community Juvenile Accountability Act, local courts and governments are encouraged to develop evidence-based programs to reduce recidivism. The state has also been a leader in efforts to make substance abuse and mental health services available to juvenile offenders.[26]

Create a competitive cost climate for businesses and residents. Local governments need to take responsibility for controlling their costs and streamlining service provision to residents, but states can help improve the fiscal milieu in which they operate and, in the process, help "level the playing field" between cities and suburbs. First, states could do several things to bolster cities' often precarious revenue situations: they could give localities greater flexibility to develop local-option revenue sources (such as excise taxes and various types of fees) so that they are not so reliant on the property tax, as well as allow—and incentivize—revenue sharing among neighboring jurisdictions so as to limit unproductive competition for retail businesses and firms. States could also do a better job of distributing local nonschool aid in a more predictable and fair way, with special attention to the needs of their struggling cities. They might, for example, create a payment-in-lieu-of taxes (PILOT) program, like that employed by Connecticut, whereby cities and other municipalities are paid a set percentage of the projected property taxes they would collect if their universities, hospitals, and other nonprofit institutions were taxable.

States can also play a major role in helping cities curb expenditures. Giving localities greater latitude to renegotiate retirement and health care packages with their employees as well as providing more transparency in the system regarding who mandates, and ultimately pays, municipal employees' pension benefits would be important first steps in helping cities rein in the skyrocketing costs of increasingly outmoded benefit systems.

Build on Economic Strengths

States need an economic development plan that focuses explicitly on reinvigorating their cities and other older communities. The most effective way to accomplish this is to build off these communities' existing economic strengths: by making targeted investments designed to renew the downtown core, by supporting industries where cities and their metros have a clear competitive advantage, and by enhancing both the physical and the economic connections between cities and regions.

Invest in downtown revitalization. Although a strong downtown doesn't necessarily assure a strong citywide economy, it certainly is a prerequisite for success. Consequently, it's vital that states help cities "set the stage" to bring people and businesses back to the core. At the most basic level, this can mean seed funding to help cities undertake a diagnostic of the downtown, including the number and type of downtown jobs and businesses, downtown's role in the metropolitan economy, the structure and state of the city's transit system, the condition of the infrastructure, and so forth. Local government, business, and community leaders can then use this information to develop a long-range strategic plan for market revitalization in which they set a concrete goal (for example, that 2 percent of all metropolitan residents will live downtown) and identify specific projects and programs the public sector should invest in to help reach it. States can target investments according to the plan by providing grants and loans to underwrite big-ticket real estate projects; by upgrading infrastructure, from mass transit to broadband in the downtown area; and by ensuring that state universities and community colleges located in or near the downtown core are key partners in the revitalization process. Following the lead of Michigan and Pennsylvania, states should require that downtowns be given first priority as locations for state-owned offices and facilities, and they should also look for opportunities to expand their suburban university and community college campuses into downtown areas.

Focus on cities' and metros' competitive niches. State leaders can help cities navigate the shift to the new economy through policies and programs designed to foster innovation and entrepreneurship and encourage growth in industries that will fuel prosperity in cities and their surrounding regions. This requires, first, that states undertake a rigorous analysis of the type and location of potential competitive clusters, including the unique opportunities, and challenges, associated with business attraction and cluster development in older communities. States then need to parlay this knowledge into a concrete plan to realign existing economic development dollars to capitalize on those strengths and niches. This might include creating and supporting programs to promote cutting-edge research and product development in universities and medical centers; investing in advanced manufacturing industries that could take advantage of cities' long-standing prowess in goods production; or providing financial and other supports, such as state-funded incubator facilities, to inspire risk taking among local entrepreneurs. One example of the last is Pennsylvania's Keystone Innovation Zone (KIZ) program, whose purpose is to align the combined resources of educational institutions, private businesses, commercial lending institutions, venture capital networks, and foundations to increase the rate of technology transfer and product commercialization.

Enhance the connectivity between regions. States can help cities forge physical and economic connections with other cities and regions in two major ways. First, state transportation dollars could be well spent on creating or expanding rail service between older industrial cities located in the orbit of larger hubs. Such links would allow workers in high-cost regions to take advantage of older industrial cities' more affordable housing, expand employment opportunities for existing older industrial city residents, as well as facilitate the ability of small and midsized cities to serve as back office or satellite locations for headquarters located an hour or two away.

States can also encourage stronger relationships among cities and regions with similar economic histories and assets. Of course, individual cities and regions must work to leverage their own unique strengths, but collaboration and planning among regions can help them and their institutions develop niches that complement and reinforce one another. Thus, rather than competing, neighboring metropolitan areas can instead work cooperatively to market the wider economic region to prospective firms and to grow strong networks of related firms, and the institutions and infrastructure needed to support them, from within. For example, the Hartford-Springfield Economic Partnership helps these two communities, located just twenty-five miles apart, to pool their resources and work together to build and market the regional economy, invest in transportation and infrastructure, and secure federal assistance. States can promote this type of collaboration through statewide economic analyses like the type described above that help individual cities and regions better understand not only their own economies but the special strengths of other areas. Moreover, states can identify ways to reorganize their agencies and programs to better align them with the spatial organization of the economy, even when it crosses state lines.

Transform the Physical Landscape

A true commitment to urban revitalization demands that states recognize and leverage the physical assets of cities that are most aligned with the needs of the changing economy, and then target their investments and amend antiquated policies accordingly. To this end, state leaders need to focus their resources on upgrading crumbling infrastructure in cities and older areas, invest in a few large-scale projects that have the power to truly catalyze a market turnaround, and give cities the tools they need to turn vacant and abandoned properties into marketable sites for development.

Fix it first. A recent issue brief by the National Governors Association offers a series of recommendations for how states can most efficiently and effectively use their limited infrastructure resources to both save money and enhance their existing assets. These include not only targeting investments toward areas of existing infrastructure but also prioritizing those investments so as to help restore the economies of particular communities.[27] This is sound advice. To achieve these goals, however, states first need to assess where current dollars are going and develop strict criteria for determining how they might be reallocated to improve the investment climate in older areas. They should also require that cities develop comprehensive plans outlining how capital, operation, maintenance, and replacement of deteriorating infrastructure systems align with neighborhood planning and economic development goals. For instance, New Jersey's Transit Village Initiative provides incentives to redevelop and revitalize communities around existing transit facilities, in accordance with municipalities' own visions and plans. Finally, states should examine opportunities to reduce costs by incentivizing cooperative agreements between neighboring jurisdictions to share overlapping or redundant services and systems.

Invest in catalytic development projects. To reinvigorate themselves, older industrial cities must once again start thinking creatively about the kinds of transformative investments that can have a true catalytic effect on urban redevelopment.[28] These might include tearing down an obsolete highway that cuts a city off from its waterfront, redesigning a large public park, or turning an abandoned wharf into a bustling shopping and entertainment district. Milwaukee spent $45 million to bring down the East Park Thruway in 2003 and restore the street grid beneath it, freeing up nearly twenty acres of land for new development;[29] and the continued development of Baltimore's Inner Harbor is one the most well-known examples of a large-scale waterfront redevelopment project in the country. Even less expensive projects can make a big difference, as evidenced by Scranton's $1.9 million investment to turn its deteriorating Nay Aug Park into a significant local amenity and regional attraction.[30] States can support such efforts by strategically targeting economic development, transportation, and other funds to locally identified projects designed to stimulate private investment. States can also catalyze local markets, as previously noted, by making smart decisions on the design and siting of state office buildings, public university campuses, museums, stadiums, and other facilities that often receive state investments.

Create marketable sites. States have an array of tools at their disposal that can help cities cope with their many vacant and abandoned properties and turn existing liabilities into market-ready development opportunities for the near and long term. In the first place, states are in a prime position to develop systems to inventory and track vacant and abandoned properties over time. States should provide funding to all local governments for the ongoing collection of parcel-based information on these sites—including information on their location, zoning, tax status, market value, and ownership—using state-established definitions and data collection criteria to facilitate collection and promote standardization across cities. This would go a long way toward helping cities identify and track opportunities to assemble and redevelop vacant lots. States should also then focus on ways to encourage large-scale redevelopment of underused sites. These should include

—Reviewing and reforming tax lien foreclosure laws to expedite the acquisition and disposition of delinquent properties, which under current systems can sit idle for years before the city can take ownership

—Developing new tools to promote brownfields development, such as an environmental insurance program (like Massachusetts'), or an environmental remediation tax-increment-financing (TIF) program

—Enabling the establishment of local land banks—as Michigan has done—that allow localities to gain clear title to vacant properties and assemble them for future use

—Continuing to allow the limited and appropriate use of eminent domain to redevelop blighted urban areas

Grow the Middle Class

Improving the economies of older industrial cities necessarily means improving the overall incomes of the families who live there. One way to do this is to make these cities more attractive to higher-income residents by improving schools, upgrading amenities, and growing high-end jobs. But this isn't enough. Older industrial cities cannot get ahead without working to alleviate poverty and increase the opportunities and wealth of their existing residents—without, in other words, growing the middle class from within. To this end, states must work with cities to improve the vocational skills of residents, ensure that workers take more money home at the end of the day, and reduce the high-cost burdens suffered by families living in poor neighborhoods.

Give residents the skills and connections they need to compete. The 1998 federal Workforce Investment Act has spurred states to streamline and enhance their workforce delivery systems. These efforts should be expanded to better serve the needs of inner-city residents. First, states should team up with local governments and nonprofits to design and fund programs to teach new and hard-to-employ workers—young adults, new immigrants, the chronically un- or underemployed—the basic skills needed to survive in the workplace. These can range from classes on the use of basic computer software programs to vocational English as a Second Language instruction to sessions teaching "soft" skills such as problem solving and customer service. States should also provide targeted resources to all types of postsecondary institutions—including vocational and technical schools, community colleges, and four-year colleges—to create or expand programs to help inner-city workers develop the "hard" skills required for jobs in growing sectors such as health care, or in specific regional industry clusters. These programs should be designed in close and ongoing collaboration with industry leaders, business groups, and private sector intermediaries and should include internship, apprenticeship, and networking opportunities that can help students make direct connections with potential employers both within the city and throughout the wider metropolitan area. Finally, states should invest directly in the creation and growth of workforce intermediaries—as Ohio, Pennsylvania, and California have done—that can help low-income workers establish career pathways to good jobs and help businesses access the job-ready employees they need to succeed.[31]

Make work pay for low-income workers. In order to help low-income residents keep more of what they earn, all states should follow the lead of the nineteen states that have enacted their own version of the federal Earned Income Tax Credit

(EITC). States should also take steps to streamline access to existing public supports for workers and their children. First, they can adopt more flexible policies and procedures for working families to enroll and remain in key state-administered benefits, such as nutritional supports, child-care assistance, and subsidized health insurance. These may include reducing onerous income and asset verification requirements; coordinating renewal periods and processes across benefit programs; permitting families to apply for programs over the phone, online, or by mail; and sharing a family's information from one program to update eligibility in other programs. Some Ohio counties, for example, allow families applying for child-care subsidies to apply for Medicaid on the same form.[32] Second, states can provide modest support to nonprofit organizations that facilitate access to key benefits for working families. Many such organizations began by conducting outreach to families eligible for federal tax credits like the EITC, but have now extended their efforts to include outreach, screening, and application for other work-support programs.[33] For instance, Pennsylvania (along with the City of Philadelphia) has provided financial support to Philadelphia's Campaign for Working Families, a collaborative of 17 organizations that provides free tax preparation and access to the EITC, other tax credits, public benefits, and asset-building resources.[34]

Reduce the costs of being poor in urban areas. States can play a major role in bringing down urban families' out-of-pocket expenses, freeing up money for investments in wealth growing assets, such as education and homes.[35] First, state leaders need to crack down on the unscrupulous business practices of mortgage lenders, check cashers, auto dealers, and others that drive up prices for the poor. Efforts could include, for example, capping the interest rates and fees set by payday lenders, as over a dozen states have done, and placing restrictions on mortgage prepayment penalties and predatory refinancing practices, as New Mexico and North Carolina have done. States can also target the demand side of the problem by helping low-income residents make decisions that are in their best financial interest. Illinois and Georgia, for instance, are among a number of states that now require a financial literacy class as a graduation requirement for high school students.[36]

Create Neighborhoods of Choice

It is now well understood that neighborhoods of concentrated poverty, many of which are located in older industrial cities, exact significant costs on families, particularly children. Residents of these neighborhoods are more isolated from jobs, are further removed from social networks, perform worse in school, and have greater numbers of health problems than those in more mixed-income communities. These neighborhoods are also costly for cities, in terms of both the high service demands and the lost opportunities they engender. State leaders need to focus on developing housing and redevelopment policies aimed at turning deprived areas where those with few options are consigned to live into high-quality communities where people of varying incomes want to live. They must also work to preserve neighborhoods before widespread decline sets in.

Support mixed-income housing. As neighborhood services and amenities improve, they naturally become more appealing to higher-income residents who have options as to where they choose to live; these residents in turn help create the market for more growth. But states can move this process along by encouraging the construction of more market-rate housing in inner-city neighborhoods. Several states, including Indiana and Massachusetts, now give preference in the allocation of their Low Income Housing Tax Credits (LIHTC) to developments that include market-rate units.[37] Such preference can be even more effective if new LIHTC developments are required to be part of a wider strategy for neighborhood revitalization.

Creating mixed-income housing isn't just about attracting wealthier residents to low-income urban areas but also requires that poor residents have housing opportunities in higher-income neighborhoods regionwide. To this end, states need to evaluate where LIHTC developments are located throughout metropolitan areas and ensure that they are being equitably distributed across communities of varying incomes. States should also encourage the implementation of local inclusionary-zoning statutes to boost the supply of affordable housing units being built in wealthier communities.[38]

Grow inner-city markets. State leaders need to work with cities and the private sector to help struggling neighborhoods attract the retail businesses, restaurants, banks, and other local-serving businesses that prospective residents seek and existing households desperately need. As a first step, states should appropriate resources to help localities collect, maintain, and promote more accurate information about neighborhood market potential through the use of innovative data collection, mapping, and other tools. They should then go further, to provide revolving loan funds and other financing mechanisms to directly support local efforts to attract supermarkets and other retailers to underserved areas, understanding that such seed money can go a long way toward helping cities acquire and assemble land, fill in financing gaps, or make vital infrastructure upgrades and traffic improvements. Finally, states should look for ways to creatively use existing resources to jump-start local markets. For instance, New York is employing its substantial depository power to encourage mainstream financial institutions to poor neighborhoods (called "Banking Development Districts") that can't attract them on their own, essentially subsidizing these banks by providing both below-market and market-rate deposits.[39]

Invest in preservation and rehabilitation. Many older industrial city neighborhoods can get caught in a blind spot where they are too well-off to qualify for many public sector community development programs, yet too run-down to attract new investment.

States can help local governments and nonprofits preserve these communities in a number of ways. In the first place, state leaders should help prevent housing abandonment through home ownership counseling programs and emergency loan, antifraud, and other laws and tools designed to prevent mortgage foreclosure and keep families in their homes. To help reduce the state's very high foreclosure rates, Ohio's Governor Ted Strickland created a Foreclosure Prevention Task Force to design a set of foreclosure prevention and intervention strategies to assist homeowners with distressed mortgages; the state is also offering a new refinancing program that will make available an affordable, fixed-rate financing alternative to home owners with mortgage loans that are inappropriate for their financial circumstances.[40]

Second, states should actively encourage the preservation and rehabilitation of aging homes and commercial areas. For example, all states should follow the lead of New Jersey, Maryland, and others that have adopted new building codes that encourage rehabilitation of existing structures by allowing greater flexibility in construction standards without compromising basic safety.[41] State leaders should also pass legislation authorizing state historic tax credit programs—as twenty-four states have already done—that give credits to home owners or developers who restore historically significant properties, many of which are located in urban neighborhoods.[42] Finally, states should create programs that provide low-interest loans and small grant funds to help low-income home owners and small business owners make necessary repairs, upgrades, and other physical improvements. Such programs can be a relatively inexpensive way to both improve the quality and livability of deteriorating properties and enhance the aesthetics of urban neighborhoods.

Conclusion

This agenda offers a new approach to state urban policy that ultimately will substantially increase the return on state investments in manifold ways. Revitalizing older industrial cities will lead to a reduction in unemployment and poverty, a rise in incomes and wealth, and an improved quality of life for urban families. It will increase the jobs, amenities, and housing choices available to suburban residents, enhance the regional market for business location, raise both urban and suburban property values, and improve the overall competitiveness of metropolitan areas. And it will enhance cities' attractiveness as places in which to live and work, leading to a more efficient use of already developed land, a decrease in energy consumption, a reduction in harmful emissions, and more sustainable metropolitan growth. Ultimately, this all adds up to stronger, healthier, more productive cities and regions that are a boon to, rather than a drain on, state budgets—evidence, to be sure, of money well spent.

But even the best of policy agendas will have little impact if local, regional, and state governments and constituencies don't have the capacity to effectively carry it out. In other words, moving forward with a real reform agenda for older industrial cities requires that these groups "organize themselves for success." In practice, this means several things. At the local level, city leaders, with support from their states, must make the competent, clean, transparent, and technologically savvy administration of government operations and services their highest priority, while working to build strong coalitions of innovative thinkers, actors, and stakeholders to develop and implement a competitive, long-term strategy for revitalization. At the metropolitan level, cities and suburbs need to work together to bolster opportunities in and the marketability of their regions as a whole, collaboration that states can help promote and incentivize. Finally, at the state level, urban leaders must band together across cities and regions to advance a state reform agenda like the one presented here. For their part, state leaders need not only engage in specific policy reforms but also look for ways to reorganize their programmatic initiatives and agencies so that they can be more effective partners in the restoration of city economies.

Implementing a real reform agenda for older industrial cities will naturally be an organic, messy, and frustrating process that will demand the patience, flexibility, and commitment of many diverse constituencies. Success won't come easy, it won't come soon, and it won't come to every city. But given the trends now afoot, there's little excuse not to try—and there's no better time to get started.

Notes

1. This chapter is based on Jennifer S. Vey, "Restoring Prosperity: The State Role in Revitalizing American's Older Industrial Cities" (Brookings Institution, 2007).
2. Douglas E. Booth, "Long Waves and Uneven Regional Growth," *Southern Economic Journal* 53, no. 2 (1986): 448–58.

3. For example, in 2005, over 95 percent of medical and biological scientists had a college education, as did at least three-quarters of those in the legal field and 65 percent of computer and mathematics specialists. See Miriam King, Steven Ruggles, Trent Alexander, Donna Leicach, and Matthew Sobek, Integrated Public Use Microdata Series, Current Population Survey: Version 2.0 (Minneapolis: Minnesota Population Center, 2004).

4. Institute for Higher Education Policy, "The Investment Payoff: A 50-State Analysis of the Public and Private Benefits of Higher Education" (Washington, 2005). The share with a bachelor's degree does not include those who have attained an advanced degree as well.

5. David M. Cutler, Edward L. Glaeser, and Jacob L. Vigdor, "The Rise and Decline of the American Ghetto," *Journal of Political Economy* 107, no. 3 (1999): 455–506.

6. From 1970 to 1990, older industrial cities such as St. Louis (−36.2 percent), Cleveland (−32.7 percent), and Detroit (−32.0 percent) lost, on net, approximately a third of their total respective populations. See U.S. Department of Housing and Urban Development, State of the Cities Data Systems.

7. Edward Beinborn and Robert Puentes, "Highways and Transit: Leveling the Playing Field in Transportation Policy," in *Taking the High Road: A Metropolitan Agenda for Transportation Reform,* edited by Bruce Katz and Robert Puentes (Brookings Institution, 2005).

8. See, for example, Gerald Prante, "Who Benefits from the Home Mortgage Interest Deduction?" (Washington: Tax Foundation, 2006), available at www.taxfoundation.org/news/show/1341.html, and Joseph Gyourko and Richard Voith, "Does the U.S. Tax Treatment of Housing Promote Suburbanization and Central City Decline?" Working Paper 97-13 (Federal Reserve Bank of Philadelphia, 1997).

9. Alan Berube and Bruce Katz, "The State of American Cities" (London: Department of Communities and Local Government, 2006); U.S. Census Bureau, "Interim State Population Projections" (2005), available at www.census.gov/population/www/projections/projectionsagesex.html.

10. U.S. Census Bureau, "Annual Estimates of the Components of Population Change for the United States, 2004–05" (2005), available at www.census.gov/popest/states/NST-comp-chg.html.

11. Recent research has shown that, over the past decade, immigrants nationwide have started a greater share of new businesses than native-born residents and have had an enormous effect on job growth and neighborhood revitalization in urban areas. In 2005, for example, an average of 0.35 percent of the adult immigrant population (or 350 out of 100,000 adults) created a new business each month, compared to 0.28 percent for the native-born adult population (or 280 out of 100,000 adults). See Robert W. Fairlie, "Kauffman Index of Entrepreneurial Activity, National Report 1996–2005" (Kansas City: Ewing Marion Kauffman Foundation, 2006). See also Jonathan Burtes and Tara Colton, "A World of Opportunity" (New York: Center for an Urban Future, 2007).

12. Census 2000.

13. Eugenie L. Birch, "Who Lives Downtown" (Brookings Institution, 2005).

14. William Frey, "Mapping Older America: Boomers and Seniors in the 21st Century" (Brookings Institution, 2007).

15. In the early 1960s, 80 percent of women had been married by the time they turned twenty-four. Today, it is not until age thirty-two that 80 percent of women have been married. See M. Hout and C. S. Fischer, "American Households through the Twentieth Century" (draft 5.1) (University of California, Berkeley, 2002), as cited in Joseph Cortright, "The

Young and the Restless in the Knowledge Economy" (Chicago: CEOs for Cities, 2005). The average household size, meanwhile, fell from 3.1 persons in 1970 to 2.6 in 2000, while the overall number of households increased by 66 percent. See Frank Hobbs and Nicole Stoops, *Demographic Trends in the 20th Century* (U.S. Census Bureau, 2002).

16. Cortright, "The Young and the Restless in the Knowledge Economy."
17. Birch, "Who Lives Downtown?"
18. Mahlon Apgar IV, "The Alternative Workplace: Changing Where and How People Work," *Harvard Business Review* 76, no. 3 (1998): 121–36; Saskia Sassen, "The Global City: Introducing a Concept," *Brown Journal of World Affairs* 11, no. 2 (2005): 27–43.
19. Robert Weissbourd and Christopher Berry, "The Changing Dynamics of Urban America" (Boston: CEOs for Cities, 2004), available at www.ceosforcities.org/research/2004/changing_dynamics.
20. Birch, "Who Lives Downtown?"
21. Jennifer S. Vey, "Higher Education in Pennsylvania: A Competitive Asset for Communities" (Brookings Institution, 2005); Initiative for a Competitive Inner City and CEOs for Cities, "Leveraging Colleges and Universities for Urban Economic Revitalization: An Action Agenda" (Boston, 2002).
22. Mark Muro and Robert Puentes, "Investing in a Better Future: A Review of the Fiscal and Competitive Advantages of Smarter Growth Development Patterns" (Brookings Institution, 2004).
23. Education Trust, "Funding Gaps 2006" (Washington, 2006). For example, after adjusting for the additional cost of educating students growing up in poverty, this study found that six states—Illinois, Michigan, Montana, New Hampshire, New York, and Pennsylvania—have funding gaps between the lowest and highest poverty districts that exceed $1,000 per child.
24. See Nancy Zuckerbrod and Melissa Trujillo, "U.S. Schools Weigh Extending Hours, Year," *ABC News,* February 25, 2007, and "Patrick Extends Himself," *Boston Globe,* February 27, 2007. These articles and additional information on extending the school day are available at the website of Massachusetts 2020 Education Opportunity, www.mass2020.org.
25. Michigan Task Force on Jail and Prison Overcrowding, "Final Report," prepared for Governor Jennifer M. Granholm, March 2005, available at http://www.michigan.gov/documents/report_119595_7.pdf.
26. National Conference of State Legislatures, "Lawmakers Visit King County, Washington, Juvenile Justice System," posted December 11, 2006, at www.ncsl.org/programs/cj/kingcounty.htm.
27. NGA Center for Best Practices, "Fixing It First: Targeting Infrastructure Investments to Improve State Economies, and Invigorate Existing Communities" (Washington, 2004).
28. See Bruce Katz, "Transformative Investments: Unleashing the Potential of American Cities," address at the Federal Reserve Bank of Philadelphia, April 5, 2006, available at www.brookings.edu/Metro/speeches/20060405_TransformativeInvestments.pdf.
29. See the website of the Milwaukee Department of City Development, "Park East," www.mkedcd.org/parkeast/index.html.
30. See the website on development in Scranton at www.scrantonpa.gov/development.html.
31. Heath Prince and Jerry Rubin, "Building New Labor Market Institutions: State Policies That Support Workforce Intermediaries" (Boston: Jobs for the Future, 2006).

32. The Center on Budget and Policy Priorities provides a comprehensive guide to simplifying and coordinating key low-income programs in states, "Program Simplification and Coordination," at www.cbpp.org/pubs/prosim.htm.
33. Many of these organizations, in turn, partner with nonprofit software developers who provide access to applications that facilitate benefit screening and enrollment. See Sean Coffey, Abby Hughes Holsclaw, and Julie Bosland, "Screening Tools to Help Families Access Public Benefits" (Washington: National League of Cities, 2005).
34. Sarah Torian, "State and Local Support for Earned Income Tax Credit (EITC) Campaigns" (Baltimore: Annie E. Casey Foundation, 2006).
35. Reducing the costs of living for low-income families by even 1 percent would add up to over $6.5 billion in new spending power. See Matthew Fellowes, "From Poverty, Opportunity: Putting the Market to Work for Low Income Families" (Brookings Institution, 2006).
36. Ibid.
37. Alastair Smith, "Mixed-Income Housing Developments: Promise and Reality" (Washington and Cambridge: Neighborworks and Joint Center for Housing Studies, 2002).
38. See Bruce Katz and others, "Rethinking Local Affordable Housing Strategies: Lessons from 70 Years of Policy and Practice" (Brookings Institution, 2003).
39. See the website of the New York State Banking Department, www.banking.state.ny.us/bdd.htm, for information on opening new bank branches.
40. The Ohio Foreclosure Prevention Task Force released its final report on September 10, 2007. See http://com.state.oh.us/admn/pub/FinalReport.pdf.
41. For more information, see Philip Mattera, "Breaking the Codes: How State and Local Governments Are Reforming Building Codes to Encourage Rehabilitation of Existing Structures" (Washington: Good Jobs First, 2006).
42. National Trust for Historic Preservation, "State Tax Incentives for Historic Preservation: A State by State Summary," chart (2003). As of 2003, California, New Jersey, New York, Ohio, and Pennsylvania are among the twenty-six states without a State Historic Preservation Tax Credit program.

3

The Talent Imperative for Older Industrial Areas

Randall Kempner

Talent is the nation's key innovation asset. America's workers and their families, present and future, are the first priority of the Council on Competitiveness's National Innovation Agenda. On an individual level, we must support workers' and families' ability to succeed, not merely survive, in a world in which skills needs are rapidly changing and the competition for jobs is global. At the national level, it's about human creativity and the human capital that drives innovation and economic growth.

—Council on Competitiveness, "Innovate America: Thriving in a World of Challenge and Change," 2005

In 2005, the Council on Competitiveness released its seminal report, "Innovate America: Thriving in a World of Challenge and Change," on what the United States must do to maintain its place as the most competitive country in the world. In "Innovate America," developed with the input of over four hundred academics, business leaders, and public policymakers, the Council lays out three broad areas of focus for the country: investment, infrastructure, and talent. Specifically, the Council identifies talent as the most important pillar that supports our national economic competitiveness. This call to action recognizes a fundamental shift in the basis of our prosperity.

In the twenty-first century, the primary drivers behind economic growth have been transformed. Where agricultural and mineral extraction drove nineteenth-century economic growth, and mass-production manufacturing drove the twentieth, it is the application of knowledge that is driving growth in the twenty-first century. This shift has created a related change in the types of inputs that are most important to economic success. In the nineteenth century, natural resources propelled wealth accumulation; in the twentieth century, it was machinery and financial capital; in the twenty-first, it is talented people.

In the "new economy," products and services can be developed and distributed throughout the world at a very fast pace. Because of the closeness, or "flatness," created by advances in communications and transportation technology, firms benefit by having access to a much broader market. Firms, regardless of location, also have much faster access to new technologies, systems, and processes. Management concepts such as total quality management are disseminated and adopted more quickly. New computer chips are simultaneously available in Texas and Thailand. As more competing global entities are able to develop (or quickly copy) similar products, the intensity of competition rises and firms are compelled to either develop new products more quickly or find another way to differentiate their offerings. This dynamic places a premium on innovation.

To succeed in the global economy, firms must continually innovate and economic regions must offer the assets necessary to support a strong innovation environment. Although there are many assets that matter for regional development—physical infrastructure, financial systems, and efficient governmental regulations among them—talented people are the engine of innovation. As a result, education has become the fundamental driver of wealth creation.

This chapter explores how older industrial areas can rise to meet this talent imperative. It begins by explaining the increasing importance of talent to regional economic development and then suggests opportunities for regions to meet their talent challenges by developing, retaining, and attracting skilled workers. The chapter reviews a variety of policies and programs that leaders from older industrial areas (OIAs) should consider when implementing a human-capital-based economic development strategy.

Talent Is the Key to Success

Throughout American history, higher education has always been correlated with higher wages. More education allowed individuals to have greater choice in their careers and access to the highest-paying jobs. Still, throughout most of our history, less-educated citizens were able to reach at least the middle class through manual labor and service work. Most industrial areas supported increases in population and wealth based on extraction industries or labor-intensive manufacturing. Firms located operations near natural resources or to take advantage of high quantities of unskilled labor. In the latter years of the twentieth century, though, the importance of education has spiked for individuals, firms, and regions.

The Returns to Education for Workers and Regions

In the three decades since approximately 1975, the income gap between the highly educated and less educated has widened significantly. According to research by the Institute for Higher Education Policy, in 2004 the average total personal annual income of workers nationwide with only a high school diploma was $25,053, more than $23,000 less than for those with a bachelor's degree.[1]

Joseph Cortright of Impresa Consulting has compared annual earnings, by education level, for the years 1975 to 2003. In 1975, advanced-degree holders earned an average of $16,725, approximately twice as much as individuals with only a high school education. By 2003 the multiple was approximately 2.75, which equated to an average salary of $75,600 for advanced-degree holders and approximately $27,900 for high school graduates.[2] On the basis of 2004 figures, the Educational Testing Service has calculated that mean lifetime earnings for male college graduates will be $2.7 million, 96 percent higher than the mean for male high school graduates. In 1979, the difference in lifetime earnings was only 51 percent.[3] Clearly, the returns to education are increasing.

So, too, are the returns to regions that host highly educated individuals. Cities with more educated residents have traditionally grown faster than those with less human capital. Research by Professor Ed Glaeser of Harvard shows that over the past century, both cities and their surrounding metro areas have seen increasing population growth linked to increasing levels of education.[4]

Traditionally, regional population growth has also been correlated closely with increases in income, but that relationship seems to have been broken. Robert Weissbourd and Christopher Berry, in their work on the changing dynamics of urban America, found that the decade of the 1990s marked the first time in modern American history that population and income growth were no longer correlated. Paul Gottlieb, a Case Western University scholar, has stated that for the first time regions could "grow without growth." On the other hand, studies have found that the relationship between education levels and regional income levels had intensified.[5]

In their comprehensive study of factors that impacted the growth of U.S. metro regions in the 1990s, Weissbourd and Berry conclude that the educational attainment of residents was the strongest driver of economic prosperity. According to their regression model, a 2 percent growth in the size of a region's college-educated population results in a 1 percent rise in regional income.[6] No other factor came close in terms of its impact on income.

Joe Cortright makes a further point: it is actually the young and educated that should be the key focus for regions that seek to thrive. By definition, young educated workers have more years to work and thus can produce more over their lifetimes than older workers. More than just productive workers, Cortright has found that members of the twenty-five-to-thirty-four-year-old age group are the most entrepreneurial in our society and are highly likely to be become civically engaged once they settle. Furthermore, as the baby boomer generation retires, members of this group will become increasingly in demand as regions will no longer have access to a large talent pool.

To succeed, regions must develop, attract, and retain college-educated workers. It is no longer the quantity of human capital that matters most, but the quality.

The Importance of Talent to Firm Location

These academic conclusions are borne out in practice. Talent tops the list when corporate executives and site selection consultants are asked to identify key factors in location decisions. This focus on talented workers is particularly critical for technology-based industries, but is increasingly important for all sectors, including manufacturing.

Bill King, chief editor, and Michael Keating, chief research editor, of *Expansion Management* magazine, explain the new calculus:

> In today's global economy, when a company is exploring possibilities for a future facility location, it is likely to have a list that includes not only U.S. cities, but also cities throughout the world. Where that company will choose to locate often hinges on labor and on which factor is more important: low costs or high skills.
>
> As a general rule, if that future facility is to be labor-intensive, it will usually end up in a low-cost location, possibly even India, China or Eastern Europe. In the cases where the labor component will constitute the bulk of the operating costs, the worker skill requirements are usually not very high. These also tend to be low-margin operations.
>
> If, on the other hand, it is to be a capital-intensive operation, it usually means that the skill set requirements for the workforce will be dramatically higher. While the labor component may still make up the majority of the

overall costs, these tend to be higher margin operations and it is the worker's brains, not brawn, that is the deciding factor.[7]

In the United States whose relative labor costs are significantly higher than those of its global competitors, corporate real estate executives and site selection consultants agree that a skilled workforce is the critical factor that allows a location to make it into the final consideration set. Consider this explanation for the decision made by Fidelity Investments to build a new 600,000-square-foot state-of-the-art operations center in the Dallas–Fort Worth (DFW) area:

> The DFW area offers the strong demographic profile that Fidelity considers important when making location decisions, including a highly talented and growing workforce, a strong business and community environment, and an opportunity to get closer to many of our customers and clients. The significant commitment and support from the Texas Enterprise Fund, along with support from the town and county, were essential in making the final decision.[8]

This description reflects the now-common approach to site selection for knowledge-based companies. First in importance is the quality of the available workforce and the likelihood that the skilled workforce can grow. Next, site selectors evaluate traditional business environment factors such as tax treatment, infrastructure, and the regulatory environment. Once regions have made it into the final round on the basis of their existing economic development assets, financial incentives often become the ultimate factor.[9]

This prioritization scheme is true even for traditionally capital-intensive industries such as auto manufacturing, and in traditionally low-cost states such as Mississippi. Jay Moon, president of the Mississippi Manufacturers Association, explains, "The automotive industry is like most manufacturers today. At the end of the day it's the workforce that builds the product and the product has to be world class because the competition is so intense."[10]

Labor Challenge for Manufacturers

Manufacturers face a growing challenge. Even though the old image of the factory floor as dark, dirty, and dumb has given way to the new reality of safe, sanitary, and smart facilities, many manufacturing-intensive regions now face a labor shortage. Most manufacturing firms that survive have invested in productivity-enhancing technology instead of more labor. Jobs in manufacturing today are less physically demanding but require increased technology skills. While the salaries are attractive, rising demand for technology-savvy laborers is increasingly hard to meet.

Over the past few years, the Council on Competitiveness has conducted interviews with hundreds of employers across the country as part of projects designed to support regional competitiveness. In regions from Spokane, Washington, to Rochester, New York, employers offered a common refrain when asked about challenges to their future success: "We have the skilled employees we need today, but are not sure about the ones we'll need tomorrow."

There is little reason to doubt that talent will continue to drive both individual and regional economic prosperity. According to the U.S. Employment and Training Administration, twenty-six of the thirty fastest-growing jobs over the next ten years in the United States will require at least some postsecondary training.[11] Between 2004 and 2014, approximately 46 percent of all job growth is expected to be generated in professions (management, technical, high-level sales) that require a college degree.[12] For the highest-paying jobs, an even greater percentage of jobs will require college training.

With no end in sight to the technological advances that enable the growth of knowledge-based industries, the need for skilled workers is unlikely to abate. Even entry-level jobs will require basic computer skills. Higher-level jobs throughout the economy will require significantly more capabilities, from technology comprehension to advanced management techniques to manage globally dispersed workers.

As the U.S. baby boomer generation retires and more global regions upgrade their ability to support high-value-added industry, U.S. metro areas will find the competition to retain highly skilled workers intensifying. As we look to the future, it seems increasingly clear that the level of education in the workforce will make the difference between regions that succeed and those that stagnate.

Talent in Older Industrial Areas

So, if talent is now the decisive driver of economic success, where do OIAs stand today? The short answer is that they are, by and large, lagging. OIAs are characterized by three common weaknesses: low educational attainment, talent flight, and weak workforce development programs. All need to be addressed for a region to succeed in the global economy.

Low Educational Attainment

In a country where educational results are faltering, the educational levels of residents of older industrial areas are falling faster than the average. Generally speaking, the U.S. talent development pipeline seems to be broken. While we are able to attract the world's best and brightest to our colleges and universities, our own secondary school system is declining in quality and is rife with inequities.

In international comparisons, U.S. high school students tend to do poorly in math, sciences, and foreign languages. And our relative standing continues to drop, even as we maintain one of the highest rates of expenditure per student in the world. To give one example, Council on Competitiveness analysis of the Program for International Student Assessment (PISA) international science assessment showed that U.S. students were twenty-second in the world in terms of math comprehension—behind emerging market countries such as Poland and Hungary—yet the United States was second only to Switzerland in expenditure per student.[13]

We are lagging in quantity as well as quality. Thirty years ago the United States could claim 30 percent of the world's population of college students. Today, the U.S. has only 14 percent, and that proportion continues to fall as other countries invest in higher education for their citizens.[14]

Within the United States, the older urban metropolitan areas (metros) fall toward the bottom for most educational indicators. From the Brookings Institution report, "Restoring Prosperity," which identified forty metro areas as weak older industrial areas[15] (table 3-1), we see that high school graduation rates in these areas lagged behind those of other U.S. metro areas by 1.6 percent. In 2005, less than 83 percent of OIA residents held high school diplomas compared to over 84 percent in the other 328 census-defined U.S. metro areas.[16]

The low performance is driven, in many cases, by the poor results of large urban school districts. In 2004, seven of the ten large urban school districts with the widest gap between their seventh- and eighth-grade reading and math test scores and their state averages were in OIAs.[17]

The disparity widens when one compares the educational attainment levels beyond high school. As we can see in table 3-2, the forty older industrial areas trail the rest of the nation in every higher education level comparison, and the gap is particularly wide at the college-graduate level. This is worrisome, for, as explained previously, a college diploma is becoming a critical credential if an individual wishes to enjoy rising wages over his or her lifetime.

Talent Flight

The plight of the OIAs is intensified by the migration of educated people away from these regions. Many of the best and brightest leave OIAs and never return. In 2004, the Census Bureau produced a special report that looked at the migration of single, young, college-educated people in metro areas. In general there has

Table 3-1. *Older Industrial Areas*[a]

Albany, Georgia
Albany-Schenectady-Troy, New York
Altoona, Pennsylvania
Baltimore-Towson, Maryland
Beaumont-Port Arthur, Texas
Binghamton, New York
Birmingham-Hoover, Alabama
Buffalo-Niagara Falls, New York
Canton-Massillon, Ohio
Cleveland-Elyria-Mentor, Ohio
Dayton, Ohio
Decatur, Illinois
Erie, Pennsylvania
Flint, Michigan
Harrisburg-Carlisle, Pennsylvania
Huntington-Ashland, West Virginia, Kentucky, and Ohio
Los Angeles-Long Beach-Santa Ana, California
Mansfield, Ohio
Merced, California
Milwaukee-Waukesha-West Allis, Wisconsin
Muncie, Indiana
New Orleans-Metairie-Kenner, Louisiana
Odessa, Texas
Pine Bluff, Arkansas
Pittsburgh, Pennsylvania
Providence-New Bedford-Fall River, Rhode Island and Massachusetts
Reading, Pennsylvania
Rochester, New York
Rocky Mount, North Carolina
Saginaw-Saginaw Township North, Michigan
Scranton-Wilkes-Barre, Pennsylvania
Shreveport-Bossier City, Louisiana
Springfield, Massachusetts
Springfield, Ohio
St. Louis, Missouri
Syracuse, New York
Terre Haute, Indiana
Trenton-Ewing, New Jersey
Utica-Rome, New York
Youngstown-Warren-Boardman, Ohio and Pennsylvania

Source: Author's compilation based on Brookings methodology.

MSA: metropolitan statistical area.

a. These forty metro areas ranked in the bottom third of an MSA Economic Condition Index on the basis of their change in employment, wages, and gross metropolitan product from 1990 to 2000 and their gross metropolitan product per job in 2000 (see also chapter 6, in this volume). In addition, each of these MSAs is home to one or more of sixty-five economically distressed cities (also identified in chapter 6).

Table 3-2. *2005 Educational Attainment in Older Urban Areas Compared with Other U.S. Metros*
Percent

Educational level	40 older industrial MSAs	328 other U.S. MSAs
Less than high school	13.1	12.0
High school	29.7	28.3
Some college	20.9	21.8
College degree (associate's or bachelor's)	23.3	24.7
Master's/doctorate	8.9	9.2

Source: Author's calculations, based on Council on Competitiveness, American Community Survey data, U.S. Census Bureau.
MSA: metropolitan statistical area.

been a flow of young, educated people out of rural areas into urban metros, and from urban metros into a small number of "hot" urban areas. From 1990 to 2000, only seventy-five metro areas saw an increase in the single, young educated population, while 243 saw a net loss of members of this group.[18]

The older industrial metros were hit particularly hard by this trend. As a group, the forty OIAs lost 15.5 percent of their young, single, educated population, while all U.S. metro areas overall lost, on average, 10 percent. Only four of the forty— Birmingham, Los Angeles, Milwaukee, and St. Louis—showed a net increase in their populations of this demographic group. The bottom five of the OIAs—New York's Syracuse and Binghamton, Arkansas's Pine Bluff, and Indiana's Terre Haute and Muncie—lost more than 30 percent of their "young and restless."[19]

The growing concentration of talented young people in fewer areas makes those areas even more attractive. Talented people seek to live with other talented people, creating a positive, self-reinforcing system. On the other hand, regions losing talented workers face a negative feedback loop that must be overcome to succeed in attracting educated residents.

Weak Workforce Development Programs

Metros need to do a better job of retaining the skilled workers who do stay. Unfortunately, workforce development programs generally do not have a strong history of success in older urban areas.

Public workforce development programs, which are primarily funded by the federal Department of Labor and administered by state agencies and local workforce investment boards, have come under criticism for failing to meet the expectations of their two ultimate clients: workers and employers.

The challenges for the workforce system begin with its fragmentation. Our federal, state, and local workforce funding programs and service delivery systems are highly diffused. At the federal level, there are multiple funding streams for services aimed at often overlapping populations. Each funding source has different rules and regulations and requires a federally authorized waiver if states wish to commingle funds. At the regional level, workforce investment boards that cover areas ranging in size from parts of cities to entire metropolitan areas oversee the provision of workforce services whose quality varies widely from place to place.

The public workforce system and regional economic development organizations have traditionally operated independently. As a result of this disconnect, workforce organizations have tended to focus on basic training and on supporting individual preferences for specialized job training, while economic development organizations have pursued target industries with an incomplete understanding of the workforce assets that exist within the region. Far too often, job training is insufficiently linked to the jobs that are being created.

With the increasing importance of human capital to regional competitiveness, there has been a growing recognition that individuals must develop a deeper set of skills and consider long-term career paths. Additionally, federal and state agencies have recognized the need to integrate workforce development, economic development, and educational strategies at a regional level and to implement systems that incorporate the skill needs of employers into the talent development system.

Progress is being made, though OIAs appear to be lagging behind. The U.S. Employment and Training Administration (ETA) tracks a variety of workforce system performance metrics at the state level, including a satisfaction survey of both employers and workers who interact with the system.[20] In each of the last three years, the three states with the majority of the OIA population—New York, Ohio, and Pennsylvania—have lagged behind other states. From 2003 to 2005, each of the states scored in the lower half of the nation in the rankings of both participant and employer satisfaction.[21]

In 2007, *Expansion Management*, a site selection trade magazine, launched its inaugural top ten list of state workforce development programs. On the basis of a survey of site selection consultants, the magazine determined that only two states with older industrial areas made the cut: Georgia and Texas. Only four of the forty metropolitan statistical areas (MSAs), which represented less than 5 percent of the total population of the OIAs, were located in states that were on the list.

If talent is the key to success, older industrial areas have a lot of work to do.

What Older Industrial Areas Can Do to Bolster Talent

For cities and regions to prosper in the knowledge economy, they must provide a high quantity of talented workers. There are three basic strategies to grow the talent force within a region: development, retention, and attraction. Of these strategies, development and retention are more sustainable and more likely to be successful in OIAs. Attracting talented people to a region can be successful, but it is usually best accomplished by targeted efforts within a particular industry cluster or by focusing on groups, such as former residents, whose members will be more likely to return. As the global market grows, it will be increasingly difficult for regions and their resident firms to attract individuals who have no ties to a particular area unless they are one of the few "hot" regions.

Workforce Development Strategies

The first and most important economic development goal for any city or region should be to develop and grow its workforce from within. This begins with ensuring that young people receive a quality education. Covering the full depth of school reform is beyond the scope of this chapter, so we focus here on a number of strategies that require special focus as part of any reform effort, including increased investments in early childhood education and making secondary education more relevant to today's economy. We also outline strategies that regions can employ to implement effective support systems for continuing education and training for those already in the workforce.

Invest in early childhood education. Human capital development should start at day one. The Nobel Prize–winning economist James Heckman has found that the greatest returns are achieved by investing in children at the earliest possible age.[22] Heckman and various other researchers, including Arthur Rolnick and Rob Grunewald, have made a strong economic case for investment in prekindergarten training. A variety of longitudinal studies have shown annualized returns on pre-K investment ranging from 7 to 18 percent.[23] The Federal Reserve Bank of Minneapolis, meanwhile, believes early childhood education to be so important from an economic perspective that it has launched a research center dedicated to the topic.[24]

Benefits from early learning are both individual and societal. On the societal side, successful early learning programs result in reduced government expenditures in special education and welfare costs and major benefits from the reduction in criminal activities. Well-trained young children receive increased earnings over their life spans and are set on a path in which they can become productive members of society and regional economies.

The Bill and Melinda Gates Foundation has recognized this opportunity and is focusing a significant portion of its philanthropy on early childhood education. In explaining its decision to develop an early learning strategy for Washington, the foundation states, "Neither our present educational system, nor our current public funding in Washington State is designed to support the fact that children's success in school and life is significantly determined before they ever enter kindergarten. By the time most funding and programs kick in to help children, many children are already behind socially, emotionally, and cognitively, and likely will never catch up."[25]

The foundation's program mentions Washington State specifically, but the lack of an effective early learning strategy is common across the country and in OIAs.

The Gates strategy, whose design is based on the foundation's assessment of early learning programs from across the nation, seeks to upgrade three related areas that will collectively affect early childhood success: parent support and education; comprehensive early learning centers that serve an entire community; and licensed child care.[26] Under this model, parents and caregivers will receive high-quality information and training on how to teach their children. To support parents and children with a diverse array of tailored services, the foundation will fund the creation of central child-care centers to serve as hubs for their communities. These hubs will also serve as models in an effort to upgrade the quality of existing licensed child-care facilities. The strategy places special emphasis on teaching children from low-income and low-education households.

Leaders in OIAs should follow the Gates Foundation demonstration project closely. Regardless of whether they choose this particular model or develop an alternative, it is important that OIA leaders develop an early learning strategy for their region.

Make secondary school training more relevant. Once children start their formal education, new challenges emerge. The first is keeping students in school and engaged in their studies. A second is ensuring that the skills these students are learning adequately prepare them for future participation in the workforce.

As indicated previously, many OIAs are struggling to provide their young residents with the basic reading, writing, science, and mathematics skills they need to succeed. Students from poor socioeconomic backgrounds or from families with low educational attainment face particularly steep barriers in reaching an acceptable level of proficiency.

Simply ensuring that students have a strong basis in core subjects is not enough, however. To thrive, students will have to be, as the New Commission on the Skills of the American Workforce, a bipartisan blue-ribbon panel of education experts, puts it, "comfortable with ideas and abstractions, good at analysis and synthesis, creative and innovative, self-disciplined and well-organized, able to learn very quickly and work well as a member of a team. They must have the flexibility to adapt quickly to frequent changes in the labor market as the shifts in the economy become even faster and more dramatic."[27]

That is a tall order, and one that can be met only if students stay in school and are being taught skills well beyond what is measured in our present standardized tests. One idea that seems to achieve this result is called *applied learning*. Research has shown that experiential learning—gaining knowledge through exercises that apply learning to actual situations—increases student engagement and overall achievement. By offering more opportunities for applied learning, particularly when it is customized to students' individual interests, urban education systems can both increase the relevance of their curriculums and boost students' interest in school. Innovative national public school operators such as Edison Schools and Big Picture Schools are incorporating this principle into their curricular approach.

Big Picture Schools starts with the concept that each high school student should select an area of interest around which a "personalized education program" is developed. Regardless of the interest area—be it dance, Latin American history, or biology—key baseline skills in math, science, and writing are incorporated into the student's curriculum through applied exercises. Students receive multiple opportunities to participate in experiential learning through internships, work with mentors, and team exercises. As a result, Big Picture students are more interested in their daily work and much more likely to stay in school than traditional high school students.

Edison has developed a curriculum that is based on traditional liberal arts training but incorporates an emphasis on helping "students develop practical skills from teamwork to technology that are crucial to success in the workplace." Edison's model incorporates significant participation of parents, mentors, and community leaders in the learning process.

An area where the applied learning approach has an obvious value is high school career and vocational education. Ironically, as the need for additional technicians and tradespeople is rising in the United States, the number of career and technical education classes has been declining. Many of these programs are expensive to operate and have come under criticism for not teaching skills relevant to the present skill needs of industry. As critical technologies change with increasing speed, it is difficult for schools to keep up.

In Florida, the Okaloosa School District has developed a program whose purpose is to ensure that the skills being learned are relevant to industry needs. Under their CHOICE Institute program, students follow a curriculum that allows them to earn high school credit, college credits, and industry certification at the same time. Students earn certifications recognized by national trade organizations in four institute areas that reflect local high-growth industries: aerospace, construction technology, creative arts, and information technology. Thus employers know exactly what they are getting when they hire students, and students have an opportunity to earn significantly higher wages right out of high school. In fact, an evaluation of CHOICE by the Haas Center for Business Research at the University of West Florida found that average CHOICE graduates can expect to make $298,000 more in lifetime earnings than the typical Florida high school graduate, even if they don't continue on to college.[28] Local business leaders are enthusiastic about the program because they are able to meet their workforce needs without recruiting outside of the area. The state of Florida recently passed a law, based on the CHOICE model, that funds career and technical institutes in every school district in the state.

OIAs—indeed, the country as a whole—should acknowledge the need for fundamental change in education. Over the past few decades, many new models and efforts to upgrade our pre-K–12 educational systems have been implemented. Two key findings are emerging from these efforts. The first is that to succeed, the change must be bold, comprehensive, and systemic. Incremental tinkering will not work. We have a new economy and it demands a new mechanism for training our children.

The second finding is that a single model of learning will not work for all students. To be sure, there is a core set of knowledge that all students need, but there are many ways to impart that knowledge. Students come to school with widely different skill sets, learning styles, and interests. A one-size-fits-all approach will not succeed and is not required, given the financial, technological, and human capital that we can employ to upgrade education.

The New Commission on the Skills of the American Workforce, launched by the National Center on Education and the Economy, gathered dozens of leading educational academics and practitioners to develop a comprehensive approach to school reform. Their report, *Tough Choices or Tough Times*, lays out a new model for training that is aligned with the demands of the global-innovation-based economy.[29] Community leaders—not just educational leaders—in OIAs should review the report and consider whether their region and state could benefit by embracing its recommendations.

Leverage new resources for public education. A comprehensive transformation of public education systems in OIAs will be time-consuming and expensive, but there is little doubt that increases in public educational funding are justified. Government, however, is not the only available source of investment. Across the country, new philanthropic foundations, such as the Bill and Melinda Gates Foundation and the Michael and Susan Dell Foundation, are supporting educational reform.

In the face of talent shortages, businesses are also increasing their involvement in educational initiatives. As Michael Bettersworth, the associate vice chancellor of the Texas State Technical College System, explains, "A few economic development organizations and chambers of commerce are increasingly realizing that improving a region's talent does not start with community arts projects, 'buffalo hunting' for firms, or TV ads on why companies should move to your area over another, but rather begins in a region's schools. An increasing number of companies of all sizes are speaking to this with their wallets, and more importantly, their time."[30]

Upgrade ongoing training and support. Improving pre-K–12 and college education will play a critical role in strengthening the future regional talent pool, but the vast majority of the people who will be in the workforce for the next twenty years are already in the workforce now. As the pace of technological change quickens, the need to upgrade and obtain new skills rises for all workers.

Today, however, on-the-job training is primarily offered to high-wage workers who work for large firms. Analysis of data from the Organisation for Economic Co-operation and Development (OECD) shows that employees earning more than $25,000 make up just half of the U.S. workforce but receive 72 percent of all employer-provided formal training. Thirty-six percent of all workers in the United States work for small companies with less than a hundred employees, but these companies account for just 12 percent of the total corporate investment in training.[31] To reach more individuals and improve their local labor pool, firms should consider developing training cooperatives, which reduce the cost of customized training. Furthermore, firms and their cluster organizations should proactively participate in the public workforce system by providing updated information on their particular skill needs and by working to improve the training services offered in local institutions.

Improve the public workforce system. Although the public workforce system has been criticized for its inefficiencies and disconnection from employers, in recent years the Employment and Training Administration has actively been trying to better link the workforce system with regional economies. Through grants and technical assistance, ETA has been encouraging improved collaboration among workforce development boards that serve the same metro area. Further, through the High Growth Job Training Initiative, it has fostered a closer collaboration between industry leaders in high-growth sectors and training providers to develop training curricula and programs that directly relate to industry skill needs.

In early 2006, ETA launched the Workforce Innovation in Economic Development (WIRED) initiative, a comprehensive effort to transform the present workforce system into a "talent development system" that better meets the needs of employers and workers. The WIRED program explicitly recognizes that innovation is the driver of economic growth and that to develop the talent necessary to fuel innovative companies the public workforce system must operate in partnership with educational and economic development partners at a regional (multicounty) level.

So far, thirty-nine pilot regions, all selected by competitive bid, have each received at least $5 million in funding from ETA to develop and implement integrated economic and workforce development strategies. Five of the OIAs—Saginaw, Flint, Scranton, Milwaukee, and Los Angeles—are participating in regional WIRED efforts.

The approach that WIRED is promoting—the creation of regional, innovation-based, integrated development strategies—is worth pursuing with or without the ETA pilot funding. Indeed, many of the regions that applied but were not selected are pursuing their strategies with other funding. States and OIAs should consider adopting the WIRED approach as part of their talent development strategies. At the very least, OIA leaders should closely follow the WIRED process and take advantage of the tools, leadership models, and programs that are being developed in other regions.

Implement lifelong learning programs. A few WIRED regions are focusing their efforts on developing a lifelong learning strategy that supports both new and more experienced workers. Incumbent workers are a particularly important group for older industrial areas. As most OIAs are losing their young, educated workers to other regions, they need to upgrade the talent that remains. To accomplish this goal, it is critical to develop approaches that incentivize ongoing skills training.

One promising approach is the creation of lifelong learning accounts, or LiLAs, portable individual savings accounts used to finance education and training that is selected by the employee. They operate in a way similar to individual retirement accounts, except the funds are used for training, not retirement.

Accounts being piloted now in Maine, Illinois, and Missouri allow individuals to enroll in accredited training programs operated by public, private, and union-based institutions.[32] The LiLA model allows for the individual accounts to accept contributions from employees and matches from other employers, states, federal programs, regional governments, and foundations.

Another related effort aims specifically to extend the careers of mature workers. Older workers typically offer more experience, more loyalty, and a stronger work ethic than employees just entering the workforce. Furthermore, since older workers are typically established residents, they are less likely to leave than younger workers. Mature workers represent an important resource that is not being fully tapped.

Employers, particularly in older industrial areas, are experimenting with alternative models for work in which older workers participate on more flexible or part-time schedules, and a few regions, such as North Central Indiana, are pursuing a more comprehensive approach to supporting these employees. The North Central Indiana initiative, Maturity Matters, is "pioneering how aging communities can better transform the untapped assets of passion, ideas, and resources that a mature worker possesses from their work and life experiences into a foundation for a vibrant future."[33]

A partnership led by the public workforce system in the region just north of Indianapolis has developed a strategy to assist both mature employees and local employers. The effort began with a baseline study about the economic status, educational characteristics, and particular employment needs of older workers. The initiative has also developed a handbook for human resource personnel that offers suggestions for how to recruit and retain older workers, as well as a series of career transition tools to assist mature workers in assessing and acting on their employment goals.[34]

Creating programs to assist workers who are already participating in the workforce offers a relatively fast and inexpensive opportunity to upgrade the regional talent base. It is certainly easier to implement a state- or region-focused training-support program than the critical but long-term reorganization of the secondary school system.

In the long run, older industrial areas that can support a successful system for adult learning may establish a competitive advantage over other regions. The Stanford economist Paul Romer has suggested that human capital is the only form of capital with infinite potential returns, but for this to be the case, human capital needs to be forged to the highest standards and continually upgraded.

Retention Strategies

Developing a well-educated and well-trained populace is a critical strategy for growing a talented workforce, but a region must also then be able to keep talent in the area if the societal and economic benefits are to accrue. There are a number of emerging strategies to retain human capital that relate to an individual's reasons for relocating.

Seize opportunities to retain talent. Americans in general are highly mobile when compared to most other nationalities, but it is young Americans—and particularly young, educated Americans—who move the most. According to Joseph Cortright's research for CEOs for Cities, the likelihood that people will move across state or metropolitan lines falls about 50 percent between a person's twenty-fifth and thirty-fifth birthday.[35]

There are three points when young adults are most likely to move: when they enter college, when they start their first job after college, and just before or after they start families. These three transition points offer opportunities for intervention with programs to encourage talented people to stay in the area.

Students entering college. The most common approach used to retain college students after graduation is preferential "in-state" tuition offered by publicly funded state universities. States provide a lower tuition rate for their native sons and daughters to ensure that taxpayers feel their funds are being used fairly and to keep talent in the state during—and then hopefully after—college.

Many states also offer scholarships to in-state students, typically based on high school success and ongoing academic achievement in college. Georgia's HOPE (Help Outstanding Pupils Educationally) scholarship program is the most established state program that awards merit scholarships. All Georgia students who graduate with 3.0 on a 4.0-point grade scale can attend a Georgia university for free as long as they maintain a 3.0 average in college. Kentucky, Louisiana, and Florida have established similar programs.

Regional organizations have traditionally played a less active role in this effort to retain students. There are few examples of regions or cities that guarantee college tuition, although some philanthropic organizations and businesses offer scholarships specifically to students from particular metro areas.

One exception is Kalamazoo, Michigan, which recently launched a program called the Kalamazoo Promise. Under this program, every graduate of Kalamazoo public schools who attends a Michigan public college or university will receive between 65 and 100 percent of tuition payments, prorated according to how many years they attended school in Kalamazoo.

Attempts to retain good students in a region are unlikely to have a significant impact on talent retention (though it may have other benefits, as will be described). Students do tend to stay in the state in which they attended college, but they are less tied to the region in which they attended college, and are even less likely to be influenced by the location of their scholarship provider. Further, requiring students to stay within the region or to return immediately after college may be counterproductive. Many educational experts suggest that the experience of living in another city and interacting with people from multiple backgrounds is part of the learning process. Still, the program substantially increases the accessibility of a college education for Kalamazoo students while contributing to the attractiveness of the city as a place in which to raise a family.

First job. Upon graduation from college, students leave their dorms and make new homes, whether just down the street or thousands of miles away. Communities with institutions of higher education have an excellent opportunity to retain students. An increasing number of regions—including many older industrial areas such as Northeast Ohio, Central Massachusetts, Boston, Hartford, Philadelphia, and Pittsburgh—have created partnerships with local educational and business institutions to attract students to the region for college and keep the human capital they have helped create.

The Philadelphia region has established itself as a leader in community efforts to attract and retain college students. Campus Philly, launched in 2003 as a collaboration between the city, state, local higher educational institutions, and nonprofits, is part of a larger regional economic development effort called the Knowledge Industry Partnership. Campus Philly pursues an integrated strategy based upon three *E*'s: enroll, engage, and employ.[36]

One of the key goals is to attract more and better students to enroll in schools in the region. Through a magazine called *Campus Visit,* the region markets its universities and colleges and explains the opportunities the region—not just its schools—offers college students. In addition, a website affiliated with the magazine offers additional information and links.

Once in the region, Philadelphia organizations seek to increase the number of students engaged in off-campus experiences. Campus Philly maintains a website that helps link students to social and cultural events in the city and offers updated information and discounts for students (www.CampusPhilly.com). In addition, the group promotes opportunities for community service and other local activities.

Finally, Philadelphia's regional universities and businesses have created an extensive internship program to encourage students to find employment in the area after graduation. In addition to traditional internship events, the Philadelphia regional partners organize fairs according to specific areas of interest such as business or arts, and host fairs geared specifically to minority and international students.

Other regions have worked to develop similar programs. In Northeast Ohio, for example, the private and philanthropic sectors have created special scholarships to help fund internships for talented students from within and outside the region. In Metro Hartford, leaders have launched a Corporate Intern Committee that supports a joint internship effort and hosts an annual "Welcome to Hartford Party" for the thousand-plus interns who come to the region every summer.[37] Other regions seek to complement internships with mentoring programs that link students to local mentors in their area of interest.

Campus Philly has implemented extensive efforts to understand the impact of its program. A 2002 baseline survey showed that only 50 percent of students planned to stay in the region, but by 2005, 65 percent of the students said they planned to stay. Actual retention has increased by more than one thousand graduates since 2004.[38] In general, Philadelphia and other regions have realized that it is helpful to build as many connections as possible between the community and its students during their college experience. The greater a student's personal engagement with the community through work, play, and service, the more likely the student is to stay in the region.

Starting a family. The third major event that often compels a move is when couples have their first child. This is the time when the preference for a large, fast-paced urban area is weighed against a desire to raise children in the comfort of a slower-paced setting, often near family. Hometowns have a chance to bring back their native sons and daughters.

Many are trying to do just that. Particularly in the Plains, the Midwest, and the Northeast, communities are embracing homecoming programs aimed at luring talented natives back. The state of Iowa has held receptions for former Iowa residents now living in Sun Belt cities with hopes of convincing them to return. Since 1977, Omaha has hosted a major reunion every two years called "Native

Omaha Days." Buffalo has a week-long event called "Buffalo Old Home Week." Although these events do not exclusively focus on bringing home families, one of the key focuses of these efforts it to promote the family-friendly aspects of the communities.

For families making a location selection, the quality of public school education is, not surprisingly, a top priority. Regions and cities that can tout above-average schools should do so. But there are many places that are "above average," so marketers need to find other distinguishing factors. The Kalamazoo Promise scholarships, for example, give the city a powerful tool in attracting families back.

As talented workers see increasing income growth, they are increasingly able to send their children to private schools or to live in select (and expensive) neighborhoods. Good schools and a safe, nurturing community are not enough for older industrial areas to regain their talented children, but they are certainly positive characteristics that can be leveraged by economic developers.

Grow the regional job market. Regardless of age or marital status, as level of education increases, so does the propensity to move. Talented workers, though, are more likely to stay in a region where they can easily find another position in the same field if their particular company or job disappears. Thus regional economic developers should *not* discard programs that are focused on the traditional economic goal of supporting firms that create high-paying jobs.

Cluster-based economic development strategies can help increase the depth of the regional job market. By fostering clusters—geographically proximate groups of firms, research centers, and associated institutions that focus on a particular industry sector or product—regions can direct resources to high-opportunity economic targets. For example, the polymer cluster in northeastern Ohio and the optics cluster in Greater Rochester, New York, are major components of their transitioning economies. By developing truly strong clusters in a few areas, regions can help boost companies' competitiveness as well as improve the labor market for workers.

Another key policy lever for talent retention is entrepreneurial support. Enabled by new information and communication technology and driven by our heritage of independence, Americans are increasingly seeking to own and operate their own businesses. In older industrial areas where the large firms that dominated regional economies are downsizing—think of Flint and GM, or Rochester and Kodak—entrepreneurship is a particularly important source of job growth. Having a strong entrepreneurial culture and support system will make it easier to retain talented residents who wish to stay in the area even after being laid off.

A variety of entrepreneurship support programs are being implemented across the country, including private and university-based business incubators, federally funded small-business development centers, entrepreneurial mentoring programs, and network development. Programs are increasingly targeted at nontraditional groups, including university faculty in areas other than business and engineering, college students, and older workers. The Kauffman Foundation, a Kansas City, Missouri–based foundation that supports entrepreneurship, has launched its Kauffman Campus Initiative to promote entrepreneurship "campus-wide," focusing specifically on nontraditional disciplines. The North Central Indiana Maturity Matters initiative also has a significant entrepreneurship component.

Over the past several decades, while the hottest markets have boomed, older industrial regions have been struggling to grow and attract firms and workers. Building clusters of industries and workers and improving opportunities for entrepreneurship are two key strategies these areas can employ to help spur a virtuous cycle of business and job growth, and ultimately build the strong human capital pools they need to thrive.

Invest in quality of place. It is increasingly possible for the most talented workers to live where they want. As a result of technology advances, an increasing number of job functions can be done off-site, or at least not at the corporate headquarters.

In response to the growing importance of human capital, companies are now commonly establishing operations around the smart people, not vice versa. And in some industries, particularly professional services such as consulting and accounting, firms are allowing their most prized workers to live where they want and telecommute. Talented people have more choices than ever in selecting how and where they live.

As a result, the lifestyle that a region offers its residents has become increasingly important in new ways. Richard Florida, a professor of business and creativity at the University of Toronto and the most influential proponent of quality-of-place strategies, explains:

> Quality of place—particularly natural, recreational, and lifestyle amenities—is absolutely vital in attracting knowledge workers and in supporting high technology firms and industries. Knowledge workers essentially balance economic opportunity and lifestyle in selecting a place to live and work. . . . The availability of job and career opportunities is a necessary but insuffi-

cient condition to attract young knowledge workers. Quality of place completes the picture.[39]

In 1990, Florida concluded that quality of place was a "missing piece of the puzzle" in regional economic development strategies.[40] Today, driven in no small measure by his work on the creative class, that part of the puzzle is no longer "missing." Regions all across the country are focusing on improving recreational amenities and environmental quality and promoting diversity as part of their talent-development strategies.

The state of Michigan has launched a "cool cities" effort to encourage the availability of art spaces and loft buildings for creative-class residents. Cincinnati, El Paso, and Memphis all have been upgrading outdoor recreational amenities in response to the types of activities that Florida argues are more attractive to younger knowledge workers. Successful talent attraction areas such as Austin, Seattle, and Portland, Oregon, which have traditionally implemented strong environmental policies in response to local concerns, now explicitly incorporate their environmental programs in their economic development marketing strategies.

When it comes to amenities, many older industrial cities start with a lead over competing regions. With their existing cultural offerings—museums, opera houses, and professional sports teams—as well as their historic architecture and streetscapes, they can offer an intimate urban environment that distinguishes them from the homogeneity of many newer areas.

To better serve the younger knowledge workers, however, civic leaders should consider making the "high" cultural activities more accessible. One common strategy is to have special nights and affinity groups for young professionals, such as that being offered by HYPE, the Hartford Area Young Professionals and Entrepreneurs. Outdoor hiking and bike trails, music venues, and cultural festivals are other nontraditional amenities that OIA leaders should consider investing more in. The key is not necessarily creating a large amount of new infrastructure, but leveraging existing resources such as parks, waterfront spaces, and performance venues that can be utilized in nontraditional ways.

Attraction Strategies

Although developing and retaining talented workers is the place to start, the ability to attract talent from outside the region is a strong sign of community health. Ideally, talented individuals from outside a region will be attracted because of the thick job market and regional quality of life. That said, talent attraction strategies

are also useful tools in building a high-human-capital region. Given their significant cost, however, it is important that any such efforts be carefully targeted.

Expand university-based programs. Efforts to attract top-notch research professors
with financial and institutional incentives have become common practice among
universities. Now, efforts to attract talent are being expanded to include student
recruitment.

In the 1980s, the University of Texas at Austin leveraged its endowment, then
flush with oil income, to attract world-class researchers and build research centers
relevant to the area's burgeoning microelectronics industry. Access to top talent
at the university was critical to the decisions of two research consortia, the Microelectronics Computing Consortia and Sematech, a semiconductor firm, to locate
in Austin.

In a similar effort, the state of Georgia, encouraged by its business community, launched the Georgia Research Alliance in the 1990s. The GRA brought
together six universities in Georgia and required them to determine the specific
research areas on which they individually wanted to focus. To sweeten the pot,
the state legislature approved additional funding for the recruitment of "star"
professors to the campuses. In addition to supporting higher salaries, the state
allocates funds—up to a million dollars—that the research professors can use to
build their laboratories.

As evidenced by the emergence of college and university consortia such as
Campus Philly and College 360, the fight for talent now extends beyond the best
professors. Colleges and universities that used to rely on local students are increasingly recruiting the best and the brightest from outside their regions. This effort
increasingly includes international students. The state of Massachusetts is considering a new program that would promote its universities to prospective Indian
and Asian students, and the New England Board of Higher Education has
planned a "Think New England Education Mission" to India in January 2008 to
promote the area to prospective students.[41]

Develop creative regional strategies. Rural areas, particularly in the Midwest, have
responded to brain drain by offering free land to people willing to move to the
region. Kansas has been the leader, with at least twelve communities that now
offer outsiders land and, in some cases, financial support in the form of help with
down payments to those willing to move to the Plains.[42]

China offers even greater incentives to lure home its natives who have studied
in the United States. The country offers financial incentives to entrepreneurs and

top-level researchers that can include direct payments, free housing, rent-free office space, and start-up funds for businesses or research centers.

The implication for older industrial areas is that they need to work closely with local business, academic, and workforce leaders to assess their talent needs. If these can't be filled by the local workforce, then attraction strategies should be considered. Free land may not be available, but other incentives such as tax breaks, low-interest loans, and business-development support can be extended to individuals. In addition, economic development leaders need to consider human capital when constructing their overall attraction strategies. A focus on firm-level attraction will not be effective unless the region can deliver a high-quality workforce and a quality of life that will keep talent in the region.

Conclusion

Today, economic development isn't just about new jobs, deals done, or tax revenue. Rather, regional prosperity is about developing, retaining, and attracting talented people.

Regional economic developers, political leaders, and community activists should embrace this reality and develop a talent strategy as a central aspect of their regional development plan. Older urban areas must determine how they will build their own human capital, keep the talented people already in the region, and implement targeted attraction efforts for the talent their firms and institutions need to support innovation.

This is no easy task, as the competition for talent is heating up globally. To win at this game, regions need to continually upgrade the resources they have to offer. These assets include the educational system; the workforce development system; the financial, physical, and institutional infrastructure that supports business development; and, increasingly, the amenities that make up quality of place.

There are some current trends that support older urban areas. Older industrial areas have many of the amenities attractive to younger talented people. Furthermore, these areas' density allows for the physical proximity of people and resources needed to create economies of scale in cluster development, training programs, transportation, and cultural assets.

Even though most older industrial areas start from a difficult set of present circumstances, they can take solace from the fact that many other regions face similar challenges—and that innovation is the driver of today's economy. If the global economy has proved anything, it is that people and regions with new ideas can leapfrog existing leaders.

Notes

1. Jennifer S. Vey, "Restoring Prosperity: The State Role in Revitalizing America's Older Industrial Cities," report (Brookings Institution, 2007), p. 23.
2. Joseph Cortright, analysis of U.S. Census Bureau, 2005 Current Population Survey data, personal communication, September 2007.
3. Educational Testing Service Policy Evaluation and Research Center, "Americas Perfect Storm," executive summary (January 2007), p. 2, available at www.ets.org/stormreport (accessed August 15, 2007).
4. Edward L. Glaeser and Albert Saiz, "The Rise of the Skilled City," report (Harvard Institute of Economic Research, 2003).
5. Robert Weissbourd and Christopher Berry, "The Changing Dynamics of Urban America" (Chicago: CEOS for Cities, 2004), p. 34.
6. Ibid.
7. Bill King, "2007 Knowledge Worker Quotient: The Top Metros in the Knowledge Economy" (*Expansion Management*, April 12, 2007), available at www.expansionmanagement. com/smo/articleviewer/default.asp?cmd=articledetail&articleid=18566&st=5 (accessed August 3, 2007).
8. Quoted in Ken Krizner, "2007 America's 50 Hottest Cities: Perception Is a Critical Factor in Attracting Expanding Companies" (*Expansion Management*, February 18, 2007), available at http://www.expansionmanagement.com/smo/articleviewer/default. asp?cmd= articledetail&articleid=18375&st=1 (accessed August 3, 2007).
9. In this case Fidelity was able to obtain $8.5 million from the Texas Enterprise Fund, a state-level "deal-closing" fund.
10. Quoted in Josee Valcourt, "Skilled Workers Essential," *Clarion Ledger*, August 14, 2005, Business Section, p. 1.
11. Council on Competitiveness, "Innovate America," p. 30.
12. Educational Testing Service, "America's Perfect Storm," p. 17.
13. Council on Competitiveness, "Competitiveness Index: Where America Stands" (December 2006), p. 91.
14. National Center on Education and the Economy, "Tough Choices or Tough Times" (San Francisco: Jossey-Bass and National Center on Education and the Economy, 2007), executive summary, p. 4, available at www.skillscommission.org/executive.htm (accessed August 13, 2007).
15. Vey, "Restoring Prosperity."
16. U.S. Census Bureau, 2005 American Community Survey data (author's analysis of data).
17. Vey, "Restoring Prosperity."
18. U.S. Census Bureau, "Migration for the Young, Single, and College Educated for the United States, Regions, States, and Metropolitan Areas: 2000," Internet release, April 13, 2004. Prior to the 2000 census there were only 318 designated metro areas in 2000; the Census Bureau increased the number of MSAs to 368 after the 2000 census.
19. Council on Competitiveness, analysis of U.S. Census Bureau, "Migration for the Young, Single, and College Educated for the United States, Regions, States, and Metropolitan Areas: 2000."
20. Standardized evaluation of workforce program performance on a regional level does not currently exist. Although evaluation of workforce investment areas is conducted, these areas range in size and very rarely align with the boundaries of the metropolitan area. For example,

the Albany, Georgia, MSA, which comprises two counties, is part of a fourteen-county workforce area; similarly, some counties in the Rocky Mount, North Carolina, MSA are included in a five-county workforce area, whereas another county has its own area designation.

21. Council on Competitiveness analysis of Employment and Training Administration data, available at www.doleta.gov/Performance/results/Reports.cfm?#wiastann (accessed August, 2007). Note that Pennsylvania did not report in 2005 and New York did not report in 2004.

22. Bill and Melinda Gates Foundation, "Investing in Children: An Early Learning Strategy for Washington State" (November, 2005), p. 10.

23. Arthur J. Rolnick and Rob Gruewald, "Early Intervention at a Large Scale" (Minneapolis Federal Reserve Bank, 2007), available at www.minneapolisfed.org/research/studies/earlychild/early_intervention.cfm.

24. For additional studies supporting the economic argument for early childhood investments, see "Early Childhood Development," Federal Reserve Bank of Minneapolis website, www.minneapolisfed.org/research/studies/earlychild/#ecd.

25. Bill and Melinda Gates Foundation, "Investing in Children," p. 6.

26. Ibid., p. 12.

27. National Center on Education and the Economy, "Tough Choices or Tough Times," executive summary, p. 8. (For further information on the commission, see www.skillscommission.org/commission_news_release1.htm.)

28. CHOICE Institutes, "Why CHOICE?" available at www.choiceinstitutes.com/why_choice.htm (accessed August 16, 2007).

29. National Center on Education and the Economy, "Tough Choices or Tough Times," executive summary.

30. Michael Bettersworth, associate vice chancellor of the Texas State Technical College System, personal communication, August 18, 2007.

31. Council on Competitiveness, "Competitiveness Index," p. 91, citing OECD data.

32. Council on Adult and Experiential Learning, "Informational Memo on LiLA Accounts," unpublished paper (2006), pp. 1–2.

33. Workforce Development Strategies, Inc., "Maturity Matters: Report and Key Findings from the North Central Indiana 60+ Success Study," available at www.wdsi.org (accessed August 15, 2007), p. 15.

34. Ibid., p. 5.

35. Joseph Cortright, "The Young and Restless in a Knowledge Economy" (Boston: CEOs for Cities, 2005), p. 7.

36. Todd Hoffman, "Growing and Keeping Your Region's College-Educated Workers," *Economic Development America,* Winter 2007, p. 24.

37. Metro Hartford Alliance, "Talent Attraction and Retention," available at www.metrohartford.com/pages/talent.html (accessed August 14, 2007).

38. Hoffman, "Growing and Keeping Your Region's College-Educated Workers," p. 23.

39. Richard Florida, "Competing in the Age of Talent: Quality of Place and the New Economy" (Pittsburgh: R. K. Mellon Foundation, Heinz Endowments, and Sustainable Pittsburgh, January 2000), p. 5.

40. Ibid., p. 7.

41. Mass Insight Corporation, "Making Massachusetts a World Class Talent Destination" (July 2007), p. 4.

42. See the website www.kansasfreeland.com, which extols the virtues of community life and inexpensive living.

4

Been Down So Long: Weak-Market Cities and Regional Equity

Manuel Pastor and Chris Benner

Traditional economic theory and standard economic development practice have tended to pose a contradiction or trade-off between efficiency and equity: what is good for one may be bad for another. The trade-off would seem to be particularly acute for cities and regions with weak economies: surely they cannot afford to pay excessive attention to issues of fairness and inclusion lest this take the eyes off the central prize of restoring competitiveness and promoting growth.

In this chapter we argue the opposite. We stress that pursuing equity is not at odds with a concerted effort to strengthen economically distressed cities; indeed, pursing inclusion, fairness, and broadened opportunity might actually be critical for urban and regional revival. To make this point, we start by exploring statistical research that looks at the relationship between key equity and growth variables in all metropolitan regions in the United States. We then develop our own model and examine how this relationship differs in regions with economically distressed central cities compared with all other regions. We find that high inequality, measured in a variety of different ways, has a negative impact on growth and that these impacts are in fact stronger in regions with what many in the literature call "weak-market" central cities.

This may not be entirely surprising for some who have been thinking about programs for struggling cities: the agenda the Brookings Institution has promoted for restoring vitality in weak-market cities, for example, combines the usual admonitions to find a competitive niche, ensure government efficiency, and redo infrastructure with calls for growing the middle class, primarily by helping the poor and near-poor, and becoming more effective at community development in lower-income neighborhoods.[1] Yet just because it seems like a good idea to promote growth and equity together does not necessarily mean that such programs will be implemented. To put such efforts into practice requires political will and strength, and putting together the necessary pro-growth and pro-equity coalition at an urban or regional level is not easy. Standing in the way is a long list of challenges, such as entrenched self-interests, historical animosities and racial tensions, unshakable political ideologies, fragmented local government structures, and eviscerated tax bases.

What are the political conditions and dynamics that can help overcome these daunting challenges in older industrial cities? To help answer that question, in this chapter we also look at the politics of growth and equity constituencies in three prototypical regions with older industrial cities: Pittsburgh, Detroit, and Milwaukee. We suggest that each has faced the challenge in a different way: Pittsburgh has been characterized by a paternalist approach, Detroit by high levels of antagonism, and Milwaukee by a certain degree of accommodation. The results, both politically and economically, have been equally mixed.

In all three regions, however, we see signs that the combination of good ideas and political will concerning the linking of equity and growth is coming together, a trend we see happening in other regions around the country as well.[2] This seems to be happening most frequently within broader metropolitan regions, rather than within individual cities. The jump to a regional scale seems to be opening up space for new and sometimes surprising political alliances, along with some increased willingness to experiment with new development initiatives that address the failings in our sprawling, fragmented, and unequal urban areas. Broadly speaking, the elements of successful strategies include a combination of robust economic growth, training for labor-market mobility, and community standards regarding wages and development. Putting all the pieces in place is hard but necessary—and an increasing number of business and community leaders are beginning to understand their complementarity.

Framing the Work

Why worry about helping economically distressed cities at all? The question is not altogether moot: David Rusk notes that when he made a visit to East St. Louis, Illinois's first African American county assessor, a native of the area, suggested that the best fix for his city's problems might be to evacuate the city completely and see whether market forces would bring it back in thirty or forty years.[3] Less extremely, one could imagine providing residents with vouchers to depart while empty lots were consolidated and converted to greenspace and urban agriculture.[4] In this view, the decline of America's older industrial areas is foreordained and our goal is to manage the decline as gracefully as possible.

Others have offered a range of reasons for preservation and indeed massive re-investment in such cities. These include a strictly economistic argument that we should capitalize on existing infrastructure—which includes anchor institutions such as universities and hospitals—and thus reinforce the agglomeration oppor-tunities of the new economy, which will eventually make their way to the places created by the old economy. There is also a sort of spiritual imperative, one that is akin to the urge that has driven Americans to save family farms: these older industrial cities are an important part of the fabric of American society, in terms of our history and architectural aesthetics.

There are also strongly held views that revitalization of weak-market or older industrial cities is critical to tackling the problems of poverty in America.[5] Indeed, although such cities house only about 9 percent of the nation's metropolitan pop-ulation, they house about 16 percent of the nation's poverty population. Racially, these cities contain only about 6 percent of the nation's white population but 13 percent of the Latino population and 20 percent of the African American pop-ulation. As a result, for those concerned about economic and racial justice, the fates of these cities is often a central part of their thinking.

Of course, the problems of inequality also exist within these cities and their regions, not just between cities and regions with strong and weak economies. Table 4-1 shows some dimensions of this inequality, comparing metros that have cities with struggling economies and those that do not. We use the classification of cities used by Jennifer Vey under the rubric of "weak markets," and link this with data we have generated on various forms of social inequality from census and other data.[6] We can see that economics is not the only relevant issue. Annual metro-politan per capita income growth over the 1990s was .4 percent lower in regions with struggling cities than those without. This was enough to let the weaker areas slip behind by about 4 percent in cumulative terms, but this seems like a small amount, one that might be recouped in a subsequent convergence to the mean.

Perhaps more striking are the sets of social differences in these areas. When we compare metropolitan statistical areas (MSAs) with struggling cities to all other MSAs, we find that city poverty rates were about 5 percent higher, whereas sub-urban poverty rates were actually lower—in short, geographic disparity was more

Table 4-1. *Comparing Inequality Measures across Metro Areas with and without Weak-Market Cities*

Unit = percentage, except as indicated

Area	Metropolitan per capita income growth (annual), 1990–2000	Central city poverty rate, 2000	Suburban poverty rate, 2000	MSA poor in high poverty census tracts, 2000	Index of racial segregation (whites-blacks), 2000	Ratio of income at the 80th percentile to income at the 20th percentile (100 = equality)
Metros with weak-market cities	1.4	21.8	8.9	48.3	62.7	440.2
Metros without weak-market cities	1.8	16.5	9.6	36.9	48.9	416.8

Source: Author's compilation.

pronounced. The concentration of the poor in the high-poverty census tracts was about twelve percentage points higher, racial segregation was far more pronounced, and the level of income inequality in the region as a whole (as measured by the ratio of the income of a family at the eightieth percentile of the regional distribution compared to a family at the twentieth percentile) was significantly higher as well.

How do we deal with these inequalities? Seeing the stark difference in America's older cities, particularly between city and suburb as well as between rich and poor, some activists have focused on trying to ensure that low-income residents get their fair share of the economic pie. The problem with this approach is that slicing up the spoils is of little comfort when the economy is itself growing slowly or shrinking. Indeed, many of the tools embraced by community advocates— pushing for living wages, insisting on community benefits, and stressing the construction of affordable housing—often seem much more suited to the stronger-market cities, for which taming and distributing growth is the central concern. Because of this, calls for "social equity" can seem like exactly the wrong remedy—perhaps the focus should be on restoring competitiveness and raising growth rates, with the hope that this will eventually benefit all residents and hence reduce disparity.[7]

We concur that economic growth is essential and recognize that many equity proponents lack a clear economic model and agenda, particularly in terms of determining which industrial sectors to support, which growth strategies to adopt, and which businesses to attract. We also think that equity proponents sometimes lack a vision of mobility, both across income and space—too often the notion is to improve people in place or simply raise the baseline wage standards for the least skilled. But we are also convinced that keeping equity among the foremost concerns will actually help promote revitalization.

Why would equity matter for growth? The reasons are complex but essentially revolve around the notion that inequity imposes high economic costs. Sharp disparities and unequal opportunities seem to be associated with an erosion of the social capital that ties regions together, leading to underinvestment in basic human capital (think families fleeing the public school system and then rebelling against taxes to support public education), significant conflict over the direction of economic development (think battles over subsidies and the location of new investments), and a general desire to jump the regional ship in favor of less problematic circumstances (think younger workers flocking to more dynamic and collaborative settings).

Research on the empirical links between social equity and economic growth that incorporates these insights has been slowly gaining ground.[8] One of the earliest studies in the United States, by H. V. Savitch and others, focused on fifty-nine metropolitan areas:[9] the main finding was that wider city-suburb disparities—one measure of fragmentation across metropolitan geography—were associated with a higher likelihood of regional stagnation.[10] William Barnes and Larry C. Ledebur subsequently examined seventy-eight metropolitan areas in the United States and found that the regions with the widest gap between central city and suburban income in 1980 had the most sluggish job growth during the following decade.[11]

Reviewing this early wave of research, Paul Gottlieb rightly noted that testing for the correlation of two variables is not the same as a multivariate analysis that considers other factors—and he also suggested that growth itself can affect equity, raising questions of simultaneity.[12] Both Richard Voith[13] and Manuel Pastor and others responded,[14] incorporating other explanatory factors and considering the feedback effects. Voith continues to find a positive association of suburban growth with city growth, and Pastor and colleagues found that various measures of inequality (the city-to-suburb poverty ratio, the geographic concentration of the poor, the change in central-city poverty, and more direct measures of income disparity) all had a negative impact on per capita income growth over the 1980s in seventy-four regions.

A more recent study covering the 1990s was published by the Cleveland Federal Reserve Board for the Fund for Our Economic Future based in Northeast

Ohio. Using a sample that included nearly 120 metropolitan areas that were similar in size to Cleveland, the researchers identified eight key factors that influence economic growth on the regional level. Using regression analysis, the researchers found that a skilled workforce, high levels of racial inclusion, and income equality do in fact correlate strongly and positively with economic growth, even controlling for other factors, including a number of more traditional business and quality-of-life variables.[15] Doing good and doing well can go hand in hand; a focus on equity can be consistent with improved results on growth.

Equity, Growth, and Distressed Cities

Does this equity-growth relationship hold true for regions with weaker central cities? There are reasons why some observers might think not: when an economy has sunk so low that economic survival is at stake, perhaps attention should be focused on anything that can retain and build industry. Fairness, in this view, is an "add-on": it should be a part of our concerns and an expression of our values, but surely it should not lead to, say, the sort of community-benefits agreements and other regulatory mechanisms that have emerged in regions with stronger economies. Moreover, much of the inequality we seek to correct may really be an outcome rather than a cause: thus, if we get the growth piece right, poverty reduction, racial desegregation, and intergenerational mobility will surely follow.

In examining this issue, we build on Pastor's recent work for the OECD in which he analyzed the relationship between competitiveness and social cohesion in over three hundred MSAs in the United States, using data from the 1990 and 2000 Census.[16] Building on the data set developed in that work, we first looked at the relationship between equity and growth in all regions, regardless of whether they contained so-called weak-market cities. We looked at the rate of per capita income growth for the MSA as a function of the following distributional or equity variables:

—Ratio of city to suburban poverty, 1990
—Percentage of poor residents in high-poverty neighborhoods, 1990
—Ratio of household income at the eightieth percentile to household income at the twentieth percentile, 1990
—Index of dissimilarity (black-white) at metro level, 1990

We also looked at a set of control variables, with the hypothesized effect indicated in parentheses:

—Percentage of working-age residents who are college educated, 1990 (+)
—Manufacturing concentration in central city, 1990 (−)
—Percentage of metro population in central city, 1990 (+)
—MSA unemployment rate, 1990 (−)
—Median household income, 1990 (ratio to U.S.) (−)

Why these signs? We expect that more college-educated residents will attract higher-value-added business enterprises and hence stir growth. The percentage of a metro area's manufacturing employment in the central city is an indirect proxy for the age of the region's manufacturing sector: in most regions, newer and more competitive manufacturing enterprises tend to have relocated to the suburbs. Following Vey and others, we assume that larger central cities will attract more economic growth for reasons of agglomeration.[17] We utilize the metro unemployment rate in 1990 as a business cycle control. Finally, the metro household income relative to the national average is assumed to have a negative impact for reasons of convergence;[18] a similar expectation (and a statistically significant sign) is found in the test on household income growth for ninety-eight cities over the 1980–2000 period performed in Furdell, Wolman, and Hill.[19]

The key variables of interest here are the measures of inequity in the initial period, which we expect to negatively impact per capita growth in the subsequent decade. Our argument is that these all reflect social and economic distance and, indirectly, proxy potential public conflict over growth, likely underinvestment in the broad workforce, and other signs of social dissolution.

The results of these regression exercises can be seen in table 4-2, in which we report beta coefficients (a measure of the degree of impact) and their t-statistics (a measure of significance).[20] All variables follow the expected pattern and have a very high level of significance. Since all these measures of distribution across place, race, and income are set prior to the income growth period being considered (along with the other variables), we are not as concerned about simultaneity or feedback issues. However, one simple argument might be that poor distributional measures at the beginning of one period reflect poor growth in an earlier period, in which case we are really just capturing the fact that these regions are on a low-growth trajectory. To look at this, we reran all the regressions, including a measure of per capita income growth from the 1980s. Growth in the 1980s did have a positive impact on growth in the 1990s, but the impact and statistical significance of all the equity measures actually rise (albeit slightly).

What are the effects of equity in regions that have so-called weak-market cities? Vey notes that such cities are disproportionately in areas where the metropolitan

Table 4-2. *A Simple Model of the Determinants of Per Capita Income Growth in U.S. Metropolitan Areas, 1990–2000*

	Coefficient	t statistic	Significance	Coefficient	t statistic
Percentage of working-age residents who are college educated, 1990	0.423	6.215	***	0.460	6.605
Manufacturing concentration in central city, 1990	−0.370	−1.755	*	−0.582	−2.657
Percentage of metro population in central city, 1990	0.466	2.117	**	0.522	2.314
MSA unemployment rate, 1990	−0.233	−4.403	***	−0.088	−1.217
Median household income, 1990 (ratio to U.S.)	−0.608	−8.715	***	−0.673	−9.600
Ratio of city to suburban poverty, 1990	−0.271	−3.788	***		
Percentage of poor residents in high-poverty neighborhoods, 1990				−0.254	−3.543
Ratio of income at 80th to the 20th percentile, 1990					
Index of dissimilarity (black-white) at metro level, 1990					
Number of observations	326			327	
R-squared	0.435			0.434	

Source: Data from Lewis Mumford Center, SUNY–Albany (http://mumford.albany.edu/census/data.html) and author calculations based on U.S. Census data Summary Files, 1990 and 2000.

***Significant at the .01 level; **significant at the .05 level; *significant at the .10 level

economy as a whole is not doing well, but there are some areas that boast stronger regional economies but distressed central cities.[21] Since the focus here is on weak-market cities, we entered a dummy variable that took the value of 1 if the region hosted a weak-market central city; these were 58 of the 331 regions for which we have all the necessary data (several of the weak-market cities share central-city status for one region, testimony to the power of neighbor effects). Not surprisingly, having a weak-market city in one's MSA has a negative and statistically sig-

Significance	Coefficient	t statistic	Significance	Coefficient	t statistic	Significance
***	0.491	7.038	***	0.386	5.702	***
***	−0.636	−2.934	***	−0.557	−2.554	**
**	0.604	2.692	***	0.443	2.006	**
	−0.041	−0.578		−0.209	−3.818	***
***	−0.716	−10.112	***	−0.568	−7.922	***
***						
	−0.349	−4.518	***			
				−0.191	−3.415	***
		327			327	
		0.447			0.433	

nificant effect on growth. But the more interesting and important question for this chapter is whether the effect of measures of inequity are more or less important for the regions in which weak-market cities are located. We thus created an interactive variable in which we tested separately for the effect of the equity measures in weak-market and non-weak-market regions (that is, regions with and without weak-market cities), pooling all the other variables across the sample as before. The results (see table 4-3) suggest, with one exception, that the negative

Table 4-3. *Social Equity Impacts on Per Capita Income Growth in Weak and Non-Weak-Market MSAs, 1990–2000*

	Coefficient	t statistic	Significance	Coefficient	t statistic
Percentage of working-age residents who are college educated, 1990	0.392	5.678	***	0.385	5.317
Manufacturing concentration in central city, 1990	−0.492	−2.265	**	−0.723	−3.282
Percentage of metro population in central city, 1990	0.587	2.600	***	0.602	2.691
MSA unemployment rate, 1990	−0.219	−4.130	***	−0.107	−1.494
Median household income, 1990 (ratio to U.S.)	−0.581	−8.235	***	−0.618	−8.681
Ratio of city to suburban poverty, 1990					
Weak market	−0.165	−3.265	***		
Non–weak market	−0.293	−3.973	***		
Percentage of poor residents in high-poverty neighborhoods, 1990					
Weak market				−0.408	−3.739
Non–weak market				−0.229	−1.946
Ratio of income at 80th to the 20th percentile, 1990					
Weak market					
Non–weak market					
Index of dissimilarity (black-white) at metro level, 1990					
Weak market					
Non–weak market					
Number of observations		326			327
R-squared		0.443			0.452

Source: Data from Lewis Mumford Center, SUNY–Albany (http://mumford.albany.edu/census/data.html) and author calculations based on U.S. Census data Summary Files, 1990 and 2000.
***Significant at the .01 level; **significant at the .05 level; *significant at the .10 level

Significance	Coefficient	t statistic	Significance	Coefficient	t statistic	Significance
***	0.413	5.854	***	0.340	4.994	***
***	−0.829	−3.828	***	−0.707	−3.211	***
***	0.723	3.273	***	0.548	2.488	**
	−0.029	−0.411		−0.186	−3.421	***
***	−0.666	−9.476	***	−0.554	−7.816	***
***						
*						
	−1.162	−4.591	***			
	−0.937	−3.697	***			
				−0.502	−3.733	***
				−0.303	−2.385	**
	327			327		
	0.476			0.450		

impact of initial inequity on growth is actually stronger (as measured by both the coefficient and the significance level) in the regions with weak-market cities.

The exception is the city-suburb poverty rate differential: although it still has a negative impact on growth, this is less pronounced in the regions with distressed central cities. This is of great political interest, given the tendency of some analysts (such as Myron Orfield[22] and David Rusk[23]) to focus on building bridges between central cities and older suburbs—it may well be that the payoff here is more with redistribution of regional resources than growth recovery. In any case, the overall pattern suggests that paying attention to equity is entirely consistent with promoting growth and may in fact be even more important in areas that have experienced economic decline.

A final word on this data analysis. Some might argue that we have not really addressed the issue of simultaneous causation—that is, whether growth in this period positively affects current distribution and so for that reason should be the main focus of policy attention. To some degree, both the choice of initial 1990 variables and the aforementioned inclusion of past income growth get at this question, but we also tried a more formal simultaneous modeling strategy in which we modeled per capita income growth as a function of all the economic variables previously discussed and the change in two distributional measures: shifts in the concentration of the poor and trends in the ratio of income for those at the key deciles of the metropolitan income distribution.[24]

We chose these two because they were themselves metropolitan-wide measures and there were good theoretical rationales for the reverse causation: since tightening labor markets tend to help the least skilled, growth would tend to improve the distribution of income and could deconcentrate poverty by providing the means for people to make different residential choices.[25] The results are a bit less well behaved—the simultaneous modeling reduces the significance of the manufacturing age and agglomeration variables—but the ongoing trends in inequity have the same negative and statistically significant impact on growth. When we split the sample to test in regions with and without weak-market cities—because the distributional variables were being allowed to be affected by growth, we could not use the interactive approach just discussed—we found that the effects for poverty concentration were stronger and more significant in the weak-market regions, whereas the negative impact of the direct income distribution measure was virtually the same in regions with and without weak-market cities.[26]

The subtleties of our regression analysis aside, the overall conclusions from these data seem clear. There may be many reasons to ignore social equity—for example, a firm belief that economic outcomes reflect skill differences, that markets are not to be tampered with, and that the government should not be in the business of addressing social ills. But there is very little evidence of what is often offered as the most compelling argument: we will kill the economic engine by focusing too much on who gets what. Instead, the results suggest that inequitable outcomes actually damage economic growth and that the effect is at least as pronounced in regions with the most distressed central cities.

What Is To Be Done?

Although providing evidence for a positive relationship between equity and growth is important, policy change requires more than just good information—it also requires mobilizing significant political will and institutional effectiveness. Such challenges may be particularly acute in weak-market cities, where a history of past distress makes political actors wary of current collaborations.

How does this play out on the ground? We provide here an assessment of the dynamics between regional growth and equity constituencies in three prototypical weak-market cities—Pittsburgh, Detroit, and Milwaukee. The three regions have all experienced dramatic social upheaval and economic distress associated with deindustrialization and globalization, but they have taken different approaches to economic restructuring and inequality in their region. In essence, the regions' stories are the following:

In Pittsburgh, elite leadership in the region has developed a clear regional economic restructuring strategy, which was initiated in the 1940s and has evolved since then. The dominant elite coalitions that developed behind this strategy also entered into paternalistic relationships with certain sectors of the equity advocacy community while excluding others—dividing the equity movement through a combination of co-optation and marginalization.

In Detroit, elite leadership in the region failed to develop a clear vision of a regional growth strategy, at least in part because this would have involved challenging the dominance of automobile manufacturing in the region. Labor unions were implicated in this acquiescence, and other social equity advocates were predominantly in an antagonistic relationship with elite leadership.

In Milwaukee, elite leadership has been successful in building a coalition around a regional growth strategy since the 1940s. Here, though, equity advocates—in the form of union leaders pursuing innovative strategies aimed at economic restructuring—have been critical partners in developing that strategy, particularly in recent times.

We examine each of these stories in more depth before turning to an examination of the growth and equity outcomes associated with these different political dynamics.

Pittsburgh

Pittsburgh is famous for its history as the core of the U.S. steel industry. At its peak, Pittsburgh produced two-fifths of the entire nation's steel and was the fifth largest metropolitan area in the country.[27] The decline of the region's steel industry actually began as early as the years immediately following World War I, but the region was particularly devastated by the recession and deindustrialization of the 1980s. In just six years, between 1980 and 1986, the region lost 42.6 percent of its manufacturing jobs, with 50 percent of this loss in the steel industry alone.[28] It is important to note that much of this decline in manufacturing was concentrated not in the city of Pittsburgh itself but in the neighboring steel mill towns that line the banks of the Monongahela, Ohio, and Allegheny rivers. Thus the landscape of decline is not as starkly driven by city-suburb divides in the Pittsburgh area as it is in cities like Detroit.

Overall employment in the region has retained some resilience, as the region's education, health care, financial, and other service sectors took up some of the slack. Thus, for example, the total population in the seven-county metropolitan area declined by only 12 percent from 1960 to 2000, dropping from 2.77 million to 2.43 million. At the same time, however, there has been a tremendous hollowing out of the city of Pittsburgh itself, and of Allegheny County, the core county in the metropolitan area. Pittsburgh itself lost 45 percent of its population between 1960 and 2000, dropping to only 335,000 in 2000. Allegheny County lost 21 percent of its population in this time, and saw its portion of the total population of the region decline from 59 to 53 percent.[29] The result of these patterns has been significant urban sprawl, disinvestment in many areas of Allegheny County (resulting in large parcels of vacant land and declining real estate and office building prices), and a significant aging of the population, as young people have migrated to other parts of the country in search of better employment opportunities.[30]

Elite leadership in Pittsburgh was successful in creating a viable regional coalition as early as the 1940s, when the Allegheny Conference on Community Development (ACCD) was established as a prominent public-private partnership, one of the earliest in the country.[31] This is in contrast to Detroit, where elite leadership in the region has never been able to unite around a common regional vision (discussed in the next section). In the face of tremendous environmental problems associated with the region's steel industry and the beginnings of signs of decline in manufacturing, the ACCD built a vision for the Pittsburgh region centered on promoting the city as a corporate headquarters and office city. From its founding in 1943 to 1970, the ACCD led a concerted redevelopment program in the city, which was later dubbed "Renaissance 1," whose expressed goal was to create a more attractive physical environment in order to retain corporate headquarters and promote office development in the downtown core of Pittsburgh.[32] The region's business and elected leadership basically gave up on trying to retain the manufacturing jobs in the region's river valleys that had sustained working-class communities since the late 1800s.

The alliance between business and political leadership in the region broke down for a period in the 1970s, when Pete Flaherty was elected to two terms as mayor of Pittsburgh on a "neighborhoods-versus-downtown" populist political agenda that garnered enough support from neighborhood-based interests to challenge the dominant Democratic Party machine. His efforts to promote more neighborhood-based development initiatives led to a breakdown in consensus between the mayor's office and the ACCD. It also, however, led to the ACCD's becoming increasingly involved in supporting particular types of community development, in part through wielding its influence over the funding of major foundations rooted in the region. By providing support for neighborhood development that focused on specific development projects and neighborhood-based revitalization, these efforts (along with a change in administration in 1977, when Flaherty left office) led to the diffusion of significant opposition to ACCD's vision for the region's future.[33]

By 1982, when the decline in manufacturing jobs that had begun as a trickle turned into a flood, the ACCD began to realize it needed another strategy beyond simply the downtown revitalization–corporate headquarters strategy that had guided their work since the 1940s. They organized an Economic Development Committee in 1981 to better understand the regional economy, eventually releasing a report in 1984 entitled "A Strategy for Growth: An Economic Development Program for the Pittsburgh Region." At the core of this new vision was a two-part strategy. First, regional leadership tried to promote high-tech industries, built around the research capacities of Pittsburgh's major universities, including Carnegie Mellon and the University of Pittsburgh. ACCD leadership played a critical role in subsequent years in supporting the creation of a range of cluster-based high-tech initiatives, including Pittsburgh Technology Council[34] (founded in 1983), the Software Engineering Institute at Carnegie Mellon (1984), the Pittsburgh Biomedical Development Corporation (1989), and, more recently, the Pittsburgh Digital Greenhouse (1999) and Pittsburgh Life Sciences Greenhouse (2001).[35]

The second major thrust of economic development strategies in the region has been to promote Pittsburgh as a cultural and entertainment hub. This has included substantial public investments in new stadium developments for the Pittsburgh Steelers (football) and Pittsburgh Pirates (baseball), a substantially renovated convention center, and efforts to create a cultural district in the downtown area with major music, theater, and arts attractions. More recently, regional leadership has tried to promote various recreational assets that take advantage of Pittsburgh's waterfront assets, including expanding bike paths, walkways, and water sports, which are seen as critical for attracting the young, highly educated, and highly mobile workforce that is the core of the region's knowledge industries. In short, since 1982 (starting much earlier than most declining industrial cities) Pittsburgh has pursued a classic "new-economy" growth strategy, centered on promoting innovation in knowledge-based industries and attracting a highly educated workforce.

There have been various movements that have challenged the ACCD-based consensus about the region's future. For example, faith-based organizers affiliated with the Industrial Areas Foundation organized a series of protests in the 1980s designed to highlight the complicity of Pittsburgh-based financial corporations in drawing manufacturing jobs away from the region (by investing in new plants in the U.S. south and overseas while refusing to invest in the renovation of Pittsburgh-area factories). These organizing efforts became increasingly confrontational over time (for example, activists dumped colored skunk water on bank executives after crashing a board of directors meeting and deposited rotting fish in bank deposit boxes after closing time on Friday evening of hot summer weekends), which eventually resulted in declining public support for their position.[36] Some innovative labor-based activists challenged the abandonment of regional manufacturing facilities, in part by promoting worker-based buyouts of declining factories and employee ownership. These efforts became institutionalized in the Steel Valley Authority (SVA), an intermunicipal economic development agency incorporated by the city of Pittsburgh and eleven riverfront Monongahela Valley municipalities in 1986, with the goal of revitalizing the region's economic base. The SVA's Strategic Early Warning Network has been valuable in identifying and helping manufacturing firms in the region that are facing challenging competitive conditions, but with inadequate public resources amid dramatic need, the SVA has struggled to have influence over regional decisionmaking processes, much less the overall direction of the regional economy.

The result is that through the 1990s, regional development was driven by a broad elite consensus in the region, centered on trying to promote "knowledge" and "culture-based" industries. Equity advocates were either captured in a paternalistic relationship focusing on neighborhood development and revitalization or marginalized outside of regional decisionmaking processes.

Detroit

The Detroit region has been hard hit over the past thirty to forty years by employment decline in the region's dominant auto industry, combined with a hollowing out of the central city. Detroit's economy has been almost synonymous with the auto industry, and at its peak, manufacturing accounted for over 40 percent of the region's workforce, with transportation manufacturing alone accounting for nearly 20 percent.[37] Manufacturing, once employing over 600,000 people,[38] by the year 2000 had shrunk to less than 340,000 of the region's workforce.[39] The region as a whole still has a higher proportion of the population employed in manufacturing than the national average, but it has struggled to diversify from its dependence on the declining automobile industry.

What is striking in the case of Detroit is how uneven much of the regional decline has been. Over the last thirty years, as the city of Detroit has declined, the suburbs have grown dramatically, as whites (and increasingly others) have fled the high tax rates and deteriorating infrastructure of the inner city to seek a better life in the surrounding areas. Between 1991 and 2001, for example, the city of Detroit experienced a 7 percent decline in employment, while employment in the suburbs grew by 25 percent; total population in the city in the 1990s declined by 7 percent and grew by 8 percent in the suburbs.[40] These patterns of flight and isolation have been accompanied by a tremendous disinvestment in the city, including abandonment of housing and properties. Detroit has almost ten abandoned buildings for every 1,000 residents, the second highest ratio of vacant buildings to population of all cities with over 1 million residents. The city is estimated to have over 10,000 abandoned buildings and the city itself owns approximately 45,000 land parcels that have reverted to city ownership because of tax delinquency.[41]

Detroit has an intense history of racial antagonism, and race relations permeate nearly all aspects of political and economic life in the region in a particularly obvious and prominent way.[42] These dynamics have left Detroit the most segregated region in the country, at least as measured by the black-white segregation index (a common measure of segregation; see table 4-1). The population of the city of Detroit itself was 81.6 percent black in 2000, whereas in the region as a whole (including Detroit), African Americans accounted for only 21.7 percent of the population.[43] Problems of disinvestment and urban decline in the Detroit region, however, are not as simple as a city-suburb divide might imply. In fact, many older suburbs in the region have also experienced deterioration of infrastructure and declining population. Between 1990 and 2000, 57 percent of Detroit's eighty-nine suburbs experienced declining population, and 13 percent declined faster than the central city.[44]

The region has responded in various ways to this crisis, but a broad governing coalition geared toward diversifying the regional economy has never been formed. Since the 1950s, automobile companies have moved plants out of the central city of Detroit to suburbs and other regions of the world. The big three auto makers retain headquarters in the region, but their focus has been more on restructuring within the auto industry rather than significant engagement in urban redevelopment and regional economic restructuring. Other local elites, based in the banking, utility, and real estate industries, have some involvement in regional development, but as service-sector offices have moved to the suburbs, these business leaders have all too easily abandoned concern with Detroit city and focused on their suburban economic base. After the riots of 1967, business leaders did create some regional organizations such as New Detroit, Detroit Renaissance, and the Detroit Economic Development Corporation, but none of these organizations has formed an effective overarching regional leadership coalition or vision.[45] According to one analysis:

> Detroit Renaissance and the Detroit Regional Chamber represent the white corporate community. Among these organizations, the Big Three automobile companies and others of the old corporate "nobility" have mainly influenced Detroit Renaissance. On the other hand, banks, utilities, and the rising service-based industries have mainly influenced the Detroit Regional Chamber. New Detroit and the Detroit Economic Development Corporation are seen as the structures for the articulation of black elite preferences and, in the latter case particularly, for the mayor. . . . These business organizations have tried to realize their own economic interests, but do not share a common vision for the region.[46]

These organizations have all played a role in promoting various projects and development initiatives in Detroit and its surrounding communities, but have been unable to bring together a viable regional coalition that is united around a cohesive vision for economic growth. As a result, Detroit has suffered at the hands of market forces and the ups and downs of the automobile industry. In essence, the strategy, by default, was to maintain a dependence on manufacturing employment as long as possible, and whatever other economic enterprises that could be developed in a localized and fragmented way.

Meanwhile, equity advocates in the region also failed to engage in developing a regional vision. Unions, dominated by the UAW (United Auto Workers), tended to focus more on meeting challenges in the auto industry and trying to hold on to whatever wage and benefit premiums they could, rather than in regional power-building strategies such as those developed elsewhere.[47] The African American community was divided between an inside and an outside strategy. The inside strategy involved contesting for formal political power, but this primarily involved gaining political power within the increasingly eviscerated city of Detroit or within business leadership positions, and then contesting for regional power in tension-filled struggles with white leadership in the suburbs.[48] The outside strategy involved community organizing and advocacy, but this was only outside in the sense of being apart from the formal political system—such efforts were rooted in the city of Detroit and centered essentially on a redistributive strategy rather than on promoting a new economic growth vision.

The white-black and city-suburb divisions among equity advocates in the region have been bridged only in recent years. Perhaps the most significant achievement in this area is by MOSES (Metropolitan Organizing Strategy Enabling Strength) a faith-based community organizing effort focused on regional campaigns that emerged from the perspectives and aspirations of their member congregations. MOSES was formed in 1997 as a regional affiliate of the national Gamaliel organizing network, with the explicit purpose of becoming a social-movement regional organization. Since its founding, MOSES has grown to include more than sixty-five congregations and five institutions of higher learning throughout the region. In addition to helping member congregations deal with neighborhood concerns such as community reinvestment and safety, it also works to address a broader set of systemic issues, including "urban sprawl, lack of affordable housing, lack of adequate transportation and education, infringement upon the civil rights of immigrants, land use, and blight."[49] The group's main campaigns in Detroit have involved attempting to gain more community control over the metropolitan transit authority and trying to smooth the way for the reuse of vacant land in Detroit. These campaigns have mobilized large numbers of urban and suburban residents and gained significant attention, both in the media and in policy arenas. Yet regional decision-making can still be described as taking place in the context of a divided leadership coalition and a largely disempowered equity advocacy movement.

Milwaukee

The national economic shift from manufacturing to a service-based economy affected the city of Milwaukee and the southeastern Wisconsin region significantly.

Between 1977 and 1987, manufacturing employment in the region declined by 19.6 percent.[50] The city of Milwaukee, the largest city in the region, was hardest hit, losing one-third of its manufacturing jobs between 1979 and 1987.[51] With the decline in employment, concentrated poverty grew. In 1979, 10.2 percent of census tracts in Milwaukee County were high-poverty tracts (where more than 40 percent of residents lived below the poverty line). By 1989, concentrated poverty had drastically spread to 47.4 percent of the county's tracts, though economic growth in the 1990s reduced this to 24.4 percent by 1999.[52]

In contrast to Detroit, in Milwaukee some of the most severe employment decline was in older, inner-ring suburbs rather than the central city. For example, despite overall regional employment growth between 1986 and 1996, eleven inner-ring suburban communities saw declines in jobs per capita, including Pewaukee (−14.8 percent), which fell from 74 to 63 jobs per 100 persons; Cudahy (−18.5 percent), which fell from 49 to 40 jobs per 100 persons; and West Milwaukee (−49.3 percent), which dropped from 81 to just 41 jobs per 100 persons.[53] Meanwhile, cities west of Milwaukee, primarily in Waukesha County, continued to lead the rest of the region in number of jobs per 100 persons, with the developing northern suburbs (in southern Ozaukee and Washington counties) gaining jobs at the fastest rate.[54]

Two factors are critical to understanding the Milwaukee region's response to these conditions. The first is the region's strong history of labor union organizing and its linkage with a generally progressive political environment. The second is the fact that the process of economic restructuring threatened, but didn't completely undermine, the traditional bases of trade union power in the region. These two factors created a fertile base for creative and innovative labor leadership to engage in innovative regional strategies.

Milwaukee's history of progressive leadership and trade union presence goes back to the early part of the twentieth century. The city has had more than forty years of being governed by socialist mayors, including the nation's first socialist mayor, Emil Seidel, elected in 1910; the longest continuous socialist administration in U.S. history with Daniel Hoan from 1916 to 1940; and arguably the last socialist mayor of a major U.S. city, with Frank Zeidler, from 1940 to 1960. Milwaukee continues to remain a Democratic stronghold in an increasingly Republican state.

Linked with this strong socialist tradition is a strong labor tradition, going back to at least the 1860s.[55] In 1865, Local 125 was formed in Milwaukee as part of the Molders Union, the nation's first modern trade union. During the Great Depression, organizing in Milwaukee's manufacturing industries led to Wisconsin's becoming one of the most unionized states in the nation (on a percentage-of-the-workforce basis). By the 1960s, 30 percent of the private sector was unionized, and in 1986, 25.1 percent of the region's workforce was still covered by a union contract, including 31.4 percent in manufacturing, 48 percent in construction, and 60.7 percent in the public sector.[56] The importance of unions in the region is not adequately captured by numbers, however—indeed, in 1986, there were fifty-one metropolitan regions in the country that had higher total unionization rates. More important was the fact that in Milwaukee, unions have been accepted as a key part of the political terrain in a way that provides key political openings for labor-based initiatives, including in the business sector.

The strong socialist and labor traditions in the region help to explain the particular nature of regional coalitions in this region. In Milwaukee, as in Pittsburgh, there has been a relatively cohesive coalition focused on regional revitalization and restructuring. A prominent player in building this regional coalition is the Greater Milwaukee Committee (GMC), which was founded in 1948 and plays a similar role in Milwaukee as the Allegheny Conference on Community Development in Pittsburgh. What is significant in Milwaukee is the extent to which unions and other civic organizations play a role in shaping GMC policies and activities. The integration of unions into Milwaukee politics is evident in the words of Julia Taylor, the president of the GMC, in an interview in 2006:

> The GMC has always had a strong labor component in our membership probably from the beginning. The GMC started back in the forties, but really got going in the fifties and sixties. I think the business leadership had a pretty good relationship with labor leaders at that time. This is a big manufacturing town, and labor was always at the table. I think both on the county executive side, as well as the business community side, they worked pretty well with the various labor leaders at that time. Our membership over the years has included key labor leadership in the membership. I've never really heard of problems working with unions as an issue in our work.[57]

It's a surprising statement from what is still primarily a business and growth-oriented entity, and one that reflects the simple fact of union power: businesses have had to get along with labor in order to get their way. The involvement of labor in the GMC probably also helps to explain why, during the economic crisis in the 1980s, the GMC focused significantly on efforts to revitalize a diversified manufacturing base in the region, in contrast to the vision developed by the ACCD in Pittsburgh.

The flip side of unions' involvement in regional politics is that Milwaukee's union leadership has had a keen sense of the importance of broader community ties with business-, government-, and community-based actors, rather than focusing simply on narrow collective-bargaining issues. This helps explain why unions in Milwaukee were successful, in 1992, in creating the Wisconsin Regional Training Partnership (WRTP), one of the most innovative and effective workforce training initiatives in the country. Starting with twelve firms, primarily in the metal-working industry, the WRTP membership has grown to include sixty companies employing 60,000 workers and fifty-six labor unions. It has built partnerships with community organizations, and partnered with the GMC in running a prominent Regional Jobs Initiative with a significant focus on disadvantaged inner-city residents.[58]

Impacts on Equity and Growth

How well did these various approaches improve growth and equity? A summary of key indicators for the three regions is provided in table 4-4. None of these city-regions has yet achieved a dramatic economic turnaround. Still, of the fifty-eight MSAs with struggling cities in our database, the Detroit, Milwaukee, and Pittsburgh MSAs all ranked in the top twenty in terms of the improvement in growth rates between the 1980s and the 1990s. This performance is particularly striking since the other regions that improved significantly from the 1980s to the 1990s were predominantly smaller metro areas, such as Shreveport, Louisiana, and Sag-

Table 4-4. *Growth and Equity Indicators for Detroit, Pittsburgh, and Milwaukee, 1990–2000*
Unit as indicated

	Growth rates			Poverty levels					
	Percentage per capita income change			Central city, percentage below poverty line			Suburbs, percentage below poverty line		
City	1980s	1990s	Change 1980s– 1990s	1990	2000	Change 1990– 2000	1990	2000	Change 1990– 2000
Detroit	13.1	19.9	6.8	30.2	24.7	−5.5	6.3	5.9	−0.4
Milwaukee	9.1	20.7	11.5	20.9	19.8	−1.1	3.2	3.5	0.3
Pittsburgh	11.7	17.0	5.3	21.4	20.4	−1.0	10.5	9.3	−1.2

Source: Data from Lewis Mumford Center, SUNY–Albany (http://mumford.albany.edu/census/data.html) and author calculations based on U.S. Census data Summary Files, 1990 and 2000.

inaw, Michigan, places in which just one new investment or positive economic shock can dramatically improve circumstances.

The achievements on the equity side are a bit more mixed. Milwaukee experienced the most improvement in the ratio of city-to-suburb poverty, with a modest decrease in central-city poverty and a slight rise in suburban poverty (though the region's suburban poverty rates were already extraordinarily low). In the Pittsburgh region, suburban poverty rates declined in tandem with city poverty rates, reflecting the fact that suburban poverty rates were already relatively high and a large share of the employment declines from deindustrialization in the region was concentrated not in the central city but in the steel towns along the region's waterways. Detroit saw a sharp fall in central-city poverty, though it still had the highest levels of central-city poverty of the three cases in 2000. As for overall regional income inequality, Milwaukee and Pittsburgh remained steady while Detroit improved slightly, presumably because of the central-city recovery. Levels of racial segregation also declined in all three cities, but this improvement was significantly less in these three regions than the norm for all weak-market regions and for the nation as a whole. Indeed, of the regions with weak-market cities, Detroit and Milwaukee ranked first and second, respectively, in both 1990 and 2000 in terms of racial segregation at the regional level.

Another and perhaps more comprehensive approach involves looking over a slightly longer period. Figure 4-1 provides such a general overview, charting the evolution of per capita income and the poverty rate for all three regions, compared with the performance for all MSAs. As can be seen, all three MSAs experienced a

City-suburb inequality			Income inequality			Racial segregation		
Ratio, city-suburb poverty levels			80/20 Ratio family income			White-Black Dissimilarity Index		
1990	2000	Change 1990–2000	1990	2000	Change 1990–2000	1990	2000	Change 1990–2000
4.8	4.2	−0.6	4.7	4.3	−0.4	87.5	84.7	−2.8
6.6	5.7	−0.9	3.9	4.1	0.1	82.8	82.2	−0.6
2.0	2.2	0.1	4.5	4.4	−0.1	70.9	67.3	−3.6

Figure 4-1. *Per Capita Income and Poverty Rates at the Metropolitan Level, Three Case Studies, 1980, 1990, and 2000*

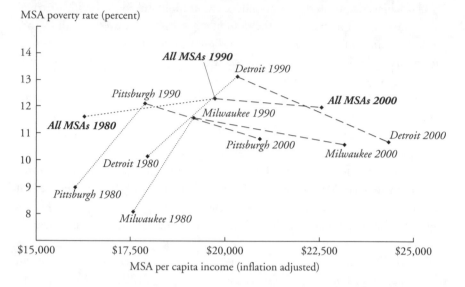

MSA poverty rate (percent)

MSA per capita income (inflation adjusted)

similar shock in the 1980s—tepid growth in per capita income compared to the national average and much sharper increases in metropolitan poverty. In the 1990s, all three cases came back to about the same level of MSA poverty, but Milwaukee experienced the biggest growth in per capita income. Also, to the extent that shifts in MSA poverty contributed to economic growth (rather than being just an outcome), the slope of the line suggests that Milwaukee might have obtained a higher growth dividend than the others for the change in underlying poverty.

Given this picture, what can we say about how the differences in political dynamics in the three regions affect the ability to link growth with equity? In some ways the picture is discouraging. In Milwaukee, where there has been more accommodation between equity and growth perspectives, regional income inequality and suburban poverty rates have actually increased in the 1990s, and rates of improvement in central-city poverty and racial segregation in the 1990s were no better or worse than in Pittsburgh and Detroit. In other ways, however, the picture is encouraging. Milwaukee experienced faster growth rates in the 1990s than the other two cities, and the absolute levels of poverty and inequality are lower, perhaps reflecting the long-term acceptance of equity perspectives in regional governance structures. What is clear is that the relationship between the level of collaboration between growth and equity constituencies on the one hand and trends in regional growth and equity on the other is complex and mediated by a wide range of other factors that we have not been able to examine here but are part of our ongoing research in progress on these issues.

Conclusions

One challenge facing equity advocates in weak-market regions is the widely held notion that pursuing equity is a luxury in the context of a declining economy. In the face of dramatic declines in manufacturing jobs, for example, many policymakers and economic developers argue that promoting growth in new industries or trying to stem declines in existing industries is more important than trying to promote equity. Policymakers often go even further than this, arguing that many equity strategies will simply undermine economic growth efforts, leading to greater poverty for a larger portion of the population. Equity efforts such as promoting increased minimum wages or development agreements, they argue, will lead potential investors to look elsewhere and make existing businesses in the region less competitive.

The research presented here suggests that equity is not a luxury but perhaps a necessity. As much as income inequality, poverty concentration, and racial segregation are outcomes of a declining city and regional economy, they are also themselves triggers of decline. Competitiveness strategies for weak-market cities should focus on the basics—infrastructure, good government, and a positive business climate—but it is good to keep the equity piece front and center as well.

Of course, the politics of doing this is not easy. The case studies reveal that there are many possible coalitions—and many different risks. Racial tensions are always a factor; as could be seen from table 4-1, racial segregation is particularly pronounced in regions with weak-market cities, and this makes for great worries that some groups will be left out when and if development is ever rekindled. Equity proponents may tend to forget or forego the economic development side, particularly as this is usually not their central concern. Business leaders are often frustrated by the poor performance of central-city leaders and tend to create "public-private" partnerships that have the putative broad aim of uniting the region—and the underlying agenda of marginalizing central-city politicians.

But putting together the politics, policies, and projects is exactly the task ahead of us. In our view, a full strategy for tackling equity in weak-market cities would combine three things. The first is a focus on economic growth, especially the targeting of driving industry clusters that can provide goods or services to markets that extend beyond the boundaries of the region; such export-oriented industries have the potential for more rapid growth and help drive demand for locally serving industries as well. We do not think that these necessarily need to be "new economy" in their orientation; the Milwaukee experience suggests that helping the manufacturing sector to be more flexible and modern also has great promise. And our discussion of Pittsburgh leads us to worry about strategies that rely primarily on using the central-city infrastructure as a gentrified playground to attract knowledge workers rather than also building on the assets, skills, and dreams of current residents.

The second component of a full strategy is a focus on the mobility of the workforce, including opportunities to move throughout the region and training systems that allow employees to improve their skills on an ongoing basis. This is a piece often left aside by place-based community activists who focus on the poor and their neighborhoods. It is, however, essential to saving such places: if we can raise incomes, people will be able to afford to rehabilitate their homes and communities. New models for labor-market intermediaries to accomplish this task have been evolving in recent years, and a better integration of workforce and economic development is key, particularly in regions with struggling cities.[59]

The last component is the maintenance and promotion of employment and community standards. These include local living-wage laws, policies to improve employment practices (such as those passed recently in Chicago and the state of Maryland aimed at large big-box retailers), efforts to support workers to form unions, community benefits agreements, and affordable housing requirements. Such efforts need to be nuanced to the region and its economy, but they should not be portrayed as antithetical to the competitiveness agenda that often dominates the policy landscape.

Combining these three strands is a challenge, but it is exactly the terrain on which leaders in cities with weak economies must operate. There is some hope that it can happen. In a fascinating study of business civic organizations, Future-Works surveyed forty-five regional business-civic organizations in twenty-nine different regions, and found that 40 percent had strategies that had implications for reducing the sort of socioeconomic disparities that we have here argued can diminish regional economic performance.[60] Some were direct, such as policies aimed at improving the economic conditions in poorer neighborhoods and reducing differences between urban and suburban school districts, whereas others were more implicit, such as targeted workforce development. Unfortunately, few of the organizations reported a high level of effectiveness in these arenas, something that tended to drive them back to the comfort zone of fighting higher taxes and encouraging more development subsidies.

Likewise, community-based organizations traditionally concerned about equity are showing a new sensitivity to the imperatives of economic growth and the potential power of the market. At the same time, few groups have actually adopted an underlying vision of how to produce rather than redistribute growth. As such organizations increasingly engage around the idea of equity at a regional scale, however, they are discovering the potential opportunities that emerge from collaborating with unlikely partners, and finding common ground with business and political interests that were often formerly considered adversaries.

It is in these political coalitions on the ground, where a new sense of common regional destiny is being formed between growth and equity perspectives, that we find hope for the future of cities in both weak and strong markets. Better research can help—and so can the sort of dialogue and conversation that is exactly the spirit of the American Assembly process.

Notes

1. Jennifer S. Vey, "Restoring Prosperity: The State Role in Revitalizing America's Older Industrial Cities" (Brookings Institution, 2007).
2. FutureWorks, "Minding Their Civic Business: A Look at the Ways Regional Business Civic Organizations Are Making a Difference in Metropolitan North America" (Arlington, Mass.: FutureWorks, 2004); Manuel Pastor, Chris Benner, and Rachel Rosner, *Edging Towards Equity: Creating Shared Opportunity in America's Regions: Report from the Conversation on Regional Equity* (University of California, Santa Cruz, Center for Justice, Tolerance, and Community, 2006).
3. David Rusk, remarks at a luncheon of executives from the Ford Foundation and the Annie E. Casey Foundation, The Victor Lofts, Camden, New Jersey, July 26, 2006.
4. See Rebecca Solnit, "Detroit Arcadia: Exploring the Post-American Landscape," *Harper's*, July 2007, pp. 65–73.
5. Radhika K. Fox and Sarah Treuhaft, "Shared Prosperity, Stronger Regions: An Agenda for Rebuilding America's Older Core Cities," monograph (Oakland, Calif.: PolicyLink, 2005).
6. Vey, "Restoring Prosperity." The methodology for identifying the weak-market cities was developed by Hal Wolman, Kimberly Furdell, Nancy Augustine, and Pamela Blumenthal of George Washington University and Ned Hill of Cleveland State University.
7. See, for example, Brookings Institution, "Back to Prosperity: A Competitive Agenda for Renewing Pennsylvania," monograph (2003). Although it raises issues of inequality, particularly spatial differences between city and suburb, the focus is resolutely on the competitiveness part of the equation.
8. The discussion here is of work on equity and growth in U.S. regions. This actually builds on a longer tradition that has looked at the relationship between distribution and growth in developing countries. For an overview, see Erik Thorbecke and Chutatong Charumilind, "Economic Inequality and Its Socioeconomic Impact," *World Development* 30, no. 9 (2002): 1477–95.
9. H. V. Savitch and others, "Ties That Bind: Central Cities, Suburbs, and the New Metropolitan Region," *Economic Development Quarterly* 7, no. 4 (November 1993): 347.
10. Ibid. In explaining the finding, Savitch and others argue that "[t]he blight of the inner city casts a long shadow. Companies will not grow or thrive in, or move to, a declining environment."

11. William Barnes and Larry C. Ledebur, *The New Regional Economies: The U.S. Common Market and the Global Economy* (Thousand Oaks, Calif.: Sage, 1998).

12. Paul D. Gottlieb, "The Effects of Poverty on Metropolitan Area Economic Performance," in *Urban-Suburban Interdependence: New Directions for Research and Policy,* edited by Rosalind Greenstein and Wim Wiewel (Cambridge, Mass.: Lincoln Institute for Land Policy, 2000).

13. Richard Voith, "Do Suburbs Need Cities?" *Journal of Regional Science* 38, no. 3 (1998): 445–65.

14. Manuel Pastor and others, *Regions That Work: How Cities and Suburbs Can Grow Together* (University of Minnesota Press, 2000).

15. Eberts Randall, George Erickcek, and Jack Kleinhenz, "Dashboard Indicators for the Northeast Ohio Economy: Prepared for the Fund for Our Economic Future," Working Paper 06-05 (Federal Reserve Bank of Cleveland, 2006). Available at www.clevelandfed.org/Research/Workpaper/2006/wp06-05.pdf.

16. For basic details on database construction, see Manuel Pastor, "Cohesion and Competitiveness: Business Leadership for Regional Growth and Social Equity," in *OECD Territorial Reviews, Competitive Cities in the Global Economy* (Paris: Organisation for Economic Co-Operation and Development, 2006). The database was supplemented for this exercise.

17. Vey, "Restoring Prosperity."

18. Median household income is also a useful control when we are looking at measures of relative disparity and want to control for the fact that higher medians may be associated with wider distributions. We also introduce dummy variables for broad regions of the United States, with no particular expectation of what the sign will be. To conserve space, we do not present either those results or the intercept, but they are included in all the regressions as appropriate. The dummies for regions of the United States were derived by using census maps to match states to broad regions; in the very few cases where a metro area overlapped two states, we used the state where the primary central city in the MSA is located.

19. Kimberly Furdell, Harold Wolman, and Edward W. Hill, "Did Central Cities Come Back? Which Ones, How Far, and Why?" *Journal of Urban Affairs* 27, no. 3 (2005): 301.

20. We use beta rather than raw coefficients to allow for some comparison between variables; beta coefficients gauge the impact of variations in the independent variables on the outcome measures, and are thus, to some degree, comparable. All regressions are weighted by the MSA populations in 2000 in order to reflect their relative importance in the sample, but the pattern holds if we drop the weights and, for example, focus on the 100 largest MSAs.

21. Vey, "Restoring Prosperity."

22. Myron Orfield, *Metropolitics: A Regional Agenda for Community and Stability* (Cambridge, Mass.: Lincoln Institute of Land Policy and Brookings Institution, 1997); Myron Orfield, *American Metropolitics: The New Suburban Reality* (Brookings Institution, 2002).

23. David Rusk, *Inside Game Outside Game: Winning Strategies for Saving Urban America* (Brookings Institution, 1999).

24. For these simultaneous tests, we chose to look at the shift in the distribution ratio for those at the sixtieth and twentieth deciles of the distribution rather than the eightieth and twentieth. The reason is that the process we use to obtain the decile cutoff is via linear interpolation. Although this is fairly accurate in the 1990 census because there were twenty-five household income categories, the 2000 census has only sixteen such categories, and the top brackets are rather broad, making linear interpolation for the eightieth now very accurate. The results for the earlier set of regressions are actually stronger if we use the sixtieth to

eightieth distribution, and the results for these simultaneous regressions are similar but less significant (and less reliable) if we use the eightieth to twentieth.

25. It was less clear why metro growth would change the relationship between city and suburban poverty or affect residential segregation in terms of race. We did initially try the city-suburb poverty differential and the results were actually amenable to our general view. We imagine that this really captured the poverty deconcentration effect, which might be more pronounced in central cities, but we did not have as good a theoretical rationale for this and so do not highlight it in the text.

26. For those more familiar with these sorts of exercises, the formal strategy was two-stage least squares, and various instruments were developed and tested. For example, the regression testing the change in poverty concentration on growth included as instruments the initial level of poverty concentration, the initial level of black and Latino segregation, and a measure of the change in recent immigrants (since they tend to cluster). Please note that in such simultaneous modeling, these is also an underlying equation for the feedback effect (from growth to equity); we did not develop an extensive model but rather a simple model of that side of the relationship and do not report on this here; instead we report on the equity-to-growth chain.

27. Stefan Lorant, *Pittsburgh, The Story of an American City* (Derrydale Press, 1999), and Edward Muller, "Industrial Suburbs and the Growth of Metropolitan Pittsburgh 1879–1920," *Journal of Historical Geography* 27, no. 1: 58–73.

28. Sabina Detrick, "The Post Industrial Revitalization of Pittsburgh: Myths and Evidence," *Community Development Journal* 34, no. 1: 4–12.

29. U.S. Census Bureau, Historical Decennial Census Population and Housing Counts, www.census.gov/population/www/censusdata/hiscendata.html (accessed April 17, 2007), author's calculations.

30. Bruce Katz, "Back to Prosperity: A Competitive Agenda for Renewing Pennsylvania," report (Brookings Institution, 2003).

31. Roy Lubove, *Twentieth-Century Pittsburgh*, vol. 1: *Government, Business and Environmental Change* (University of Pittsburgh Press, 1969).

32. Louise Jezierski, "Pittsburgh: Partnership in a Regional City," in *Urban Affairs Annual Review*, edited by H. V. Savitch and Ronald Vogel, vol. 45, pp. 159–81 (Thousand Oaks, Calif.: Sage, 1996).

33. Lubove, *Twentieth Century Pittsburgh*, vol. 2: *The Post Steel Era* (University of Pittsburgh Press, 1996).

34. See www.pghtech.org.

35. See www.pittsburghlifesciences.com.

36. Lubove, *Twentieth Century Pittsburgh*, vol. 2; Sidney Plotkin and William Scheurman, "Two Roads Left: Strategies of Resistance to Plants Closings in the Monongahela Valley," in *Dilemmas of Activism: Class, Community and the Politics of Local Mobilization*, edited by Joseph Kling and Prudence Rosner (Temple University Press, 1990).

37. Je Jo Hyung, "Regional Restructuring and Urban Regimes: A Comparison of the Pittsburgh and Detroit Metropolitan Areas," Working Paper: UMTRI 2002–20 (University of Michigan Transportation Research Institute, Office for the Study of Automotive Transportation, 2002), p. 10.

38. William J. V. Neil, "Industrial Policy in Detroit: The Search for a New Regional Development Model in the Home of Fordism," *Local Economy* 6, no. 3 (1991): 250–70.

39. Hyung, "Regional Restructuring."
40. Fox, "Shared Prosperity."
41. Ibid.
42. June Manning Thomas, *Redevelopment and Race: Planning a Finer City in Postwar Detroit* (Johns Hopkins University Press, 1997).
43. U.S. Census Bureau, available at www.census.gov/main/www/cen2000.html for Census 2000.
44. Fox, "Shared Prosperity."
45. Marion E. Orr and Gerry Stoker, "Urban Regimes and Leadership in Detroit," *Urban Affairs Quarterly* 30, no. 1 (1994): 48–73.
46. Hyung, "Regional Restructuring," p. 16.
47. Lowell Turner and Daniel Cornfield, eds., *Labor in the New Urban Battlegrounds* (Ithaca, N.Y.: ILR Press, 2007).
48. Wilbur Rich, *Coleman Young and Detroit Politics: From Social Activist to Power Broker* (Wayne State University Press, 1989); Richard Child Hill, "Crisis in the Motor City: The Politics of Economic Development in Detroit," in *Restructuring the City,* edited by Susan S. Fainstein, Norman I. Fainstein, Richard Child Hill, Dennis R. Judd, and Michael Peter Smith (New York: Longman, 1986).
49. See the MOSES website, www.mosesmi.org/new %20website/history2.htm for MOSES' scope of work.
50. Mark V. Levine and Sandra J. Callaghan, "The Economic State of Milwaukee: The City and the Region," report (University of Wisconsin-Milwaukee, Center for Economic Development, 1998).
51. Matthew Zeidenberg, "Moving Outward: The Shifting Landscape of Poverty in Milwaukee," report (Madison: Center on Wisconsin Strategy, 2004).
52. Levine, "Economic State of Milwaukee"; Zeidenberg, "Moving Outward."
53. David E. Wood, Myron Orfield, and Joel Rogers, "Milwaukee Metropatterns: Sprawl and Social Separation in Metro Milwaukee" (Madison: Center on Wisconsin Strategy and the Metropolitan Area Research Corporation, 2000).
54. Wood, "Milwaukee Metropatterns."
55. For more information, see www.wisconsinlaborhistory.org/milestones.html.
56. Bureau of Labor Statistics, BLS CPS data for Milwaukee-Racine CMSA; Barry T. Hirsch and David A. Macpherson, "Union Membership and Coverage Database from the Current Population Survey: Note," *Industrial and Labor Relations Review* 56, no. 2 (January 2003): 349–54, available at www.unionstats.com.
57. Julia Taylor, author interview, Milwaukee, March 10, 2006.
58. Annette Bernhardt, Laura Dresser, and Joel Rogers, "Taking the High Road in Milwaukee: The Wisconsin Regional Training Partnership," in *Partnering for Change: Unions and Community Groups Build Coalitions for Economic Justice,* edited by David Reynolds (Armonk, N.Y.: M. E. Sharpe, 2004).
59. See Chris Benner, Laura Leete, and Manuel Pastor, *Staircases or Treadmills: Labor Market Intermediaries and Economic Opportunity in a Changing Economy* (New York: Russell Sage Foundation, 2007).
60. FutureWorks, "Minding Their Civic Business: A Look at the New Ways Regional Business-Civic Organizations Are Making a Difference in Metropolitan North America" (Arlington, Mass., 2004).

5

Effective Chambers of Commerce:
A Key to Regional Economic Prosperity

Stephen Moret, Mick Fleming, and Pauline O. Hovey

"Human prosperity does not abide long in one place." Herodotus' observation in the fifth century B.C. should serve as a reminder to high-growth regions about the frailty of their wealth, as well as confirmation that weaker markets *can* come back. Whether they serve in growth regions or struggling communities, public and private sector leaders who seek sustainable prosperity must attend to the fundamentals that can improve the likelihood of economic success.

Other chapters in this volume highlight the causes and extent of the current disparity between regions. Market forces will, for the most part, determine levels of success in sectors, communities, and regions. At the same time, each regional market and the communities contained therein can be positioned to exploit opportunities, build on strengths, and address weaknesses that come with population and investment shifts. It is in no one's interest to have unbridled (unsustainable) growth in one urban market and an economic death spiral in another. It is also wrong to assume that intervention and activism aimed at improving weak markets cannot work.

With that in mind, more and more chambers of commerce, economic development entities, and other corporate-civic groups are establishing or recharging organizations in order to better position their respective metropolitan areas for sector-diverse, sustainable economic growth.

Increasingly, chambers of commerce are being charged with much more than organizing civic-business functions and welcoming new businesses to communities. The era of chambers as purveyors of "pancakes and parades" has disappeared in most parts of America over the last few decades. In many ways, chambers are returning to their century-old roots as builders and promoters of local and regional economies. They are being tasked more and more with designing and leading economic transformations in communities, regions, and states. Heightened expectations and performance levels have placed business-led civic organizations in the key role of securing prosperity in the territories they serve.

Widespread misunderstanding exists among the general public, media, and elected officials about how chambers of commerce and similar organizations operate. There is no "head office" of the international or American chamber movement. No Vatican-like hierarchy controls the positions or work of individual chambers. Each chamber is a fiercely independent advocate for its member companies, all of which contribute voluntarily to the organization. Chamber footprints overlap and seldom match any political boundaries, making them natural regionalists. Governments do not run—and rarely provide much funding for—chambers in the United States, except when paying for specific contracted functions.

Some chambers are substantial nonprofits with scores of employees focused on macro issues in megatropolis environments. Others are small, retail-focused entities operating out of storefronts or borrowed office space. Still other business-civic organizations serve the corporate elite—Fortune 500–level CEOs. The missions of chambers vary, but all must work to solve the puzzles that prevent or accelerate economic vitality in their various jurisdictions.

Box 5-1. *What We Mean by* Chamber

The terms *chamber of commerce* and *chamber* are used in this document to refer to any business-led or business-funded nonprofit organization whose purpose is to serve the business sector in a region—all employers and not just a single industry sector—and encourage economic and community development. Thus, though some may protest the shared genealogy, we consider boards of trade, business councils, growth councils, committees of 100, business and industry associations, and economic development councils to be chambers, provided their governance, leadership, staffing, and funding come largely from the private sector. When referring to public sector–dominated economic development entities in this paper, we use the term *EDO* (economic development organization or office).

Why are chambers and other heterogeneous, business-funded organizations taking on this larger role in today's economic development equation? There are three primary reasons:

1. The nature of economic development, as described elsewhere in this volume, has changed from an endeavor focused on "incentives, inventory [facilities], and industry," to one largely centered on the three *P*'s: people, place, and positioning. American chambers have been responsible for the three *P*'s since the first chamber of commerce was formed under a tree near Wall Street nearly three hundred years ago.

2. Frustration with the unavoidable political and bureaucratic hassles of government-led economic development efforts has grown, leaving business leaders who want their communities to prosper with little choice but to do it themselves—and a chamber, or chamber-like organization, is their logical vehicle.

3. The increasingly regional nature of development work makes jurisdiction-based initiatives less relevant. With chamber territories bounded only by tradition and courtesy, they can more easily adapt to regional thinking than governments can.

The nature of chambers and the shift in thinking about how growth occurs make a compelling argument for chambers to take a more active role within their communities in reversing poor, or sustaining strong, regional economic performance. This chapter focuses on how chambers of commerce can serve as vehicles within their regions to drive sustainable economic prosperity, outlines the need for a regional approach to economic development activities, and then describes how chambers need to evolve to tackle the challenges of wider regional economic growth. Since effective implementation of regional economic development strategies requires an emphasis on both business development (marketing) and product development, success factors for both types of activities are also included. The final consideration in any regional initiative is how to garner widespread support. Throughout the chapter we will provide examples of what chambers have done to promote economic growth in their regions.

The Regional Nature of Economic Development

Several substantial trends have emerged within the chamber and within economic development worlds in response to the rapid changes in the global and national economies. The most striking is that development efforts increasingly are focused on *regional* rather than *local* economies. Another is the advent of new professional specializations. Site selectors and corporate real estate officers hunt for sites. They are the *buyers*. People who are employed at chambers and economic development organizations, as well as their representatives, are the *sellers*. They try to sell the site selectors or real estate officers on choosing their locale.

When counseling development professionals and communities, site-selection consultants routinely advise them not to market themselves as a single town or city, or even as one county, but as part of a region. Because businesses looking to grow or invest are focusing more attention on the overall strength of a place in which they are doing or might do business rather than just on the guts of a deal, regional approaches are critical. Workers and markets are no longer local, and neither are investment location decisions.

A leading site-selection consultant, Mark Sweeney of McCallum Sweeney Consulting, sees it this way: "Our clients are not in the employment or job-creation business. We're looking for a location that allows them to succeed in their business. The political boundaries between municipalities and counties often are important to public officials, but they mean nothing to company executives deciding where to locate a project. What matters is the site and the characteristics of the region in which it is located."

Sweeney and his counterparts from the other side of the aisle, such as Mac Holladay of the location marketing firm of Market Street Services in Atlanta, stress that a company trying to quickly understand what a region has to offer appreciates having information packaged and presented at the regional level through a single contact. A regional business development program, orchestrated by a powerful regional, business-led organization, meets the need for both convenience and confidentiality.

With so many communities across the country fighting for a limited number of major facility-attraction projects, name recognition becomes an important asset in trying to distinguish one's region from other locations. Smaller locales, as well as those struggling to overcome less-than-appealing perceptions of their location, are less likely to be known to prospective businesses, so it becomes advantageous for them to leverage the public's awareness of their more widely known neighbors. "Regional identity is easier to develop because you're building on a [better-known] name," says Sweeney. That existing identity could be the difference maker in landing the next big deal.

It is also important to remember that somebody must fund place-building and business development activities. Many large regional economic development and chamber of commerce entities engage in multiyear, special campaigns funded via checks and pledge commitments from the private sector. Often these include a match or contribution of some kind from the public sector (local, state, or county governments) as well. These campaigns sometimes focus on marketing the region as a place to move or grow a business, but other times they are used to improve the "product" through improvements in workforce development, industrial parks, major developments, infrastructure lobbying, or whatever fits a planned strategy.

Regional multiyear strategic-growth campaigns tend to be much more attractive to large private sector corporations that usually fund economic development programs (banks, energy firms, health care institutions, law firms, insurance companies, and regional retail). Multijurisdictional fundraising campaigns have been highly successful in markets as varied as Memphis ($61 million for a multistate, multiyear initiative) and northeastern Ohio ($3 million annually, covering ten counties).

No regional economic development program is without challenges. Practitioners and public officials in rural areas situated on the outskirts of major urban centers tend to be skeptical about participating in regional economic development efforts. Whereas most top business leaders intuitively embrace the regional concept, public officials and some development professionals representing smaller communities sometimes fear that their interests will be neglected—or even actively undermined—by their larger neighbors. Within a regional context, individual local governments as well as chambers of commerce and even government economic development departments or agencies must strike a balance between the immediate needs and missions of specific constituencies and larger regional development strategies. Where and when does each group's support for regional principles trump the need to keep supporting funders happy? A tension line must be established, but then flexed, every day.

Motivating players within a region to work together can be difficult when each locality, mayor, or economic developer has his or her own priorities. A number of strategies can be employed to alleviate these concerns.

One factor that usually breaks down parochial barriers is desperation. An economic death spiral has the power to focus attention much like the sight of a gallows to a condemned man. When Erie, Pennsylvania, lost a significant portion of its manufacturing base just before and after 9/11, Brian Bosworth of the consulting firm FutureWorks was hired by the Erie Chamber to advise local business leaders. His caution was stark and direct—Erie was simply headed for economic collapse unless action was taken.

This "seismic shock" of an informed pronouncement to the region provided motivation to craft, fund, and support a collaborative multijurisdictional approach.

A new thirty-eight-municipality development entity, the Erie Regional Chamber and Growth Partnership, was created to tackle the issues of economic diversification, postsecondary education, and infrastructure.

Taking a regional approach makes it possible to create economic growth programs tailored to the needs and preferences of customers (that is, prospective employers and existing ones who are expanding), as well as leverage the diversity of resources represented by the communities that make up a region. While population and job growth in most parts of the Midwest have been anemic at best, and downright negative in the worst cases, the labor force in the Springfield region in Missouri has been expanding about 2.6 percent per year and is the fastest-growing area in the Midwest, according to the Springfield Area Chamber of Commerce.[1]

Back in 1991, business and community leaders recognized that Springfield was not competing in the modern economy. They proactively came together to build a common vision and market the area's resources and assets to new businesses and a skilled workforce. The Springfield Chamber took the lead in an effort to unite ten counties, seventy cities, and other chambers in signing a public-private partnership agreement to create a regional program. Called the Ozarks Regional Economic Partnership, this organization has the support of city councils, the public utility board, and other key stakeholders that support sustained development throughout the southwestern Missouri region. The regional approach is working. The Springfield metro area has accounted for more than one-third of Missouri's total job growth over the last ten years and doubled its gross metro product. In 2007, *Expansion Management* magazine named the Springfield MSA (metropolitan statistical area) one of the top mid-size metros for recruiting workers and attracting businesses.[2] Recently, *Inc.* magazine recognized Springfield as one of the top twenty midsize cities in America for entrepreneurs.

Localities are not the only place where regionalism is changing the way economic development is practiced. Statewide business organizations will also be affected by the growing influence of regions. State chambers' struggles to influence the cost of doing business will not wane, but proactive legislative initiatives to enhance incentive programs, training priorities, and infrastructure investment may be increasingly influenced by regional development voices.

While some markets such as Boston and Los Angeles seem to thrive without aggressively pursuing regional agendas, most metropolitan areas—Chicago, Orlando, Denver—are taking regional approaches to solving problems and positioning themselves for more prosperous futures. For struggling older markets, like those in the Great Lakes and other areas affected by the rapid transformation of the manufacturing sector, regional thinking is absolutely critical to any hope for turnaround.

Effective Chambers and Healthy Regions

As chambers of commerce and similar organizations grapple with a wider realm of responsibilities, many are radically changing strategies and structure to have a greater impact on both business development and product and place development. *Business development*, as used in this chapter, covers activities designed to influence the decisions of corporate leaders, entrepreneurs, developers, and even government leaders to select a particular market for investment. *Business attraction*, one of the core economic development activities, would fall under this rubric. *Product development*, on the other hand, includes activities designed to increase the attractiveness of a place (neighborhood, city, community, region, state) for investment. Assets such as a well-functioning transportation system, effective public education, a tolerable tax climate, access to skilled workers, and affordable housing all contribute to the attraction of a location.

Successfully *implementing* effective, regional economic strategies requires emphasis on both *business* development and *product* development. An effective, private sector–driven organization with the right volunteer and professional leadership is essential to the advancement or recovery of any community or region. To create or grow capacity in chambers, everything from governance to staffing may need to change.

Today, chamber CEOs and their professional staff must carry most of the load. This results in both higher skill requirements and greater expectations of these professional leaders, who must possess the right mix of communication and influencing skills, fundraising and coalition-building capacity, and advocacy muscle, as well as passion, vision, and tenacity.

A variety of models for regional economic development organizations are in place around the country. The most common forms include economic development programs established within regional chambers of commerce or dedicated regional economic development corporations, which themselves often are subsidiaries or affiliates of chambers. The most successful programs tend to be based on a business-led, public-private partnership in which governments, as well as leading businesses, participate in governance *and* funding of the organization.

Public and private sector interests tend to align more closely in relation to *business* development efforts, than in *product* development arenas. Prioritizing improvements is difficult when resources are limited and stakeholders are numerous. Communities face large-*P* and small-*p* political concerns about how to solve certain problems. Often, the many factions simply cannot reach a consensus, if, for example, one entity or party favors emphasis on schools while another wants a highway.

For this reason, many communities, counties, and regions have separate organizations—often with quite different jurisdictional footprints—to deal with these two broad avenues of economic development. Sometimes, a dedicated economic development organization leads business development activities and a chamber of commerce leads product development activities. Some communities have created two complementary entities with separate boards that operate under one office, in order to reduce competition for funding, recognition, and identity. There is no single organizational and governance model that will work for every region. Politics, organizational histories, and even leadership personalities all play a role in determining levels of involvement and divisions of labor by various parties.

Regardless of the structure, however, certain key features must be present to ensure desired outcomes: leadership, organizational capabilities, and funding strategies.

Leadership

The single most important ingredient in a successful chamber or EDO is leadership. It has been noted that ". . . corporate elites may be increasingly disengaging from civic efforts, largely as a result of pervasive economic trends. . . ."[3] A core group of business leaders must buck this trend toward civic disengagement and willingly devote their reputations, political capital, time, and energy (leading by example through their financial commitments) to ensuring that economic development ambitions are met. Governing boards of business organizations focused on regional economic development should be made up predominantly of private-sector CEOs—people with the power to move influential political, media, and community leaders.

Increasingly, however, it is the professional community leader, the primary paid executive of the private sector regional development entity, who must provide visible, consistent leadership of the processes and people focused on economic success in the region. In the past, the paid leader—the CEO of the chamber—took his or her lead from the volunteer board. The board *proposed* and the staff *disposed,* to use a government separation-of-powers analogy. This is no longer the case. There has been a general decline in the personal, active involvement of business leaders in civic affairs, as discussed in reports published by the Brookings Institution, in a book by the Harvard public policy professor Robert Putnam, and others.[4]

Organizational Capabilities

In the twenty-first century, economic development is increasingly complex and fast paced, requiring new strategies for targeting prospective business investors and demanding rapid, accurate turnaround for information requests. Business leaders increasingly are asking the organizations they fund to tackle complex public policy issues that require detailed planning and robust advocacy campaigns for success. At the same time, these leaders are less engaged in civic activities. The result of these trends is a need for highly professional leadership and staffing of both chambers and government-led economic development organizations.

Successful development efforts in the third millennium likely will require larger, more capable, and better-compensated teams of professionals than were needed in the last century of the previous millennium. Key capabilities include business and public policy research, lobbying, public and media relations, marketing and fundraising, partnership management, and an intellectual curiosity sufficient to seek out and understand complex issues. Successful chambers of the future will be more akin to high-caliber professional service firms than traditional nonprofit organizations.

Funding Strategies

Money matters. If the work, territory, and complexity are growing, so too must funding streams. Building and running a strong regional economic or community development organization requires appropriate levels of funding for staff, office, travel, marketing, administrative expenses, and lobbying work, among other activities. For midsize and larger regions, annual operating budgets of several million dollars should be expected and creative funding strategies are necessary. The largest strategic funding campaigns, covering economic development in major metro markets, have budgets that now reach into the tens of millions of dollars over three-to-five-year horizons.

Funds are generated through a variety of means, including private sector fundraising, dedicated public taxes, contracts with local governments, application of dues (and special chamber member assessments), and foundation grants. These exceptional funding initiatives can be problematic in weaker markets because turnarounds take time, while funders (both of the private and tax-supported varieties) often demand measurable, short-term results from their investments. Making the case for long-term, sometimes multicampaign support can be tough in circumstances in which data on perceived recovery are elusive. *There is, however, no way to successfully fight for future regional prosperity other than to invest in the activities that have proved to lead to greater economic health.*

Business Development Success

Only recently have chambers of commerce taken a more active role in business development efforts. One of the most compelling reasons for chambers to increase their involvement in business development is that company executives and site-selection consultants do not just evaluate sites—they evaluate regions. Successful business development efforts, therefore, must be organized at the regional level. Perceptions of balkanized, town-by-town marketing in weaker markets can retard investment interest by both out-of-town site selectors and resident employers considering expansion. It is often easier for chambers and other business-led organizations to reach out across political boundaries to develop a location solution that works best for the client.

In high-growth markets such as Charlotte, North Carolina, with a highly integrated multicounty, even multistate, regional development network, there is seldom confusion about where to go for development assistance. The Pittsburgh region's coordinated coalition in the late 1990s enabled growth in the services sectors to backfill against the decades-long decline in local steel industry employment.[5] The Detroit Regional Chamber, on the other hand, has fought a frustrating battle for decades against the many insular policies and traditions of the region—city versus two counties, white versus black, inner city versus suburbs. Over the last six months, Detroit business leaders launched the "One D" initiative. One D is a program that enables regional collaboration while removing roadblocks to cross-jurisdictional and cross-organizational cooperation. The initiative is headed by Edsel B. Ford II, and all of the major development entities in southeastern Michigan are on board as participants.

Business development activities can also lead to a better understanding of what businesses desire from a community. Working with business leaders, entrepreneurs, developers, and site selectors provides chambers with a clearer sense of what might be missing or deserving of ongoing support on the product development side of the equation. There are a number of strategies that chambers can employ to boost regional business development efforts.

Box 5-2. *Case Study 1: Providence, Rhode Island*

Background

The capital of Rhode Island has a population estimated at 179,000, but Providence MSA is about 1.6 million, which includes the state and parts of southern Massachusetts. Providence is situated in the heart of the Northeast Region of the United States, within hours from Boston, New York City, and Cape Cod.

Despite its central location, in the early 1980s, Providence found its businesses and manufacturers moving out, leaving behind vacant buildings and a steadily declining economy. Concerned business and civic leaders joined forces with the Greater Providence Chamber of Commerce and, over a twenty-year period of planning and development, transformed Providence and the surrounding area into an attention-grabbing "hot spot," cited on the "best" lists of *Forbes American-Style, Entrepreneur, Money,* and *US News & World Report.*

Today U.S. Census Bureau figures show that Providence is one of New England's fastest-growing cities. And the growth is not limited to population. According to *The 2007 New Economy Index* released by the Kauffman Foundation and the Information Technology and Innovation Foundation, Rhode Island was among the four states in the nation that made the greatest economic strides from 2002 to 2007.

How did a lackluster industrial town in the smallest state of the union achieve such a dramatic economic comeback in less than twenty years? The answer lies in its regional approach to economic development.

Taking Stock of Its Strengths—How Providence Slowed the Decline

In the midst of its economic decline, Providence area leaders began to take a strategic look at its place in the New England economy and the Northeast Region, as well as its underutilized, and in some cases hidden, assets. Business leaders, city and state officials, chamber executives, planners, architects, and artists collaborated in identifying the state's strengths and advantages within various global industry sectors. The partnership identified several clusters—insurance, defense, boat building, biotechnology, and information technology—important to the area and sought ways to grow those industries while also building on existing strengths.

Realizing the city, founded in 1636, had unique, underused assets in its architecture, business leaders and city officials made a conscious effort to preserve historic properties. Crucial to getting the area's resurgence going was the passage of the state's historic investment tax credit, which was instrumental in transforming historic cast-iron, brick, and granite buildings into residential space, hotels, office space, and restaurants.

Recognizing that its unique collection of waterways was another advantage, the city literally uncovered a river that had been paved over. The project initiated more collaborative waterfront efforts. In 1999, organizers, with public and private support, created an arts culture and tourism initiative called Waterfire, a performing arts and entertainment event centered around the new mid-city river. The event, taking place every two weeks during about six months of the year, draws an average of 50,000 people as well as positive media coverage for the area. Tax revenues from the event total about $2.4 million each season.

(continued)

Box 5-2. *Case Study 1: Providence, Rhode Island (continued)*

Another draw to the Providence area is the prevalence of respected and sought-after institutions of higher education, such as the Rhode Island School of Design, Brown University, Johnson & Wales Culinary Institute, and the University of Rhode Island. Area leaders devised a strategy to encourage graduates who could populate the ranks of young professionals and entrepreneurs to stay in the area, but there is significant work to be done in this arena. The Rhode Island Economic Policy Council's Brain Drain/Gain Index, which measures net retention of college graduates in the Providence Metro, indicates there is still a net loss.

Twenty-Plus Years of Planning and Cooperation
The Rhode Island Economic Policy Council, composed of representatives from business, labor, higher education, and government (the governor, mayors, and leaders of the Rhode Island General Assembly), was formed to respond to strategic challenges facing the state's economy and to develop new initiatives to seize key opportunities. The Council then mobilized the public and private resources to ensure that its initiatives would succeed (for more on the activities of the Council, see www.ripolicy.org).

In 1998, the Council hired a consultant to conduct a regional analysis to determine the best ways to expand businesses and create jobs. Adopting a regional approach to economic development mandated the creation of joint marketing efforts involving cities, counties, and the state.

—Coordinated, regionwide business solicitation led to the attraction of Southwest Airlines to the Providence airport in nearby Warwick in October of 1996, thus positioning it as a low-cost hub. According to Rhode Island Airport Corporation figures, a total of 2.2 million passengers used T. F. Green Airport in 1995; by 2004 that number had risen to 5.5 million.

—A regionwide study assessed the competitive advantages of the state's nonprofit institutions such as hospitals, colleges, and universities, to determine how research and development (R&D) strengths could be commercialized. The Rhode Island Economic Policy Council, using National Science Foundation estimates, reports that in 2005 $1.7 billion was spent on R&D by industry, universities, and federal labs, up from $553,000 in 1987.

—The state invested in land development and infrastructure, which paid off with new sites available and ready to occupy when new businesses were seeking places to relocate. This speed-to-market advantage was one reason Providence attracted Fidelity Investments from Boston in 1998, leading to a significant expansion of the company in 2005.

—In seeking to attract a certain biotechnological company that was considering relocating to the area but wanted manufacturing laborers with bachelor's degrees, the Rhode Island Economic Policy Council was instrumental in creating a dedicated training program for biotech workers through the University of Rhode Island.

Box 5-2. *Case Study 1: Providence, Rhode Island (continued)*

Lessons Learned

The revitalization and renaissance of Providence and the surrounding region required visionaries with strong leadership skills—"shrewd business leaders with a civic conscience," as one observer noted. The leadership understood the importance of not underestimating the value and ingenuity of the region's artists, upper-level graduates, entrepreneurs, and inspired architects. Once industries and assets were identified, a regional partnership, led by the Greater Providence Chamber of Commerce, worked to pass legislation to encourage growth within those markets.

According to Janet Raymond, senior vice president, operations and economic development for the chamber, early buy-in is critical, and stakeholders must be in it for the long term, as projects will require long-term commitment—transformation won't happen overnight. As Raymond explained, the resurgence of the Greater Providence area has been twenty years in the making and they have only been seeing the fruits of their labor for the last half decade. In the process, they celebrated small steps with public acclaim. Today, after more than twenty years of concerted efforts to reenergize the region, the state, city, chamber, and economic development groups continue to work together to build on the area's strengths and assets.

Objectively Assess Strengths, Weaknesses, and Unique Challenges

A critical starting point for any regional business development effort is conducting a third-party evaluation of strengths and weaknesses. Without first understanding how a region stacks up against its competitors, it is impossible to develop a marketing strategy with a high potential to succeed. The results of such assessments can provide valuable information about what kinds of public policy issues may need to be addressed to generate long-term success. Consistently underperforming markets either avoid acknowledging the warts they see in the mirror, or focus on these competitive disadvantages to such a degree that they lose sight of their many strengths. Either extreme is dangerous for those who are responsible for pulling struggling economies away from despair.

Economic development and site-selection consultants are capable of providing a candid third-party assessment. Ideally, such an assessment should include not only an evaluation of strengths and weaknesses but also an articulation of short-term and long-term recommendations for improvement. Whether the evaluation is undertaken by internal or contracted sources, key factors for evaluation at the regional level should include factors as varied as available sites, incentive options, workforce characteristics, infrastructure capacity, and labor harmony.

Often a regional assessment of strengths and weaknesses reveals insights concerning previously unrecognized strengths and weaknesses. For example, leaders in the Baton Rouge area who completed a regional assessment learned that the regional economy's high concentration in the petrochemical industry had resulted in average manufacturing wages much higher than those of any of its peer regions—with many associated implications for future development. In Portland, Oregon, an examination of the boundaries and jurisdictions of the metro area determined that there were twenty-five cities within thirteen counties covering about a million residents, which helped the state legislature recognize the need to consider a metrowide government structure that would provide transportation, planning, waste management, and park, convention, and cultural activities across the entire region. Cleveland's regionwide economic evaluation concluded that the lack of adequate inclusion of the minority community in the workforce and private industry was a contributing factor to the region's less-than-satisfactory economic performance.

Target the Right Industry Sectors

Successful business development is about matching a region with industry sectors for which the particular area has competitive advantages. Too often, in weaker markets, public and private sector funders do not possess an accurate profile of their region's strengths and weaknesses, mistakenly thinking that they know best what kinds of businesses should be attracted to their area. Going with one's "gut" will often lead to failure. In addition, weak markets suffer from fear of alienating or offending precious local employers whose industry type does not match the target profile. Again, a powerful, well-funded, and supported corporate-civic entity is the only organization in a position to tell it like it is, basing its assessment on a professionally developed regional analysis of strengths and weaknesses. For each target industry (selected for fit and future growth potential), an aggressive and very specific marketing and lead-generation plan should be developed *for just that sector!*

Cultivate Business Growth Opportunities

Although the media tend to focus their attention on the recruitment of new businesses, business editors often miss the fact that over 75 percent of all new jobs will come from the expansion of existing firms. This is true in virtually every region in the United States, but especially in weaker markets that struggle to gain attention from national and international site selectors. Critical retention and expansion activities center on relationships and research.

One method is to identify the top economic-driver firms and interview multiple individuals at these firms—from the human resources director to the chief financial officer to the environmental engineer—to understand their needs, challenges, and frustrations with the local scene and dreams of business expansion. Follow-up must be obsessively persistent to ensure rapid answers to questions and elimination of as many obstacles to success as possible. Sophisticated software systems can assist economic development offices and chambers in tracking and serving the needs of current employers. The San Antonio Chamber leadership—which comprises both paid professionals and heavy-weight corporate representatives—takes these visits to an even higher level, flying to the East and West coasts each year to meet with parent companies of branch facilities based in south-central Texas.

Over time, the results of consultation visits can be analyzed to identify common concerns (for example, an unorthodox business tax levied by the state, or the lack of direct flights at the airport), and these can be addressed via *product* development efforts.

Strive for Seamless Public Sector Coordination

Business development victories typically include a variety of local, regional, and state inducements, including things such as tax or cash incentives, zoning accommodations, workforce development grants, and roads and other infrastructure improvements. Because multiple public and nonprofit organizations are usually involved in finalizing a deal, the extent to which various public authorities and assets across a region are managed is critical. Whenever uncertainty exists relative to the process for securing a particular inducement, prospective companies and site-selection consultants will discount its potential value. A development community in a weak-market region that is seen as unable to provide more than "fuzzy" or dependent promises of incentives and support will find it hard to attract or grow new investment.

Cultivate Relationships with Site-Selection Consultants

With roughly fifteen thousand economic development organizations in the United States competing for fewer than five hundred major site-selection projects (*major* means new projects offering at least one hundred new jobs) each year,[6] the competition is fierce. Industry estimates suggest that roughly 40 percent of these site-selection decisions are heavily influenced by a site-selection consultant.[7] Because of the huge influence they wield, leading site-selection consultants have a substantial impact on the economic development success of every region in the country.

Weak markets often miss out on the investment attraction opportunities that more naturally flow to strong, growing regions, so it is particularly important for these communities to cultivate positive relationships with these individuals. Many weaker, older industrial markets are simply not well known by consultants. Perceptions of rust and decline may be decades out of date, but old images die hard. Persistent, personal contact (at trade shows, intercity visits, sales calls, and so forth) is as critical to breaking down inaccurate perceptions as any collateral material a region may design and distribute.

"We had to do a better job of making economic opportunities known to investors outside the region," said Jacob Rouch of the Regional Chamber and Growth Alliance in the slowly recovering market of Erie, Pennsylvania. The chamber took a proactive approach by building a database of potential investors and putting information about new developments in the Erie region in front of those investors monthly. "Erie has to exist in their realm of possibility," Rouch said. The number of potential new projects in the region has increased substantially since the chamber started to take this proactive approach.

First Impressions Count

Site selection really is better described as site *elimination.* Company executives and site-selection consultants often start with several hundred potential sites for a project and aim to quickly reduce the list to just a few prospective sites for serious evaluation. Staying *on* the list through the initial round(s) of cursory assessment is critical. A less-than-coordinated, weakly prepared response by a resource-strapped development office to an initial blind inquiry can be fatal to a deal that could have provided a strong boost to a struggling regional economy.

Each region's primary economic development entity—whether public or private in nature—must be showcased with a professional, well-designed website and marketing material (brochures, research presentations, and so forth). The information contained in electronic and print media must be up-to-date in regard to regional strengths, sites, workforce characteristics, incentives, relevant legislation, and quality-of-life features. Competing with the biggest and richest metro markets on glamour and gloss is virtually impossible for many communities and regions, but highly reliable, timely, creatively analyzed data, powerful testimonials, and clear writing can be developed and delivered with sweat equity rather than checks.

Educate about and Publicize Return on Investment (ROI)

Business recruitment deals often are rightly scrutinized by the media and others for the amount of public money used to lure them. Effective economic development professionals have therefore learned the importance of justifying the level of incentives in a particular deal by commissioning a credible third-party economic impact analysis, including not only the number of direct and indirect jobs created but also the forecast for new tax revenue.

Rigorously Monitor Progress and Communicate Success

Every EDO and chamber is accountable to its board of directors, as well as to its funders. Accordingly, each funding source should receive regular progress reports that include not only marketing and recruitment activity but also hard numbers indicating progress (such as potential deals brought to the table, improving retention numbers, new jobs or capital investment). Credibility, public support, and future funding often depend on the extent to which this activity occurs on a regular basis. In communities struggling with higher-than-average unemployment, outmigration, and shriveling public coffers, making sensible and transparent use of all economic development funds—both public and private—is especially important. Regular communications with funding sources can help manage expectations, which is particularly important when a community faces significant business development obstacles.

Go the Extra Mile

After the culling process, in the final competition between two or three communities on the short list, creativity and personal effort go a long way. Organize the job fair for a prospective new employer before the prospect is even landed, as Baton Rouge did for a Staples investment. Push for one more supporting testimonial phone call from a resident CEO. Take one extra flight during the deliberation period to meet with one more person who has influence in the company hierarchy.

Product Development Success

A persistent, organized, regional approach is not just important in pursuing specific business retention, expansion, and attraction projects—it also is critically important in fostering a healthy business environment. Many pressing issues that affect economic growth are regional in nature (for example, traffic congestion, workforce housing, air quality, tax and regulatory policies, public education, workforce development); accordingly, they require regional solutions. Poorly performing regions must realize that fixing, or at least improving, the most obvious and visible barriers to investment may be the only way to turn their economies around, since most businesses and people will not come to or remain in a region with a poor business and employment climate.

Every industry and business is different when it comes to the site location characteristics it considers most important. A particular region can be very competitive for one industry (say, shipbuilding) while generating no interest whatsoever from another (say, biotech). Nevertheless, there are a number of major *product* features of regions that have broad appeal for corporate decisionmakers. Some of these factors, such as risk of natural disasters, are largely outside the control of regional business leaders. However, factors such as workforce quality and infrastructure can be directly or indirectly influenced by regional product development efforts. Accordingly, the areas mentioned here warrant attention from chambers seeking to remove or at least mitigate weaknesses, as well as to bolster existing strengths and create new opportunities.

Create a World-Class Workforce

The most important factors evaluated in many site-selection decisions are the quality, size, and cost of the workforce in a particular region. Chambers must focus their lobbying, influence, and research to ensure that higher education institutions with specialized skills-training programs in *their* regions are offering quality programs that link with the current and expected demand of business and industry (particularly target industry sectors).

In some weaker markets, the struggle to build a viable workforce (and therefore strengthen the future economy) takes unusual turns. In Santa Ana, one of the pockets of economic hardship in Orange County, California, the business community has launched an aggressive, privately funded multi-million-dollar "learn English" campaign. According to the Santa Ana chamber's extensive research, roughly 75 percent of the jobs in the region require English and 70 percent of the residents don't speak it. The goal for the new language initiative is fifty thousand newly trained English speakers in four years. Workforce pressures are so important to regional economic growth that *whatever* is required must be attempted.

Unfortunately, regions with relatively high poverty levels must, when speaking to development prospects, combine a short-term strategy of emphasizing their higher-performing districts and private schools with a long-term strategy of pursuing education reform. Although this issue is difficult and politically charged, chambers must still focus on raising educational attainment in the form of more high school graduates—both to encourage perception of the region as "educated" and to create a ready pool of potential employees who are trainable for future positions.

As wealth and economic opportunity increasingly accrue to those with high-level capabilities or specialized skills, higher education is emerging as one of the most important economic development assets in any region. Universities, four-year colleges, and community colleges have the potential to attract talent, boost skill levels, and train professionals critical to the functioning of modern economies, such as accountants, engineers, attorneys, nurses, and technicians. In many markets, attaining a bachelor's degree is becoming more important than ever before. It should also be emphasized, however, that chambers in weak markets must take advantage of myriad higher education opportunities that do not involve earning bachelor's degrees. The pursuit of chamber and business objectives and strategies regarding higher education can take many forms, from partnering to form university incubator centers to joint lobbying to funding exciting on-campus applied research to future-oriented curriculum design. The biggest role a chamber-like organization plays, however, is to serve as a constant link between higher education institutions and the community and businesses in the region.

Prioritize Infrastructure Needs

From agriculture to entertainment, energy to information technology, business health and growth depend on effective transportation and infrastructure. The provision of roads and other public infrastructure is one of the most important roles of government, yet many communities have fallen short because of political infighting, lack of planning, redirection of funds to social programs, and shrinking revenue sources for public infrastructure. Key infrastructure issues include road quality and capacity, sewer capacity and linkages, water quantity and quality, and a ready supply of affordable energy. For struggling communities trying to compete for a major new investment, these mundane issues can prove to be the make-or-break criteria that incentives and glamorous presentations cannot overcome. The development community must "play" constantly in this arena to ensure that projects are strategically planned, funded, and prioritized to reflect real needs—not political forces.

Normalize the Business Climate

It is critical that regions and the states in which they operate avoid unorthodox tax and regulatory policies. The appearance of "normalcy" in terms of tax treatment and rate structures may be as important as the overall actual tax burden a prospect company may expect to bear. Similarly, communities should ensure that their regulatory agencies, planning commissions, and permitting offices are as easy (fast, predictable, and consistent) to deal with as possible.

Seek Balanced Environmental Policies

The quality of the environment in a community can have a direct impact on its ability to attract new business investment. Communities that have air pollutant concentrations that exceed national health standards are subject to severe penalties, including restrictions on new industry, required gasoline formulations, and recurring fines on existing industry for nonattainment of environmental standards. Business-led groups that are perpetual obstructionists in dealing with environmental issues will find themselves politically marginalized. A more productive model is for employer-led groups to work to ensure that community responses to air, water, and waste issues are balanced across industry and consumer interests.

Foster Tolerance and Inclusion

The most vibrant economies increasingly are those that have learned to embrace diversity. Many weaker markets in the Great Lakes region have been fighting segregation for decades, but they are still relatively segregated.[8] MSAs such as Cleveland, Buffalo, and Detroit all show inordinate signs of racial separation and inequity, as well as struggling economies. Southern metro regions such as Atlanta, which became less segregated during the civil rights era than their regional peer communities, have grown faster.

Research done at the Wharton School of Business suggests that inclusive workplaces have lower recruiting costs and higher employee productivity. Nearly 90 percent of Fortune 500 firms already have gone beyond federal statute, adopting policies to prevent discrimination on the basis of marital status, political affiliation, race, and sexual orientation.[9] These companies—enviable recruitment prospects for any developer—are simply more likely to locate in communities that are inclusive and welcoming. As the economic mix continues to shift away from traditional industries to more knowledge-based work, the correlation between inclusion and level of attraction to investors will grow. The business leadership in every region can and must take a major role in breaking down barriers to entry into the highest corporate circles, fighting institutional discrimination, and opening doors of opportunity at both the staff and board levels of chamber activity. Efforts to break down neighborhood segregation are also important. The Greater Cleveland Partnership developed a comprehensive matrix approach, which is described in chapter 13 of this volume (see chapter 13, figure 13-1). Every major metropolitan community should consider taking such an approach.

Expand Workforce Housing

The cost and availability of housing are often overlooked as significant factors in economic development. The lack and poor quality of available workforce housing (referred to as "affordable" housing before the term became emotionally charged) has become a significant obstacle or motivator for regional economic development. An article in *Forbes* magazine in July 2007 pointed to the correlation between the fastest-growing suburban communities and housing affordability.[10] Since everything from traffic patterns to school quality is influenced by housing stock and cost, the issue of housing supply must be faced by business-led development organizations as a part of regional product development. Chambers have taken the lead in communities as different as Washington, D.C, Long Island, San Jose, and Palm Beach, by providing powerful research on the impact of building permits, zoning, and real estate practices on workforce housing availability. The U.S. Department of Housing and Urban Development has an entire department dedicated to assisting communities in establishing policies, regulations, and practices to expand, rather than contract, workforce housing availability.

Address Quality-of-Life Issues

With place now as important as position in determining where highly mobile talent will land, quality-of-life factors are critical to keeping and attracting employers who depend on that workforce. Successful metro economies of the future will likely have vibrant, recognizable downtowns, relatively low crime, a clean appearance, well-maintained park systems, diverse recreational opportunities, and cultural amenities. Extensive research by the California-based author and consultant Joel Kotkin and others has made it clear that suburbs will continue to appeal to a majority of Americans for the foreseeable future, but even outer-rim communities must develop unique public assets if they want to expand their prosperity (even if not their populations).[11]

Promote a Positive Vision and Mind-set

The final area of product development in which chambers often are involved is vision and mind-set. Often overlooked among attractiveness of place is the importance of a community's mind-set—its optimism, its outlook, its receptiveness to growth. Where larger regionwide metro chambers can and must influence many product development features such as transportation and education, local chambers usually play a variety of roles focused on improving community-specific quality of life. Among the most important of these is the articulation of a vision for the future of the community, and celebrating the actions and individuals that move the community closer to that vision. Such intangibles can have a major impact on site-location decisions. A visibly positive, engaged, and committed group of business leaders is critical to establishing and maintaining that mind-set.

Moving the Ball

Although solutions to regional public policy issues may vary dramatically, depending upon the local and regional context, a number of strategies for success are universal. There are proven ways to "move the ball," and many of them involve working effectively in the policy arena. Whether fighting to improve schools, build bridges, or break down tax and regulatory roadblocks, it will be necessary to influence and change policies through heavy involvement in the public policy arena. Advocacy work of chambers occurs in many venues, only one of which is legislative. Chambers need to build relationships and expand their spheres of influence to include regulatory agencies, mayoral offices, university bureaucracies, and, very important, other organizations located in the region in order to affect public policy. Success depends on many factors.

Influence Your "Publics"

The importance of the media in influencing public opinion and the perspectives of key public officials cannot be overstated, but paying for sufficient advertising to shift opinions is seldom in the financial ballpark for chambers. One powerful strategy for creating a platform for free (earned) media attention for your group's organizational priorities is to become the leading source of information and analysis on all issues relating to regional economic development.

The Buffalo-Niagara Partnership is fighting to restore western New York as a viable business and investment destination by taking on the most complex financial issues. Their research work on public budgets and finance is quoted extensively in regional and statewide media. Since the local tax burden is seen as a major disincentive for employers, the research is critical to economic recovery. The Baton Rouge Area Chamber built a strong research capability not only to publish an annual economic outlook but also to quickly analyze and prepare comments on any potential economic story *ahead* of press inquiries.

Every media inquiry can be used to frame an economic event or story in a way that supports the public policy priorities critical to the economic success of the

Box 5-3. *Case Study: Pittsburgh-Allegheny Region*

Background

During and after the Industrial Revolution, Pittsburgh, Pennsylvania, was among the wealthiest areas in the country. Known for the manufacturing of steel, aluminum, and glass and the area's reserves of coal, petroleum, and natural gas, Pittsburgh remained a major industrial center through the 1970s. When, during the 1980s, the steel industry went bust, the region experienced what could only be described as a depression, losing 100,000 jobs in three years—a greater loss than anywhere else in the country. Although the Pittsburgh region's population had been in the top ten in the 1970s, by 2000 it had declined to twenty-first place, back to the same population it had had in 1940: 2.7 million people. And the drop continued through the early part of the twenty-first century, as Pittsburgh remained one of only three major metropolitan statistical areas where deaths outpaced births.

Restructuring the Economy

Efforts to restructure the Pittsburgh area's economy had begun long before the steel industry went bust. In 1946, as World War II ended, high-level corporate leaders formed a partnership called the Allegheny Conference on Community Development to work in conjunction with government officials to deal with environmental issues that were a legacy of the region's industrial heritage—specifically, pollution abatement and flood control. The Conference later turned its energies to supporting regional infrastructure projects. By the 1980s the economic impact of the fundamental changes in the steel industry drove the Conference to launch initiatives to diversify the local economy, improve transportation networks, and promote advanced manufacturing, research, and development.

In the 1990s the Conference undertook a sustained effort to evaluate and strengthen the economy. Recognizing the need to think and act regionally, it launched the Southwestern PA Growth Alliance—comprising nine counties and the city of Pittsburgh—to present a unified regional voice in Harrisburg and in Washington, D.C. As a result of these efforts, and at the direction of the newly named Allegheny Conference's leadership, the organization broadened its "service area" and began to restructure itself, adding three other organizations—the Pennsylvania Economy League of Southwestern Pennsylvania, the Greater Pittsburgh Chamber of Commerce, and the Pittsburgh Regional Alliance—as affiliates. Each organization has a specific role, yet, joined together through their board leadership and structure, they share a common vision, a common action agenda, and a common staff; thus, the expanded Allegheny Conference is well positioned to improve the business climate and quality of life in southwestern Pennsylvania and to market the region worldwide.

As part of its restructuring, the Conference formed the Regional Investors Council, comprising private sector leaders of more than three hundred member companies from across the region and more than five hundred small-business chamber of commerce members, who advise the boards of the Conference. Meeting quarterly, investors volunteer

(continued)

Box 5-3. *Case Study: Pittsburgh-Allegheny Region (continued)*

their time, resources, and their pool of talent to the boards, task forces, and committees that provide oversight to the projects and programs that advance the agenda for regional excellence.

First Signs of Economic Successes

The transformed, broader-based Allegheny Conference focused on tackling the tough problems of infrastructure and government consolidation to create a business climate that could attract the people and capital required for a world-class economy. Determined to grow world-class industry sectors, the Conference focused its attention and resources on data-verified technology drivers: advanced materials, information technology, and life sciences. Today the Pittsburgh region has more than two thousand companies that employ more than 107,000 people in these three sectors alone.

These regional efforts have started to show tangible results:

Business tax competitiveness. One of Pennsylvania's most uncompetitive taxes, the Capital Stock and Franchise Tax, was phased out. Conference efforts also led to a new tax treatment for operating losses, which is critical for start-up companies.

Air quality—PM 2.5. In 2005 the Conference successfully lobbied federal compliance officials for a change in the U.S. Environmental Protection Agency's interpretation of new air quality regulations to ensure continued employment, negating what would have been a major impediment to economic development in the region.

Regional Air Service Partnership and other infrastructure improvements. In 2001, the Conference created the Regional Air Service Partnership (RASP), a public-private partnership to improve the region's air transportation. RASP conducted extensive research to identify markets critical to the region's travelers and raised corporate funds to help support the marketing of new air service. This effort succeeded in attracting Independence Air (2004), Southwest Airlines (2005), and JetBlue (2006) to the Pittsburgh International Airport. The results have been a record number of boardings at PIA and lower costs. RASP also created a coalition to lobby for airport-related infrastructure and succeeded in getting state roads designated as Interstate Highway I-376, thus qualifying for ongoing federal highway funding. RASP also secured $6.9 million in grants and loans for new water and sewer lines needed by three major new industrial parks near the airport.

Other tangible successes of the Conference include the following:

—Influenced almost $2 billion of private and public sector capital investment in developing land for commercial and residential use in the Pittsburgh International Airport region, nearly doubling the anticipated growth targets for the 2003–06 period.
—Developed master plans for three thousand acres of Airport Authority property and one thousand acres of former strip mines, while securing $6 million for a new business park that is expected to attract 1,356 new jobs and $33 million in private investment.

Box 5-3. *Case Study: Pittsburgh-Allegheny Region (continued)*

—Received approval of more than $4 million for outlying industrial and mixed-use employment centers expected to create or save nearly three thousand jobs and bring in hundreds of millions in private investment.

—During the 2005 Base Alignment and Closure rounds, mobilized a grassroots community network that ultimately succeeded in retaining the region's primary military base, the Pittsburgh Air Reserve Station, home of the 911th Airlift Wing.

Lessons Learned

The partnership must have a vision and focus on results. The Conference leadership developed a vision that is now embodied in the organization's two initiatives: promoting the Pittsburgh region through business development and improving the competitiveness of the region's business climate. Each goal has a series of objectives and measurable results that are tracked quarterly on a "dashboard," where board members report their progress to one another.

Strong leadership is critical to success. The Allegheny Conference came about because the region's high-level corporate leaders wanted a new model for civic leadership. Corporate leaders showed their commitment to the "affiliate" model, joining the Chamber, Pennsylvania Economy League, the former Allegheny Conference on Community Development, and Pittsburgh Regional Alliance through increased funding and increased leadership engagement.

A commitment to continuous improvement is necessary. In broad terms, the focus of the Conference's current three-year agenda—including taxes and regulation, infrastructure, workforce, and local government reform, coupled with business development activities for the region—has not varied greatly from the goals of its founders over sixty years ago. Over the years and over this recent organizational transformation, the key has been a commitment to continuous improvement.

region. Whether the goal is to restore confidence and hope in the region, identify obstacles to growth, or foster support for specific employers, the media can be key to economic recovery efforts.

Establish Working Relationships

Laws and administrative policies are enacted by people—all of whom are motivated to act, or not act, by more than just the simple facts of a particular public policy matter. To ensure that policy changes move in the right direction, chambers and business leaders must establish positive working (personal) relationships with key political leaders and opinion makers months before a particular issue comes to the fore. Relationships must be built *before* they are needed, and commitments of support should be secured well before a formal decision point is reached. Asking a previously unknown legislator for support in a complex issue during a busy legislative session typically is not successful. Additionally, lawmakers tend to trust those who consistently provide them with reliable, fact-based information on issues.

Governmental affairs professionals, chief executives at chambers, and others seeking to influence public officials need to understand who each official is as a person and what he or she wants to achieve (policy priorities and political aspirations). Find out what key elected officials believe is the reason they were elected. In many cases, some of the reasons will dovetail more than expected with the product development goals of the chamber. Identifying major donors to a particularly important lawmaker and engaging them in the process can be especially effective. And, of course, effective use of PAC contributions can take relationships to a different level.

Maintain Focus

Organizations in regions facing economic hardship often feel overwhelmed by the sheer magnitude of product negatives stacked against them: poor schools, crumbling roads, weak support for the arts, high taxes, tough regulations, poor public safety. They select and tackle too many problem areas simultaneously, reducing chances for success in any. They take aggressive positions on issues with relatively little importance, burning up valuable resources and political capital. A hard, comprehensive look at a region's strengths and weaknesses (highlighted earlier) can help to focus regional efforts on enhancing strengths while diminishing weaknesses.

It is also tempting for broad-based business groups such as chambers to become distracted by the "other guy's" priorities. Every organization in the region—from the heart association to the library—may approach the chamber to assist in advocacy work on behalf of their getting vital tax resources or for their particular community asset. Sometimes, these appeals even come to the organization via volunteer members serving on the board of directors. It's tough, but in weak markets especially, the chamber must accept the fact that it can do anything . . . but not everything.

Employ Appropriate Tactics

To achieve success on a tax or regulatory issue, "victim" testimony from affected employers can be a powerful tactic in an overall direct legislative strategy. To achieve success on zoning changes or government efficiency improvements, grassroots neighborhood work is the most effective tool. Changing community college curricula to include new employer-based programs might be best handled by calls from donors to the governor that can result in administration "suggestions" to the college president. In some cases, wide-ranging coalitions involving lions and lambs, Davids and Goliaths, work, whereas in others, quiet one-on-one lobbying wins the day. Some issues and campaigns last for days and others for years.

Sometimes, the way to make a critical change to develop the product and improve the region is the do-it-yourself method. In Springfield, Missouri, for instance, the Ozarks Regional Economic Partnership mentioned earlier pays directly for a program to help local employers work through the maze of legal and cultural issues surrounding hiring immigrant workers.

Even selecting the venue in which to do battle is part of this strategy. For instance, in their efforts to integrate city and county services in Chicago, Metropolis 2020 and the Chicagoland Chamber worked more effectively in the state house than in local legislative chambers.

Partner . . . It's Lonely Out There

The business community acting alone, or even in concert with other organizations focused on economic growth, can seldom succeed on big regional initiatives if acting alone. Partnerships in the policy arena are not till-death-do-us-part marriages. They are mutually beneficial, temporary, initiative-specific alliances aimed at achieving specific outcomes. Whereas coalitions of chambers and other business organizations (builders' associations, manufacturing councils, and so forth) sometimes can and do last for decades, the most effective advocacy partnerships are crafted around specific pieces of legislation, causes, or projects. To increase the likelihood of victories, chambers may be aligned with homeowners one year and high-volume electricity users the next.

Know the Process Cold

Political decisionmaking processes, particularly legislative processes, involve a broad range of maneuvers that can derail or support the progress of a policy proposal. Since the defining factor is the process itself, it is absolutely critical for governmental affairs professionals to understand in detail the operations of the agency, department, or legislative entity in question. Volunteer business leaders and board members, no matter how well meaning, do not understand—and seldom have time to learn—the real nitty-gritty of how policy changes move from idea to law. Securing matching funds from several sources for new sports or cultural facilities is a perfect example of a complex process involving every possible political, legal, and procedural nuance. No matter how good the idea and how unanimous the support, ideas can still go up in flames if players take the wrong steps. This presents difficulties for organizations working with limited resources in struggling markets, but failure to retain and pay policy professionals will doom recovery initiatives. For the biggest projects with the highest payoffs, funds should be raised to retain the services of professional campaign managers.

Use Celebration as Leavening

Each policy success related to improvement of prospects for a weak region should be celebrated and leveraged as an opportunity to create future wins. Sometimes, restoring hope for positive change in a struggling economy is all that is needed to spur additional investment, the return of home-grown talent, or the attention of government funding sources. Successes should be assertively communicated to the public and key stakeholders, with care taken to provide ample recognition for decisionmakers and other supporters who helped achieve the policy victory. Often it is necessary to break out of the "not-in-my-term-of-office" (NIMTO) mode to achieve major successes—but this can be politically risky in the extreme. Acknowledging the courage of those who *do* will help build organizational credibility and political capital for future battles.

View Occasional Failures as Unavoidable . . . and Acceptable

Defeats, or delayed victories, in certain individual policy battles are inevitable with ambitious regional agendas. If there are no setbacks, it probably means the regional agenda is not ambitious enough. Volunteer and professional leadership of chambers must accept and can learn from these setbacks. Every failed policy effort aimed at improving the quality of life or business competitiveness of the region should be examined for flaws to avoid in the future.

In Des Moines, Iowa, communities in a tri-county area voted in July 2007 on whether or not to support a tax proposal, put together by the Greater Des Moines Partnership, that would distribute revenue in the Des Moines metro area. The proposal, called "Yes to Destiny," was to raise the sales tax from 6 to 7 percent in three counties for ten years, so as to generate $750 million, to be split among property tax reduction, new regional facilities, and cultural and green initiatives. Of the forty-one communities voting on the proposal, thirty-nine voted it down. Why? Postmortem analysis indicated that the proposal was too complicated. Voters saw it as an unnecessary tax increase that would put more money into the hands of government. Promoters of the plan may have failed to clearly communicate their message of why an environment that attracts and retains young professionals is beneficial to the entire Des Moines region. The partnership and its allies have already begun work on plan B.

Conclusion

Why do communities and regions fight so hard to establish a platform to assure future economic growth? Why do they—and we—bother? Because growth produces prosperity for *everyone*. A common misperception is that economic growth helps only those at the top of the wage scale, but the data say otherwise. Chamber leaders and economic development professionals work so hard at finding regional remedies and stimulants to economic growth because such expansion increases personal incomes, tax revenue for public goods, and charitable giving while enriching the lives of the citizenry.

Today, those solutions are more likely to be regional than local, and more likely to be found in the supply of good people than in the supply of good buildings. The diverging lines on graphs that compare regional economies can be disturbing, but their paths are not inevitable. The anthropologist Margaret Mead said, "Never doubt that a few thoughtful people can change the world. Indeed nothing else ever has." In most regions in this country, some of the very best of the thoughtful people are striving as board members, funders, and executives in corporate-civic organizations, EDOs, business councils, boards of trade, and chambers. And their world—our world—is changed by their work.

Finding ways to effectively advocate, partner, communicate, plan, and lead down the path to regional economic prosperity takes wits, courage, money, and luck, in just about equal proportions. There has been no mention of government mergers in this chapter about regionalism. Regional thinking and action might be aided by joining governments together, but it is not a necessary prerequisite. Likewise, it makes little sense to portray elected officials as the enemy of economic growth. It would be easy to blame one party, politician, or civic leader for economic hardship in a community or region, but the reality in this changing world is that many factors influencing health and wealth are beyond the control of those who are charged with leadership.

In many cases, heroic efforts have been needed by public and private sector leaders simply to stay above water following massive economic dislocation caused by technology changes, global trends, and transformations of corporate ownership. The "few thoughtful people" fighting every day to find the talent, investment, and opportunity to help their growth-starved regions are not able to point to sexy job statistics as evidence of their success in these hard-market towns.

"Could have been worse" is not a campaign slogan that will convince many private sector investors or taxpayers to step up to the plate with added support for these dedicated professionals and volunteers. But they keep at it anyway.

Buffalo moves up a notch or two on MSA comparison charts because of its successful work in marketing cross-border business opportunities throughout a binational region. Detroit breaks down decades of city-county squabbles, bringing the leadership of all governments in southeastern Michigan together to promote development in and around their international airport to join the elite aerotropolis centers of global commerce. Hartford business leaders fund a multijurisdictional economic partnership to overcome a decade of insurance industry job losses around that capital.

The lessons and counsel contained in this document are all drawn from professionals in markets large and small, strong and weak, who are already working successfully to grow, restore, or save their economies in the face of sometimes overwhelming odds. With even more focus on regional approaches that build on partnerships, cooperation, shared assets, and future-oriented development strategies, their impact will be even greater.

Notes

1. See www.ozarkspartnership.com/regional_profile/welcome_to_the_ozarks.
2. See "SBDC Investor Brief 2007," at www.springfieldchamber.com/regional_economy/ sbdc_newsletters/june_2007_investor_brief/6_top_midsize_metro.
3. Royce Hanson, Hal Wolman, David Connolly, and Katherine Pearson, "Corporate Citizenship and Urban Problem Solving: The Changing Civic Role of Business Leaders in American Cities," report (Brookings Institution, September 2006).
4. Robert D. Putnam, *Bowling Alone: The Collapse and Revival of American Community* (New York: Simon & Schuster, 2000).
5. Pauline Hovey and Allegheny Conference on Community Development, "Pittsburgh-Allegheny Regional Action Plan" and Interviews (Pittsburgh, July–August, 2007).
6. Conway Data, Inc., "New Plant Database" (Norcross, Ga., 2006).
7. Eric Canada, of Blane-Canada Ltd., and James McGraw, of KMK Consulting, during consulting project for Baton Rouge Area Chamber, September 2007.
8. See Gordon Trowbridge, "Locale Links Segregated Cities," at www.detnews.com/special reports/2002/segregation/b03-390169.htm.
9. Human Rights Campaign, "The State of the Workplace," annual report to the nation from the Leadership Conference on Civil Rights (Washington: 2006–2007).
10. See "America's Fastest-Growing Suburbs," *Forbes,* July 2007, available at www.forbes.com/ realestate/2007/07/16/suburbs-growth-housing-forbeslife-cx_mw_0716realestate.html.
11. See Joel Kotkin, "Rule, Suburbia," *Washington Post,* February 6, 2005, available at www.washingtonpost.com/wp-dyn/articles/A364-2005Feb5.html.

PART TWO

Analytics

6

Understanding Economically Distressed Cities

Harold L. Wolman, Edward W. Hill, Pamela Blumenthal, and Kimberly Furdell

Even though American cities as a whole have been gaining jobs and residents over the past two decades, numerous cities continue to have serious economic problems.[1] These cities, many of which have a manufacturing legacy, have been unable to make the adjustments necessary to meet the challenge of changing economic circumstances. They have suffered economic and population decline or stagnation, and their residents, on average, have had little or no improvement in their standard of living. Understanding the nature and causes of this economic distress, and both the potential and limitations of public policy in addressing it, is essential for effective policymaking.

This chapter attempts to shed some light on which cities are underperforming economically when compared with their peers, and why. We begin by identifying a set of economically distressed cities and examining the relationship of these cities to their metropolitan economies (the term metropolitan as used in this chapter refers to a metropolitan statistical area, or MSA). We then explore the extent to which cities have moved into and out of the economically distressed

We appreciate the financial support received from the Fannie Mae Foundation and the Brookings Institution's Metropolitan Policy Program, which over the past two years has supported our research on the economies of cities and their metropolitan regions.

category (that is, the extent to which economic distress is a chronic condition), identify some of the factors that account for the economic health (and, therefore, degree of distress) of cities, and offer explanations as to why some cities have been successful while others have not.

Economically Distressed Cities

Economically distressed cities are cities whose economies are performing poorly and whose residents have, on average, low levels of economic well-being. To identify these cities, we use a set of economic indicators to construct two broad measures of the economic health of cities: the growth of (or change in) a city's economy during the 1990s and a measure of the level of the economic well-being of city residents in 2000. We then use these measures to create a typology of central cities. Within this typology, the set of cities exhibiting the most severe levels of economic difficulty and whose residents are the least well off in the aggregate is designated as economically distressed.

Our data set comprises the 302 central cities that met at least one of the following criteria either in 1990 or in 2000:[2]

—Cities with populations of at least 50,000 that were the primary city in a metropolitan area
—Cities with populations of at least 50 percent of the population of the primary city in their metropolitan area
—Cities with populations of at least 150,000, regardless of whether they were the primary city in a metropolitan area

We created two indexes for the cities in our dataset: the City Economic Condition Index, which measures change in the competitiveness of a central city as a place of business activity, relative to other central cities, from 1990 to 2000, and the City Resident Economic Well-Being Index, which measures the economic well-being of residents of the city as of 2000. The City Economic Condition Index consists of three indicators measuring growth between 1990 and 2000: growth in employment, growth in annual payroll, and growth in the number of establishments.[3] The City Resident Economic Well-Being Index consists of five indicators measuring city residential well-being as of 2000: per capita income, median household income, poverty rate, unemployment rate, and labor-force participation rate. (See table 6-1A for variable definitions and data sources.)[4]

Table 6-1. *Typology A: City Resident Economic Well-Being and City Economic Condition, 2000*

City economic condition	City resident economic well-being		
	High	Medium	Low
Strong	57	28	16
Moderate	36	45	19
Weak	7	28	65

Source: Authors' calculations.

To create each index, variables were standardized through the use of z-scores, which were then summed across the variables within each index to create a summary score for each city on each index, thereby weighting each of the variables equally.[5] We then ranked each city on the indexes according to the index scores.[6]

We used the two indexes to create a typology of central cities. For each index we divided the cities into thirds on the basis of their rankings. For the City Economic Condition Index, the top third of cities were considered *strong* on that index, the middle third *moderate,* and the bottom third *weak.* For the City Resident Economic Well-Being Index, the top third was considered *high,* the middle third *medium,* and the bottom third *low.* Typology A was created by grouping cities according to the nine possible combinations created by crossing the three categories of the two indexes. Sixty-five of the 302 central cities were considered both weak on the City Economic Condition Index and low on the City Resident Economic Well-Being Index. These sixty-five cities were designated as economically distressed, or weak-market, cities.[7] (See table 6-2 for the list of these cities.) These cities were declining locations for business activity relative to other central cities during the 1990s, and their residents, on average, experienced low levels of economic returns and activity in the labor market.[8]

Over half of the economically distressed cities (58.0 percent) are concentrated in just eight states: Connecticut, Indiana, Massachusetts, Michigan, New Jersey, New York, Ohio, and Pennsylvania. (Cities in these states made up only 20.5 percent of all central cities in the set.) This reflects the difficulties facing the metropolitan areas in the northeastern and east north-central regions of the country, a large portion of the so-called "Rust Belt," as they attempt to revitalize their stagnant regional economies and stem the decline of their central cities. The three states with the highest proportion of cities that are economically distressed are Pennsylvania, with nine of its ten cities considered to be weak-market cities, New York (seven out of eight), and Ohio (eight out of eleven). Although heavily

Table 6-2. *Economically Distressed (Weak-Market) Cities*[a] *(N = 65)*

Albany, Georgia	Flint, Michigan	Milwaukee, Wisconsin	Saginaw, Michigan
Albany, New York	Fresno, California	Muncie, Indiana	San Bernardino,
Allentown,	Harrisburg,	New Bedford,	California
Pennsylvania	Pennsylvania	Massachusetts	Santa Maria,
Altoona, Pennsylvania	Hartford,	New Haven,	California
Baltimore, Maryland	Connecticut	Connecticut	Schenectady, New
Beaumont, Texas	Huntington, West	New Orleans,	York
Binghamton,	Virginia	Louisiana	Scranton,
New York	Jackson, Mississippi	Newark, New Jersey	Pennsylvania
Birmingham, Alabama	Kalamazoo,	Odessa, Texas	Shreveport,
Bridgeport,	Michigan	Philadelphia,	Louisiana
Connecticut	Lancaster,	Pennsylvania	Springfield,
Buffalo, New York	Pennsylvania	Pine Bluff, Arkansas	Massachusetts
Canton, Ohio	Long Beach,	Pittsburgh,	Springfield, Ohio
Cincinnati, Ohio	California	Pennsylvania	St. Louis, Missouri
Cleveland, Ohio	Los Angeles,	Port Arthur, Texas	Stockton, California
Danville, Virginia	California	Providence, Rhode	Syracuse, New York
Dayton, Ohio	Macon, Georgia	Island	Terre Haute,
Decatur, Illinois	Mansfield, Ohio	Reading, Pennsylvania	Indiana
Detroit, Michigan	Merced, California	Richmond, Virginia	Trenton, New Jersey
Erie, Pennsylvania	Miami, Florida	Rochester, New York	Utica, New York
Fall River,	Milwaukee,	Rocky Mount, North	Warren, Ohio
Massachusetts	Wisconsin	Carolina	Youngstown, Ohio

Source: Authors' calculations.

a. Cities in bottom third of both City Economic Condition Index and City Resident Economic Well-Being Index.

concentrated in the northeastern quadrant of the nation, economically distressed cities are scattered across the nation; seven of California's thirty-three cities fall into this category.

Characteristics of Economically Distressed Cities

How did the sixty-five economically distressed cities differ from the nondistressed cities? We look first at the values of the individual indicators that make up the two indexes.[9] The set of distressed cities was characterized by slow economic growth, or deterioration in many cases, and high levels of city resident economic distress. Although the overall mean index score for both indexes is approximately zero, the mean City Economic Condition Index score for the weak-market cities is −0.89, or approximately one standard deviation below the mean for all cities. Likewise, the mean City Resident Economic Well-Being

Index score for the weak-market cities is −0.96, about 1.1 standard deviations below the overall mean (see table 6-2A for summary statistics). On average, economically distressed cities

—lost 8 percent of their jobs from 1990 to 2000, while employment among the nondistressed cities increased 18 percent;

—experienced payroll growth of only 50 percent (in current dollars), while payroll grew 91 percent in the nondistressed cities;

—saw the number of establishments grow just 1.4 percent, while the number grew 18 percent in the nondistressed cities;

—had an average per capita income in 2000 that was only 78 percent of that in the nondistressed cities ($16,019 compared to $20,424);

—had a median household income that was 76 percent of the average of the nondistressed cities ($29,138 versus $38,510);

—had an unemployment rate of 10 percent, compared to 6 percent in the nondistressed cities;

—had a labor-force participation rate of 59 percent, compared to 65 percent in the nondistressed cities;

—had a poverty rate of 23 percent, compared with 15 percent in the non-distressed cities.

The weak-market, or economically distressed, cities also differed from the non-weak-market cities on a variety of other variables that were not entered in either of the two indexes, but are nonetheless interesting. (We emphasize that the following are descriptive differences, not causal. Some of them are obviously the products of economic distress rather than causes; others might well contribute to the causes of distress.) Weak-market, or economically distressed, cities were more likely than other cities (on average) to be older cities (91.7 years since the central city first reached 50,000 population, compared to 50.7 years). They were also more likely to have

—lower shares of MSA population (28.9 percent compared to 37.0 percent) and employment (33.4 percent compared to 48.6 percent),

—a higher percentage of workers employed in the manufacturing sector (14.3 percent compared with 12.1 percent),

—lower median home values ($80,600 compared to $122,400) and higher vacancy rates (9.9 percent compared with 6.0 percent),

—lower home ownership rates (49.3 percent compared with 55.7 percent),

—a lower percentage of residents with college degrees (16.7 percent compared with 26.6 percent),

—a higher percentage with no high school diploma (26.9 percent compared with 17.3 percent) and with only a high school diploma (58.0 percent compared with 43.4 percent),

—a higher share of single-parent households (45.1 percent compared with 31.3 percent),

—a higher percentage of black non-Hispanic residents (31.4 percent compared with 14.7 percent),

—a higher murder rates (1.49 per 10,000 compared with 0.64),

—greater racial segregation (as measured by both dissimilarity and exposure indexes),

—higher rates of concentrated poverty (22.8 percent of poor in high-poverty neighborhoods compared with 12.1 percent),

—greater income inequality (ratio of poor to high-income households).

Economically Distressed Cities and Their Metropolitan Areas

Cities exist as parts of metropolitan economies. Substantial research has indicated that city economic health is tied inextricably to the economic health of the metropolitan area's economy.[10] To examine the relationship between city and metropolitan economic condition, we created an MSA Economic Condition Index for the 255 MSAs of all the central cities in our data set.[11] The four indicators used to form this index are the change in MSA-level employment, wages, and gross metropolitan product from 1990 to 2000 and the gross metropolitan product per job in 2000.[12] (See table 6-3A for the list of indicators, their definitions, and data sources.) As with the other two economic health indexes, these indicators were standardized using z-scores, summed across the standardized values and divided by the number of indicators to create each city's index score. We then ranked the MSAs according to their index scores and divided them into thirds to get weak, moderate, and strong groups, which are shown in typology B.

This analysis demonstrates a strong link between the economic condition of cities and that of their MSAs (see table 6-3).[13] The sixty-five weak-market, or economically distressed, cities (those with weak city economic conditions and low city resident economic well-being) were in MSAs with an average MSA Economic Condition Index score of −0.51, compared with a mean index score of 0.15 for the MSAs of the non-weak-market cities. Only three economically distressed cities were in MSAs that had strong scores on the MSA Economic Condition Index (Bridgeport, Conn.; Richmond, Virginia; and San Bernardino, California). Fifteen were in MSAs

Table 6-3. *Typology B: City Economic Condition and MSA Economic Condition, 2000*

City economic condition	MSA economic condition		
	Strong	Moderate	Weak
Strong	72	24	5
Moderate	28	42	30
Weak	6	30	63

Source: Authors' calculations.

with moderate MSA Economic Condition Index scores, and the majority, forty-six cities, were in MSAs with weak index scores, as shown in table 6-4.

As table 6-4 indicates, the problems of economically distressed, or weak-market, cities are inextricably related to the problems of the metropolitan area in which they are located. As a consequence, it may well be that efforts to improve the conditions of economically distressed cities must be metropolitan area–wide in scope.

Economic Distress and Change over Time: Can Cities Overcome Their Problems?

To what extent is economic distress a chronic condition for cities experiencing it? Can cities that are economically distressed in one era improve their conditions and

Table 6-4. *Typology C: City Resident Economic Well-Being, City Economic Condition, and MSA Economic Condition, 2000*

City economic condition	Residential economic well-being			MSA economic condition
	High	Medium	Low	
Strong	42	21	9	Strong
Moderate	15	13	0	
Weak	1	2	3	
Strong	13	7	4	Moderate
Moderate	13	15	14	
Weak	3	12	15	
Strong	2	0	3	Weak
Moderate	8	17	5	
Weak	3	14	46	

Source: Authors' calculations.

Table 6-5. *Cities That Were Economically Distressed in 1990 But Not in 2000 (N = 17)*

Akron, Ohio	Lafayette, Louisiana	Spokane, Washington
Anderson, Indiana	Lake Charles, Louisiana	St. Joseph, Missouri
Battle Creek, Michigan	Louisville, Kentucky	Toledo, Ohio
Chattanooga, Tennessee	Mobile, Alabama	Waco, Texas
Chicago, Illinois	Monroe, Louisiana	Yakima, Washington
Duluth, Minnesota	Pueblo, Colorado	

Source: Authors' calculations.

escape that status in the next? To examine this question, we created City Economic Distress indexes (the intersection of the weak City Economic Condition Index and low City Resident Economic Well-Being Index cells of the two indexes) for 1990 and compared the cities that were distressed in 1990 ($n = 56$) with those that were economically distressed in 2000 ($n = 65$). Of the fifty-six weak-market cities in 1990, thirty-nine were still classified as weak-market cities in 2000, but seventeen (or 30 percent) had moved out of the weak-market category. These can be thought of as transitional cities. They were replaced by twenty-six cities that were not economically distressed in 1990 but were in 2000.[14]

In what ways did the cities that were classified as weak markets in 1990 but moved out of that category in 2000 differ from those that were classified as weak markets in 1990 and remained so? The transitional weak-market cities (those that moved out of the category between 1990 and 2000) were statistically significantly different from the cities that were classified as weak markets over both

Table 6-6. *Cities That Were Economically Distressed in 2000 But Not in 1990 (N = 26)*

Albany, New York	Long Beach, California	Rochester, New York
Allentown, Pennsylvania	Los Angeles, California	Rocky Mount, North
Birmingham, Alabama	Macon, Georgia	Carolina
Bridgeport, Connecticut	Merced, California	San Bernardino, California
Decatur, Illinois	Miami, Florida	Santa Maria, California
Fall River, Massachusetts	New Bedford, Massachusetts	Schenectady, New York
Fresno, California	New Haven, Connecticut	Stockton, California
Hartford, Connecticut	Odessa, Texas	Syracuse, New York
Lancaster, Pennsylvania	Richmond, Virginia	Trenton, New Jersey

Source: Authors' calculations.

decades: at the beginning of the period (1990) they were characterized by the following:

—Higher employment growth in the prior decade from 1980 to 1990 (a 5.9 percent increase, compared to a 1.1 percent decline)

—A lower rate of decline in the number of establishments between 1980 and 1990 (a decline of 9.1 percent compared to 16.2 percent)

—Greater shares of metropolitan area employment in 1990 (59.6 percent, compared to 39.5 percent), and of population (43.6 percent, compared to 29.2 percent)

—Higher per capita income in 1990 ($11,800, compared to $10,933)

—A lower unemployment rate in 1990 (9.2 percent, compared to 10.7 percent)

—A lower murder rate in 1990 (1.13 per 10,000 residents, compared to 2.39)

—Lower income inequality in 1990

—A slightly higher home ownership rate in 1990 (57.1 percent, compared to 52.2 percent)

—A higher share of adult residents with at least some postsecondary education in 1990 (43.1 percent, compared to 36.6 percent), and lower shares of their adult populations who terminated their education with either no high school diploma (27.5 percent, compared to 32.3 percent) or only a high school diploma (56.9 percent, compared to 63.4 percent)

—A lower share of single-parent households in 1990 (34.9 percent, compared to 42.1 percent)

—A lower share of black non-Hispanic residents in 1990 (21.9 percent, compared to 33.8 percent).[15]

In short, the escapees from economic distress were in many ways poised to do so at the beginning of the period, as they were already performing better than the consistently weak cities on a range of indicators. Overall, while the City Economic Condition Index scores of the two groups of cities were not significantly different as of 1990, the City Resident Economic Well-Being Index scores of those that moved off the list were higher in 1990 than those of the chronically distressed cities.

The Causes of City Economic Distress

The prior section leads us to ask an important yet vexing question: What are the determinants of city economic condition and, given that it is so tied up with the metropolitan economy, of metropolitan area economic condition? In order to answer these questions and to begin to sort out causal links, we conducted a multivariate regression analysis first of change in central-city employment (by place of work) between 1990 and 2000 and then of changes in three measures of metropolitan area economic condition over the same period: employment, earnings, and gross metropolitan product.

The base model we used for all of these regressions includes a set of variables to capture economic structure, urban spatial structure, demographic structure, labor-market conditions, amenities, and the area environment for economic activity.[16] (See table 6-4A for variable definitions and data sources.) The dataset was made up of 224 metropolitan statistical areas (MSAs), which contained the 268 cities that had populations of at least 50,000 in both 1990 and 2000 and met at least one of the criteria set forth previously (see p. 152).[17]

Economic Structure

We consider three aspects of economic structure: industry composition, economic diversity, and whether the region contains a state capital city.

To address industry composition, we included the location quotients for the manufacturing sector and for the finance, insurance, and real estate (FIRE) sector, using the Standard Industrial Classification (SIC) definitions.[18] We would expect a low manufacturing location quotient in 1990 to be associated with increased employment growth and high earnings growth between 1990 and 2000. These expectations are consistent with the findings of Edward L. Glaeser, Jose A. Scheinkman, and Andrei Shleifer, who found the share of employment in manufacturing in the beginning of the time period they studied to be negatively related to income and population growth.[19] We chose FIRE as an example of a growing high-wage sector. We expected the FIRE location quotient to be positively associated with growth in both gross metropolitan product (GMP) and employment, because FIRE was a growing sector during the 1990s, so an area that was well positioned in FIRE in 1990 was likely to benefit from growth in that sector over the decade.

Economic diversity was measured through a portfolio measure of employment concentration, a variant of the Hirschman-Herfindahl Index (HHI).[20] Using a portfolio measure is a reasonable way of gauging the diversity of an area's economy because the way an area's pool of jobs is distributed across industries is in a real sense the area's portfolio of work and income-earning opportunities. We expect that greater economic diversity will be positively associated with city employment growth and with all three economic outcomes that we model at the metropolitan-area level.

The presence of a state capital in an MSA (or the city's being a state capital) is expected to be associated with employment and earnings growth, since state government employment, much of which is located in the state capital city, has been growing over several decades.

Urban Spatial Structure

An area's comparative advantage is based on both the quantity and quality of the factors of production that are associated with its spatial structural characteristics. Three area characteristics are particularly important: agglomeration economies, city economic age, and connectivity to the national and international economy.

Agglomeration economies are production cost savings for economic activity that result from large and diverse labor markets, support services, and consumer demand. Production cost savings associated with agglomeration economies are hypothesized to be positively associated with population size. Increases in metropolitan size have been related to increased productivity and higher average wages.[21] We measure agglomeration economies as the natural logarithm of the population of the metropolitan area for the three metropolitan change models and the city employment change model.[22]

A region's spatial form—its physical structure and infrastructure—is partially a reflection of when the region's core city first reached its economic maturity. Regions that have evolved out of older cities have greater building density, narrower streets, and highways that are retrofitted into an existing streetscape rather than a streetscape that is built to match the demand for, and pattern of, highways. Therefore, they also are more likely to have aging infrastructure and be less friendly to motor vehicle transportation. Age also determines the characteristics of the housing stock. Newer metropolitan areas have newer housing stock that better meets the consumption desires of families today.

We operationalize the concept of area age as the economic age of the city or, for the metropolitan models, the age of the oldest city in the MSA. Age is calculated as the number of years, as of 2000, since the city first passed the 50,000 mark in population in a decennial census. We expect area age to be negatively related to our four measures of economic performance.

Although old regions may have less connectivity by roads than newer regions that were designed for automobiles rather than streetcars and trains, connectivity to the global economy is now accomplished through air travel. Jan K. Brueckner found that every 10 percent gain in airport traffic is related to a 1 percent gain in service employment.[23] A preliminary study by Richard K. Green (2007) found that boardings, originations, and hub status predict an increase in economic activity.[24] We measure this connectivity of both people and goods in relative terms by calculating the number of scheduled airline flights per 1,000 population in the

MSA in the first quarter of 1991.[25] On the basis of prior studies, we expect airline departures to be positively associated with employment growth as well as earnings and GMP growth.

Demographic Structure

The primary impact of demographic structure on metropolitan economic performance is its relationship to the labor force. Demographics shape the supply side of the labor market. Therefore, we include variables that measure the portion of the population that is not of traditional working age and therefore is not likely to be part of the labor force. We call this portion the dependent population because most members of this group depend directly or indirectly on the wages of others to live. We split the dependent population into two subgroups: the population that is age seventeen and under and the population that is age sixty-five and older. We use the percentage change in these variables to capture any increase in the size of this segment of the population, capturing increases in the operating costs for businesses as a result of the tax load required to pay for growth in the region's social overhead burden. We expect both of these variables to be negatively associated with economic growth, since these two populations tend to increase social burdens through higher use of services such as public schools and health care services, without adding to the tax base.

Racial composition, the percentage of the city's or metropolitan area's population that was black non-Hispanic in 1990, has also frequently been associated with poor economic performance. This results partly from the historic legacy of discrimination and the strong correlation between percentage of black population and the poverty status of the population.[26] However, the relationship often holds even after controlling for educational attainment, suggesting that the quality of education in schools that the average black student attends is not as good as the quality of education in schools that white students attend. Thus a black resident with a high school education may have gained less knowledge, and received lower economic returns, than a white resident with a high school education from a different school system. This leads us to expect a negative relationship between this variable and the dependent variables.

Labor-Market Conditions

Two facets of the labor market are consistently found to be major factors in businesses' location decisions: the human capital of the labor force (the availability of skilled workers) and labor cost.[27]

The work of Glaeser and others has consistently found that human capital is positively related to economic growth. Robert Weissbourd and Christopher Berry found that education was the biggest driver of positive economic outcomes when measured by average wage per job.[28] However, formal education is not the only route to sustained higher incomes; training and spillovers also positively increase productivity. David E. Marcotte found that taking courses at a community college has a positive effect on earnings, even if the students did not obtain a credential, such as a certificate or an associate's degree.[29] This suggests that the labor market values some aspect of postsecondary (higher) education or the motivation of those who pursue it, in addition to the labor-market signaling effect of a college degree. Although educational attainment is most frequently measured by the percentage of the population with a bachelor's degree, we chose to use the percentage of the population with some college education both for empirical reasons and to reflect the work of Marcotte.[30] Consistent with the prior studies, we expect the percentage of the population with some college education to be significantly and positively related to economic growth across all three measures.

Labor cost also affects an area's comparative advantage. Relatively high wages in a metropolitan area have been found to reduce employment.[31] We expect higher average wages in 1990 to be negatively related to employment and GMP growth. Since wages for central-city workers are set in the metropolitan labor market, we use average wage per job in the metropolitan area as a measure of labor cost for all of our models, including central-city employment change.

Amenities

Economic growth has been found to be associated with desirable climate, low crime rates, and other amenities.[32] Like post–high school education, desirable climate (often defined as dry and temperate) consistently has been found to be significantly and positively associated with both population and wage growth at both the city and metropolitan levels.[33] Colder weather is associated with lower growth in wages. We expect warmer temperature to be positively associated with positive economic outcomes. We use average July temperature as a measure of climate-related amenities.[34]

Safety is a critical amenity that has been related to positive economic outcomes. Julie Berry Cullen and Steven D. Levitt have found that rising crime rates in cities are significantly related to decreases in population.[35] We originally expected high city crime rates to reduce not only city but also metropolitan area economic outcomes, since city crime rates may lead regionally mobile households and business investors to perceive, whether accurately or not, that high crime rates are typical throughout the metropolitan area. Accordingly, the three metropolitan models initially included city crime rates, but as they were not significant in any of the models, they were eliminated for reasons of parsimony. This result suggests that perceptions of city crime do not affect regional economic outcomes. However, it may influence the intraregional location of economic activity.

Environment for Economic Activity

In connection with the rise of what Glaeser termed the "skilled city," innovation is increasingly considered to be an important driver of economic growth.[36] Positive impacts have been found between science and research and development activities and economic development.[37] These results suggest that the presence of research universities will aid economic growth. Institutions of higher education can be thought of as multiproduct firms, with each product making a unique contribution to the city and regional economy.[38] The presence of universities has been found to be positively related to per capita income growth.[39]

For all four models, we measure this type of innovation by using a variable that combines the number of universities with high research activities and very high research activities in a metropolitan area in 1990, as defined by the Carnegie college and university classification system.[40]

In state capitals across the nation, policymakers and legislators express a great deal of concern about what the state business climate is and how the state's tax and regulatory policies affect business investment. Researchers frequently try to develop an all-encompassing index to measure state business climate. However, this concept is difficult to measure because of the many facets of a state's business climate and the range of demands placed on a state by different industries.

We use a single variable that employers may associate with perceived business friendliness: right-to-work laws.[41] Robert Tannenwald examined studies of right-to-work laws, finding that they had a positive and statistically significant association with economic activity, but raised concerns of endogeneity and other problems with studies that used the variable.[42] Timothy J. Bartik found that unionization levels had a negative effect on employment, and the existence of right-to-work laws had a positive effect on manufacturing plants' location decisions, which suggests that metropolitan areas in states with right-to-work laws are more attractive to manufacturers, and perhaps to other businesses.[43]

Finally we added regional variables to control for other factors that might vary by region and that we did not want to mistakenly attribute to characteristics of cities within those regions.

Regression Results

The models captured much of the variation in the dependent variables. The city economic change model had an adjusted R2 value of 0.593, whereas the adjusted R2 values for the metropolitan outcome models were 0.626 for metropolitan employment change, 0.523 for growth in gross metropolitan product, and 0.457 for growth in the metropolitan average earnings per job. (See table 6-5A for regression results.)

Economic Structure

The only economic structure variable that was significantly related to city employment growth was economic diversity; it was also significantly related to metropolitan employment growth at the 0.10 level.[44] However, at the metropolitan level an area's location quotient in manufacturing was positively related to all three measures of metropolitan economic performance. This result was surprising in light of our expectation that metropolitan areas dominated by manufacturing employment (as many of the cities in economic distress were) were likely to be at severe risk for relative economic decline. It may be that most of the expected decline occurred from the late 1970s through 1990 and that areas with a high manufacturing location quotient in 1990 were areas that were left with, or had developed, high-productivity manufacturing activity.

Urban Spatial Structure

Agglomeration economies, as measured by metropolitan population in 1990, were positively related to city economic change and to growth in GMP and metropolitan employment. An approximate doubling of a metropolitan area's 1990 population was associated with a 2.81-percentage-point increase in city employment, a 4.23-percentage-point increase in metropolitan area job growth, and a 7.03-percentage-point increase in gross metropolitan product growth.

Economic age was negatively related to central-city job growth and to metropolitan job and GMP growth. Each additional year of age for a city reduced central-city employment growth by 0.18 percentage point, meaning that a city that was a decade older than the average would, ceteris paribus, have experienced a job growth of 1.8 percentage points less than it otherwise would have. At the metropolitan level the effect on job growth was slightly lower, with each additional year of age being associated with a 0.11-percentage-point decline in job growth as well as a 0.17-percentage-point decline in GMP growth. This was consistent with our expectation that metropolitan regions with older cities are negatively affected by their older infrastructure and more sclerotic institutional arrangements and thus have lower economic performance, particularly lower growth rates in GMP and employment.

Connectivity as expressed by scheduled airline flights per capita (which we take to be a measure of connection to the global economy) was positively associated both with city and metropolitan employment growth and with growth in GMP.

Demographic Structure

Changes in dependent population as a proportion of total population have the expected negative impact on outcomes at both the city and metropolitan-area levels. Each percentage point increase in the central-city population under seventeen years of age is associated with a 1.5-percentage-point decline in city employment. At the metropolitan level, increases in the proportion of population over sixty-five are negatively associated with growth in all three outcomes, with a particularly strong impact on GMP change (each increase of 1 percentage point in the percentage of the population age sixty-five and over was associated with an 8.76-percentage-point decline in GMP). Change in the share of the population age seventeen and younger is also negatively associated with change in metropolitan-area employment.

The effect of the race variable was as expected. For all three measures of metropolitan economic performance, race (the percentage of black non-Hispanics in the population in 1990, the beginning of the period) was negative and significantly different from zero.[45] However, race did not have a significant effect on city employment change.

Labor-Market Conditions

Both human capital and labor cost were significant and in the expected directions in all four models. For each additional percentage point of city residents with at least some college education in 1990, city employment grew by an additional 0.42 percentage point between 1990 and 2000. The percentage of the population with at least some college education is predictive of growth in all metropolitan-area models as well. A one-point increase in the percentage of the population with at least some college in 1990 is associated with a 1.06-percentage-point increase in metropolitan GMP between 1990 and 2000, a 0.60-percentage-point increase in metropolitan employment, and a 0.35-percentage-point increase in metropolitan earnings.

As expected, wage per job in 1990 was negatively related to job growth at both the city and metropolitan levels and to GMP growth. The places that had high average wages in 1990 experienced lower rates of employment growth and GMP growth. An increase of $1,000 in 1990 metropolitan area wages was associated with declines of 1.9 percentage points in city employment change and 1.6 percentage points in metropolitan-area employment change between 1990 and 2000.

Amenities

The 1990 city crime rate (larcenies and murders per 10,000 residents) was negatively related to city employment growth between 1990 and 2000.[46] The crime variables were not significant in any of the metropolitan models, so were removed from the models. The lack of statistical significance between these variables and the dependent variables in the metropolitan-area models suggests that crime affects intrametropolitan location but not intermetropolitan location.

Climate, even after controlling for region, was positively associated with two of the metropolitan-level outcomes: the higher the July temperature, the greater the growth in metropolitan jobs and gross metropolitan product.[47] It was not related to city employment growth or metropolitan earnings.

Environment for Economic Activity

Innovation, as we measured it (the number of very high and high activity research universities in the metropolitan area), was not significantly related to either city employment change or to any of the metropolitan-area outcomes.

The presence of right-to-work laws was unrelated to city employment change. However, location in a state with right-to-work laws was significantly and positively related to change in metropolitan employment, GMP, and earnings per job. Being a right-to-work state, on average, is associated with a 9.5 percent increase in GMP, a 5.0 percent increase in earnings per job over the decade, and a 4.0 percent increase in employment growth rates. These results support the findings of prior research that found that right-to-work laws are a factor in business location decisions and provide an advantage for attracting business investment to a metropolitan area.

Public Policy and Economically Distressed Cities

What do we know about public policy and economic distress? Did cities that were distressed in 1990 but not in 2000 engage in different kinds of public policy activities than those that were distressed in 1990 and remained so in 2000?

Unfortunately, we do not know the answer to this question, nor was it possible to include a comprehensive set of public policy variables in our regression models. However, results from case studies of thirteen cities that had either over-performed or underperformed between 1990 and 2000 relative to expectations (that is, given their characteristics at the beginning of the period) provide some indications.[48]

In general our research suggested that deviations from expected performance result largely from factors that are unrelated to public policy, at least in the short run. This is the case partly because other forces are quite powerful, partly because in many cases there is a substantial lag between policy application and its effect, and partly because of the nature of many of the policies that target city problems. In the longer run we believe that many of the forces affecting residential and firm location decisions are susceptible to public policy through efforts to improve a city's competitive advantages as a location for high-wage employment and through efforts to improve a city's public services and amenities.

Most city governments are active in designing policies to improve city life and outcomes for their residents and many state governments pursue urban-related policies as well. However, in many cases the policy actions are either manifestly too limited, mostly symbolic, or too poorly designed to account for the unexpected overperformance relative to expectations. On the other hand, our conclusion is not symmetrical; we did find many cases where policies appeared to have contributed more substantially to the underperformance of cities relative to the outcomes predicted by our models.

We found that older cities experience less employment growth, reflecting both older infrastructure and entrenched institutional arrangements. We also found that key to "overperformance" was a city's ability to attract in-migrants from elsewhere—foreign immigrants, in-migrants from outside the metropolitan area, and in-migrants from its own suburbs. This was essentially a two-step process. To attract in-migrants a city had to be part of a metropolitan area in which the economy was dynamic, growing, and creating high-wage jobs. However, a growing metropolitan economy does not guarantee that in-migrants will locate in the central city rather than in the suburbs or that the central city will be successful in attracting suburban residents.

A city's perceived vitality and the public value proposition (the package of services provided and amenities received for taxes paid) can play a major role in its attractiveness to metropolitan-area in-migrants. And this in turn is at least partly a product of public activity and leadership. Effective leadership and civic engagement more broadly constructed, rather than government activity more narrowly construed, often were seen to be the critical factors in a city's vitality. Among the common characteristics of the leadership we encountered is that the vision was practical, involved the physical reshaping and repositioning of the downtown, and formed politics so that the vision became part of the political fabric of the community.

Our research suggests that broader contextual public activities at the city and state levels, city vitality and the quality of city leadership, local tax and service packages where the taxes are seen to produce quality services rather than inefficiency or rent-seeking payments, state and city business climates favorable to economic activity, and institutional arrangements that provide cities adequate autonomy and resources are all likely to have an impact.

Conclusion: Summary of Findings and Policy Implications

Examining the differences between cities that were distressed in 1990 but not in 2000 and those that were distressed in both periods, as well as examining the results of our regression analysis, it is clear that the following characteristics are important determinants separating economically healthy from distressed cities. Economically distressed cities, compared with nondistressed cities

—are in metropolitan areas that are not economically healthy;
—arc in metropolitan areas that have lower levels of connectivity to the global economy;
—have a lower share of the metropolitan-area population and employment;
—are older;
—are smaller (that is, have lower agglomeration economies);
—have lower levels of human capital (as measured by educational attainment);
—are in high-wage labor markets;
—have higher crime rates;
—have a higher proportion of residents who are not of labor-force age.

What policies do our findings suggest for coping with economically distressed cities? As the foregoing discussion indicates, economically distressed cities face difficult and long-term problems, yet although many appear to be chronically distressed, it is not inevitable that they be so, evidenced by the fact that close to a third of cities in our study that were distressed in 1990 had moved out of that category by 2000.

Economically healthy cities are part of a healthy metropolitan economy. There are very few instances of economically healthy cities in economically distressed metropolitan areas. Efforts, both public and private, to deal with the problems of economically distressed cities must be directed in large part to metropolitan-level economic development.

Conversely, however, if the metropolitan economy is thriving, it is not inevitable that the central city will be doing well (or not be economically distressed); a thriving metropolitan area is a precondition but not a guarantee. If the region is thriving economically, then effective municipal public and private leadership can generate city vitality and make the city an attractive place to live within the metropolitan area. This suggests that such cities should be encouraged to direct their policy efforts toward building on their assets and developing amenities for city residents within the context of the metropolitan economy.

It also suggests efforts to provide high-quality public services at reasonable tax levels. In particular, the perception of a safe public environment—not only low crime (our regression indicates that high crime rates deter city employment growth) but also low grime—is critical. This mixture can satisfy residents who do not place a high value on the quality of the K–12 educational system.

Poorly performing educational systems, particularly at the middle and upper school levels and particularly for minority children, remain a major problem for cities in attracting and retaining households with children and in educating a skilled labor force. Our case studies suggest that virtually no city has figured out how to do this, yet that did not prevent at least some of them from being healthy places that attract in-migrants.

Our findings that city age is strongly related to economic distress do not, of course, suggest some anthropomorphic aging process of cities akin to human aging, decline, and death. Indeed, some older cities are doing quite well. City age is associated with decline because it is related to

—a physical form put in place in an era of less-developed technology (particularly transportation, but communication as well);

—older infrastructure;

—long-established governmental institutions and practices that provide patronage and rewards to supporters (and therefore require high levels of taxation) but do not necessarily result in efficient delivery of public services equivalent to the high levels of taxation they require;

—a low-growth portfolio of mature tradable goods and services.

Efforts to adapt a city's form (to the extent possible) to twenty-first-century economic needs, to build and maintain a modern infrastructure, and to engage in political reform that results in basic core services being delivered effectively and efficiently at reasonable tax levels can overcome the problems of city age.

In short, what our analysis suggests is that the problem of economically distressed cities needs to be addressed at two levels: an economic development effort to create a growing, high-wage economy, which must be focused mostly at the metropolitan level, and a community development and governance effort to make the central city within the metropolitan area a place where residents and businesses want to locate. Efforts to engage solely in economic development within the central city as a means of solving the problem of city economic distress are almost certainly, however paradoxically, doomed to failure. Equally, efforts to create a thriving metropolitan economy without making the central city a desirable place for human activity will have the same result.

Table 6-1A. *Indicators Used to Measure City Economic Health*[a]

	Definition	*Source*
City economic condition indicators		
Change in employment	Change in the number of jobs by place of work, 1990–2000	State of the Cities Data Systems, census data, 1990 and 2000
Change in annual wages	Change in annual wages of the county containing the majority of city residents, 1990–2000[b]	County Business Patterns, 1990 and 2000
Change in establishments	Change in the number of establishments in the central county, 1990–2000[b]	
City resident economic well-being indicators		
Median household Income	Median income of city households 2000	State of the Cities Data Systems, census data, 2000
Unemployment rate	Employed residents as a percentage of residents in the labor force, 2000	
Poverty rate	Percentage of residents with household incomes below the poverty line, 2000	
Labor-force participation rate	Percentage of working-age residents in the labor force, 2000	
Per capita income	Total income per city resident 2000	U.S. Census of Population and Housing, 2000

Source: Authors' compilation.

a. Variables measured at city level unless otherwise indicated.

b. If city population was more or less evenly split between two counties, both were included. The five counties that are contiguous with the New York City boundaries were combined.

Table 6-2A. *Summary Statistics of Weak-Market Cities Compared with*
Non-Weak-Market Cities[a]
Unit as indicated

Statistic	Weak-market cities	Non-weak-market cities	All central cities
City Economic Condition Index	−0.888 (0.25)	0.243 (0.84)	−0.001 (0.89)
Change in employment	−8.29% (9.58)	17.95% (20.03)	12.30% (21.23)
Change in annual payroll	50.19% (12.92)	91.19% (36.44)	82.34% (36.90)
Change in establishments	1.43% (6.15)	17.99% (15.82)	14.42% (15.84)
City Resident Economic Well-Being Index	−0.960 (0.42)	0.263 (0.74)	−0.0001 (0.85)
Median household income	$29,138 (3,134.1)	$38,510 (8,532.3)	$36,493 (8,605.6)
Per capita income	$16,019 (1,756.1)	$20,424 (4,249.5)	$19,476 (4,254.7)
Unemployment rate	10.04% (2.14)	6.46% (2.12)	7.23% (2.58)
Poverty rate	22.98% (3.64)	15.22% (5.42)	16.89% (6.01)
Labor-force participation rate	58.83% (3.11)	65.48% (4.59)	64.05% (5.11)

Source: Authors' calculations.
a. Each cell shows the mean value, with the standard deviation in parentheses.

Table 6-3A. *Indicators Used to Measure MSA Economic Condition*[a]

MSA economic condition indicators	Definition	Source
Employment growth	Change in the number of jobs by place of work, 1990–2000	State of the Cities Data Systems, Census Data 1990 and 2000
Earnings growth	Change in total earnings, 1990–2000	Economy.com
GMP growth	Change in gross metropolitan product, 1990–2000	
GMP per job	Gross metropolitan product per job, in thousands of current dollars, 2000	

Source: Authors' compilation.
GMP: gross metropolitan product; MSA: metropolitan statistical area.
a. All variables are measured at the metropolitan-area level unless otherwise indicated. MSAs are defined using the Office of Management and Budget's 2003 metro area definitions.

Table 6-4A. *Variables and Their Definitions for the Regression Analysis*

	Variable	Definition	Source
Dependent variables			
	Change in MSA employment	Percentage change in employment by place of work, 1990–2000, MSA	State of the Cities Data Systems, Census data 1990 and 2000
	Change in GMP	Change in gross metropolitan product, 1990–2000	Economy.com
	Change in central-city employment	Percentage change in central-city employment by place of work, 1990–2000	
Independent variables			
Economic structure	Location quotient for manufacturing[a]	Ratio of MSA manufacturing share to national manufacturing share (see formula below), 1990	State of the Cities Data Systems; Census 1990 data for the MSA jobs by place of work data; Census data 1990 for the national employment data
	Location quotient for FIRE	Ratio of MSA FIRE share to national FIRE share, 1990	State of the Cities Data Systems; Census 1990 data for the MSA jobs by place of work data; Census data 1990 for the national employment data
	Economic diversity[b]	Index of the MSAs' diversity among industries, 1990 (see formula below)	Calculated using State of the Cities Data Systems; Census 1990 jobs by place of work data
	State capital	State capital dummy variable	
Urban spatial structure	Population	Natural log of MSA population, 1990	Calculated using State of the Cities Data Systems; Census 1990 population data
	MSA age	Number of years in 2000 since the oldest city in MSA passed 50,000 in population in a decennial census	Historical census data

(continued)

Table 6-4A. *Variables and Their Definitions for the Regression Analysis (continued)*

	Variable	Definition	Source
	Airport departures	Number of scheduled airport departures in first quarter of 1991 per 1,000 population in MSA	Bureau of Transportation Statistics, regional air carrier summary data
Demographic structure	Change in population age 17 and under	Percentage-point change in the percent of the population that was age 17 or under, 1990–2000, MSA	State of the Cities Data Systems, Census data, 1990
	Change in population age 65 and over	Percentage-point change in the percentage of the population that was age 65 or over, 1990–2000, MSA	State of the Cities Data Systems, Census data, 1990
	Black non-Hispanic residents	Percentage of the population that was black (non-Hispanic) in 1990, MSA	State of the Cities Data Systems, Census data 1990
Labor-market conditions	At least some college	Percentage of the population that had at least some college in 1990, MSA	State of the Cities Data Systems, Census data 1990
	Average wage	Average wage per job 1990, MSA	Bureau of Economic Analysis
Amenities	July temperature	Average July temperature, 1990	countrystudies.us http://countrystudies .us/united-states/ weather/arkansas/ index.htm
Innovation	Research institutions	The number of institutions in the MSA categorized in 1990 as either very high research activity or high research activity	Carnegie classifications of institutions of higher learning
State business climate	Right-to-work state	Right-to-work state dummy variable	National Right-to-Work Legal Defense Foundation

Source: Authors' compilation.

MSA: metropolitan statistical area.

a. Location quotient = [(MSA manufacturing jobs / MSA total jobs) / (national manufacturing jobs / national total jobs)]. In other words, ratio of the MSA share of jobs that are in manufacturing to the national share of jobs in manufacturing

b. Diversity index = $1 - \Sigma (n/N)^2$, where n = number of jobs in a particular industry sector and N = number of jobs in all sectors, or in other words, $1 -$ the sum of the squares of all the industry-sector shares in the MSA.

Notes

1. See Kimberly Furdell, Harold Wolman, and Edward W. Hill, "Did Central Cities Come Back? Which Ones, How Far, and Why?" *Journal of Urban Affairs* 27, no. 3 (2005): 283–305; Edward W. Hill and John Brennan, "America's Central Cities and the Location of Work: Can Cities Compete with Their Suburbs," *Journal of the American Planning Association* 71, no. 4 (Autumn 2005): 411–32; John F. Brennan and Edward W. Hill, "Where Are the Jobs? Cities, Suburbs, and the Competition for Employment," Survey Series (Brookings Institution, November 1999), available at www.brookings.edu/es/urban/hillexsum.htm.

2. Because of missing data, we were unable to compute a City Economic Condition Index score for Carson City, Nevada.

3. Because of data availability constraints, the earnings and establishments variables were measured at the county level.

4. We used Cronbach's alpha to confirm that our indicator groupings represented two internally cohesive sets of variables. The alpha coefficient in both cases shows a high degree of reliability: for the indicators in the City Economic Condition Index, 0.8598; for the City Resident Economic Well-Being Index, 0.8991.

5. A common method of standardizing data is to use z scores so that the data can be combined and compared in a meaningful way. A z score for any city for a variable is the number of standard deviations the variable value is from the average score of all the cities on that variable. For variables for which a lower value indicates a lesser degree of economic distress, such as poverty rate, the signs on the z scores were reversed so that a higher z score always indicated better economic health. To get each city's index scores, we added the z scores for each of the variables in the index and then divided by the number of variables in the index. As a result, the index scores for each index were on roughly the same scale and can easily be compared.

6. The Pearsonian correlation coefficient between the two indexes was 0.4597, meaning they are measuring two relatively distinct aspects of economic health. The rank-order correlation between the two indexes was 0.5033. For index scores and corresponding rankings of the 302 cities, see Jennifer S. Vey, "Restoring Prosperity: The State Role in Revitalizing America's Older Industrial Cities" (Brookings Institution, 2007), available at www.brookings.edu/metro/pubs/20070520_oic.htm.

7. In this chapter we use the terms *economically distressed* and *weak market* interchangeably to represent what Vey has termed "older industrial cities."

8. We recognize that this is a rough and ready way of identifying economically distressed cities. Given our methods, one-third of the cities in the data set will always be, by definition, in weak economic condition and one-third will have low City Resident Economic Well-Being Index scores. The degree of overlap of cities in the intersection of these two sets will determine the number of economically distressed cities (that is, cities that appear in the weak or low cell on both indexes are defined as economically distressed).

9. Since the typology is based on the index values, and since the index values result from the variables that are part of the index, substantial differences between economically distressed and noneconomically distressed cities are to be expected for the variables used to form the indexes.

10. See, for example, Edward W. Hill, Harold L. Wolman, and Coit Cook Ford III, "Can Suburbs Survive without Their Central Cities? Examining the Suburban Dependence

Hypothesis," *Urban Affairs Review* 31, no. 2 (November 1995): 147–74; Richard P. Voith, "City and Suburban Growth: Substitutes or Complements?" *Federal Reserve Bank of Philadelphia Business Review,* September–October 1992, pp. 21–33.

11. Because of missing data, we were unable to calculate an MSA Economic Condition Index score for the Danville, Virginia, MSA.

12. We again used Cronbach's alpha to test the cohesion of the index's four indicators, and found a relatively high degree of internal validity (= 0.7785).

13. The correlation coefficient between the City Economic Condition Index and the MSA Economic Condition Index was 0.7473.

14. Of the seventeen cities that were distressed in 1990 but not 2000, four were in metropolitan statistical areas (MSAs) whose economic condition was moderate in 1990, and the remainder were in weak MSAs in 1990. Of those that transitioned out of the weak-market category, seven of the seventeen improved on the City Economic Condition Index, five improved on the City Resident Economic Well-Being Index, and five improved on both indexes. Of the twenty-six cities that were not economically distressed in 1990 but were in 2000, nine were in MSAs with weak or moderate economic conditions in 1990, and the remainder were in MSAs with strong economic conditions.

15. We stress that these differences are descriptive rather than causal.

16. Unless otherwise stated, the explanatory variables for the change in the central-city employment model are measured at the city level, whereas those for the metropolitan change dependent variables are measured at the metropolitan level.

17. In this portion of the analysis the data set was confined to cities whose population exceeded 50,000 in both 1990 and 2000 ($N = 268$) and that met the other stated criteria in 2000, whereas in the prior analysis the data included cities whose population exceeded 50,000 in either 1990 or 2000 ($N = 302$) and that met the other two criteria in either year.

18. A location quotient (LQ) is simply the ratio of the proportion of an area's employment in a specific industrial sector to that of the proportion of the nation's employment in that sector. An LQ substantially higher than 1.0 for a sector indicates that the area specializes and has a competitive advantage in that sector. The location quotients for both manufacturing and FIRE use employment data from HUD User State of the Cities Data Systems Census files. We use SIC (Standard Industrial Classification) codes rather than NAICS (North American Industry Classification System) codes, since NAICS codes were not available until 1998. We have also used the SIC codes for the economic diversity index, discussed below.

19. Edward L. Glaeser, Jose A. Scheinkman, and Andrei Shleifer, "Economic Growth in a Cross-Section of Cities," NBER Working Paper 5013 (Cambridge, Mass.: National Bureau of Economic Research, 1995).

20. The HHI is an index that sums the squares of the market shares of firms in an industry as a measure of market concentration; it is a widely used measure of the diversity of holdings in an investment portfolio. We sum the squares of the decimal shares of regional employment that each two-digit SIC industry has and then subtract that sum from 1 so that larger numbers reflect greater employment diversity across industries. Diversity is calculated according to the following formula: $1 -$ construction share$^2 -$ manufacturing share$^2 -$ TCU share$^2 -$ wholesale trade share$^2 -$ retail trade share$^2 -$ FIRE share$^2 -$ business and repair services share$^2 -$ personal services share$^2 -$ professional services share$^2 -$ public administration share$^2 -$ not classified elsewhere share^2. The sum is subtracted from 1 so that larger numbers reflect greater diversity. The values in our universe ranged from .743 to .885, with a mean of

0.85 and a standard deviation of 0.02, for the metropolitan-area models and ranged from .655 to .886, with a mean of 0.84 and a standard deviation of 0.03, for the city model.

21. Patrick Beeson, "Agglomeration Economies and Productivity Growth," in *Sources of Metropolitan Growth,* edited by Edwin Mills and John McDonald (New Brunswick, N.J.: Center for Urban Policy Research, 1992); Edward L. Glaeser, Jed Kolko, and Albert Saiz, "Consumer City," *Journal of Economic Geography* 1, no. 10 (2001): 27.

22. The models were also run using the square of the natural logarithm of the MSA population in addition to the natural logarithm in an attempt to capture any nonlinearities that may exist in the relationship between the independent and dependent variables. However, this specification did not improve the fit of the models and the results are not reported.

23. Jan K. Brueckner, "Airline Traffic and Urban Economic Development," *Urban Studies* 40, no. 8 (2003): 1455.

24. Richard K. Green, "Airports and Economic Development," *Real Estate Economics* 35, no. 1 (2007): 91.

25. This variable includes scheduled passenger flights and cargo flights, such as UPS and FedEx.

26. Edward L. Glaeser and Jesse Shapiro, "Is There a New Urbanism? The Growth of U.S. Cities in the 1990s," NBER Working Paper (Cambridge, Mass.: National Bureau of Economic Research, 2001).

27. Natalie Cohen, "Business Location Decisionmaking and the Cities: Bringing Companies Back," Working Paper (Brookings Institution, Center on Metropolitan Policy, 2000). www.brookings-institution.com/dybdocroot/ES/urban/COHEN.pdf (accessed April 24, 2007); Arthur O'Sullivan, "Where Do Firms Locate," *Urban Economics,* 5th ed. (Boston: McGraw-Hill, Irwin, 2003), p. 65.

28. Robert Weissbourd and Christopher Berry, *The Changing Dynamics of Urban America* (Chicago: CEOs for Cities, 2004).

29. David E. Marcotte, "The Earnings Effect of Education at Community Colleges," IZA Discussion Paper 2334 (Bonn: IZA [Institut zur Zukunft der Arbeit—Institute for the Study of Labor], 2006).

30. Results in our models were similar using percentage holding a bachelor's degree instead of some college. Percentage with some college accounted for greater variance in all but the earnings growth model, and had a closer association with the dependent variables in the other three equations.

31. Vernon Henderson, Ari Kuncoro, and Matt Turner, "Industrial Development in Cities," *Journal of Political Economy* 103, no. 5 (1995): 1067.

32. Stuart A. Gabriel, Joe P. Mattey, and William L. Wascher, "Compensating Differentials and Evolution of Quality-of-Life among U.S. States," Working Paper (University of Southern California, Lusk Center, 1999).

33. Glaeser and Shapiro, "Is There a New Urbanism?"

34. The relationship between average July temperature and the dependent variables in the models has been treated as linear, although we recognize its form is undoubtedly not linear. We ran regressions using the square of average July temperature, but this added nothing to the model, so it was eliminated.

35. Julie Berry Cullen and Steven D. Levitt, "Crime, Urban Flight, and the Consequences for Cities," NBER Working Paper 5737 (Cambridge, Mass.: National Bureau of Economic Research, 1996).

36. Edward. L. Glaeser and Albert Saiz, "The Rise of the Skilled City," Brookings-Wharton Papers on Urban Affairs (Brookings Institution and Wharton School, 2004), p. 47.
37. Daniel Felsenstein, "The University in the Metropolitan Area: Impacts and Public Policy Prescriptions," *Urban Studies* 33, no. 9 (1996): 1565; Edward W. Hill and Iryna Lendel, "The Impact of the Reputation of Bio-Life Science and Engineering Doctoral Programs on Regional Economic Development," *Economic Development Quarterly* 21, no. 3 (August, 2007): 223.
38. Timothy J. Bartik and George Erickcek, "Higher Education, the Health Care Industry and Metropolitan Regional Economic Development: What Can 'Eds & Meds' Do for the Economic Fortunes of a Metro Area's Residents?" Paper prepared for Conference on Urban and Regional Policy and Its Effects (Brookings Institution, Washington, March 29–30, 2007); Harvey A. Goldstein and Catherine S. Renault, "Contributions of Universities to Regional Economic Development: A Quasi-Experimental Approach," *Regional Studies* 38, no. 7 (2004): 733; Initiative for a Competitive Inner-City, "Leveraging Colleges and Universities for Urban Economic Revitalization: An Action Agenda" (Chicago: CEOs for Cities, March 2002), available at www.ceosforcities.org/rethink/research/files/colleges_1. pdf (accessed April 24, 2007).
39. Janet Pack, *Growth and Convergence in Metropolitan America* (Brookings Institution Press, 2002).
40. The models originally used a variable that combined universities with very high research activity, high research activity, and research and doctoral institutions. However, that variable was insignificant in the models and was too broad to capture the element of innovation. The location of the data, which used the Carnegie classification system in effect in 2005, is specified in table 6-1A.
41. We use right-to-work rather than unionization for three reasons: it better reflects the business climate aspect in which we are interested, unionization is highly related to industrial structure, and union membership is increasingly dominated by public sector employee unions.
42. Robert Tannenwald, "State Regulatory Policy and Economic Development," *New England Economic Review,* March–April 1997, p. 83.
43. Timothy J. Bartik, "Business Location Decisions in the United States: Estimates of the Effect of Unionization, Taxes, and Other Characteristics of States," *Journal of Business and Economic Statistics* 3, no. 1 (1985): 14.
44. Except where noted otherwise, all findings reported are significant at the .05 level; in other words, they could be expected to occur by chance only 5 percent of the time.
45. The race variable was significant only at the .10 level rather than the .05 level for change in metropolitan earnings.
46. The city murder rate per 10,000 was significant only at the .10 level rather than the .05 level.
47. Average July temperature was significant only at the .10 level rather than the .05 level for metropolitan employment change.
48. The thirteen case study cities were Sacramento and San Francisco, California; Aurora and Chicago, Illinois; Grand Rapids and Lansing, Michigan; Charlotte and Durham, North Carolina; Portland, Oregon; Philadelphia and Pittsburgh, Pennsylvania; and Seattle and Tacoma, Washington. For a full discussion of the results from the case studies, see Harold Wolman and others, *States and Their Cities: Partnerships for the Future* (Washington: Fannie Mae Foundation, 2007), available at www.knowledgeplex.org/showdoc.html?id=236675.

7

Placing Labor Center-Stage in Industrial City Revitalization

Ann Markusen and Greg Schrock

Many U.S. cities, especially those with venerable industrial traditions, have had a difficult time recovering from accelerated world market integration and structural change in particular sectors. They have struggled to retain existing industries and firms and attract new ones. They have experimented with new ways to retrain the resident labor force for new and existing lines of work. They have hired more professionals to pursue economic development strategies. And they have spent considerable resources doing these things, with quite mixed success.

Part of the problem is the continued reliance on old ideas of how development happens and whom and what should be given priority. Most economic developers still operate as if firms and industries were the most important decisionmakers in the economy, underestimating the semi-autonomous significance of skilled labor both as a source of new product and skill development and as makers of location decisions based on quality-of-life factors as well as job offers. Most still believe that only productive activities whose output is exported outside the region are worthy of nurturing and underestimate the potential of the existing consumption base to generate new jobs and sectoral strengths. Most still devote the lion's share of their attention and resources to physical capital rather than to human-capital formation and underinvest in the latter.

In this chapter we summarize new thinking in economic development theory that broadens the conceptualization of urban economic development and places labor alongside capital as a coequal factor. We develop the notion of occupation as an organizing principle for understanding the labor complexion of a regional economy and show how an analysis of employment by occupation complements the conventional way of studying an area by industry. We use occupational profiles of selected cities to demonstrate the insights possible with this approach and also demonstrate that a metro area's industrial structure does not dictate its occupational structure.

Although some states and cities have merged their economic and workforce development agencies, few do it well. They are not using an occupational approach in fashioning strategy or evaluating incentives, even though data are easily available. We outline how city and state agencies can use occupational analysis and targeting to strengthen economic development policy. Such an approach requires that economic developers create new relationships with organizations that train, organize, and network by occupation: professional associations, unions, colleges, technical schools, and community-based organizations.

First we summarize the outdated thinking that still encumbers urban economic development policy, including an undue preoccupation with the export base and dismissal of the consumption base. In the second section we lay out the occupational approach, explaining that the links between industry and occupation—between employers and workers—have weakened over the past few decades, and why economic developers need to work with an occupational as well as an industrial lens in research and practice. In the third, we explore changing occupational structure in the fifty largest U.S. metros over the past two decades, showing that heightened competitiveness increased the distinctiveness of labor specialization among both the export and distinctive consumption bases of metros. However, manufacturing is still a significant base component—a number of metro areas retain strength in particular skilled blue-collar occupations, often as an outcome of strategic policies and institution building. In the last section we explore the implications of an occupational emphasis in economic development practice, and suggest how older industrial areas can better craft economic development strategies that play to labor strengths.[1]

Beyond Export Base, Physical-Capital, Location-Theory Mind-Sets

Metro regions have posted dramatically divergent employment growth rates over the past two decades (table 7-1). Atlanta, Denver, Portland, and Dallas have posted the highest growth rates, while Pittsburgh and Cleveland have posted the persistently lowest. But one decade's experience was not necessarily replicated in

Table 7-1. *U.S. Metro Areas, Total Employment Growth, 1980, 1990, 2000*
Percent, except as indicated

Metropolitan area	Change 1990–2000	Change 1980–90	Total jobs, 2000
Atlanta	34	48	2,098,444
Denver	30	18	1,119,460
Portland-Vancouver (Oregon, Washington)	28	22	968,429
Dallas	25	34	1,740,247
Minneapolis-St. Paul	18	23	1,621,047
Houston	18	17	1,902,637
Seattle	17	33	1,271,126
Washington, D.C. (Maryland, Virginia, West Virginia)	8	36	2,597,544
Chicago,	7	9	3,893,737
San Francisco-Oakland[a]	7	20	2,065,065
Detroit	7	7	2,047,169
San Diego	6	44	1,328,893
Cleveland	6	1	1,059,388
San Jose	4	22	844,738
Pittsburgh	3	–1	1,075,837
Boston (Massachusetts, New Hampshire)	3	12	1,748,374
Miami	2	21	922,717
Philadelphia (Pennsylvania, New Jersey)	0	16	2,361,552
New York-Bergen County (New York, New Jersey)[a]	0	11	4,548,029
Los Angeles	–6	21	3,957,917

Source: HUD State of the Cities Data System, Employment by Place of Residence, 1980, 1990, and 2000, based on U.S. Census Bureau data. Data are based on 1990 Metropolitan Standard definitions for individual metropolitan statistical areas, except where noted (note a), where multiple areas have been aggregated for comparability purposes.

a. Consolidated MSAs. All others are PMSAs (primary metropolitan statistical areas).

the next. Some metro areas grew rapidly in the 1980s but stalled in the 1990s, whereas others that hosted slow or negative growth in the 1980s rebounded in the 1990s. Denver and Portland did better in the 1990s (a slower growth decade overall for large metros) than in the 1980s, whereas Washington, San Jose, and Philadelphia slowed abruptly in the later decade.

In response to these upheavals, cities are struggling to present a more distinctive face to the larger world and to their own citizens. Powerful integrating forces have undermined regional manufacturing strengths and unique local consumption offerings, obliterating traditional sources of identity and distinction. Blue-collar workers face blistering competition from low-wage workers elsewhere who have access to the same technologies but few benefits or workplace rights. Sprawling suburban developments, look-alike downtown entertainment complexes, and big-box retail stores disappoint visitors looking for the unique, unusual, and lovable in another metro. To compete, leaders cultivate new production niches while shoring up and maintaining traditional strengths. They aspire to attract and hold skilled workers. They try to tailor and market cultural and environmental assets that will help them stand out in the crowd.

In these efforts, we argue, cities and their metro regions suffer from a poverty of theory. The impulse to foster distinctiveness as a development strategy is stoked by theories that emphasize export base activities, investments in physical capital, firms as decisionmakers, and industries as groupings of like-producing firms. These theories, while containing grains of truth, are not sufficient. They do not accurately reflect significant causal forces that shape contemporary urban economies.

Beyond the Export Base: Bringing the Consumption Base into the Mix

The export base orientation, a peculiarly North American innovation, grew out of an exceptional history of land settlement on the mercantile outposts of emerging European industrial society.[2] Economists crafted a theory to match this experience, arguing that to maintain livelihoods and quality of life, regions must rely on an export base that will be resistant to import competition and generative of good jobs over the long haul. Trade theorists, meanwhile, added the insight that increasing returns to scale offer regions opportunities to construct comparative advantage in key industries by making investments, often behind trade barriers, to ramp production capacities up to scale.[3]

The heart of the export base argument is as follows: In a trade-integrated world, regions outside of one's own are superior producers of many goods and services consumed locally, in one's own area. In order to be able to pay for these imports, the region must specialize in its own exportable goods and services. If new export activities cannot be found, overall growth and employment will be constrained. Everything not in the export sector is conceived of as local consumption (or the residential sector), including retail, health care services, local government, and personal services. The size of the residential sector bears a fixed relationship to the export base, where dollars earned from export activities are respent on goods and services produced locally.

In the mid-twentieth century, with its sophisticated globe-transcending transportation systems that reached far into little hamlets everywhere, this theory seemed powerful and obvious. Mining towns became ghost towns once their singular export was tapped out. Farm communities, despite exporting ever-larger quantities of agricultural produce, could not find jobs for residents made redundant by huge gains in productivity. Economists codified the theory into the export base model, ubiquitously used to this day in forecasting, multiplier analysis, and economic impact analyses of everything from new branch plants or call centers of multinational firms to stadiums and museums.

But from the beginning, the theory had its critics. In his famous debate with Douglass North, Charles Tiebout pointed out several logical flaws in the theory.[4] Though the world economy as a whole continues to grow in terms of production and jobs, it does not export! In addition, a regional economy's ability to provide for itself increases as its income from exports grows, resulting in the area's reaching minimally efficient production scales in new sectors and thus becoming able to substitute local production for imports. Tiebout argued for an endogenous theory of regional growth, whereby a deepening division of labor internal to the region spurs regional growth without exports at all. Lindstrom's study of nineteenth-century Philadelphia's economy, for instance, shows that not exports but growing exchange between local manufacturers, farmers, and craftspeople explained its growth.[5]

Over the decades, practitioners of economic development have vigorously debated and experimented with import substitution and export base strategies for regional and national development, especially in the developing world. The apparent failure of import substitution in postwar Latin America brought an emphasis on export base strategies back into fashion. Yet the evidence on the relationship between output growth and export growth is far from established. In recent decades, economists have demonstrated empirically that export growth bears little relationship to GDP (gross domestic product) growth, both in developing and developed countries.[6] There is thus room to explore alternative theories of regional growth, including the possibility that changes in consumption patterns can contribute to employment creation.

In practice, export base theory has been applied principally to raw materials and manufactured products sold to producers and consumers in other regions. In the 1980s, as resource exhaustion, employment-undermining gains in agricultural productivity, and industrial restructuring revealed the limits to export promotion strategies, economic developers began extending the economic-base conception to include services, especially tourism. The spectacular success of the Las Vegas region, the fastest-growing U.S. metro in the 1980s and 1990s, demonstrates that visitors' consumption expenditures of dollars earned elsewhere can drive a regional economy.

The consumption spending of existing residents and consumption-oriented investments by city governments can also produce longer-term employment growth by substituting for spending on imports, nurturing new export sectors, and improving the quality of life to attract and retain skilled workers and entrepreneurs who do not have to change regions to find work. Research on smaller towns demonstrates how investments in local cultural capital capture a larger share of residents' discretionary spending than was the case before such investments were made, and also attract artists, retirees, and small businesses with mobile incomes.[7] And distinctive local consumption patterns can jump-start new exporting industries: Joseph Cortright shows, for example, how micro-breweries' experiments for the Portland metro market, flush with avid and discriminating beer drinkers, resulted in the creation of quality brews that subsequently found an export market.[8]

Investments in the consumption base may play a role in attracting and retaining skilled labor, too. Relatively footloose workers, especially those with high rates of self-employment, such as artists, web designers, and truckers, may choose to reside in a region because of its amenities and to export their work and services elsewhere. They may choose a region first and then seek work with area employers. In turn, amenity-seeking workers may make location in the region more attractive to export-sector managers, who may themselves be attracted by consumption offerings. Since amenities to one person may be disamenities to another—for example, some are drawn to a hot young music scene that can be a noisy nuisance or security concern to others—we can expect regions to play to their distinctive strengths in marketing themselves as places to live. Thus we can integrate into regional macro growth theories the implications of microeconomic migration and location models that permit amenities and consumption potential as well as costs of production and job prospects to influence, simultaneously, the distribution of employers and workers across regions.

This reasoning and evidence of the limits of export base theory open up possibilities for new local consumption–based investment as a complement to the attraction and retention of businesses that export goods and services elsewhere. Our view is that certain consumption base activities can be targeted for job growth. Their expansion is amenable to policy influence, and they should be included in a portfolio approach to economic development investments.

Beyond Physical Capital: Adding Human Capital

The export base mind-set is linked in economic development practice to a bias toward investments in physical capital rather than human capital. Akin to the way that twentieth-century architects and engineers shaped the built environment of cities without regard to the inhabitants' human and social needs, local economic developers have been blinkered into a myopic focus on physical capital. Business incentives for investments in plant and equipment have become the staple of development practice, while human capital—increasingly recognized as a very crucial driver of economic development—has taken a back seat, often shunted off into the domain of "workforce development," where it is divorced from key investment decisions.

In the making of the North American continent, huge public investments in land, canals, railroads, ports, and highways drove and integrated the American and Canadian economies in the nineteenth and twentieth centuries. These investments enabled a boom in internal trade, tying agriculture and industry together across regions, and, since labor was relatively scarce, given the amount of land to exploit, prompted large commitments of private capital.[9] Similarly, public investments in power, electricity generation and transmission, water and sewer systems, and, more recently, Internet connectivity have been heralded as powerful growth engines.

Although government investments are vitally important to economic growth, there are downsides to such investments in physical capital, whether publicly built or induced through subsidies and tax holidays. First, many physical infrastructure investments simply favor one place over another, even within metro regions, often undermining existing production complexes and causing underutilization of capacity. Second, while transportation infrastructure may facilitate exports, it also enables import penetration. The interstate highway system in the United States, along with container-port facilities on the East and West coasts, has enabled manufactured goods made in China, often by U.S. companies, to reach dispersed small settlements cheaply, undercutting domestic producers. A third problem with public and private physical infrastructure projects, often celebrated as job creators, is that many of them employ as many as ten times the number of workers to construct them as to operate them, creating a boom and bust cycle that can be debilitating to inner cities and smaller towns. A fourth problem: Capital-intensive projects also nourish a large construction sector that can become a powerful political actor. In many regions, more urban redevelopment and transportation projects are underwritten than are justified by their future returns, simply because the combined lobbying of the construction, real estate, auto, and other sectors is so powerful in legislatures and city councils.

In contrast, only small portions of regional development moneys go toward human-capital investments. In many of the multi-million-dollar incentive packages offered by states to woo large plants, as much as 5 percent may be used for training new workers, but this is still a tiny fraction. Some governments have created entrepreneurial training programs and built business incubators to foster new firm formation, but the amounts devoted to them are similarly small. Workforce development programs exist at subnational levels in the United States, but are funded at only a fraction of physical-capital-related outlays, especially when tax expenditures are included. To the extent that states or localities own and fund elementary, secondary, technical, and university educational systems, human capital is fostered, though generally not under the rubric of regional development. In the United States over the past decade, academic critiques and organized protests on the part of regional governments, planners, workers, and citizens have grown in volume against the excesses of state and local government subsidies to firms for private sector physical capital investments.[10] Hefty incentives packages, often given without performance requirements or unenforced in cases of failure to perform, allow companies to bargain their way out of years of future tax payments while receiving large grants of infrastructure and land for newly constructed plants, office buildings, warehouses, and retail outlets on the promise of job creation. In this environment, interest in human-capital-oriented regional development strategies is growing.

To develop more effective strategies, economic developers must comprehensively assess the respective contributions of capital and labor to long-term development and design a portfolio that includes investments in human capital as well as physical capital. The significance of human capital has long been appreciated by development economists, reflected in national governments' commitments to support education at all levels, from elementary through graduate school. But at the subnational level, economic development practice has evolved in agencies that have no connection with regional education policy or schooling. Workforce development programs, which typically target difficult-to-employ segments of the population (disadvantaged job seekers and displaced workers), are lodged in separate agencies and funded through entirely different expenditure streams. Emerging respect for the importance of entrepreneurship, a human-capital trait, has been only modestly integrated into economic development strategies.

Adding in Workers as Place Makers

Enhancing the role of human capital in economic development entails incorporating workers as a distinct set of decisionmakers whose choices affect regional development outcomes. These choices are distinct from those that firms make and may be amenable to policy influence. The economic-base mind-set and its companion preference for physical capital are linked to a narrow vision of who are the significant actors in the regional economy, privileging firms and their managers as the only location decisionmakers who matter. As a result, economic development has become preoccupied with increasingly costly efforts to induce firms to locate and remain in a region.

Yet workers and households are semiautonomous decisionmakers who invest in human capital and decide where to live and work. When choosing among competing jurisdictions for education and careers, they base their decisions both on work possibilities (including nonpecuniary aspects of jobs) and on quality of life. Because workers have strong preferences for non-work-related features of regions, firms must take this into account when making their location decisions. The significance of worker spatial choice reinforces our case for the significance of the consumption base in a region, because the character of consumption opportunities contributes to the regional quality of life and can be addressed with policy and resource commitments.

A well-developed body of industrial location theory serves as a companion to export base theory. Most states and local governments seek to develop a distinctive export base by spending the greatest share of their energies recruiting and targeting private sector firms. The recruiting effort will often involve detailed analyses of courted firms' financial condition, product or service line, expansion plans, and competitors, and an understanding of the larger industrial context in which each operates.[11] Branch plant sitings and even relocations of corporate headquarters have become a business highly mediated by site consultants, who often exploit information asymmetries to the disadvantage of competing governments.[12]

In comparison to this focus, both in theory and in practice, on firms and their investment and location decisions, the choices made by individual workers and households have received relatively little attention in the economic development field. Largely overlooked is the possibility that export base expansion may also result from residents' decisions to start new firms and from burgeoning pools of skilled labor formed via many individual workers' decisions to acquire skills and live in the region. To limit key targets of economic development efforts to firms only, especially those outside the region, is to unduly restrict economic development options for the region.

Individual workers and members of their households make ongoing choices regarding the acquisition of education and skills. Youthful households make decisions about where to reside, where to send their children to school, and how much energy to put into their children's learning at home. They decide whether to encourage their children to pursue postsecondary vocational training or college education and whether to earn and set aside income for this purpose. Households and individuals may come from abroad to acquire a good education for themselves and their children, or from rural areas, or from low-quality-education states to higher-quality ones. As adults, individuals decide whether to pursue additional skill formation and whether to do so through schools, apprenticeship programs, or on-the-job training. Some will choose career paths that involve greater skill acquisition up-front, even at the cost of deferred income. Some will leave jobs, change careers, or respond to a layoff by seeking additional education and training later in life. Workers and households also make decisions about where to deploy their human capital. Some make that decision when they leave home to go to college and then remain in their college towns after graduating. Others make conscious choices, during early stages of their careers, to accept the best job offer wherever it may be, to move without a prior job offer to a region well endowed with large labor pools and multiple employers in their fields, or to choose a region based on quality of life or family ties and then search for a job within it. Some refuse good job offers in remote places where they would be too dependent on a single employer or industry, while others will highly value any one of dozens of environmental features from culture (from opera to the club scene) to sports (spectator or participatory) to clean air and clean water in making their location choice. On retirement, workers make decisions about where to live, often taking their pensions and other assets, including skills, earned in one region and spending or using them in another.

The plurality of decisions that people make in acquiring and using their human capital offers regional policymakers a number of options for encouraging skill accumulation. One approach is to "home-grow" skills through investments in education, from early childhood through postgraduate studies. Governments, nonprofits, and, increasingly, for-profit organizations offer education and training services through an elaborate system of schools, vocational schools, colleges and universities, web-based curricula, and workforce development programs. Regions rich in educational options are more likely to achieve baseline levels of workforce human capital necessary to attract and sustain knowledge-based economic activity. They also give workers and their employers a wider array of opportunities to update and upgrade their skills as the economy changes, enhancing a region's economic resilience.

But because workers can take their skills and human capital and move to other places, regions face the equal challenge of attracting and retaining human capital. Reflecting the traditional people-follow-jobs perspective, academic and policy discussions of the chronic problem of "brain drain" have typically revolved around a mismatch between a place's educational offerings and the needs of the local employers.[13] Yet this understates the extent to which investments in quality of life may help regions attract and retain talent. Managers, skilled workers, and individuals with entrepreneurial aspirations may make their own trade-offs between income prospects and quality of life in choosing among cities. To the extent that quality of life matters, government must balance investments in clean air, parks, and cultural and sports facilities against investments (including tax expenditures) to attract and retain export-oriented employers.

Economists have often assumed that physical capital, because it is fixed and endures over long periods of time, is more likely to be committed to place than people. But in the past decade, the reliability of firms and establishments has also diminished, reflecting in part the accelerated obsolescence of physical capital and technology. Many communities have spent tax resources and subsidies, often mortgaging their futures, for manufacturing plants, call centers, and privately run prisons, only to find that the companies running them pull out after only a few years. On the other hand, individuals also make significant investments in housing and social capital in communities, what the economist Roger Bolton calls "the economic value of a sense of place."[14] Many locally educated individuals choose to stay in their communities, especially given work and family ties, and those who leave in their twenties may choose to return later in their work lives. We have no aggregate evidence on long-term commitment of either firms or individuals. But it should not be taken for granted that workers are more highly mobile interregionally than firms.

Complementing Industrial with Occupational Analysis

To implement a skilled-labor dimension to economic development practice, we need an occupational lens. Regional economies can be conceptualized as comprising occupations, not just industries. An industry-based approach analyzes employment in enterprise units grouped as industries such as manufacturing, utilities, and finance. We can also study regional employment as consisting of occupations such as managers, professionals, production workers, clerical workers, and health care workers. Each approach gives us a very different window into job generation. The first stresses what workers make—jobs are grouped by their attachment to output such as software and steel. The second stresses what workers do—what their skills are and what activities they perform at work: writer, lawyer, doctor, home health aide, and so on. The former is in sync with an emphasis on physical capital and firms' location calculus, whereas the latter emphasizes human capital and workers' location choice.[15]

Why an Occupational Approach?

The increasing interest in an occupational approach to regional economic development reflects substantial and fundamental shifts in the way economic activity is organized within and across places. In the last several decades we have witnessed dramatic changes in the organization of the economy. Firms have restructured away from the multidivisional, vertically integrated corporations that dominated most of the twentieth century, in an effort to become "lean and mean" and more responsive to market fluctuations.[16] Although the establishment of branch plants, satellite operations, and joint ventures for research, production, and distribution is not necessarily new, the extent to which firms are constantly shifting, reorganizing, and recombining themselves on a global scale is. Companies such as Boeing are emblematic of the "virtual corporation," with top corporate executives in Chicago, scientists and engineers in Seattle, lobbyists and media consultants in Washington, D.C., and New York, and skilled machinists and routine assemblers in far-flung locations from Kansas to China. This is also occurring in countless and less dramatic instances as businesses shift toward flexible, network-based modes of organization.

These changes have important implications for how skills and new ideas are used in the economy. First, the relationship between workers and employers has been weakened, with neither party as committed to the other as it once was.[17] Workers—especially younger ones—increasingly expect to build careers that span employers and industries, which lessens the incentives for firms to make investments in workers' skills as the returns on those investments become increasingly uncertain. Firms are thus increasingly sensitive to the skills available in regional labor pools, while workers are more dependent on externalized training in universities, community colleges, and other educational providers, which are organized along skill and occupational lines.

Second, as outsourcing and subcontracting proliferate, skills are shared and cross-fertilized more liberally across industries. Actors and directors create videos for medical instrument companies, while software engineers program for film companies and arts organizations. Occupations that appear to be local-serving, because their sales are local, may in fact enhance the productivity of other export-oriented sectors in the regional economy. Functions, skills, and networks among skilled workers become more important economic facts than organization, and these are best studied via occupational groupings.

Third, the fast-paced and flexible economy places a premium on innovation and entrepreneurship. Firms large and small are constantly developing new ideas for proprietary products and services, which often have the effect of carrying them beyond previous industrial categories. The core skills and knowledge giving rise to these innovations, however, are likely to be occupationally grounded.

Finally, the digital revolution has made it easier to work from remote job sites, permitting many individuals greater autonomy in choosing locations based on amenities, connectivity, and quality of life. Workers are more likely to be committed to their city, region, and neighborhood than to the firm or industry.[18]

The consequence is that *industries*—aggregations of what products and services are made—are becoming a less and less coherent framework as a way of viewing a region's economic activities. As firms reorganize themselves in ways that separate different functional activities spatially, and as individuals and households make similar semiautonomous decisions about where to live and work, we can expect *occupational* structure to take on greater coherence as an indicator of urban economic activity.

Treating a region's labor expertise separately from its industrial prowess is particularly important because the correspondence between industrial and occupational structures across regions is on the wane. For eleven California metropolitan areas, an effort to infer occupational composition from industry structure found that the latter was often a relatively poor predictor of unique metro occupational structure.[19] This is especially true for the crucially important and fast-growing high-tech and business-services industries. Policymakers for the California metro areas studied would have over- or underestimated their pools of scientists, engineers, and computer professionals by as much as 38 percent by failing to analyze occupational structure separately (see table 7-2). Regional economic intelligence must be developed by probing occupational structure in its own right.

Developing an Occupational Lens

Despite these reasons why occupations are becoming more important as a basis for thinking about regional economies, economic development practice remains largely stuck inside the industry box. Public data collection continues to privilege industries over occupations in summarizing employment structure in a region. This has considerable implications for the way we think about the economy and what interventions are possible or desirable. After all, no economist, citizen, or policymaker ever "sees" a regional economy. Instead, they develop mental maps based on conceptual categories that frame the metro area's spatial, structural, and organizational dimensions. These mental maps showcase certain decisionmakers, or actors, as key to economic development. And to date, the dominant industrial lens trains economic developers' sights on industries and the behavior of firms

Table 7-2. *Incidence of Three High-Tech-Related Occupations in Six California Metropolitan Areas, 1997*
Units as indicated

Occupations	San Francisco	San Jose	Oakland	Los Angeles	Orange County	San Diego
Computer and IT professionals						
Location quotient[a]	2.0	3.3	1.7	0.9	1.3	1.3
Employment share unexplained by industry (percent)	32	38	33	–25	2	11
Number of jobs unexplained by industry	8,961	18,348	8,448	–13,433	572	2,277
Selected engineers						
Location quotient[a]	1.2	4.6	1.7	0.9	1.5	1.7
Employment share unexplained by industry (percent)	10	37	28	–6	10	21
Number of jobs unexplained by industry	623	9,888	2,755	–1,383	1,104	2,274
Natural scientists						
Location quotient[a]	1.8	1.7	1.9	0.8	0.9	1.8
Employment share unexplained by industry (percent)	33	18	37	–12	–4	3
Number of jobs unexplained by industry	1,504	756	1,872	–1,023	–125	142

Sources: Elisa Barbour and Ann Markusen, "Regional Occupational and Industrial Structure: Does the One Imply the Other?" *International Regional Science Review* 30, no. 1 (2007): 1–19; data from California Employment Development Department, Industry-Occupation Matrix, and Bureau of Labor Statistics, National Historical Industry-Occupation Matrix Time Series, 1983–98.

a. Location quotients (LQ) calculated as the ratio between an occupation's share of total employment in the region and its share nationally. An LQ of greater than 1 implies overconcentration of that occupation within the region.

within them. It's no wonder that firm incentives and fiscal and regulatory changes dominate practice.

Rather than a regional economy that treats workers as members of industries, imagine that we view employment in terms of what workers do, not what they make, captured in the category of "occupation." Some workers manage entire chains of conceptualization, production, and marketing processes (managers). Some create, implement, and monitor technologies (scientists and engineers). Some develop, write, adapt, and trouble-shoot information systems (systems analysts and software programmers). Some educate (teachers, trainers, and coaches). Some adjudicate, advocate, and make law (judges, lawyers, and legislators). Some run, interact with, and maintain machines (assembly line workers). Others build structures and repair them (craft workers). Others move commodities and services across space and out to consumers and other users (longshoremen; truckers; and retail, wholesale, and warehousing clerks). Yet others care for the sick, elderly, and children (nurses, home-care, and child-care workers). And still others entertain us (musicians and athletes).

A mental map of a regional economy based primarily on occupation would depict the San Jose metro as composed of technology managers, venture capitalists, aeronautical and electrical engineers, inspectors and testers, and commercial artists, and Los Angeles of aircraft assemblers and engineers, sewing machine operators, broadcast technicians, musical instrument repairers, camera operators, and other workers in the film industry. The occupational lens helps us to see the relatively unique pools of talent possessed by each city. Each occupation is distinguished by its skill, educational content, and work tasks. Individual workers are key decisionmakers in an occupational framework, because they decide whether to acquire skills and how to deploy them, given their options in labor markets. Other decisionmakers are also important to the skilled-labor equation: those who supply skills and training, including schools and colleges and private sector firms.

Approaching economic development as an occupational rather than an industrial phenomenon opens up alternative paths for economic developers. For instance, when an industry is in structural decline because its products are cheaper to produce elsewhere or because substitutes are destroying its market or because the market itself dries up, working with occupational groups offers an alternative to simply trying to prevent plant closings or convincing firms to convert to new product lines. Rather than approach the problem of huge layoffs among aerospace workers as synonymous with an imploding aerospace industry, as Southern Californians did in the 1990s, an occupational approach might have enabled a more creative and less expensive economic development approach. For instance, engineers exiting aerospace brought knowledge about exotic substances developed with military research dollars into sports and sportswear lines such as golfing and athletic clothing.

What would occupational profiles of individual cities look like and what insights do such profiles offer? Such profiles can be constructed to show over- and underrepresentation of occupations and changes over time. For the Twin Cities metro area, occupations prominent in 1998 (the year before occupational codes last changed) and increasingly so over the decade from 1989 to 1998 are shown in table 7-3. Here the labor-force diversity of the Twin Cities as an employment center and the region's good positioning in fast-growing jobs are apparent. Computer professionals are highly concentrated in the region, with a regional work-force share 62 percent higher than the nation's, and the region's science and technology expertise is reflected in high and growing location quotients for life and physical scientists, architects, engineers, and science, engineering, and mathematical technicians. But the metro area's strength lies in more than high tech. The prevalence of urban and regional planners, government leaders, air traffic controllers (the latter two occupations not shown), and social and recreational workers suggests a strong public sector and urban amenities that attract and keep a skilled workforce. Above-average pools of machinists and assemblers are present, as are personal-service occupations (accounted for by the metro's relatively large pools of home health aides and child-care workers) and sales workers other than retail and cashiers, the latter likely attributable to the tourist-oriented Mall of America.

Metro leaders can use occupational analysis to understand their region's strengths vis-a-vis those of its competitors for jobs and residents. California's largest metros exhibit very different occupational specializations (see table 7-4). Los Angeles' strengths lie in aerospace, garment making, and media-related occupations, whereas architects and legal occupations are most prominent in San Francisco. Oakland, which is near the University of California–Berkeley and its research spin-offs, also has important public transportation functions and hosts high shares of life scientists, civil and operating engineers, and recreation workers. Construction workers and real estate agents, as well as electrical engineers, are overrepresented in San Diego, a fast-growing metro.

Cities or metros can also scrutinize unexpected gains and losses by occupation. In the 1990s, seven smaller (suburban and stand-alone) California metros posted surprising gains in a number of occupations, as shown in table 7-5. Analyses like these alert planners to promising occupations in ways that reflect competitive labor strength; they are likely to prove to be more reliable than questionable job vacancy data to inform workforce development and industry targeting.

Table 7-3. *Growing Concentrations of Specialized Occupations in the Twin Cities, 1989–98*

Occupation	Location quotient, 1998[a]	Location quotient change, 1998[a]	1998 Employment
Urban and regional planners	2.19	0.35	910
Computer and IT professionals	1.62	0.25	41,593
Adjusters, investigators, and collectors	1.44	0.11	24,912
Engineering technicians	1.34	0.16	12,317
Life scientists	1.33	0.46	2,714
Science and mathematics technicians	1.31	0.42	3,573
Management support occupations	1.26	0.13	64,597
All other sales and related workers	1.25	0.14	106,729
Personal-service occupations	1.23	0.11	36,894
Physical scientists	1.22	0.23	2,880
Architects and surveyors	1.19	0.11	3,279
Engineers	1.13	0.11	19,455
Mail clerks and messengers	1.12	0.09	3,288
Social and recreational workers	1.06	0.06	10,680
Hand workers, including assemblers, fabricators	1.06	0.06	38,792
Other clerical, administrative support workers	1.04	0.03	171,552
Machine setters, operators, tenders	1.02	0.10	62,379
Psychologists	1.02	0.33	1,750
Statistics			
Totals, growing concentrations	1.16	0.11	608,294
Growing concentrations' share of region total (percent)			36.7
Total employment, Twin Cities			1,655,792

Sources: Computations by the Project on Regional and Industrial Economics, University of Minnesota, from data from the Minnesota Department of Economic Security, based on the Minnesota Department of Economic Security 1989 and 1998 base-year occupational employment estimates from projections series for the seven-county Minneapolis–St. Paul metropolitan region. National data based on U.S. Bureau of Labor Statistics, National Industry-Occupation Employment Matrix, 1983–1998.

a. Location quotients (LQ) calculated as the ratio between an occupation's share of total employment in the region and its share nationally. An LQ of greater than 1 implies overconcentration of that occupation within the region.

Diverging Patterns of Urban Occupational Distinctiveness

Researchers conventionally distinguish city and regional economies from each other and the nation by the over- and underrepresentation of employment by industry, and they can easily do this by occupation. Just how distinctive are metro-

Table 7-4. *Top Occupational Specializations, California's Largest Metros, 1997*

Occupation	Specialization ratios (location quotients vis-à-vis U.S.)			
	Los Angeles	San Francisco	Oakland	San Diego
Aircraft assemblers, precision	6.1			
Sewing machine operators, garment	4.7	2.5		
Aeronautical and astronautical engineers	3.2			3.2
Jewelers and silversmiths	3.1			
Broadcast technicians	2.8			
Architects, except landscape and marine		3.5		
Messengers		3.2		
Lawyers		2.7		
Paralegals		2.5		
Civil engineers, including traffic engineers			2.9	
Life scientists			2.3	3.4
Operating engineers			2.0	
Recreation workers			2.0	
Science and mathematics technicians			1.9	
Drywall installers and finishers				2.5
Electrical and electronics engineers				2.4
Sales agents, real estate				1.9

Source: Ann Markusen and Elisa Barbour, "California's Occupational Advantage" (San Francisco: Public Policy Institute of California, 2003), available at www.hhh.umn.edu/projects/prie/pub.htm.

politan labor pools and which are gaining or losing ground in key occupations? The coefficient of localization can be used to separate occupations that are heavily skewed across the set of metros, thus distinctive, from those that are relatively evenly spread and thus presumably are local-serving. The coefficient is defined in Walter Isard, *Methods of Regional Analysis: an Introduction to Regional Science.*[20] The skewed occupations consist of those that are heavily engaged in exporting, but also those where distinctive local consumption patterns support unusually high numbers of workers. Examples of the latter might be performing artists and recreational workers, whose exceptional presence signals high consumption levels of their services.

Major occupational groupings show highly divergent patterns of skewness across the top fifty U.S. metros (see table 7-6). Some highly skewed groupings are mathematical, computer, life sciences, physical and social science, and legal and artistic occupations. Others, such as management, sales, education, and personal-care occupations, are distributed in tandem with overall employment. At the top of the

Table 7-5. *Top Four Occupations with Unexpected Gains, California Suburban and Stand-Alone Metros, 1988–97*

Occupation (N.E.C. = *not elsewhere classified*)[a]	San Jose	Orange County	Riverside–San Bernardino	Bakersfield	Fresno	Sacramento	Redding
Managers and administrators, N.E.C.	6,072					2,474	
Management support workers, N.E.C.							
Electrical and electronics engineers	7,665						
Computer and IT professionals, N.E.C.	12,667					1,820	
Teachers		4,532	8,965	2,255	2,162		
Clinical lab technologists and technicians		15,705					
Professional workers, N.E.C.					1,969		321
General office clerks				1,163			
Police patrol officers						1,980	
Correction officers				1,073			
Food counter, fountain, related workers							570
Janitors, cleaners, maids, housekeepers		3,606	10,575			2,142	
Service workers, N.E.C.				1,711			592
Blue-collar worker supervisors					1,173		
Sewing machine operators, garment		4,333					
Truck drivers, light and heavy			6,099				512
Machine operators, assemblers, N.E.C.	13,115		24,834		3,288		

Source: Ann Markusen and Elisa Barbour, "California's Occupational Advantage" (San Francisco: Public Policy Institute of California, 2003), available at www.hhh.umn.edu/projects/prie/pub.htm.

a. N.E.C. groupings are often large residuals of occupational groupings.

Table 7-6. *Occupational Localization in the Fifty Largest U.S. Metros, 1980–2000*
Unit as indicated

Occupational group	Index C.O.L.[a]	Change in C.O.L., 1980–2000 (percent)	U.S. E growth,[b] 1980–2000 (percent)	U.S. employment, 2000
Export base occupations (index C.O.L. > 1.75)			10	22,889,810
Farming, fishing, and forestry	3.26	23	−37	954,755
Life, physical, and social sciences	2.36	20	36	1,203,513
Computer and mathematical	2.35	20	316	3,162,637
Legal	2.01	−12	112	1,423,337
Arts, design, entertainment, sports, media	1.94	3	61	2,477,332
Craft and assembly production	1.85	20	−17	11,003,719
Engineering and architecture	1.85	10	15	2,664,517
Local consumption base occupations (index C.O.L. < 1.75)			40	106,826,838
Health care support	1.55	41	66	2,579,656
Protective service	1.54	2	64	2,553,136
Construction and extraction	1.32	−28	26	7,150,604
Community and social services	1.14	−9	81	1,945,926
Installation, maintenance, and repair	0.93	1	21	5,110,115
Health care practitioners and technical	0.93	42	69	5,985,446
Food preparation and serving	0.92	−10	33	6,263,129
Business and financial operations	0.92	−2	95	5,551,438
Building, grounds cleaning, maintenance	0.91	44	25	4,250,257
Transportation and materials moving	0.89	4	14	7,959,078
Personal care and service	0.86	−11	66	3,630,598
Management	0.71	20	69	11,884,694
Education, training, and library	0.70	−5	53	7,331,579
Sales and related	0.56	−29	56	14,604,836
Office and administrative support	0.42	−38	13	20,026,346
Total, all occupations			33	129,716,648

Source: Ann Markusen and Greg Schrock, "The Distinctive City: Divergent Patterns in Growth, Hierarchy, and Specialization," *Urban Studies* 43, no. 8 (2006): 1301–23, table 5. Data from U.S. Census Bureau, decennial Population Census Public Use Microdata Sample (PUMS) 5 percent file, accessed from Integrated Public Use Microdata Series, Minnesota Population Center, University of Minnesota.

a. C.O.L. = coefficient of localization. C.O.L.s are indexed to average between 1980, 1990, and 2000. A high C.O.L. means that the occupation is highly skewed across the fifty-metro set.

b. E = Employment.

table are occupations for which job competition among cities is fierce: high-tech, arts and media, legal, and craft and assembly occupations. Products and services embodying their work are either exported or provide distinctive local consumption amenities to firms, workers, and their households. These specialized occupations encompassed just 18 percent of total employment across the fifty metropolitan areas in 2000.

Economists and practitioners generally assume that if an industry or occupation is overrepresented in a region, it is because it is exporting its output elsewhere. But this may not be the case at all, suggesting caution against using location quotients and concentration ratios as ways of delineating the export base. For instance, the arts, entertainment, and sports occupations, among the highly skewed, are engaged mainly in serving the local population in most metros, with the exception of Los Angeles and New York. Cities may vary dramatically in their residents' expenditures on these activities and on the investments they make in providing them. Such investments may be key to attracting and retaining skilled labor and firm managers, and may also draw tourist visits. Thus certain consumption base sectors are worthy candidates for economic development practice.

Most of the specialized export and consumption base occupations increased their differential distribution across the fifty largest metros between 1980 and 2000 (table 7-6, third column), which reveals deepening interurban division of labor. High-tech occupations, arts, media, and architecture are now more competitive and specialized across metros than they were in 1980. Although craft and assembly occupations fell dramatically, they were more concentrated across major metros in 2000 than they were twenty years earlier. Only the legal occupations showed a tendency toward deconcentration.

Occupations that demonstrate higher and increasing skewness among metro areas from 1980 to 2000 are prima facie candidates for targeting, whether for education and training investments, attraction, or retention, because they are occupations that cluster and whose members are "on the move." For each of these occupations, a closer look at skill formation and training locales, distribution across industries, migratory choices of members, and presence in one's own metro will help economic developers understand which might serve as key occupational targets for their city. Although these occupational groups are becoming more concentrated in certain regions, it does not follow that metro economies overall are becoming more distinctive from each other. Because some key, chiefly export-oriented occupations, especially those in the craft and assembly lines of work, are on the decline, some cities are less distinctive in their export base activities than they were two decades previously.

In the 1980s especially, the implosion of craft and assembly occupations that often were anchored in particular industries was a major contributor to the loss of distinctiveness in a number of metros. For example, Pittsburgh, Cleveland, and Youngstown metros lost more than two-thirds of their steelworkers in this era. In many of these, such losses were by and large not counterbalanced by new export or consumption base activities. Between 1980 and 2000, the fifty metros studied lost more than 2.2 million jobs in the production occupations and sustained additional job erosion in resource-oriented occupations.

Yet even with these deep losses, manufacturing and resource-related occupations in 2000 accounted for 48 percent of all specialized-base jobs, belying the notion that manufacturing is no longer a significant city function. Craft and assembly jobs have shifted to smaller towns, rural areas, and abroad, and have also lost ground to imports, but they form a crucial component of the urban economy in absolute numbers, amounting to 11 million export-oriented jobs in 2000. They still bestow distinction on many cities: New York's garment workers, Detroit's autoworkers, Pittsburgh and Cleveland's steelworkers, Tampa's cigar makers, Seattle's aircraft engineers and mechanics, and Silicon Valley's chip makers.

These findings vindicate what manufacturing modernization researchers have argued since the 1980s, ever since Dan Luria and Jack Russell's precocious study, *Rational Reindustrialization:* that goods production is far from dead and that attention to upgrading and innovation in these sectors can be a smart investment in employment retention for many cities.[21] Dozens of excellent projects linking research to practice have pioneered displaced workers' programs, high-performance work systems, and manufacturing extension services to stabilize and revitalize the economies of host regions.[22] They may not yield surges in future employment or enable an older industrial city to compete with Las Vegas's growth trajectory, but they play a key role in sustaining well-compensated, export-oriented jobs that in turn support additional consumption base jobs in the local economy. They produce equitable outcomes as well as efficiencies essential to successful competition.

In practice, economic developers must look carefully at their region's particular occupational strengths to see whether these might buck overall trends. Manufacturing may still hold considerable traction for some cities. Consider, for instance, the stake that certain metro areas have in several large, blue-collar occupations such as textile and apparel workers, plastics and metal production workers, and assemblers (see table 7-7). Textile and apparel workers were more concentrated in the largest metro areas in 2000 than they were in 1980, a function of large plant closings from the Carolinas to Texas and of tightening spatial ties between big city–based fashion decisionmakers and their manufacturing suppliers. Cities as

Table 7-7. *Specialization of Selected Craft and Assembly Occupations, by Metro, 1980–2000*
Units as indicated

Metro	Location quotient, 2000	Location quotient, 1980	2000 LQ as percentage of 1980 LQ
Textile, apparel workers			
Greensboro–Winston-Salem	3.38	3.23	105
Los Angeles	2.61	1.18	220
Charlotte (North and South Carolina)	2.20	3.05	72
Providence (Rhode Island, Massachusetts)	1.77	2.12	84
New York (New York, New Jersey)	1.73	1.62	106
Miami	1.31	1.81	72
Orange County	1.21	0.40	304
50 Metros	0.89	0.75	118
Metal, plastic workers			
Grand Rapids	2.58	2.09	123
Milwaukee	2.09	1.95	107
Detroit	2.04	1.89	108
Cleveland	1.97	1.86	106
Hartford	1.68	2.07	81
Providence (Rhode Island, Massachusetts)	1.59	1.62	98
Indianapolis	1.25	1.49	84
50 Metros	0.76	0.90	85
Assemblers, fabricators			
Grand Rapids	2.31	1.59	145
Detroit	2.19	1.62	135
San Jose	1.94	2.30	84
Nashville	1.48	0.98	150
Milwaukee	1.37	1.73	79
Cleveland	1.35	1.31	103
Indianapolis	1.34	1.67	80
Orange County	1.34	1.53	87
Salt Lake City	1.27	1.15	111
Greensboro–Winston-Salem	1.22	1.14	107
Minneapolis–St. Paul (Minnesota, Wisconsin)	1.21	1.34	91
50 Metros	0.83	1.01	82

Sources: Ann Markusen and Greg Schrock, "The Distinctive City: Divergent Patterns in Growth, Hierarchy, and Specialization," *Urban Studies* 43, no. 8: 1301–23, table 5. Data from U.S. Census Bureau, decennial Population Census Public Use Microdata Sample (PUMS) 5 percent file, accessed from Integrated Public Use Microdata Series, Minnesota Population Center, University of Minnesota.

disparate as Greensboro and New York increased their apparel and textile employment specializations over the period. The Los Angeles metro area added huge numbers of apparel workers in the 1990s, mainly Latina women, which helped to counter severe blue-collar and engineering employment losses in the region's post–Cold War defense industries.[23]

Metal and plastics workers, a group underrepresented and declining across the large metro set, are concentrating in the Grand Rapids, Milwaukee, Detroit, and Cleveland metros, many of them working to supply the still large, if beleaguered, midwestern auto complex. Assembly and fabrication workers are prominent and increasing their significance in cities such as Nashville, Cleveland, and Salt Lake City, signaling their continuing competitiveness in these occupations and host industries.

Occupational targeting, then, resembles industrial targeting in that each city must figure out its economic development goals and its existing strengths and weaknesses, and whether it wants to pursue a strategy of bolstering current concentration skill sets, diversifying to other promising skill sets, making up deficits in skills that are underrepresented, or a combination of these. No one generic formula can accomplish this, just as no simple ranking scheme can tell us which cities have the "best" and "worst" occupational structures. All cities' labor pools are constantly being replenished and remade, as the occupations within them are subjected to the impacts of broader technological and knowledge trends.

Conclusion: A Labor-Centric Revamping of Urban Economies

Older industrial cities can secure a distinctive and sustainable labor pool by selectively "growing," attracting, and retaining workers in key occupations, which they can identify by means of the methods described here, consonant with their goals. In this final section, we propose a labor-centric economic development practice that partners with occupational intermediaries such as professional associations, unions, and training institutions and uses an "occupational lens" to screen projects and initiatives. Such a practice can link with community development efforts to ensure that programs promote equity among groups of workers as well as vibrant neighborhoods by targeting the ones with concentrated employment needs.

Conceptualize and Secure a Distinctive Labor Pool

A robust industrial city relies on its ability to supply and retain topnotch talent—both home grown and imported—around its occupational specializations. If successful, it is a "place to be" for certain occupations: New York for aspiring dancers,

Detroit for automotive engineers, Silicon Valley for systems analysts, and Boulder for outdoor gear designers. This means funding education and training institutions and systematically connecting them to the demand side of the labor market, allowing firms to recruit local graduates before they leave for greener pastures, and helping mid-career workers to update their knowledge.

Efforts to recruit and retain individuals in targeted occupations can work through occupational intermediaries. Or, states and localities can market themselves directly to individuals within key occupations by advertising in occupation-specific trade publications and marketing themselves to education and training institutions. For example, Michigan recently established the Michigan Recruitment Alliance to connect job seekers, businesses, and educational institutions around its targeted areas of life sciences, information technology, and advanced manufacturing occupations. Recruiters can also work with lists from local universities and colleges encouraging alumni to come home to work. They can also work with the headquarters offices of national labor unions, which may be able to help displaced workers in one region move to similar jobs in regions where such jobs are increasing.

What about nonprofessional occupations? Many aging industrial regions owe their distinctiveness at least in part to cadres of skilled blue-collar workers. Where these groups are in short supply, either because of retirements or rapid growth in demand, a partnership can be built among labor unions, community groups, employers, and education and training institutions to shore them up. In Milwaukee in the 1990s, when large-scale retirements and an undersized younger blue-collar workforce threatened to hamper the competitiveness of venerable Milwaukee producer goods manufacturers and to discourage new businesses from starting up, trade unionists initiated the Wisconsin Regional Training Partnership (WRTP) to forge such a coalition. They were successful and went on to disseminate their model throughout the state.[24] Other cities and states have used training subsidies as part of packages to recruit new firms. But the WRTP model pioneered the idea of working outside of the walls of any particular firm, so that the regional economy as a whole would benefit from skill building and labor pool formation.

Although they are not generally conceived of as economic development agencies, education and training institutions play a large role in building regional occupational distinctiveness in both blue-collar and professional occupations. Some universities and colleges self-consciously target certain undergraduate and professional programs as being key to their regions' futures. For public universities, legislators sign on to these strategies by providing extra funding for expansion in these fields. Unfortunately, they often do so by following the fashions of the times, such as supporting biotech research and education in the current decade, or computer science in the 1980s. These specializations are not always appropriate for the region and often result in "brain drain" when the graduates of the training programs leave to take jobs in other regions.[25] Some regions have dealt with the brain drain problem by targeting graduates who have left the region and recruiting them back on the basis of family ties, familiarity with the landscape, and financial incentives.

Adding the occupational to the industry lens could improve the efficacy of legislative commitments. Particularly key is the balance of emphasis on research versus occupational training. Many states have recently made commitments for large capital outlays to biotechnology research facilities at universities and beyond, with disappointing results.[26] It is the training rather than the research function of postsecondary educational institutions that translates consistently into regional job growth.[27] Community colleges and technical schools are crucial elements in this complex because of their role in providing and upgrading skills.

Screen Economic Development Projects with an Occupational Lens

A labor-centric practitioner will scrutinize business incentives packages in the deal-making phase for the character of the workforce entailed, since each such expansion shapes the area's labor pool. Will the jobs be skilled, pay well, provide mobility over time, and add to existing or new skill specializations in the region? Will the jobs go to newcomers from elsewhere, who will require new public services, or is the firm committed to training and hiring existing residents, and ameliorating unemployment either by directly hiring the unemployed or by creating job openings for them as employed workers move into the new jobs?[28] Such screens can help prioritize who receives incentives, how large the packages are and for how long, and what kinds of performance criteria and clawbacks (requirements to pay incentives if jobs do not materialize) will be applied to ensure that the promised job creation takes place.[29]

Occupational analysis has often been used as a subsidiary exercise when targeting industries in economic development. Once industries are chosen, their occupational structure is examined for ways to harness the workforce development system to the effort. Yet occupational analysis could play the lead role in economic development efforts. Turning the tables, economic development planners and policymakers could choose a set of target occupations and then use them as a screen for deciding how employer-based incentives might be allocated.

Occupational analysis involves two key steps: first, prioritizing key occupations using a range of criteria such as their current presence in the city or region, capturability (their potential for localization and agglomeration), pay and bene-fit levels, long-term growth potential, connectivity across industries and entre-preneurship potential, and fit with existing labor-force skills and aptitudes; and second, researching the locational dynamics and development potential for those occupations. These exercises should encompass consumption-serving as well as export-oriented occupations. The resulting occupational set can be matched to the occupational composition of a prospective employer's workforce or that of a current employer who is asking for retention incentives.

Work with Professional Associations and Unions

To encourage entrepreneurship, streamline education and training systems, and uncover barriers and problems in attracting and retaining skilled workers, eco-nomic developers can forge connections with professional organizations, unions, and training institutions. This is analogous to economic and workforce develop-ers cultivating relationships with business and industry associations to develop employer-friendly and targeted industry policies. Targeted occupational strategies can include entrepreneurial training and business technical assistance provided by professional associations and trade unions that could also be consulted on issues of physical space, network enhancement, and challenges unique to their members' skill sets and experiences.

Professional associations establish standards for education and certification, provide forums for networking and technical debate, do research on pay and ben-efits, offer support on issues of contracts and property rights, and monitor relevant public policy issues. On the local level, they can serve as vehicles for networking and professional development, but unfortunately they are rarely engaged by economic developers. They could, for instance, be conduits for tailored entrepreneurial training or channels for recruiting their university and past work colleagues back to the region. For industrial occupations, trade unions are appropriate partners, as they have been in the Wisconsin case described earlier, for telecommunications equipment installers in several cities and for cultural workers in New York and Los Angeles.[30]

Cities can also market collectively for an occupation, an analog to the way they underwrite trade missions for firms or pitch tourist attractions to potential visi-tors. For instance, advertising art fairs and art crawls helps generate business for artists, as do artist-dedicated websites such as MNArtists.org. They can also help professional associations and unions develop Internet training and websites that will raise the visibility of their skill sets and provide a virtual market for matching up workers with employers.

Link Labor-Centric Initiatives with Community Development

Too often, economic development initiatives to promote the growth of key indus-tries are carried out without regard to their impacts on particular places and pop-ulations within the city or region. As a result, traditional economic development strategies, such as business attraction incentives, often fail to generate benefits for disadvantaged populations and low-income communities. Community-based organizations (CBOs) often target the vitality of industry sectors and occupations that match the experience and qualifications of residents. In the 1980s, for instance, the city of Chicago's Local Industrial Retential Initiative relied on CBOs to help area businesses find good employees. One successful example of a Chicago CBO connecting skilled workers and businesses who need their skills is the Jane Addams Resource Corporation, a CBO whose metalworking training program feeds skilled workers to manufacturing businesses throughout the city and region.[31]

Efforts to create districts that harbor particular occupations and related work are another option. In the arts, economic developers are beginning to understand that funding large destination arts facilities surrounded by parking lots is an expensive way of remaking an area and often fails to create synergies in the imme-diate neighborhood. Shaping revitalization around artist live-work buildings, instead, has required modest funds but has brought large payoffs for areas such as St. Paul's Lowertown neighborhood, where such spaces have been created in sev-eral beautiful and once-vacant old warehouses. Artists residing in concentrated numbers have spurred commercial and retail growth, the revival of the farmer's market, and spring and fall arts crawls where thousands come to visit artists show-ing their work in their studios. Neighborhood effects can be enhanced and medi-ated as part of this effort to build a distinctive sense of place. Planners can change zoning laws to permit members of key occupations to live as well as work in what once were warehouses or districts zoned only for commercial uses. Similarly, sup-porting smaller-scale arts performance spaces and cultural centers throughout the city rather than concentrating investments in a single cultural district offers the potential for much greater participation and higher consumption spending on the arts and cultural events, thus bolstering the ranks of artists and related workers.

Community-based organizations are often the most articulate interpreters of desirable amenities that attract and hold city residents. They can help eco-nomic developers and city leaders weigh targeted occupational and industry initiatives against investments to enhance the qualities of the living and work-ing environment.

We welcome further debate about our claims for the centrality of labor, occu-pations, and amenities in development practice. Other innovations—metrowide economic development planning, greater consensus on and more explicit statements of development goals, a unified economic development portfolio approach that combines tax expenditures and direct economic development spending in a single accounting framework—would facilitate the agenda sketched out here. Overall, we believe that an approach that puts labor center stage, by focusing on the training, location, and entrepreneurial potential of workers grouped by occupation rather than industry, will produce strong and more effective economic development practice for revitalization in older industrial cities. Because the consumption base can be an autonomous source of growth, not fully dependent on export base employment, policymakers should pay more attention to the distinctiveness of their cities as places to live and work. Investments in quality-of-life assets such as recreational infrastructure, arts and cultural offerings, and clean air and water can divert local consumer expenditures into more local job-sustaining activity. At the same time, these consumption base offerings will help retain skilled labor, recruit new workers and firms, and encourage entrepreneurs to set up their new businesses in the region. Cities should avoid being drawn into escalating incentive competition over mobile firms and plants and take a broader, more strategic view of their human and physical capital and cultural and environmental assets.

Notes

1. This chapter, though written for this volume, draws on Ann Markusen and Greg Schrock, *The Distinctive City,* an unpublished book manuscript, University of Minnesota, Humphrey Institute of Public Affairs, Project on Regional and Industrial Economics, August 2007.
2. Export base theory began with Harold Innes's insights on the Canadian staples trade (*Essays in Canadian Economic History* [University of Toronto Press, 1956]) and was codified by Douglass North (*Economic Growth of the United States, 1790 to 1860* [New York: Norton, 1966]) in his work on the evolution of the American economy, especially the role of slave-grown cotton in the antebellum South.
3. For a review of these developments, see Candace Howes and Ann Markusen, "Trade, Industry, and Economic Development," in *Trading Industries, Trading Regions,* edited by Helzi Noponen, Julie Graham, and Ann Markusen (New York: Guilford Press, 1993), pp. 1–44. Strategic trade theory is summarized in Paul Krugman, *Geography and Trade* (MIT Press, 1992).
4. Charles Tiebout, "Exports and Regional Economic Growth," *Journal of Political Economy* 64, no. 2 (1956): 160–69.
5. Diane Lindstrom, *Economic Development in the Philadelphia Region, 1810–1850* (Columbia University Press, 1978).
6. See, for example, Edward Ghartey, "Causal Relationship between Exports and Economic Growth: Some Empirical Evidence in Taiwan, Japan and the US," *Applied Economics* 25, no. 9 (1993): 1145–52, and Subhash Sharma, Mary Norris, and Daniel Wai-Wah-Cheung,

"Exports and Economic Growth in Industrialized Countries," *Applied Economics* 23, no. 4A (1991): 697–708.

7. Ann Markusen, "A Consumption Base Theory of Development: An Application to the Rural Cultural Economy," *Agricultural and Resource Economics Review* 36, no. 1 (2007): 1–13.

8. Joseph Cortright, "The Economic Importance of Being Different: Regional Variations in Tastes, Increasing Returns and the Dynamics of Development," *Economic Development Quarterly* 16, no. 1 (2002): 3–16.

9. See Ann Markusen, *Regions: The Economics and Politics of Territory* (Totowa, N.J.: Rowman & Littlefield, 1987), chapter 4, for an account of this history.

10. See Kenneth Thomas, *Competing for Capital* (Georgetown University Press, 2002); Greg LeRoy, *The Great American Jobs Scam: Corporate Tax Dodging and the Myth of Job Creation* (San Francisco: Berrett-Koehler, 2005); Ann Markusen, ed., *Reining in the Competition for Capital* (Kalamazoo, Mich.: W. E. Upjohn Institute for Employment Research, 2007).

11. For a methodology of how to analyze regional growth prospects by studying firm behavior, see Ann Markusen, "Studying Regions by Studying Firms," *Professional Geographer* 46, no. 4: 477–90.

12. Leroy, *Great American Jobs Scam;* Ann Markusen and Katherine Nesse, "Institutional and Political Determinants of Incentive Competition," in Markusen, *Reining in the Competition for Capital,* pp. 1–41.

13. Paul Gottlieb, *The Problem of Brain Drain in Ohio and Northeastern Ohio: What Is It? How Severe Is It? What Should We Do about It?* (Case Western Reserve University, 2001), prepared for the Ohio Board of Regents and the Jobs and Workforce Initiative of the Greater Cleveland Growth Association.

14. Roger Bolton, " 'Place Prosperity' vs. 'People Prosperity' Revisited," *Urban Studies* 29, no. 2 (1992): 185–203.

15. For seminal work on an occupational approach, see Wilbur Thompson and Philip Thompson, "From Industries to Occupations: Rethinking Local Economic Development," *Economic Development Commentary* 9, no. 3 (1985): 12–18; Edward Feser, "What Regions Do Rather Than Make: A Proposed Set of Knowledge-Based Occupation Clusters," *Urban Studies* 40, no. 10 (2003): 1937–58; Ann Markusen and Elisa Barbour, *California's Occupational Advantage,* Working Paper No. 2003;12 (San Francisco: Public Policy Institute of California, May 2003); Ann Markusen, "Targeting Occupations in Regional and Community Economic Development," *Journal of the American Planning Association* 70, no. 3 (2004): 253–68.

16. Bennett Harrison, *Lean and Mean: The Changing Landscape of Corporate Power in the Age of Flexibility* (New York: Basic Books, 1996).

17. Susan Christopherson, "Emerging Patterns of Work," in *Skills, Wages and Productivity in the Service Sector,* edited by Thierry Noyelle (Boulder: Westview, 1990), pp. 11–30; Paul Osterman, *Securing Prosperity: The American Labor Market—How It Has Changed and What to Do about It* (Princeton University Press, 1999).

18. Ann Markusen, "Sticky Places in Slippery Space: A Typology of Industrial Districts," *Economic Geography* 72, no. 3 (1996): 293–313.

19. Elisa Barbour and Ann Markusen, "Regional Occupational and Industrial Structure: Does the One Imply the Other?" *International Regional Science Review* 30, no. 1 (2007): 1–19.

20. Walter Isard, *Methods of Regional Analysis: an Introduction to Regional Science* (The MIT Press, 1960), pp. 252–54.

21. Dan Luria and Jack Russell, *Rational Reindustrialization* (Detroit: Widgetripper Press, 1981). Other seminal calls for industrial revitalization policies in this period include Barry Bluestone and Bennett Harrison, *The Deindustrialization of America* (New York: Basic Books, 1982); Ann Markusen, *Steel and Southeast Chicago: Reasons and Remedies for Industrial Renewal,* Report to the Mayor's Task Force on Steel and Southeast Chicago (Evanston: Northwestern University, Center for Urban Affairs and Policy Research, 1985); Steven Cohen and John Zysman, *Manufacturing Matters* (New York: Basic Books, 1987).

22. Philip Shapira and Jan Youtie, *Coordinating Industrial Modernization Services: Impacts and Insights from the U.S. Manufacturing Extension Partnership* (Georgia Institute of Technology, Economic Development Institute, 1996); Ann Markusen and Laura Wolf-Powers, *Lessons from Defense Workers' Experience in the 1990s* (Washington: Economic Policy Institute, 1998); Eileen Applebaum, Thomas Bailey, Peter Berg, and Arne Kalleberg, *Manufacturing Advantage: Why High-Performance Work Systems Pay Off* (Ithaca: Industrial and Labor Relations Press, 2000); Eric Parker and Mia Gray, *Prescribing the High Road: A Comparative Case Study of the Pharmaceutical Industry* (Rutgers University, Project on Regional and Industrial Economics, 2003).

23. Markusen and Barbour, *California's Occupational Advantage.*

24. Eric Parker and Joel Rogers, "Sectoral Training Initiatives in the U.S.: Building Blocks of a New Workforce Preparation System?" in *The German System of Skill Provision in Comparative Perspective,* edited by Pepper D. Culpepper and David Finegold (Oxford: Berghahn Books, 1999), pp. 326–62.

25. A study of Cleveland found that the city's colleges and universities were producing far too many graduates in fields with little regional expertise or demand while underproducing graduates in occupations that local firms were more interested in hiring; see Gottlieb, *Problem of Brain Drain in Ohio and Northeastern Ohio.*

26. A study of biotech employment found that few new U.S. biotech firms that were formed as start-ups from regional universities and research centers generated much regional employment. Instead, the bulk of associated employment gains were registered in New Jersey, where labor pools and firm agglomerations with expertise in testing, clinical trials, advertising and marketing, and packaging were concentrated; see Mia Gray, "The Micro-Level Matters: Evidence from the Bio-Pharmaceutical Industry," *Zeitschrift für Geographie* 46, no. 2 (2002): 124–36.

27. An early study of the success of high-tech industries found that U.S. metropolitan high-tech enterprise and job growth were negatively correlated with university R&D spending but positively associated with postsecondary educational offerings. See Ann Markusen, Peter Hall, and Amy Glasmeier, *High Tech America: The What, How, Where and Why of the Sunrise Industries* (Boston and London: Allen & Unwin, 1986).

28. Tim Bartik, "Who Benefits from Local Job Growth: Migration or the Original Residents?" *Regional Studies* 27, no. 4 (1993): 297–312, argues that hiring local residents has a far greater overall positive impact, and yet in the United States, an excess of 70 percent of new subsidized jobs created go to outsiders. See Joseph Persky and Daniel Felsenstein, "Evaluating Local Job Creation: A 'Job Chains' Perspective," *Journal of the American Planning*

Association 73, no. 1 (2007): 23–34, on how creating a new job for an existing resident opens up jobs for others in the region.

29. Rachel Weber, "Negotiating the Ideal Deal: Which Local Governments Have the Most Bargaining Leverage?" In Markusen, *Reining in the Competition for Capital,* pp. 141–59; Leroy, *Great American Jobs Scam,* 2005.

30. On telecommunications, see Laura Wolf-Powers, "The Role of Labor Market Intermediaries in Promoting Employment Access and Mobility: A Supply- and Demand-Side Approach," Ph.D. dissertation, Rutgers University, 2003; on unions in the culture industries, see Ann Markusen, Sam Gilmore, Amanda Johnson, Titus Levi, and Andrea Martinez, *Crossover: How Artists Build Careers across Commercial, Nonprofit and Community Work* (University of Minnesota, Project on Regional and Industrial Economics, 2006).

31. See accounts of Chicago's efforts in Joan Fitzgerald and Nancey green Leigh, *Economic Revitalization: Cases and Strategies for City and Suburbs* (Thousand Oaks, Calif.: Sage, 2002), and Amy Glasmeier, Candace Nelson, and Jeffrey W. Thompson, *Jane Addams Resource Corporation: A Case Study of a Sectoral Employment Development Approach* (Washington: Aspen Institute, 2000).

8

Occupational Clusters, Employment, and Opportunity for Low-Skilled Workers

Mark Turner, Laurel Davis, and Andres Cruz

L ow-skilled workers vying for employment in the U.S. job market face many challenges in today's global economy. Manufacturing jobs and, increasingly, skilled occupations (such as accounting and software programming) are moving overseas, where labor costs are dramatically lower. Many service occupations, which have historically provided a strong job base, have become obsolete due to technological advancements and automation. As a result of these changes in the U.S. job market, there are fewer career paths left for low-skilled workers, who lack the education and training to compete against a growing pool of highly skilled yet underemployed and nonemployed citizens and immigrants. The jobs that are within reach often do not provide fringe benefits, living wages, or career pathways.

In the country's older industrial cities, the impacts of these changes are especially serious because of the loss of traditional employment sectors. The number of factory jobs in steel mills, automobile manufacturing plants, and textile warehouses has diminished substantially. These jobs offered large numbers of low-skilled workers stability, a steady salary, the ability to advance in their jobs, and a variety of on-the-job and retirement-based benefits. The number of these jobs in today's marketplace is much lower, and new prospects for careers with the opportunities afforded by these past occupations are lacking.

These changes present large numbers of low-skilled workers in American cities with a serious and pressing dilemma, and force researchers and local governments to look for solutions. One approach may be to work to reattract the types of jobs that large cities have lost. But another, more realistic approach may be to aim to reattract the manufacturing, skilled-labor, and service occupations lost to technical innovation and international outsourcing, in order to determine what other occupations could be viable choices for low-skilled workers.

Basis of This Study

A recent report by Jobs for the Future (JFF) attempted to define nationally relevant job clusters for low-skilled workers using a model based on Bureau of Labor Statistics (BLS) data.[1] The authors' methodology looked at BLS's Standard Occupational Code list and narrowed that list using data on earnings, accessibility, availability, and advancement potential.[2] The resulting list of occupations is then narrowed again on the basis of the level of risk to offshoring, technological innovation, and overall industry decline. Finally, interviews were conducted with both employers and job training providers to garner detailed information on the nature of the work, hiring practices, training, advancement potential, and the stability of demand.

JFF's analysis resulted in six viable occupation clusters: nurses, customer service representatives, automotive and truck technicians, computer support specialists, building trades workers, and commercial drivers of heavy vehicles. JFF discusses these occupations in detail, providing useful information on their viability as a job opportunity for low-skilled workers, and beginning the discussion of how both public and private investment could aid workers in entering into those fields.

Purpose, Goals, and Preliminary Results of This Research

JFF's model to identify occupational clusters for low-skilled workers at the national level is useful to congressional leaders and policymakers but is not designed to guide state and local officials. A model that is tailored to specific metropolitan area conditions (incorporating industrial-occupation mix, labor-market conditions) could prove to be more useful to business leaders and policymakers as they seek to identify and build occupational clusters that will provide sustainable, living-wage jobs to low-skilled workers.

The research described in this article used the strong analytical foundation conceived by Jobs for the Future to create customized models for six metropolitan statistical areas (MSAs): Baltimore, Detroit, Los Angeles, Las Vegas, Orlando, and New Orleans. This chapter presents a preliminary quantitative analysis that identifies viable job clusters for low-skilled workers that are specific to each metropolitan area.

The results of this preliminary analysis suggest that there are unique occupations in each of the six sites, and that there are also many employment clusters that exist across some or all of the six metropolitan areas. Unique employment clusters were often directly tied to the distinctive features of the metropolitan area's industrial comparative advantage, history, and environment. Those that were common to many sites included registered nurses, computer support specialists, purchasing agents, automotive service technicians and mechanics, and electricians. Some of these occupations are the same as those found in the nationally based JFF study.

In deriving these occupations, every effort was made to obtain clusters that have the possibility of growing better-quality jobs for low-skilled workers. By defining viable employment opportunities for this population, and helping these workers to gain entry into the selected occupations, it may be possible to help alleviate the large numbers of individuals and families living in persistent cycles of poverty as a result of changes in the economic fabric of our nation's cities.

Site Selection

In selecting the study sites for this project, the research team aimed to select locations where there is significant need and where the results could affect a large number of individuals. Additionally, the research team recognized the importance of selecting locations with different spatial and economic characteristics. A final goal was to work with the Ford Foundation to select sites that would complement their current initiatives or work being done by other philanthropic organizations on restoring economic prosperity in older industrial areas.

To achieve these goals, the team completed a three-step process. First, it divided the nation's MSAs into three geographical regions. Second, data were reviewed to discern locations with large numbers of low-skilled workers, demonstrated long-term unemployment, and significant poverty levels. Third, the team applied external knowledge of these locations possessed by the research team and representatives of the Ford Foundation to finalize the list of selected sites.

Data Reviewed

The research team used data from three sources: the 2005 listing of MSAs from the United States Census Bureau, the 2000–2005 Current Population Survey (CPS) data sets, and the 2005 American Community Survey (ACS). The team began by narrowing the list of MSAs to only those with a total population of 1 million or more residents. This list was then divided into the three geographical regions: East, West, and South. The delineation of these regions was based partially upon existing Census Bureau divisional boundaries, but given that MSAs often cross state boundaries, the boundaries of the three regions were adjusted to avoid the overlap of a single MSA into multiple regions. Figure 8-1 shows the three geographical regions that the research team defined.

After dividing the large MSAs into three regions, the research team performed an analysis of selected data variables from the CPS and ACS to describe each MSA, and to help determine which MSAs in each region would be most appropriate for further study. The variables reviewed included information on individual income by education level, percentage employed by education level, household income,

Figure 8-1. *Regional Classification of States*

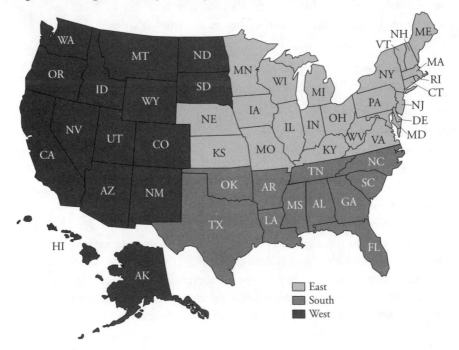

percentage of families below the federal poverty level (FPL; set by the U.S. Department of Health and Human Services), ethnicities of the population, and percentage employed in key industries.

The team used a combination of variables to cross-query and develop a list of top sites for consideration. These were sites that had, in comparison to the other sites in the region:

—Low income levels
—A high percentage of individuals with low-educational-attainment levels
—An extremely high percentage of individuals from one or more minority groups
—A high percentage of families below the FPL
—A large percentage of workers employed in key low-skilled industries

The research team used these data and the team's external knowledge of the top sites to finalize the preliminary selection of six sites, two in each region. The funds allocated for this work and the time frame for its completion limited the number of study sites selected to six. In each region, both sites selected were in need of investigation of employment options and potential future interventions, but they were somewhat different in nature. The research team hypothesized that by selecting a more diverse sample, the study would provide a richer pool of viable employment clusters for the low-skilled population, thus providing a larger return on the funds invested in this work.

The research team presented the preliminary site selection to the Ford Foundation, and the initial selection was modified to reflect information provided by the Ford Foundation regarding other projects in which they were engaged.

Selected Sites

The sites selected by the research team and the Ford Foundation for inclusion in this study were Baltimore, Detroit, Los Angeles, Las Vegas, Orlando, and New Orleans. This section presents summary information on each of the selected sites that was critical to the site's selection and provides a brief overview of the unique factors associated with each location. Tables 8-1 and 8-2 present data for each site, which is referenced in each summary.

East: Baltimore and Detroit. In the East region, the research team chose two old, industrial cities. Baltimore is historically a port city, located at the head of the Chesapeake Bay. Over the last three decades, Baltimore has experienced the same

Table 8-1. *Characteristics of Recommended Sites, 2005*
Unit as indicated

	East		West		South	
	Baltimore	Detroit	Los Angeles	Las Vegas	Orlando	New Orleans
2005 Current Population Survey						
Median respondent income (weekly)	$710	$680	$560	$575	$600	$570
If GED	$560	$484	$400	$481	$475	$461
If some college	$600	$500	$500	$540	$509	$481
Percentage employed respondents	95.8	92.7	95.7	96.7	96.6	95.7
Percentage if GED	91.9	88.7	94.6	96.3	93.9	92.4
Percentage if some college	95.0	91.5	95.1	95.9	96.6	95.2
2005 American Community Survey						
Population	2,583,923	4,428,941	12,703,423	1,691,213	1,903,273	1,132,036
Median household income	$57,447	$50,787	$51,824	$49,571	$44,543	$39,879
Percentage residents with high school diploma only	27.4	29.3	21.1	30.8	29.5	31.3
Percentage of families below the FPL	6.6	9.9	11.7	8.7	9.0	14.5
Percentage Hispanic ethnicity	2.7	3.4	43.9	26.2	21.2	5.0
Percentage African American ethnicity	28.0	22.8	7.2	9.5	14.7	37.7
Percentage Asian ethnicities	3.5	3.2	13.8	6.8	3.6	n/a

Source: As listed in table.

Table 8-2. *Workers Age Sixteen and Over Employed, by Industry*
Percent

	East		West		South	
Industry	Baltimore	Detroit	Los Angeles	Las Vegas	Orlando	New Orleans
Construction	7.3	6.0	7.2	11.9	9.8	6.6
Manufacturing	6.6	20.5	13.3	3.6	5.1	7.8
Retail	11.2	10.8	10.5	11.1	12.1	12.1
Hospitality and food service	5.5	6.4	6.4	16.5	10.2	8.9
Total	30.6	43.7	37.3	43.1	37.3	35.4

Source: Authors' compilation, based on U.S. Census Bureau, 2005 American Community Survey data.

problems as many other older, industrial cities: shrinkage in the manufacturing sector, dilapidated housing stock, problem-plagued schools, and a loss of population to the suburbs. In 2005, the Baltimore MSA had a population of 2,583,923. Of that, 635,815 residents lived within the boundaries of the city of Baltimore, and the remaining 1,948,108 lived in the surrounding suburbs. Between 1990 and 2005, the city of Baltimore had lost approximately 100,000 residents, or 13.6 percent of its population, to the suburbs.

Although Baltimore's problems are vast, the city also has immense resources to build on, including professional sports teams, historical heritage, reinvestment in the downtown waterfront, and well-funded hospitals and universities. In choosing Baltimore as a study site, the research team hopes to build upon the reinvestments that are occurring, and to help low-skilled workers obtain higher wage-paying jobs in viable sectors.

Detroit was for many decades the center of the automobile manufacturing industry in the United States, hence its nickname, the Motor City. As the manufacturing sector declined and many of the automobile manufacturing plants began to close, Detroit experienced a tremendous decline in its traditional job center.

The pain caused by this change in employment dynamics is reflected in current data on the city and surrounding area. As shown in table 8-1, in 2005 approximately 10 percent of the families in the Detroit MSA were living below the FPL. Data from the 2005 Current Population Survey list Detroit's employment rate as 92.7 percent, but that number drops significantly, to 88.7 percent for those with only a GED (high school equivalent) or less education.[3] In selecting Detroit, the research team hopes to define employment sectors for the low-skilled population that are an alternative to the traditional manufacturing jobs that have long been Detroit's employment core.

South: Orlando and New Orleans. In the aftermath of Hurricane Katrina, many New Orleanians have been displaced from their homes as well as their jobs. Those who remain and those who are returning are faced with the challenge of rebuilding their lives in a much changed Gulf Coast region. With the recent nature of this catastrophic event, the data sets used for the site-selection portion of this project do not show the changes in the region's economy and population post-Katrina; however, these effects have been validated extensively by other authors and news outlets. These other external qualitative data coupled with historical descriptive data of the New Orleans population led the research team to suggest it for inclusion in this study, as it is a location in dire need of all possible assistance. The team sees the possibility of helping to define viable employment clusters as a way to help settle the lives of the low-income individuals who were displaced as a result of the storm.

The 2005 data (pre-Katrina) in table 8-1 demonstrate that New Orleans has an extremely large population with only a high school degree, a large number of residents living below the FPL, and low income levels, especially for those individuals with only a GED or some college. Table 8-2 shows the high percentage of employed residents working in the retail and accommodation and food service industries.

In contrast, Orlando, with a 2005 population of almost 2 million permanent residents, is a city with a strong and vibrant tourism-based economy. In this type of setting, many of the jobs available to low-skilled workers are in the service industry. In 2005, 12.1 percent of Orlando's employed population aged sixteen and over were employed in retail, and another 10.2 percent were employed in the accommodation and food service industry. Thus the difference in income for the low-skilled population and that of the overall population is striking (see table 8-1). The research team hopes that in choosing Orlando as a study site, we will be able to help define employment clusters for the unskilled population that are more independent of the major theme parks and tourist attractions of the city.

West: Los Angeles and Las Vegas. Los Angeles is one of the largest cities on the West Coast—indeed, one of the largest metropolitan areas in the country: in 2005 the Los Angeles MSA had a population of over 12 million. The area has been long plagued by immense population growth and its ensuing sprawl. The fact that the city is very spread out often makes it difficult for the low-skilled to obtain transportation to and from the better jobs. By identifying the most viable employment clusters for the low-skilled, the research team may be able to aid low-skilled residents in finding higher-wage jobs closer to their homes.

Furthermore, a large proportion of Los Angeles's population is racial-ethnic minority groups. As shown in table 8-1, Hispanics make up 43.9 percent of the population, African Americans, 7.2 percent, and Asian ethnicities, almost 14 percent of the population. Recent statistics suggest that these groups move into the middle class at a slower rate than other ethnic groups and are disproportionately working at lower-paying dead-end jobs.

Las Vegas is experiencing extreme levels of population growth, as the city transitions from being solely a tourist mecca into a city with a sizable number of permanent residents. This transition is putting an immense strain on Las Vegas's infrastructure and public services. The majority of jobs have traditionally been service based, but as the population grows and there are more permanent residents, the need for added infrastructure and public services will continue to expand, creating a market for new, higher-wage jobs. In 2005 (see table 8-2), 16.5 percent of Las Vegas's employed residents aged sixteen and over were employed in the accommodation and food service industry; 11.1 percent, in retail; and 11.9 percent, in construction. The research team hopes to be able to use these known changes in Las Vegas's physical and economic environment to define employment sectors with strong and stable wage-earning potential for the low-skilled.

Methodology and Data Sources

The research team's methodology was modeled on that of a study undertaken by Jobs for the Future, which examined nationally relevant job clusters for low-skilled workers. This study differed in that it examined specific locations (MSAs) to determine locally relevant growth occupations. This provides a more focused look at relevant occupations in a variety of settings. The majority of the data used to determine growth occupations were collected at the MSA level, either directly through the Bureau of Labor Statistics (BLS) or through local and state agencies. Where data were not available at the MSA level, national-level data from the BLS were used.

Identification of Potential Growth Occupations

To identify growth occupations that may be viable occupational clusters, four categories of variables were used to screen each occupation: availability, accessibility, advancement potential, and annual openings. Availability refers to the number of available job openings per occupation annually, and is defined by the research team as the sum of new or growth openings and replacement openings for a given occupation in a given year. Accessibility is defined as the education and training necessary for entrance into an occupation. Advancement potential represents an individual's ability to ascend to a higher position or salary while employed in a single occupation. The research team calculated advancement potential as the difference between the top and bottom 10 percent of earnings in each occupation. Earnings were defined as gross annual income paid by a job, measured by the median annual earnings for each occupation. Table 8-3 lists each category, the specific variable used to represent that category, a definition for each variable, and the data sources used by the research team.

As noted earlier, availability measures how many openings occur in a particular occupation annually. This variable is an essential component to the study because of the need to decipher which occupations have a significant number of openings. If an occupation has only a few openings per year in a given location, it would not be an occupation to target for the location's low-skilled workers, as the chance of obtaining a job in that field would be minimal.

The data selected to calculate this variable were taken from state-level data produced in cooperation with the BLS. Each state calculates its own set of projections using the Occupational Employment Statistics (OES) survey as the basis for its information.[4] This data set was then used to produce information at the MSA level. National occupational projection data are produced by the BLS using only CPS data. (The CPS data could be aggregated to MSAs, but we were concerned that the sample size would be too small to make the results meaningful.)

Availability is the sum of new or growth openings and replacement openings for a particular occupation annually. *New or growth openings* refers to completely new openings in an occupation or the change in employment of an occupation over the projection period divided by the number of years in the projection period. *Replacement openings* refers to the number of job openings that result when workers leave the occupation permanently.

Accessibility is a measure of the level of education necessary to enter a particular occupation. The MSAs selected for inclusion in this project did not all have localized data sets available for this measure, and those that had collected this information had not followed a set methodology for doing so. Therefore, the research team used national-level data to measure this variable. The BLS created a broad system of categories called "educational attainment clusters," which included high school, some college, and college, ratings for each occupation. This system provides a hierarchical sorting of occupations that reflects increasing skill levels, and accounts for multiple paths of entry into the various occupations.[5] As a separate, secondary,

Table 8-3. *Variables: Definitions and Data Sources*

Category	Variable	Definition	Data source
Availability	Total growth and net replacement openings	This variable is measured as the sum of new or growth openings and replacement openings for a given occupation.	Local OES data found on state websites. See also www.laworks. net/Downloads/LMI/ 20042014 Questions onProjections.pdf
Accessibility	Education and training necessary for entrance into an occupation	The educational attainment cluster is a broad system of educational categorization that includes high school, some college, and college. This system provides a hierarchical sorting of occupations that reflects increasing skill levels, and accounts for multiple paths of entry into various occupations. As a separate, secondary variable, postsecondary training categories are applied to each occupation through internal BLS staff and interviews with employers.	National data from the Bureau of Labor Statistics and American Community Survey for regional education data. For BLS data, see http:// data.bls.gov/oep/ servlet/oep.noeted. servlet.ActionServlet? Action=empeduc
Advancement potential	Wage growth	This variable is used to judge advancement potential within a field, calculated by the difference between the 10th percentile of BLS earnings data and the 90th percentile of BLS earnings data. BLS collects hourly wage data, and then multiplies by 2,080 hours or the total number of working hours in a year.	See http://data.bls.gov/ oes/search.jsp
Earnings	Median income	Earnings are measured as the annual median income in dollars for an occupation.	See http://data.bls.gov/ oes/search.jsp

Source: Authors' compilation.

variable, postsecondary training categories are applied to each occupation through internal BLS staff knowledge and interviews with employers.[6]

Advancement potential and earnings were estimated with data compiled at the MSA level, which used the OES as the basis for its calculation. The BLS collects hourly wage data in the OES and then multiplies it by 2,080 hours to calculate the annual wage.[7] The median annual earnings for each occupation was this study's measure of total earnings, and the difference between the top and bottom 10 percent of wage earners in each occupation provided the measure of salary growth (and hence advancement potential) in the occupation.

The variables outlined above were merged into one data set using the Standard Occupational Classification (SOC) system created in 2000 by the BLS. The SOC is used to classify each worker surveyed into one of approximately 820 occupational categories. SOC codes served as unique identifiers in combining tables through a one-to-one relationship in Microsoft Access.

Once the data were combined into a single data set, a multistep query was used to narrow the list of occupations. Thresholds were determined for each variable to filter out the occupations that were not considered viable. The threshold for accessibility included all occupations that required an associate's degree or below. Thus occupations requiring college were eliminated, and the secondary filter removed occupations from other educational cluster groupings for which a college degree was the main entry mechanism. The threshold for advancement potential was a greater than 60 percent wage growth for employees in the top and bottom deciles. The threshold for earnings was set at 185 percent of the federal poverty level,[8] chosen because it is the cutoff for many federal and state assistance programs, such as Head Start, Food Stamps, and the National School Lunch Program.[9] This threshold filtered out all jobs with median incomes of less than $18,888.50 per year.

The thresholds needed to be set in a way that would yield a reasonable number of occupations for study. Recognizing the scope limitations of this stage of the study, we tried to obtain a list that would not be excessively large, thus allowing the team to reasonably consider each occupation listed. To accomplish this, the availability threshold was applied after the other three variables and limited the results to the top fifteen jobs based on the total number of annual openings.

The data ranges for each variable and the specific thresholds used for each of the six study sites are shown in tables 8-4 through 8-9.

Limitations of the Approach

The main challenge encountered while trying to obtain the data for this study was the collection of data sets aggregated to the appropriate geographic MSA

Table 8-4. *Information on Baltimore Variables*

Category	Variable	Data range	Variable or variable range to be used
Availability	Total growth and net replacement openings	Minimum, 5 Maximum, 4,845	Greater than or equal to 200 total openings per year
Accessibility	Education and training necessary for entrance into an occupation	Minimum HS Maximum C	Less than or equal to SC/C degree
Advancement potential	Wage growth	Minimum, $4,670 Maximum, $121,630 (excluding occupations with null values)	Producing wage growth greater than 60 percent between the 10th and 90th percentiles
Earnings	Median income	Minimum, $18,960 Maximum, $99,930 (excluding occupations with null values)	185 percent of poverty guidelines set by the Department of Health and Human Services. Greater than or equal to $18,888.50.

Source: Authors' compilation.

Table 8-5. *Information on Detroit Variables*

Category	Variable	Data range	Threshold to be used for selection
Availability	Total growth and net replacement openings	Minimum, 1 Maximum, 3,143	Greater than or equal to 100 total openings per year
Accessibility	Education and training necessary for entrance into an occupation	Minimum HS Maximum C	Less than or equal to SC/C degree
Advancement potential	Wage growth	Minimum, $7,130 Maximum, $129,290 (excluding occupations with null values)	Producing wage growth greater than 60 percent between the 10th and 90th percentiles
Earnings	Median income	Minimum, $18,960 Maximum, $98,050 (excluding occupations with null values)	185 percent of poverty guidelines set by the Department of Health and Human Services. Greater than or equal to $18,888.50.

Source: Authors' compilation.

Table 8-6. *Information on New Orleans Variables*

Category	Variable	Data range	Threshold to be used for selection
Availability	Total growth and net replacement openings	Minimum, 10 Maximum, 1,060 (excluding occupations with zero values)	Greater than or equal to 300 total openings per year
Accessibility	Education and training necessary for entrance into an occupation	Minimum, HS Maximum, C	Less than or equal to SC/C
Advancement potential	Wage growth	Minimum, $4,240 Maximum, $125,940 (excluding occupations with null values)	Producing wage growth greater than 60 percent between the 10th and 90th percentiles
Earnings	Median income	Minimum, $19,120 Maximum, $96,430 (excluding occupations with null values)	185 percent of poverty guidelines set by the Department of Health and Human Services. Greater than or equal to $18,888.50.

Source: Authors' compilation.

Table 8-7. *Information on Orlando Variables*

Category	Variable	Data range	Threshold to be used for selection
Availability	Total growth and net replacement openings	Minimum, 1 Maximum, 3,099 (excluding occupations with zero values)	Greater than or equal to 100 total openings per year
Accessibility	Education and training necessary for entrance into an occupation	Minimum, HS Maximum, C	Less than or equal to SC/C degree
Advancement potential	Wage growth	Minimum, $4,500 Maximum, $127,250 (excluding occupations with null values)	Producing wage growth greater than 60 percent between the 10th and 90th percentiles
Earnings	Median income	Minimum, $19,080 Maximum, $96,690 (excluding occupations with null values)	185 percent of poverty guidelines set by the Department of Health and Human Services. Greater than or equal to $18,888.50.

Source: Authors' compilation.

Table 8-8. *Information on Los Angeles Variables*

Category	Variable	Data range	Threshold to be used for selection
Availability	Total growth and net replacement openings	Minimum, 2 Maximum, 5,010	Greater than or equal to 200 total openings per year
Accessibility	Education and training necessary for entrance into an occupation	Minimum, HS Maximum, C	Less than or equal to SC/C degree
Advancement potential	Wage growth	Minimum, $3,670 Maximum, $129,680 (excluding occupations with null values)	Producing wage growth greater than 60 percent between the 10th and 90th percentiles
Earnings	Median income	Minimum, $18,970 Maximum, $97,420 (excluding occupations with null values)	185 percent of poverty guidelines set by the Department of Health and Human Services. Greater than or equal to $18,888.50.

Source: Authors' compilation.

Table 8-9. *Information on Las Vegas Variables*

Category	Variable	Data range	Threshold to be used for selection
Availability	Total growth and net replacement openings	Minimum, 1 Maximum, 2,711	Greater than or equal to 100 total openings per year
Accessibility	Education and training necessary for entrance into an occupation	Minimum, HC Maximum, C	Less than or equal to SC/C degree
Advancement potential	Wage growth	Minimum, $1,259 Maximum, $100,004	Producing wage growth greater than 60 percent between the 10th and 90th percentiles
Earnings	Median income	Minimum, $19,030 Maximum, $145600 (excluding occupations with null values)	185 percent of poverty guidelines set by the Department of Health and Human Services. Greater than or equal to $18,888.50.

Source: Authors' compilation.

boundaries. For many states local data were not congruent with MSA boundaries,[10] which sometimes forced the research team either to use nationally collected data or to include data for a slightly different geographical area. These differences were generally minimal and the team did not feel that they significantly affected the quality of the results produced by the study. For example, Orlando maintained data sets according to workforce area definitions,[11] which were similar to the Orlando MSA; the difference between the two areas in population was minimal, approximately 3 percent.[12] The state and national definitions of the New Orleans MSA differed by one parish; the population difference was just 2 percent.[13]

The Maryland Department of Labor, Licensing, and Regulation uses a geographical area called a workforce investment area (WIA) to measure the total annual job openings, which is different from the Baltimore-Towson MSA.[14] WIAs are groupings of counties with 200,000 or more residents and a common labor pool, and data were available only for the twelve WIA groupings, not the individual counties making up the WIA.[15] The Baltimore-Towson MSA did not match the WIA groupings, and the team was faced with the dilemma of either not including some counties in the Baltimore-Towson MSA calculation of annual openings or including more counties than were actually part of the MSA. For instance, Queen Anne's County was combined with Caroline, Dorchester, Kent, and Talbot counties to create the Upper Eastern Shore WIA. But the Baltimore-Towson MSA includes Queen Anne's County only, and not the other four counties in the WIA. In this instance, Queen Anne's County was not included in the MSA calculation. The research team was comfortable with this decision because Queen Anne's County is a rural county located on the Eastern Shore of Maryland, and is not near the city of Baltimore. Thus individuals living in that county tend to commute via car to jobs in the Baltimore area, and they are not the target group for this research. Additionally, Queen Anne's County does not provide a large number of jobs and because of its location would not be accessible to the residents of the city of Baltimore and the surrounding suburbs. The Susquehanna WIA comprised Harford and Cecil counties. The same decision was made for Harford County as for Queen Anne's County. Thus the two counties were removed from the calculation.

Additional limitations of this study are associated with peripheral variables, not explicitly considered at this stage. These include whether an occupation provides insurance coverage and other fringe benefits to employees and whether an occupation generally employs individuals on a part-time, full-time, or seasonal basis. The research team hopes to fully consider these data during later phases of the study.

Results of the Study

The product of the analysis process was a group of fifteen to twenty site-specific occupations that are considered viable growth occupations for low-skilled workers in each of the six economically troubled metropolitan areas. These occupations represent opportunities for low-skilled workers with little or no additional education to obtain a job that offers a living wage and a career pathway through salary advancement. The jobs selected for each site also are available within the metropolitan area, as evidenced by the substantial number of annual job openings reported in the result tables.

These occupations will be further researched in the future and will be narrowed to remove occupations that are at risk of becoming obsolete or are exposed to other national or local factors that may not have been apparent from our review of the data.

Growth Occupations for Each Study Site

Queries were applied to each site's data set in a two-step process. First, the research team created a multivariable query that applied thresholds for earnings, wage growth, and the educational attainment level. The team then sorted the results of this survey by the number of annual openings, and the top fifteen occupations were chosen on the basis of the total number of openings. In some instances, numerous occupations had the same number of openings, so the list for that site had more than fifteen occupations. All of the occupations listed are accessible to individuals with less than a college degree.

East: Baltimore and Detroit. Table 8-10 lists the survey results for the Baltimore MSA and shows a wide range of growth occupations. The availability of jobs such as teachers and police officers is indicative of the persistent high crime rates and poor education systems plaguing the city of Baltimore and the surrounding areas. Of note is the high number of jobs available for registered nurses (4,845 per year), which is likely a direct reflection of the growth in the health care services and research industry in the area.

Other occupations on table 8-10 are a direct reflection of the immense need for goods and services in the densely populated Baltimore-Washington metropolitan region, including retail and nonretail sales managers and other sales-related workers.

The median annual income of selected occupations for Baltimore ranges from $31,950 to $99,930. These occupations have a strong salary with a large range for

Table 8-10. *Results of Baltimore Query*
Unit as indicated

Group label	Occupation	Annual ($) median earnings	Wage growth ($)	Total annual openings	Educational attainment cluster[a]
Management occupations	Managers, all other	99,930	93,790	470	HS/SC/C
Business and financial operations occupations	Purchasing agents, except wholesale, retail, and farm products	56,760	55,740	185	HS/SC/C
Business and financial operations occupations	Compliance officers, except agriculture, construction, health and safety, and transportation	46,130	55,850	265	SC/C
Computer and mathematical occupations	Computer support specialists	44,460	42,370	415	SC/C
Education, training, and library occupations	Self-enrichment education teachers	31,950	73,410	510	SC/C
Health care practitioners and technical occupations	Registered nurses	68,860	44,090	4845	SC/C
Protective service occupations	First-line supervisors, managers of police and detectives	70,510	50,300	245	SC/C

Sales and related occupations	First-line supervisors, managers of retail sales workers	36,720	42,510	505	HS/SC/C
Sales and related occupations	First-line supervisors, managers of nonretail sales workers	74,630	107,180	225	HS/SC/C
Sales and related occupations	Sales representatives, wholesale and manufacturing, except technical and scientific products	54,480	77,730	905	HS/SC/C
Sales and related occupations	Sales and related workers, all other	37,140	52,020	190	HS/SC/C
Office and administrative support occupations	First-line supervisors, managers of office and administrative support workers	45,860	41,920	1035	HS/SC/C
Construction and extraction occupations	First-line supervisors, managers of construction trades and extraction workers	54,500	46,350	350	HS/SC
Installation, maintenance, and repair occupations	First-line supervisors, managers of mechanics, installers, and repairers	58,520	48,760	255	HS/SC
Installation, maintenance, and repair occupations	Automotive service technicians and mechanics	33,730	42,050	250	HS/SC
Production occupations	First-line supervisors, managers of production and operating workers	52,570	49,700	315	HS/SC

Source: Authors' compilation.

a. HS = high school; SC = some college; C = college.

wage growth and advancement—$41,920 to $107,180—over the course of an individual's employment in the field. Thus they present strong, long-term options for low-skilled workers in the Baltimore MSA.

Table 8-11 shows the survey results for the Detroit MSA. The occupations' median earnings range from $22,920 to $75,290, with a wage growth potential of $13,650 to $44,390 over the course of a person's employment in the occupation. These numbers are not as high as Baltimore's, and indicate the economic market in Detroit, a city that has lost a large number of jobs. One result has been a severe drop in home prices.

The large presence of production, mechanical, and transportation-related occupations reflects Detroit's heritage as the leader in the automobile manufacturing industry. In general, this industry has declined in recent years, and many of Detroit's facilities have shut down or have scaled back the number of workers. Still, this industry remains one of the city's core employers. Sustaining the remaining auto-related jobs will be a challenge for Detroit in coming years, as additional technological innovations emerge and factories are moved to cheaper labor markets.

Other occupations on this list may reflect future directions for the city, and should be considered as viable employment options for the low-skilled, including those in the construction trade, such as carpenters, electricians, plumbers, pipe fitters, and steam fitters. New employees can often enter these occupations as apprentices and obtain training while working on the job. The jobs in these fields are reliable and present long-term employment options for workers because they are always needed in a densely populated area.

South: New Orleans and Orlando. Results of our New Orleans survey are shown in table 8-12. Median annual earnings range from $24,730 to 59,750, with a potential wage growth of between $32,790 and $73,940 over the course of employment in the occupation.

Unique to this area are occupations that exist because of New Orleans's location on the Gulf of Mexico, including sailors and marine oilers, ship engineers, pumpers, petroleum pump system and refinery operators, and captains, mates, and pilots of vessels. These occupations are often accessible with on-the-job training and little to no formal education past a high school diploma. And, given the city's location, they will likely continue to be in demand regardless of what changes arise in the city after the post-Katrina rebuilding is completed.

It is important to note that the data sources used to determine these occupations did reflect the damage caused by Hurricane Katrina. While the base year for the employment projections data was pre-Katrina, the 2004–14 projections

Table 8-11. *Results of Detroit Query*
Unit as indicated

Group label	Occupation	Annual median earnings ($)	Wage growth ($)	Total annual openings	Educational attainment cluster[a]
Business and financial operations occupations	Purchasing agents, except wholesale, retail, and farm products	63,300	35,710	226	HS/SC/C
Computer and mathematical occupations	Computer support specialists	43,440	25,700	214	SC/C
First-line supervisors, managers of retail sales workers	First-line supervisors and managers of nonretail sales workers	75,290	44,390	193	HS/SC/C
First-line supervisors, managers of retail sales workers	Sales representatives, wholesale and manufacturing, technical and scientific products	72,210	39,780	273	HS/SC/C
First-line supervisors, managers of retail sales workers	Sales representatives, wholesale and manufacturing, except technical and scientific products	56,460	30,010	970	HS/SC/C
First-line supervisors, managers of retail sales workers	Sales and related workers, all other	38,290	17,700	170	HS/SC/C
Office and administrative support occupations	First-line supervisors, managers of office and administrative support workers	48,050	31,540	450	HS/SC/C

(continued)

Table 8-11. *Results of Detroit Query (continued)*
Unit as indicated

Group label	Occupation	Annual median earnings ($)	Wage growth ($)	Total annual openings	Educational attainment cluster[a]
Construction and extraction occupations	First-line supervisors, managers of construction trades and extraction workers	64,890	43,070	216	HS/SC
Construction and extraction occupations	Carpenters	47,470	28,020	389	HS/SC
Construction and extraction occupations	Electricians	66,210	36,190	237	HS/SC
Construction and extraction occupations	Plumbers, pipe fitters, and steam fitters	60,160	32,720	245	HS/SC
Installation, maintenance, and repair occupations	First-line supervisors, managers of mechanics, installers, and repairers	65,750	38,430	206	HS/SC
Installation, maintenance, and repair occupations	Automotive service technicians and mechanics	43,830	20,960	392	HS/SC
Production occupations	First-line supervisors, managers of production and operating workers	60,640	35,890	274	HS/SC
Production occupations	Welders, cutters, solderers, and brazers	45,540	23,800	184	HS/SC
Transportation and material moving occupations	Cleaners of vehicles and equipment	22,920	13,650	233	HS

Source: Authors' compilation.

a. HS = high school; SC = some college; C = college.

Table 8-12. *Results of New Orleans Survey*
Unit as indicated

Group label	Occupation	Annual median earnings ($)	Wage growth ($)	Annual total openings	Educational attainment cluster[a]
Management occupations	Managers, all other	59,750	73,940	120	HS/SC/C
Business and financial operations occupations	Compliance officers, except agriculture, construction, health and safety, and transportation	38,990	45,190	30	SC/C
Health care practitioners and technical occupations	Registered nurses	55,420	35,030	360	SC/C
Protective service occupations	Protective service workers, all other	25,990	33,000	50	HS/SC/C
Sales and related occupations	First-line supervisors, managers of nonretail sales workers	54,000	71,280	30	HS/SC/C
Sales and related occupations	Parts salespersons	30,320	33,810	30	HS/SC
Sales and related occupations	Sales representatives, wholesale and manufacturing, technical and scientific products	58,790	68,390	40	HS/SC/C
Sales and related occupations	Sales representatives, wholesale and manufacturing, except technical and scientific products	48,100	55,110	190	HS/SC/C
Office and administrative support occupations	First-line supervisors, managers of office and administrative support workers	35,970	37,960	150	HS/SC/C
Construction and extraction occupations	First-line supervisors, managers of construction trades and extraction workers	46,530	37,000	60	HS/SC

(continued)

Table 8-12. *Results of New Orleans Survey (continued)*
Unit as indicated

Group label	Occupation	Annual median earnings ($)	Wage growth ($)	Annual total openings	Educational attainment cluster[a]
Installation, maintenance, and repair occupations	First-line supervisors, managers of mechanics, installers, and repairers	47,930	44,940	60	HS/SC
Installation, maintenance, and repair occupations	Automotive service technicians and mechanics	32,900	40,310	90	HS/SC
Installation, maintenance, and repair occupations	Installation, maintenance, and repair workers, all other	24,730	34,460	30	HS/SC
Production occupations	First-line supervisors, managers of production and operating workers	43,100	44,750	50	HS/SC
Production occupations	Petroleum pump system operators, refinery operators, and gaugers	55,210	38,110	50	HS/SC
Production occupations	Inspectors, testers, sorters, samplers, and weighers	30,950	39,540	30	HS/SC
Transportation and material moving occupations	First-line supervisors, managers of transportation and material-moving machine and vehicle operators	46,150	46,560	30	HS/SC
Transportation and material moving occupations	Sailors and marine oilers	28,060	32,790	110	HS/SC
Transportation and material moving occupations	Captains, mates, and pilots of water vessels	55,540	56,730	80	HS
Transportation and material moving occupations	Ship engineers	45,590	59,530	30	HS/SC
Transportation and material moving occupations	Pump operators, except wellhead pumpers	38,120	40,570	30	HS/SC

Source: Authors' compilation.
a. HS = high school; SC = some college; C = college.

include employment changes that occurred throughout the state as a result of Katrina. Historical employment is a key source used to develop industry projections, and reflects the drop in employment in the last quarter of 2005, among other factors.[16] Wage estimates produced from the OES come from mailed surveys conducted two times a year. The years included in the wage estimates are 2006, 2005, 2004, and 2003; thus the estimates take into account Hurricane Katrina's impact on the New Orleans economy.[17]

Orlando is home to numerous theme parks and tourist attractions, including Walt Disney World and Universal Studios, which serve as destinations for tourists and as employers for large numbers of local residents. The occupations listed in Orlando's results (see table 8-13) range from $26,540 to $72,820 in annual median earnings. The potential wage growth is between $29,980 and $86,050.

Many of the selected occupations are directly related to the service industry associated with theme park and tourist destinations. Although many of the occupations related to these types of industries do not provide living wages and career pathways, the selected occupations appear to have substantial wage growth, and may be viable career pathways for low-skilled workers.

Other interesting results in the Orlando MSA include real estate agents and construction-related occupations, which may be linked to the growth in vacation home sales and time shares, and to more permanent residents settling in the area.

West: Los Angeles and Las Vegas. Table 8-14 shows the occupational results for the Los Angeles MSA. These occupations range from $31,720 to $89,720 in median earnings. They have a potential wage growth of between $45,370 and $97,240. The strong median salaries and large wage growth range are reflective of the high cost of living in the Los Angeles area.

The types of occupations listed for Los Angeles are indicative of the large and varying economy in this sprawling metropolitan area. The occupations derived from the analysis vary substantially, and include occupations related to the entertainment industry, personal care and pampering, law, and mechanics. These occupational areas all present entry-level positions accessible with only on-the-job training and also show a strong salary increase over the time an individual is employed in the occupation, with no occupation having less than a $40,000 increase.

The occupations selected for the Las Vegas MSA are listed in table 8-15. These occupations range from $20,560 and $63,220 in median earnings. The possible wage growth while employed in these occupations ranges from $53,223 to $87,728. This growth range represents a large window for advancement over the course of an individual's employment in a given occupation.

Table 8-13. *Results of Orlando Query*

Unit as indicated

Group label	Occupation	Annual median earnings ($)	Wage growth ($)	Total annual openings	Educational attainment cluster[a]
Management occupations	Food service managers	48,890	61,580	134	HS/SC/C
Management occupations	Managers, all other	72,820	80,280	198	HS/SC/C
Business and financial operations occupations	Cost estimators	45,780	54,450	133	HS/SC/C
Computer and mathematical occupations	Computer support specialists	35,790	33,770	210	SC/C
Installation, maintenance, and repair occupations	Automotive service technicians and mechanics	35,300	36,730	348	HS/SC
Transportation and material moving occupations	Truck drivers, heavy and tractor-trailer	29,680	29,980	526	HS/SC
Transportation and material moving occupations	Truck drivers, light or delivery services	26,540	36,920	349	HS/SC
Personal care and service occupations	First-line supervisors, managers of personal service workers	39,890	35,640	141	HS/SC

Sales and related occupations	First-line supervisors, managers of retail sales workers	37,990	47,220	438	HS/SC/C
Sales and related occupations	Sales representatives, services, all other	46,120	68,680	314	HS/SC/C
Sales and related occupations	Sales representatives, wholesale and manufacturing, technical and scientific products	59,440	86,050	133	HS/SC/C
Sales and related occupations	Sales representatives, wholesale and manufacturing, except technical and scientific products	48,840	74,980	714	HS/SC/C
Sales and related occupations	Real estate sales agents	33,720	73,770	507	HS/SC/C
Office and administrative support occupations	First-line supervisors, managers of office and administrative support workers	40,200	41,040	431	HS/SC/C
Construction and extraction occupations	First-line supervisors, managers of construction trades and extraction workers	50,490	41,160	425	HS/SC
Construction and extraction occupations	Tile and marble setters	36,950	36,190	180	HS

Source: Authors' compilation.

a. HS = high school; SC = some college; C = college.

Table 8-14. *Results of Los Angeles Query*
Unit as indicated

Group label	Occupation	Annual median earnings ($)	Wage growth ($)	Total annual openings	Educational attainment cluster[a]
Management occupations	Managers, all other	89,720	97,240	668	HS/SC/C
Business and financial operations occupations	Cost estimators	57,170	64,630	162	HS/SC/C
Legal occupations	Paralegals and legal assistants	49,540	51,500	279	SC/C
Arts, design, entertainment, sports, and media occupations	Camera operators, television, video, and motion picture	75,030	70,620	162	SC/C
Health care support occupations	Massage therapists	33,910	47,440	232	SC/C
Protective service occupations	Firefighters	73,660	47,420	256	HS/SC
Personal care and service occupations	Fitness trainers and aerobics instructors	38,460	52,070	259	SC/C
Sales and related occupations	First-line supervisors, managers of nonretail sales workers	64,440	82,560	239	HS/SC/C
Sales and related occupations	Advertising sales agents	47,160	81,560	191	SC/C
Office and administrative support occupations	First-line supervisors, managers of office and administrative support workers	47,160	45,370	1,370	HS/SC/C

Construction and extraction occupations	First-line supervisors, managers of construction trades and extraction workers	62,330	49,260	341	HS/SC
Construction and extraction occupations	Electricians	48,230	54,230	364	HS/SC
Installation, maintenance, and repair occupations	First-line supervisors, managers of mechanics, installers, and repairers	56,950	55,310	376	HS/SC
Installation, maintenance, and repair occupations	Automotive service technicians and mechanics	32,040	50,830	747	HS/SC
Production occupations	First-line supervisors, managers of production and operating workers	44,930	50,410	482	HS/SC
Transportation and material moving occupations	First-line supervisors, managers of transportation and material-moving machine and vehicle operators	50,710	55,310	278	HS/SC
Transportation and material moving occupations	Industrial truck and tractor operators	31,720	46,540	586	HS

Source: Authors' compilation.

a. HS = high school; SC = some college; C = college.

Table 8-15. *Results of Las Vegas Query*
Unit as indicated

Group label	Occupation	Annual median earnings ($)	Wage growth ($)	Total annual openings	Educational attainment cluster[a]
Health care practitioners and technical occupations	Registered nurses	63,220	53,223	836	SC/C
Protective service occupations	Security guards	22,800	85,567	840	HS/SC
Food preparation and serving-related occupations	Cooks, restaurant	26,720	81,654	741	HS
Food preparation and serving-related occupations	Bartenders	21,180	87,728	811	HS/SC
Building and grounds cleaning and maintenance occupations	Janitors and cleaners, except maids and housekeeping cleaners	24,100	84,679	1518	HS
Building and grounds cleaning and maintenance occupations	Maids and housekeeping cleaners	25,220	83,720	1374	HS
Building and grounds cleaning and maintenance occupations	Landscaping and groundskeeping workers	21,070	84,592	969	HS
Sales and related occupations	First-line supervisors, managers of retail sales workers	32,750	79,329	601	HS/SC/C
Sales and related occupations	Retail salespersons	20,560	85,375	2149	HS/SC/C
Office and administrative support occupations	Bookkeeping, accounting, and auditing clerks	29,360	79,264	658	HS/SC
Office and administrative support occupations	Customer service representatives	29,000	80,731	702	HS/SC/C
Office and administrative support occupations	Office clerks, general	23,860	84,790	939	HS/SC
Construction and extraction occupations	Carpenters	40,980	74,465	1161	HS/SC
Installation, maintenance, and repair occupations	Maintenance and repair workers, general	37,310	79,003	606	HS/SC
Transportation and material moving occupations	Taxi drivers and chauffeurs	24,450	82,020	764	HS/SC
Transportation and material moving occupations	Laborers and freight, stock and material movers, hand	22,700	84,650	1713	HS/SC

Source: Authors' compilation.
a. HS = high school; SC = some college; C = college.

Overall, these occupations fall into two main categories. First are those related to the service and tourism industries of the large casinos and hotels, which are the historic basis of Las Vegas's economy, including bartenders, retail salespersons, maids, taxi drivers and chauffeurs, cooks, and security personnel. These occupations provide stable wages with some possibility of advancement, although in many instances the career ladder can be short, with raises in salary coming more from the length of time on the job and the quality and efficiency of the work done than from the ability to rise to higher positions.

Second are the occupations centering on the expansion of the city's infrastructure and services. For many years, Las Vegas was predominantly a vacation destination and tourist mecca, but in recent years an increasing number of individuals are moving to the city as a permanent home. This has put pressure on the existing resources of the city, and as a result, occupations such as construction workers and registered nurses are more in demand than ever before in this area. If the city continues to grow, occupations related to the expansion of critical infrastructure, construction, and health services will continue to be viable career pathways for the low-skilled.

Overall Findings: Similarities and Differences among the Sites

Some growth occupations are relevant to multiple sites, including registered nurses, computer support specialists, purchasing agents, automobile technicians and mechanics, and electricians. Some of these occupations are the same as those found in the nationally based Jobs for the Future study. First-line supervisors and sales representatives in multiple fields were prevalent throughout the six sites. Table 8-16 shows all selected occupations and the sites where each was relevant.

Most of the occupations identified through this study were unique to one site. Often these occupations were directly tied to the distinctive features of the location's history, economy, and environment. New Orleans's results showed many occupations unique to its location on the Gulf of Mexico. Orlando's and Las Vegas's results demonstrated that there are viable options for low-skilled workers in a tourist-based economy. Las Vegas's results reinforced the theory of the viability of occupations related to the expansion of the city's infrastructure and services. The uniqueness of many of the selected occupations can also be seen in table 8-16.

Future Research

The employment clusters derived from this research show promise as growth occupations with viability for low-skilled workers trapped in persistent poverty due to a lack of suitable employment options. Additional research is needed to

Table 8-16. *Comparison of Growth Occupations across Study Sites*
Unit as indicated

Occupation	Baltimore	Detroit	New Orleans	Orlando	Los Angeles	Las Vegas
Food service managers				x		
Purchasing agents, except wholesale, retail, and farm products	x	x				
Compliance officers, except agriculture, construction, health and safety, and transportation	x		x			
Cost estimators	x			x	x	
Computer support specialists		x		x	x	
Paralegals and legal assistants						
Self-enrichment education teachers	x					
Camera operators, television, video, and motion picture					x	
Registered nurses	x		x			x
Massage therapists					x	
First-line supervisors, managers of police and detectives	x					
Firefighters					x	
Security guards						x
Cooks, restaurant						x
Bartenders						x
Janitors and cleaners, except maids and housekeeping cleaners						x
Maids and housekeeping cleaners						x
Landscaping and groundskeeping workers						x

First-line supervisors, managers of personal service workers			x		
Fitness trainers and aerobics instructors	x		x		
First-line supervisors, managers of retail sales workers		x	x		
First-line supervisors, managers of nonretail sales workers	x	x	x	x	
Parts salespersons				x	
Retail salespersons			x		
Advertising sales agents	x	x	x	x	
Sales representatives, wholesale and manufacturing, technical and scientific products		x	x	x	
Sales representatives, wholesale and manufacturing, except technical and scientific products		x	x	x	
Real estate sales agents		x	x	x	
First-line supervisors, managers of office and administrative support workers	x	x	x	x	
Bookkeeping, accounting, and auditing clerks	x		x		
Customer service representatives	x	x			
Office clerks, general	x		x		
First-line supervisors, managers of construction trades and extraction workers	x	x	x	x	
Carpenters			x		
Tile and marble setters	x		x		
Electricians	x		x	x	
Plumbers, pipe fitters, and steam fitters			x		
First-line supervisors, managers of mechanics, installers, and repairers	x	x	x	x	

(continued)

Table 8-16. *Comparison of Growth Occupations across Study Sites (continued)*
Unit as indicated

Occupation	Baltimore	Detroit	New Orleans	Orlando	Los Angeles	Las Vegas
Automotive service technicians and mechanics	x	x	x	x	x	
Maintenance and repair workers, general						x
First-line supervisors, managers of production and operating workers	x	x	x		x	
Welders, cutters, solderers, and brazers		x				
Petroleum pump system operators, refinery operators, and gaugers						
Inspectors, testers, sorters, samplers, and weighers			x			
First-line supervisors, managers of transportation and materials-moving-machine and vehicle operators			x		x	
Truck drivers, heavy and tractor-trailer				x		
Truck drivers, light or delivery services				x		
Taxi drivers and chauffeurs						x
Sailors and marine oilers			x			
Captains, mates, and pilots of vessels			x			
Ship engineers			x			
Industrial truck and tractor operators					x	
Cleaners of vehicles and equipment		x				
Laborers and freight, stock, and material movers, hand						x
Pump operators, except wellhead pumpers			x			

Source: Authors' compilation.

determine whether shifting national and local market forces have put the occu-pations at risk. Occupations that may become irrelevant in the immediate to near future are not sustainable career pathways for low-skilled workers. However, the results of the research to date do present occupations that can and should be dis-cussed by local leaders and policymakers in the six study areas.

Need for Additional Refinement

In future iterations of this study, the research team will work to eliminate non-viable occupations from those selected by conducting a risk analysis and by con-sulting policymakers, economic development officials, and workforce officials from each metropolitan area. The level of risk associated with each employment cluster will be assessed via a qualitative analysis, in order to account for current policy developments, economic trends, or trade policies that may not have been captured in the quantitative analysis. Risks associated with offshoring, techno-logical innovations, and industry decline will be taken into account, and employ-ment clusters with high levels of risk in any of these areas will be removed from the list of viable opportunities.

Industry sources such as employers, job trainers, and local economic develop-ment leaders in each study site will also be consulted, in order to finalize the list of viable employment clusters. The information gained will help discern whether the occupations previously identified have other risks or challenges associated with them that were not evident in the quantitative data analysis or the qualitative risk analysis.

Potential Uses by Policymakers and Local Stakeholders

Policymakers and local stakeholders have long been in agreement regarding the need to find better-quality jobs for low-skilled workers. Determining viable employment opportunities for the low-skilled population and helping these workers to gain entry into these occupations may help reduce the large numbers of individuals and families living in persistent and repetitive cycles of poverty. Policymakers and local stakeholders are faced with putting the measures in place that will accomplish this task.

Cooperation from all stakeholders—policymakers, educators, local businesses leaders—will be pivotal to effecting change. The research presented in this paper provides local leaders and stakeholders with a short list of starting points. Although these occupations still need refinement, they offer a foundation for discussion among the stakeholders. Holding forums, focus groups, or other types of discussions that bring these individuals together to discuss the viability of the occupations is an essential starting point. Having all relevant parties present and included in the dialogue will help ensure that potential roadblocks are avoided. The discussions can start by generally discussing the viability of each occupation and narrowing the list and can then flow into more detailed strategy development. Strategy will likely include plans to recruit low-skilled individuals for the targeted occupations, train them for the jobs, and, finally, ensure that they are hired by local employers in these occupations. The development of marketing techniques and placement programs may facilitate this strategy.

Notes

1. Jobs for the Future (JFF) is a Massachusetts-based research, consulting, and advocacy non-profit group. For more information on JFF, visit their website at www.jff.org/index.php.
2. Susan Goldberger, Newell Lessell, and Radha Roy Biswas, *The Right Jobs: Identifying Career Advancement Opportunities for Low-Skilled Workers* (Boston: Jobs for the Future, 2005).
3. Employment rate is defined as the number of employed prime-aged adults (age eighteen to fifty-five) divided by the total number of prime-age individuals in the labor force.
4. For state projections information, see www.projectionscentral.com/projections.asp?page= About. Each State Employment Security Agency in cooperation with the Bureau of Labor Statistics uses the Occupational Employment Statistics (OES) survey to gather occupational employment data. These OES data are the basis for the occupational data used in the projections. The data collected reflect the Standard Occupational Classification (SOC). Many occupations are not identified separately in the SOC and are included in aggregate categories not shown on this site.
5. Bureau of Labor Statistics, *Occupational Outlook Handbook,* 2006–07 edition, available at www.bls.gov/emp/optd/optd001.pdf.
6. Ibid.
7. For more information on annual wages, see Bureau of Labor Statistics, "Technical Notes for May 2006 Estimates," at www.bls.gov/oes/current/oes_tec.htm. Annual wages were calculated by multiplying the hourly mean wage by 2,080 hours; where an hourly mean wage is not published, the annual wage has been directly calculated from the reported survey data.
8. For information on programs using the guidelines (or percentage multiples of the guidelines) in determining eligibility, see http://aspe.hhs.gov/poverty/07poverty.shtml. These programs include Head Start, the Food Stamp Program, the National School Lunch Program, the Low-Income Home Energy Assistance Program, and the Children's Health Insurance Program. For a detailed list of programs that do and do not use the guidelines, see the Frequently Asked Questions (FAQs).
9. Ibid.
10. This was determined via a review of state projection websites and the corresponding data they contained. For more information, see www.projectionscentral.com/projections.asp? page=ProjSites.
11. For a list of counties included in the workforce area, please see www.labormarketinfo.com/ library/ep.htm.

12. The workforce area's geographical definition was compared with the Bureau of Labor Statistics' geographical definition of each MSA to see which counties corresponded to both definitions. For a definition of the Bureau of Labor Statistics' MSA boundaries, see www.bls.gov/oes/current/msa_def.htm.

13. The information on the geographical construction of the MSA was taken from the New Orleans website and compared with the Bureau of Labor Statistics website to see which counties were included in both the national and state definitions. The counties that did not correspond were researched on the CPS website to determine the population in relation to the rest of the MSA. For the state definition of the New Orleans MSA, see www.laworks.net/LaborMarketInfo/LMI_OccTopDemand.asp?years=20042014.

14. For further information on WIAs, see www.dllr.state.md.us/employment/jtpa.html.

15. For a list of the counties included in the workforce investment area, see "2006 Maryland Occupational Wage Estimates," www.dllr.state.md.us/lmi/wages/TOC000.htm#footnote.

16. Louisiana Department of Labor: www.laworks.net/LaborMarketInfo/LMI_employment projections.asp.

17. For information regarding pre- and post-hurricane data, see "Questions about Projections," at www.laworks.net/Downloads/LMI/20042014QuestionsonProjections.pdf. The 2004–14 projections include employment changes that occurred throughout the state as a result of the hurricanes. Historical employment by industry trends, which are used as one data source in the development of industry projections, reflect the drop in employment in the last quarter of 2005, the shifts in employment as employers move, closed and reopened businesses, and the gradual rebuilding of the largest metropolitan area in Louisiana.

9

Manufacturing, Regional Prosperity, and Public Policy

Daniel Luria and Joel Rogers

U.S. manufacturing employment declined 20 percent over the decade from 1998 to September 2007. Having peaked near 20 million in 1979, the number of manufacturing jobs has dropped to 14 million, its lowest level since the early 1950s, and as a share of national employment to barely 10 percent.[1] About 40 percent of this recent job loss was visited on the traditional northeastern and north-central "industrial heartland"—Illinois, Indiana, Michigan, Ohio, Wisconsin, and the western parts of Pennsylvania and New York—which contains most of the "older industrial areas" that are the topic of this Assembly.[2]

The broad relevance of manufacturing to these areas is obvious. Its dominance is what made them "industrial" in the first place. Its decline is what now makes them weak. Parts of its legacy—brownfields and blight, older non-college-educated workers with health care and pension claims—now burden their movement forward. What is less obvious is manufacturing's relevance to their future, or that of the United States generally, much less what can or should be done about it. That is the topic of this chapter.

A dominant view is that declining manufacturing employment is explained by causes either natural or positive: a long-term shift in consumer demand away from manufactured goods toward services, and a massive recent increase in manufacturing productivity.[3] An allied view is that although most "routine" American manufacturing jobs will soon be lost to lower-cost foreign competition, the harm to the U.S. economy is small or even negative. American consumers gain low-cost foreign goods; U.S. firms and their workers can, by innovating new products, still capture value in profits and the design and marketing (if not fabrication) of them.

Many, of course, hold a less sanguine view. The U.S. labor movement (now representing only 7 percent of private sector workers, but those still dispropor-tionately manufacturing based) has for years called for some measure of trade pro-tection. Others, recognizing the consequences of manufacturing-job loss on older cities and the minorities and non-college-educated within them, express hope for a partial revival there of "advanced manufacturing," but without indicating how that might proceed.[4] Still others frankly wish that all of manufacturing would sim-ply go away, leaving an America fully occupied by college-educated workers with little to no connection to making physical things. They regard manufacturing's latest gasps as progress in its creative destruction, which will clear the way to real-izing a fully postindustrial society.

Uncontested in this welter of diagnosis, reaction, and prescription is the fact that the United States currently has no national strategy on manufacturing. This nonevent is virtually unique among nations, most of which are far more attentive to the state of their manufacturing base. That they are may reflect their noticing that no successful large nation has ever survived without some self-sufficiency in physical goods, or that foreign policy autonomy is nearly impossible without such. Or it may simply reflect their greater appreciation of the contribution that man-ufacturing makes to their present national economies, or its role in the innovation process necessary to future prosperity. Whatever the reason, we have little of that in the United States.

Here, instead, we hear a good deal about manufacturing's decline and impend-ing death, but very little about what might make it important and worthy of attention. Even today, however, manufacturing accounts for nearly two-thirds (64 percent) of U.S. exports, as well as almost 80 percent of imports. Even though increased exports of services and decreased imports of oil are certainly part of the solution, it is very difficult to see how the United States might balance its chronically negative current account without some significant improvement in our merchandise trade balance. Manufacturing has historically accounted for some two-thirds of private sector expenditures on R&D. In this way and many others, it is deeply implicated in the discovery and innovation process that fuels long-run productivity and national wealth.[5] Average annual compensation in manufacturing, even after a long period of stagnation, leads the private sector—in 2006, $68,859 versus $55,470 in all of the private sector. Its jobs are particularly important for those unfashionably non-college-educated workers who happen to constitute 70-plus percent of our current workforce. Of particular interest to those concerned about economic development, manufacturing has an exceptionally high direct employment multiplier of nearly 2.4—meaning that the 14 million reported remaining manufacturing jobs hold up nearly 20 million others. And so on.[6]

Of importance to the argument that follows is the fact that we also hear almost nothing about differences within manufacturing—no effort is made to distinguish jobs as bad as the worst the service sector has to offer from jobs that involve some of the most skilled application of technology on earth. To introduce here the terms we shall use later in our discussion, no effort is made to distinguish *low-road* manufacturing—typically low-paying, unsafe, environmentally degrading, marked by little investment in training or new technology, competing on commodity production of essentially commodity products—from *high-road* manufacturing—typically "advanced" or "high-end" and certainly "modern" in its use of equipment, marked by relatively high investments in training and new technology, dedicated to continuous process improvement and product innovation, covering some portions of design as well as production, and compensating its workers much better.[7] This failure to make distinctions between different sorts of manufacturing firms breeds unnecessary confusion. More important, it increases the risk of losing, through public inattention, manufacturing jobs that should uncontroversially be worth saving. To put the matter directly: Why, given the at least arguably great importance of manufacturing in our national economy, and the presence of many good jobs within it, would we not want at least to keep those jobs, assuming they could be kept?

To ask this question and think it worth answering does not require blindness to manufacturing's long-term decline, both in absolute and share numbers, in this and other advanced industrial nations; nor does it imply valuing manufacturing activity over other ones (education, health care, even financial and other business services); nor certainty that manufacturing's past importance portends disaster upon its loss. It requires only a bit of common sense. Assume that we want an economy of shared prosperity, good jobs, and the competitive practices that sustain them. We want that in all conceivable sectors of the economy. Why not in manufacturing?

We pursue this question here. Our discussion goes as follows. In the first section, we criticize some of the conventional explanations of manufacturing's decline. In the second section, we identify that portion of it that we think is both worth saving and capable of being saved. In the third, we indicate the sorts of actions required at both the regional and national levels to do that. A conclusion draws lessons from the manufacturing case for regional development policy generally.

Manufacturing Reality

How concerned you are about manufacturing decline depends not just on what value you attach to manufacturing jobs but also how you explain their loss. One common and comforting view on recent job loss is that it is both explained and excused by a tremendous increase in the sector's productivity, coupled with indifferent growth in domestic demand. An allied view puts the United States in the context of the world economy. It holds that high-wage nations will inevitably have less, but could have much better, manufacturing than in the past. "Routine" manufacturing will be shed to low-wage nations, but if rich nations continue to innovate they can retain a large share of manufacturing value even as they lose a good deal of the work and jobs.

We find the first view mistaken, and the second misleading.

Regarding the first—the rising-productivity, sagging-demand story—it is true that aggregate productivity growth in manufacturing has outpaced that of nonfarm business generally, by about 60 percent. But most of that overall growth in productivity is attributable to spectacular productivity growth in a critical but relatively small subsector of manufacturing, namely, computer and electronic product manufacturing (NAICS [North American Industry Classification System] code 334). Measured either on an output-per-hour or multifactor basis, overall manufacturing productivity increased about 50 percent from 1990 to 2004, for a crisp annual rate of growth of 4.4 percent. But NAICS 334, which accounts for under 9 percent of total manufacturing employment, posted gains roughly ten times as great (426 percent on an output-per-hour basis from 1990 to 2000 alone), and was responsible for about 80 percent of the total increase.[8] Productivity growth in the rest of the sector, accounting for more than 90 percent of its employment, was anemic at best, averaging only about 1 percent annually. So job loss couldn't be attributable to great productivity gains, since there simply was little where most of the jobs were.

Even this record may be overstated by the rise in manufacturing offshoring to low-wage countries. As Susan Houseman has recently pointed out, there are anomalies in how the value of inputs from such countries are imputed in final-shipped manufacturing product. At a given level of domestic demand, labor cost savings from offshoring are registered as a decline in inputs, and thus result in an overstatement of domestic output and productivity in meeting it.[9] NAICS 334, a prominent site of offshoring, is a particularly potent possible site of this over-statement. A less fashionable sector, furniture production, is another. Imports there almost doubled from 2000 to 2006 (from $17.2 billion to $30.3 billion), almost all coming from China, and the domestic industry lost more than 20 per-cent of its jobs. But U.S. government figures show an actual increase in domestic production over the period and, given far fewer domestic workers in it, a sub-stantial increase in productivity. *Business Week* recently estimated the existence of some $66 billion in "phantom GDP" over the 2003-to-2006 period because of this overstated domestic output. Sixty-six billion dollars is a small share of an over $13 trillion–dollar economy, but enough to explain 40 percent of imputed gains to manufacturing output over the period.[10]

Finally—less important to the manufacturing productivity numbers but also driving them down—employment in the manufacturing sector is being under-estimated and productivity therefore further overestimated by manufacturing's growing use of (often part-time) contract personnel. Current conventions in gov-ernment accounting assign these to the "employment services" sector, rather than the "manufacturing" sector in which they are working. How big is this phenom-enon? The Employment Policies Institute estimates that the number of contract personnel in manufacturing rose from 34,000 in 1972 to 707,000 in 1997. Con-verted to full-time-equivalent employees, the increase is even more dramatic—from 25,500 to 625,100—because many contract personnel now work much longer hours. In 2004, the Congressional Budget Office estimated that between a bit under a quarter to a bit under a half of all claimed 2.2 million manufactur-ing employment losses from 1979 to 2000 were attributable to the expansion of such contract personnel. A more recent estimate has employment services (those supplying contract workers) adding 8.7 percent to manufacturing employment by direct-hired workers in 2004 (up nearly fourfold from the 2.3 percent they added in 1989).[11] That would reduce productivity estimates by an equivalent amount.

If productivity does not seem to explain manufacturing job loss, perhaps declining growth in demand for manufactured products does. There is, in fact, little evidence of this. Taking cyclical variations into account, U.S. demand for manufactures has remained stable, at about 15 percent of GDP, for the past half century: demand for manufactures grew right along with the rest of the economy. But the Federal Reserve's measure of industrial production shows value-added in manufacturing rising just 21.3 percent over the 1998–2005 period, or 2.8 percent a year, somewhat under the growth in GDP. In manufacturing durables, the increase was even more meager: just 10.8 percent over the period, or 1.3 percent annually, even though durables included the output of NAICS 334, just discussed.

In nondurables, the increase was a much healthier 35.9 percent. But if petroleum, coal, and chemicals (whose output growth was inflated by sharp price increases) are excluded, nondurables output grew a more modest 18.3 percent over the period, or just 2.1 percent annually. Excluding oil-coal-chemicals from both durables and nondurables gives a seven-year output rise of just 1.7 percent annually.[12] It might appear from these weak numbers that manufacturing job loss need not be explained by spectacular productivity gains. Combined with lackluster growth in demand, even very modest increases in productivity—albeit much larger than those we just computed—might suffice. And indeed, everything else equal, they might.

But in fact everything else was not equal. What changed most significantly was trade. Stepping back to get some perspective, we see that from the 1920s through the early 1970s the additive share of imports to and exports from the U.S. economy and the rest of the world was relatively slight, and stable, averaging around 10 percent of GDP. Since the mid-1970s, however, that has more than doubled and now averages about a quarter of GDP. While real GDP has more than doubled since 1978, imports—80 percent of which, again, are nonoil manufactured goods—have quintupled, rising 410 percent in real terms, from $328 billion to $2 trillion in 2006 (in chained 2000 dollars). The increases from 1978 to 1988 were concentrated in steel, automotive, and consumer electronics. Thereafter, and particularly since 1998, the increases have been more broad-based across sectors.[13] Our chronically negative merchandise trade balance shows that U.S.-based manufacturing has simply not nearly kept pace: by 2006, the U.S. merchandise trade balance was $818 billion in the red. Some $233 billion of that was in a massive deficit with China. But negative balances were registered nearly everywhere: with Europe (−$142 billion), Latin America (−$112 billion), Asia and Pacific (−$409 billion), the Middle East (−$36 billion), and even Africa (−$62 billion).[14]

Thus it is not so much that domestic demand is not growing fast enough but that more and more of it is being met from abroad. From 1990 to 2000, the value of manufactured products consumed in the United States actually grew slightly as a share of GDP, from 17.8 to 18.5 percent. But whereas in 1990 domestic manufacturing value-added, at 16.3 percent of GDP, met 92 percent of that demand, by 2000, at 14.5 percent of GDP, it met only 78 percent. By 2006, U.S. demand for manufactures was down to 16.3 percent of GDP, but the share of that met by domestic supply, at 12.1 percent of GDP, was down further, to just 74 percent of the total.[15] The rest—1.5 percent of GDP in 1990, 4.0 percent in 2000, and more than 4.2 percent in 2006—was accounted for by net imports. Total U.S. manufacturing output over the period was flat, increasing less than 1 percent; manufactured imports over the period increased 25 percent. Whatever one thinks of gains from trade, there is no way to explain manufacturing job loss without reference to it. We will return to this.

Moving to the second story—about retaining value, if not jobs—why do we find that misleading? For starters, there is no reason to think that the manufacturing jobs lost in the United States were merely, or even predominantly, the routine jobs that many are happy to see go to other nations. If in doubt, ask any unemployed auto worker. More generally, if "routine" manufacturing were being shed, we would expect substantial growth in the average wages for U.S. manufacturing workers, since the "routine"—low-paying—ones were eliminated. But that is not the case. From 1990 to 2005, the data show, real U.S. hourly wages grew only 5.9 percent, a dismal 0.38 percent annually. Even including benefits, the increase was only 14.9 percent, still less than 1 percent annually.[16]

Two recent studies of consumer electronics—of laptop computers and Apple's iPod—still suggest the plausibility of the retained-value thesis. In both, the United States retains the largest share of income because, even though nearly all the manufacturing jobs are low wage and offshore, most of the profits go to U.S. firms such as Dell, HP, Apple, FedEx, and Best Buy.[17] Does this allay our doubts? Not really, since there are relatively few decently paid U.S. workers employed at these companies. Obviously, computer electronics are an extreme case, and obviously innovation for new products is, ceteris paribus, something the United States should strive for. But for that innovation to directly benefit workers in or around manufacturing, those workers will have to be seen as making some contribution of value. And in the cases given, they generally were not. We did a rough spreadsheet analysis, modeled on the studies cited, for automobiles purchased in the United States. In the auto case, unlike in the consumer electronics examples, the U.S. share of jobs and profits are about the same. This is obviously more favorable for U.S. workers. Yet autos are considered a near disaster, and laptops and iPods are American success stories, despite the untoward distributional consequences.

The deeper problem with this view, however, it what it says about the relationship of innovation to manufacturing, as currently mediated by U.S.-based multinationals. Precisely how much knowledge of making something is needed to know how to improve it is anyone's guess, and almost certainly varies across industries and kinds of product. But we do know that thousands of studies of innovation suggest a pretty close connection between fabrication and invention, especially the multiple incremental innovations that eventually bring whole new worlds into view.[18] And we know that modern production is a famously complex process, typically involving networks of firms and diverse suppliers, with different sorts of spillovers in knowledge and innovation among them, that are hard to build again from scratch once they are lost. We also know that most other countries think of themselves, far more self-consciously than the United States does, not just as stable producers at whatever point their "natural" industrial advantage (say, low labor costs) suggests. They aim to improve their position within that value system, and to reach the point where they, too, can make critical innovations, capture first-leader status, lock in monopoly positions, and otherwise be off to the wealth-generating races. That is why poorer countries such as China and India are investing so heavily in education, and bargaining access to their internal market for multinational promises to locate R&D and other knowledge-intensive activities in them. Certainly, and entirely properly, they have no intention of stopping at commodity assembly of laptops for American middle-schoolers. We also know that U.S. multinationals, whose offshored and then reimported products make up more than 40 percent of U.S. manufactured imports, have no particular interest in improving the position of U.S. workers, nor of the U.S. economy.[19] They are certainly not seeking national comparative advantage, but only a firm-based absolute advantage based on labor arbitrage, which has nothing to do with trade at all. Put these elements together, and it does not seem at all implausible to us that the U.S. domestic economy could eventually lose big chunks of innovative capacity as its lead firms become more and more remote from actual production processes—and that U.S. workers would naturally suffer those losses.

Of course, destroying parts of a country's domestic capacity and moving it offshore may not be good for its population, and is nowhere recommended in the articles of economic science, but it may benefit others. And no moral person would wish unnecessary poverty on anyone, including the roughly 40 percent of the world's population that survives on less than two dollars a day, some billions of whom happen to live in India and China. But the thought that a concern for the poor now motivates U.S. multinationals and banks is risible, and that globalization's effects have been overwhelmingly positive for them only slightly less so.[20] The first responsibility of any democratic government is to its citizens. Other countries manage, without war or rank protectionism, to build and defend comparative advantages that benefit their populations. There is no reason why the United States should not also do so.

To summarize, then, manufacturing in the United States did not shed jobs principally because of a spectacular sectorwide productivity advance in the face of stagnant domestic demand. In fact, the sector is a bit bigger, and a lot "fatter" (that is, less productive), than the conventional story suggests. Increased and almost uniformly negative net balances on trade explain the greater part of recent losses; and about half of this loss is due to U.S. firms themselves. To get a better story on numbers of manufacturing jobs, the United States will have to get a much more accountable set of multinationals, a more competitive domestic manufacturing sector, or both. To get better-quality jobs—meaning jobs that pay better and are safer, less environmentally degrading, and ideally, more interesting to those who have them—the United States not only will have to do these things but also will have to aim deliberately at high-road manufacturing, which means also closing off low-road manufacturing that is stealing some of their business. That will almost surely mean many fewer manufacturing jobs, but ones that are, on average, better.

Making Distinctions

Thus far we have considered variation within manufacturing—for example, the tremendous contribution to stated average manufacturing productivity increases made by NAICS Code 334, the manufacture of computers and electronic products—largely for critical purposes. We now look at variation for constructive ones, to guide the task of raising living standards.

The first and obvious point of variation is sectoral. Looked at through the lens of appropriate regional or even national economic development, the particular shape of this variation—the region's areas of sectoral specialization—is tremendously important. Indeed, we would first define an economic "region" by its common specializations, and a successful region as one that is deep enough in those specializations to be relatively self-sufficient (less needful of imports) in their supply.[21] Current contrary fashions notwithstanding, we take it as all but settled that some measure of specialization is needed for productivity growth and innovation, which are the bases of high wages and dynamic growth.[22] Specialization, of course, has risks, but then so do most useful things; consider fire. It is *neglected* specialization that typically carries the great risk. The iconic case of overspecialization in the United States is the industrial heartland that is so dependent on the auto industry; it effectively makes this point. What first drove its decline was not that it produced too many cars, but that other countries figured out how to build better ones.

Specializations also generally take time and cost to create. So for economic developers, the current range of specialization should effectively be taken as given. It follows that the starting point for almost any effort to increase regional wealth nearly always lies in or around existing specializations. The most promising place to look for adding wealth are specializations with high multipliers and a legacy of past success. Improving them, or combining them in new ways with others, or jumping off from them to something at least proximate, is almost always more rewarding than taking on the task of creating entirely new specializations.[23] This applies to regions specialized in manufacturing no less than others.

Looked at another way, however, through the lens of industry upgrading, the particular identity of sectors subject to such treatment is not important at all. What is important are firms. If broad and rising value-added per unit of labor and capital is what we're finally after, note first that interindustry variance in total factor productivity (output relative to the input of labor, capital, and energy) is much less than variance in value-added per full-time employee (VA/FTE) alone. But note, second, that variance in VA/FTE within sectors is enormous. Returning to the case of manufacturing, for example, at its center—within discrete industries such as electrical appliances; metal-forming; machined dies, molds, and prototypes; and plastics processing—about a third of firms have VA/FTE of less than $60,000; another third, up to $90,000; and the upper third, a median that approaches $120,000, including firms with a VA/FTE upward of $300,000. As you go up the VA/FTE chain within particular subsectors, firms become recognizably more "modern" (using current technology), more "systematic" (applying consistent methods throughout their operations), and more "distinctive" (occupying valued market niches that they defend through continuous innovation).[24] They do things that are new, innovative, nonroutine, and difficult to perform, producing things that are valued well above their cost. They typically spend a great deal on training and new equipment. They generally export out of the region and often out of the country. We shall call such firms more or less *advanced*. By *high-road* we mean advanced firms that share the benefits of the premiums they can charge their customers with the typically better-trained, more involved workers who help produce that premium.

Manufacturing is dominated in its physical operation and employment by 300,000-plus smaller units of fewer than five hundred employees. They constitute the overwhelming share of plants—depending on how measured, between 85 and 99 percent—and about two-thirds of all manufacturing employment.[25] Within this large group as well as beyond, performance on VA/FTE is not, importantly, a function of plant size. There are firms or plants as small as twenty employees that are high-road, and there are firms or plants with five hundred or more employees that are distinctly low-road.

This means that there is widespread opportunity for manufacturing upgrading— here finally defined, simply, as moving firms up the VA/FTE ladder within their industry. We know that higher VA/FTE—not limited by size—is possible, since other firms have already achieved it. And although achieving a higher VA/FTE is not a cookbook exercise, industrial engineers and consultants know in most cases what individual firms need to do to achieve it. There are studies of the effectiveness of interventions made with these small firms, principally through the Manufacturing Extension Partnership (MEP) program of the National Institute of Standards and Technology, which has affiliates in every state. At quite reasonable costs, MEP specialists can achieve very significant—on average, 5 percent, but in some cases 20 to 50 percent—increases in small-firm productivity.[26] The reasons small firms do not typically do this on their own are familiar. They typically lack knowledge of best practice in their industry, and in particular the sorts of practices achieved by the best firms. And they lack incentive to change. Firms do not maximize productivity, but profit, and they can often maintain profits, or at least large salaries for their owner-managers, without the burdens of the changes in equipment, training, labor relations, and much else that are typically required to get on the high road. We will return to the incentive problem later, but the information problem, the MEP experience shows, is definitely soluble.

The vast range of performance across firms suggests not only the opportunities open to them but also a simple distinction between three sorts of manufacturing firms: first, the plants or firms with five hundred or more employees, either big suppliers to OEMs (original equipment manufacturers) or OEMs themselves. The second and third categories, accounting for about two-thirds of all manufacturing employment, include *bad smalls* and *good smalls*. Given their number, and the fact that they present the easiest opportunities for useful intervention and policy discrimination, we concentrate on them here, though throughout what is said of these two groups could be said of their bigger counterparts.

In their present state and inclination, bad smalls, accounting for nearly 50 percent of current manufacturing employment, deserve little policy attention. Their pay and productivity are too low. They tend to have weak regional multipliers, since they do little within-region purchasing. They are not an impressive source of value in their own operations, or through value they bring through export. And by capturing some of the more routine work that better firms could be doing, and typically need to do to amortize their higher investments in new equipment and training, they make the life of the good smalls, or those that want to be good, that much harder.[27]

Then there are those firms, the good smalls, that do deserve policy attention. They could be known immediately by exceptional VA/FTE, and especially also by exceptional wages. But these firms, though certainly worth attending to, definitionally need little help immediately. It is the firms that are just above average but trying to get to exceptional that are the sweet spot for policy. They might be recognized by high performance on some of the known industry practices causing high performance on desirable attributes mentioned earlier, such as modernity, systematicity, and distinctiveness; VA/FTE at least above average for their sector; an average hourly wage about three times the present federal minimum; total compensation for hourly workers of at least half their value-added; health care insurance coverage for most (at least 80 percent) hourly workers, with an employer health care premium of at least $3,000 per covered worker; widespread employee use of computers (more than 67 percent); and low employee turnover (less than 20 percent annually).

Recognizing the distinction between good and bad smalls is probably the single most important step in a policy response to our manufacturing problems. If we fail to make this distinction, a great deal of money could be wasted on firms that, absent wholesale protectionism, have no serious chance of survival, and whose success would do little good for anyone but their owners, beyond providing low-skill employment to those who have not found their way yet into other more promising sectors of the economy. Those workers should be helped, in ways suggested by other chapters in this volume, but not the firms that currently employ them.

The Hard Case

Another way into the tasks of upgrading is to consider limiting cases of competition. Despite the trade figures reported above, American manufacturing obviously competes effectively in international markets all the time. Manufacturing exports, while obviously lagging imports, have also grown spectacularly over the past twenty years. The obvious sometimes bears restating. The United States is still the world's leading manufacturing exporter, and its manufacturing sector still produces, to take a prominent point of comparison, something like two and half times the output of China. But as low-wage countries take a larger share of U.S. imports—either directly or through American multinationals operating there— the question is naturally asked: Isn't this hopeless? Don't other countries' labor-cost advantages make such competition impossible?

The short answer is no, at least not for the "good smalls" (and again, their corresponding "bigs"). Table 9-1, based on case studies culled by the authors from a variety of industries, including access to several proprietary firm studies by the management consulting firm McKinsey & Co., reports unit costs for landed goods from a hypothetical median U.S. and low-wage country (LWC) competitor. It makes a number of stylized assumptions about the cost structures these competitors face. Among these assumptions: that LWC shop-floor wages are only about a tenth of U.S. ones, but productivity is only about a quarter; that purchased services are about two-thirds the cost of U.S. purchased services; that the LWC waste rate (scrap, rework, rejects) is five times the U.S. one, but that material and energy costs are almost as high as U.S. costs; and that the LWC must add 12 percent to its costs

Table 9-1. *Comparison of Costs for Stylized $10 Million Manufacturer,*
United States and Low-Wage Offshore Country, 2006
U.S. dollar, except as indicated

Type of cost	United States	Low-wage country
Manufacturing costs	7,500,000	5,782,793
Nonmanufacturing costs	1,000,000	717,563
Inventory interest expense	49,498	76,330
Receivables interest expense	61,250	61,250
Own-country cost	8,610,748	6,637,936
Duty and freight	. . .	531,035
Logistics and oversight	. . .	166,379
Cost of time on the water	. . .	27,658
Landed cost per $10M sales	8,610,748	7,363,008
Landed cost index	116.95	100.00

Source: Daniel Luria, "Is Manufacturing in the US Toast?" *ManufactLINE*, September 2007, pp. 10–12.

to cover freight, duty, and logistics and asks what the landed difference is in unit costs. The net is that unit costs of the median U.S. firm are only about 17 percent higher than the landed cost of the median LWC competitor. As might be expected, the gap results almost entirely from the much lower wages and fringe benefits of workers in LWC firms. Although half of that gap is offset by the LWC's lower median productivity, and some more of it is reduced by the cost of servicing the U.S. market from offshore (freight, duty, cost of capital for time on the water), a substantial price difference remains.

Now consider what U.S. firms could do about this. Table 9-2 presents their typical options, weighting the effect of 10 percent improvements in different areas by the contribution of the area to firm cost. So, for example, firms could reduce waste further, but since waste is now only about 2.5 percent of costs, that would reduce product costs by only 0.25 percent. More substantial gains can be had by cutting material costs, typically by designing material content out of the product. Lighter products are valued by customers because of their own transportation and handling costs, and this area presents a more promising potential for gain on the order of 4.3 percentage points. Equivalent gains could be had by cutting labor costs, but we exclude that as undesirable. So that leaves increasing productivity and materials savings or, covering the aggregate, devaluing the dollar.

Firms obviously cannot control the dollar's value, but many have already pressed hard on the major levers—in materials and productivity—that are available to them. That they have done so is shown by the fact that, depending on

Table 9-2. *Payoff to Improvement Initiatives*
Unit as indicated

Improvement initiative	Impact of initiative	Landed cost, percentage of low-wage-country median	Reduction in gap
Memo: baseline median		116.95	
Reduce waste 10 percent	Cuts labor, material, and capital cost of scrap, rework, and rejects	116.70	0.25
Reduce material cost 10 percent	Cuts material and weight	112.63	4.32
Reduce pay 10 percent	Reduces labor cost, but tends to increase employee turnover	113.12	3.83
Increase productivity 10 percent	Cuts overtime and employment unless firm grows	112.44	4.51
Devalue U.S. dollar 10 percent	Raises most offshore costs	106.54	10.41
Material + productivity		108.12	8.83
Material + productivity + U.S. dollar		97.71	19.24

Source: Daniel Luria, "Is Manufacturing in the US Toast?" *ManufactLINE,* September 2007, pp. 10–12.

industry, between 15 and 33 percent of U.S. firms already have lower costs than the offshore low-wage median, and the data show that almost all of those that do have higher labor productivity and more product design responsibility than the 67 to 85 percent in their industries that do not.[28] Not a great deal of effort would be needed to move these firms higher up the higher-value-added, lower-cost chain.

All of this said, U.S. manufacturers are competing with a moving target. An International Labour Organization (ILO) report suggests that, in China at least, productivity in the export-oriented portion of the manufacturing sector is growing at close to 7 percent annually.[29] Many U.S. manufacturers, therefore, will need not only to take a qualitative step forward in productivity but also to accelerate their ongoing year-over-year performance. This again, we think, recommends careful targeting of individual firms for assistance—something MEP does not currently do.

But the ILO report also recommends seeking maximum cross-firm efficiency in the supply of upgrading services and support. In addition to reserving these services for firms that either are or are close to being cost-competitive, the easiest efficiencies are achieved by shared supports: quasi- or full-fledged public goods, again in information, but also in worker skills, physical goods such as mass transit or other infrastructure, and institutional supports in the form of higher standards, government purchasing conformed to those standards, and so forth. All of these productive public goods (some call them *productivity amenities*) share two features: they increase firms' efficiency without requiring large increases in private investment, and they raise the living standards associated with a given money wage. Typically, they are most efficiently supplied in cities.

This is potentially of great relevance to the topic of this assembly. In *Metro Futures: Economic Solutions for Cities and Their Suburbs,* we showed that sixteen metro areas had borne the entire brunt of the 1978–88 manufacturing decline.[30] Since then, those and other cities and metros have continued to lose manufacturing at a higher rate than the country as a whole, but the rest of the United States has been hemorrhaging factory jobs as well. Despite the continuing decline in urban manufacturing employment, there is some evidence that incomes in some of the largest cities may be improving as compared to those in nonurban areas. Nonmetro places, which did relatively well in the early 1980s as firms fled high-wage, unionized cities, have since then fared only a little better than metro areas in factory jobs, and they have fared much worse in earnings. Between 1979 and 2001, metro earnings per job rose $7,500, or 23 percent, with half the increase occurring just between 1995 and 2000. During the same twenty-two-year period, nonmetro earnings rose just 1 percent.[31] As table 9-3 shows for the five heartland states mentioned earlier, the largest metropolitan areas all have seen pay increases larger than their states' averages, and larger than those in smaller metro areas.

Historically, metro areas have also enjoyed a significant productivity advantage over nonmetro areas, which helps explain this pay gap.[32] Urban productivity and pay advantages are probably rooted in the sheer scale of cities and in the richer mix of manufacturing-related activities in and around those cities' areas of specialization.[33] This may not bode well for smaller cities, a point we shall return to. In the meantime, however, for all the reasons that cities' density has always helped underwrite a more abundant supply of public goods, they would again be the natural target for the public goods useful in manufacturing.

The Right Policies

What would it take to encourage high-road manufacturing in the United States? Essentially what it takes to build the high road anywhere: higher standards of firm performance, and help in meeting those, in ways that effectively ground capital— retain it in place.

Table 9-3. *Comparison of Employment Profiles and Hourly Wages in Five Western Great Lakes States and Selected Metros, 1998 and 2006*

Units as indicated

State or metro	Manufacturing jobs, 1998	Manufacturing jobs, 2006	Change in manufacturing jobs (percentage)	Manufacturing wage, 1998 (dollars)	Metro percentage of state wage, 1998	Manufacturing wage, 2006 (dollars)	Metro percentage of state wage, 2006	Wage change (percentage)
Wisconsin	593,200	505,000	−14.9	14.02		16.54		18.0
Milwaukee	170,000	132,600	−22.0	14.99	106.9	18.02	108.9	20.2
Appleton-Oshkosh	60,000	48,400	−19.3	15.22	108.6	17.59	106.3	15.6
Michigan	969,700	630,900	−34.9	17.61		21.83		24.0
Detroit-Livonia-Dearborn	142,500	97,100	−31.9	19.63	111.5	25.32	116.0	29.0
Grand Rapids	91,700	73,500	−19.8	14.74	83.7	17.86	81.8	21.2
Ohio	1,030,700	788,100	−23.5	15.79		19.16		21.3
Cleveland-Elyria	198,800	147,600	−25.8	15.45	97.8	19.10	99.7	23.6
Cincinnati-Middletown	149,300	121,700	−18.5	15.20	96.3	19.58	102.2	28.8
Dayton-Springfield	81,900	56,500	−31.0	16.89	107.0	20.28	106.2	20.1
Indiana	688,200	565,900	−17.8	14.97		18.57		24.0
Indianapolis-Carmel	112,500	100,300	−10.8	15.60	104.2	20.82	112.1	33.5
Fort Wayne	46,600	38,000	−18.5	14.89	99.5	17.69	95.3	18.8
Illinois	896,600	680,900	−24.1	13.75		16.03		16.6
Chicago	544,400	390,200	−28.3	13.49	98.1	15.77	98.4	16.9
Rockford	46,200	33,300	−27.9	15.53	112.9	17.87	111.5	15.1

Source: Bureau of Labor Statistics (2007), http://data.bls.gov/PDQ/outside.jsp?survey=sm (2006) and http://data.bls.gov/PDQ/outside.jsp?survey=sa (1998).

One form that this might take for multinationals and trade has recently been proposed by the Horizon Project.[34] It would close the gap between their interests and those of the nation in favor of the latter. Trade deficits could be capped by Congress and enforced either through temporary tariffs or restricted import licensing. The inherent conflicts in the office of the U.S. Trade Representative, which is currently charged with both expanding trade and enforcing trade rules, would be relieved by separating such promotion and enforcement. All current incentives to offshoring would be eliminated, while new incentives would be built into the tax system encouraging high-value-adding domestic investment. World Trade Organization–enforceable labor and environmental rights would be built into all new agreements, and grandfathered into old ones. Of course, there are innumerable problems in actually achieving these results with any certainty or precision, and without the corruptions that have previously attended active trade regulation. In principle, however, the basic mechanisms (or closely allied ones) are straightforward enough, and the goals are clear: box in multinationals that want access to the U.S. market to invest heavily in it. Make the United States thereby more self-supplied. Move VA/FTE up in individual industries.

The Horizon Project posits coupling this constraining program with a more mainstream, "softer" one, centered on increasing human capital, improving physical infrastructure, expanding social insurance, promoting labor-industry partnerships, and more deliberately organizing efforts to promote innovation. This softer program is now widely embraced and is the centerpiece of groups such as the Hamilton Project, whose participants find directive constraints on multinational capital such as those recommended by the Horizon Program anathema.

Our own view is that both programs are welcome, with, again, the caveat that in the Horizon program, much rests on the execution of the details. We are, for example, entirely in favor of partitioning the Office of the U.S. Trade Representative and of abolishing all subsidies to offshoring. We are much more nervous about how import licenses would be allocated in an already preposterously business-dominated polity. And we are more interested in things the United States might do to encourage export-oriented economies such as China to grow their domestic markets.

And, such national and international ambitions aside, we are interested in what a regional approach to high-road manufacturing might look like.

What Does a High-Road Region Look Like?

High-roading firms seek to drive the value of their products well above their cost. They add as much value, and eliminate as much waste as possible, within their sector and share the gains from doing so with workers. A high-road region does much the same, but here the productive unit is not the firm, but the democracy. We stipulate a high-road region to be one that similarly organizes itself to add value, reduce waste, and capture and more equitably share the benefits of doing both, largely through democratic organization. High-road regions seek to accommodate and satisfy capital's interest in profit-making while subordinating that to public interests in equity, sustainability, and democratic power. They do so by providing both resident firms and individuals a range of location-specific public goods, typically beyond the means and certainly the incentive of individual firms to provide, that enable firms abiding by public standards to succeed.

This infrastructure helps such firms directly—with, for example, wage or environmental standards that drive out their low-road competitors, modernization services to upgrade firms, joint marketing, effective transit systems, lowered energy costs, and R&D of all kinds. It also helps them indirectly by its aids to individuals and regional efficiency and equity. It expands opportunities for individual residents to add their own value (education institutions, training) and reduce their own waste (transit again, smart growth patterns to reduce unnecessary individual consumption, energy efficiency in housing). It helps organize regional assets toward the same aims (integrating often-scattered human-capital systems to increase movement through them, pooling regional savings for investment, aggregating other dispersed assets—such as individual energy efficiency—for trading in markets). And, more generally and familiarly, it permits individual residents to enjoy higher levels of shared consumption irrespective of individual income (public safety, education, health care, insurance of all kinds, a clean environment, culture, and so forth). This wrap of social protections and services, and even more traditional public goods, relieves high-road firms of obligations that, because able to, they might otherwise be forced to meet.

The bottom line is this: the abundant provision of these productive public goods in places attracts high-roading capital to those places by increasing its return. But as capital's strategies and local investment come to rely on their supply, the immobility of these goods also serves to *ground capital*. Thus the ability of places to bargain with capital is restored. Regions can demand more of capital—less pollution, higher wages, better labor relations, more investment in the community—than is now demanded by competitive markets, in exchange for the infrastructure that allows capital to meet those demands profitably under competitive conditions. With a nod to Don Corleone, high-road regions can make capital an offer it can't refuse, and should not want to. Such offers go on all the time in the real world, with productive regions exchanging their wealth-generative capacities to get more out of a grounded capital.

But note, finally, the effects in the unreal world sometimes imagined in economic theory or pop journalism and increasing feared by the vulnerable—in which capital is fully mobile and investment across places responds immediately to expected after-tax rates of profit. Under such conditions, the rate of profit is the same everywhere. No single place can lower it. But, equally, none can raise it. So in such a world, non-mobile local populations (among the chief victims of internationalization) get all the benefits of increased efficiency in the places they call home.

We earlier stated that a successful region is one that shares a set of common large-scale specializations, and is deep enough in those specializations to be relatively self-sufficient (less needful of imports) in them. Successful regions are naturally high-road in that they almost naturally add value and capture the benefits of doing so locally. Specialization and self-supply are the key to that. Specialization is needed for wealth generation. Depth in specializations, to the point of self-sufficiency in them, helps ensure regional value capture, while promoting agreement on public goods that will further improve area productivity and efficiency. Finally, success in that helps underwrite the more familiar, favorably redistributive but less immediately industry-tied public goods.

What Should Regional Economic Development Do?

Our prescription for regional development of high-road manufacturing follows, straightforwardly, from everything said thus far. Regions first need to understand the universe of firms they contain, starting but not ending with those in significant areas of specialization. What does the region do more of than other places, and at what scale? How well does it do it compared to other regions, the nation, and world benchmarks—what is its relative productivity? Where in the region is the specialization most concentrated? To whom and where does the specialization sell its output? From whom and where does it buy its inputs? In effect, regions need to map themselves.

We did the beginnings of such a map in the western Great Lakes region in our work on component manufacturing. It showed, not surprisingly, auto parts and machinery as large-scale specializations. Together they made up close to a quarter of all manufacturing output and employment, and an absolute majority of regional exports, and had large if declining regional multipliers. We also discovered that the region buys more and more auto parts and machinery inputs from outside the region and that a large proportion of these purchased imports were products with high electronic content. The products produced by the region's areas of specialization had greatly increased electronic content—for example, engines and automatic transmissions now had electronic controls—but area firms were importing much of that, reducing the regions' level of self-supply.[35] That told us what specific areas the region should concentrate on attracting, what would buttress its existing strengths—and should tell policymakers the same. More generally, while retaining and even increasing its specialization, the region should enrich its mix within the specialization. In this case, that would mean incorporating better activities (more design and engineering), emerging processes (more composites and other lightweight materials), and stronger companies (for example, in the auto industry, more successful firms like Honda, Bosch, and Aisin, and fewer weak ones like Ford, Delphi, and Dana).

With the targets better known, all sorts of strategies can be pursued to reach them. Some of these are individual firm interventions, of the type made by Manufacturing Extension Partnership affiliate centers. Other public goods are improved logistics, energy use, transportation, and community college training that could help support the region's industries. These should, on our recipe, all be targeted efficiently, and that means toward dense areas, where they will also find a disproportionate share of high-road firms and would-be high-roaders. And then there is state purchasing, which should explicitly favor high-roading firms, especially those that are purchasing supplies within the region. No support should be provided to low-roading firms, and as little as possible should be given to those that are not in dense regions. Specialization, scale, self-supply, reconcentration, discrimination. It's not a pretty mantra, but it is the one worth repeating endlessly.

While the heavy lifting must occur in the regions, and especially in their cities, the federal government, too, has a major role to play in making this approach to regional upgrading work to plan. Restructuring will inevitably be business-led, but there is no reason it need be as pathologically business-dominated as it has been to date. Regional efforts to discriminate in favor of high-value activities and the firms that engage in them should be explicitly encouraged. That would be greatly aided by a progressive federalism that sets higher national floors on wage protection, national insurance, and other basic benefits and citizen privileges, but then lets states experiment freely above that level, including on labor rights; gives states the financial wherewithal to experiment (by removing unfunded federal mandates, constraining fiscal competition among states by harmonizing their tax systems, and adopting some measure of the "fiscal federalism" common to other federal polities); and then shares the results of those experiments.[36]

Weak-Market Cities in a Weakened Region

Admittedly, applying this recipe to weak-market cities will be difficult. We are all for making old cities safe and attractive to individuals who possess human capital, but we would not want to place bets on the speed of recovery this strategy will guarantee. And "eds and meds"—educational institutions and medical centers—will likely add little real value to older cities without genuine regional specializations. The quality of "eds and meds" jobs can surely be improved through unionization, higher wage standards, and more worker involvement in making decisions, but will not, except in the rarest of cases, add up to a dominant strategy. The same goes for jobs in the hospitality sector, arts, recreation, and the other amenities sought by the creative class. Markets are quite able to place those services near the spending power of affluent seniors or their children.

A better strategy for an older industrial region, we should think, would be to place fewer but larger bets by concentrating creative thinking on a relatively small number of midsize and larger cities.[37] There, the focus should be on building on proven specializations by deepening local supports for firms in both sourcing and skill supply. Within that focus, there should be active discrimination in favor of good and improving companies, subject to their cooperation in sourcing locally. A region's first priority must be on developing a much richer understanding of its economy. For the western Great Lakes region, we can already describe on a preliminary basis some promising measures to deepen regional specialization.

Metropolitan manufacturing might. Imagine several of the region's governors and big-city mayors launching an initiative to map the economies of their major metropolitan areas. Imagine, further, that having identified more or less noncompeting specialties of each, they lobbied for and won a pilot program among their MEP affiliates to pinpoint world-class performance in those specialties. Imagine, finally, that they put the region's best minds to work pulling many more local firms up to that level.

Attraction of appropriate activity. Imagine the aforementioned governors, armed with their economic maps, identifying holes in the region's self-supply. Imagine, further, a coordinated effort to focus business attraction efforts on plugging those gaps, including a multistate effort to train the attracted firms' workforces. Imagine, finally, that a key attraction inducement would be to connect the newcomers to the increasingly world-class local supply base. With many of the region's specialties involving engines and torque transfer products, it is not hard to enumerate the list of large companies whose presence and sourcing within the region would provide significant new markets to existing manufacturers.

Sewers, cement, steel, and cities. Regions will be spending billions—indeed, collectively, trillions—to renew their water and sewer infrastructures over the next two decades. In-region purchasing of the goods and services associated with this recapitalization could help make many regions richer and more self-supplying. Imagine the governors and mayors mapping sewer and water refurbishment as a multistate regional project. Imagine them organizing the financing and purchasing on a regional basis, turning this critical, metro-focused need into something rivaling the 1930s WPA: steel from Gary and Cleveland, trenching equipment from Peoria, process controls from Milwaukee.

Reducing energy imports. Despite the United States' producing close to two-thirds of the fossil fuels it consumes, most regions are large net importers of petroleum products, natural gas, and coal. The five western Great Lakes states that we describe in this chapter collectively consume more than $100 billion in out-of-region fossil fuels, exceeding even the expenditure on their burgeoning imports of components for cars, trucks, and machinery. The resulting leakage of income saps regional economies of purchasing power that could make their economies larger, and of tax revenues that could make them more livable. Sensible public subsidies for and encouragement of in-region supply of conservation and alternative energy investments make obvious sense. The overlaps among automotive, construction equipment, aerospace, and wind-turbine-component requirements have been widely, and rightly, noted.[38]

Conclusion

Almost any region of reasonable size has organizable assets that, if properly managed, can lift it from chronic economic depression. The lessons to be drawn from manufacturing's decline, we think, have broad applicability to efforts in other sectors. Again, the problem is usually not specialization per se, but inattention to its management. In the case of manufacturing in the older industrial area that has concerned us, it was incompetent specialization within a nation unwilling to share basic social costs across generations, and long fixated on an outmoded economic ideology on trade. Smaller weak-market cities may be sacrificed to this. But the blame has much less to do with transitioning from a manufacturing-based to a knowledge-based economy than with the political failure to organize assets, to dynamically adjust the mix of manufacturing activities, products, and production recipes in anticipation of, and in reaction to, changes in those activities, products, and recipes in competitor regions around the globe.

Second, and in our view critical, regions should aim at self-supply and concentration. The latter is needed for efficiency in public goods, if nothing else. And they are needed for upgrading, and for their welfare effects in a time of relentless downward pressure on wages. And self-supply? Well, self-supply is needed for a quiet life, and a more democratic one. Enthusiasts of business-dominated globalization like to remind us that we need, every day and in every way, to be running and figuring out new ways to outcompete others, whom we bombard with exports as they bombard us. A little more true comparative advantage (natural or acquired) governing trade among regions and nations, less but better trade, less forced integration and more local policy autonomy, less unbridled capitalism and more human development that was environmentally sustainable, would not be such a bad thing.

Notes

1. Bureau of Labor Statistics, B-3, "Employees on Nonfarm Payrolls by Major Industry Sector and Selected Industry Detail, Seasonally Adjusted," September 2007, available at www.bls.gov/pub/suppl/empsit.ceseeG3.txt.
2. Howard Wial and Alec Friedhoff, *Bearing the Brunt: Manufacturing and Job Loss in the Great Lakes Region, 1995–2005* (Brookings Institution, Metropolitan Policy Program, 2006), offer the same share results, but for a slightly earlier period (1995–2005) and larger group of states (including all of Pennsylvania and New York).
3. See Congressional Budget Office, "What Accounts for the Decline in Manufacturing Employment," CBO Economic and Budget Issue Brief, February 18, 2004, available at www.cbo.gov/ftpdocs/50xx/doc5078/02-18-ManufacturingEmployment.pdf.
4. Jennifer S. Vey, *Restoring Prosperity: The State Role in Revitalizing America's Older Industrial Cities* (Brookings Institution, Metropolitan Policy Program, 2007), points repeatedly to "advanced manufacturing" (see pp. 6, 8, 50) as a potential niche for distressed cities, but nowhere defines its attributes or provides guidance on how it might be developed.
5. For recommendations on an explicit innovation policy, see Robert Atkinson and Howard Wial, "Boosting Productivity, Innovation, and Growth through a National Innovation Foundation," draft paper from the Brookings Institution.
6. See Joel Popkin, "Securing America's Future: The Case for a Strong Manufacturing Base" (Washington: Joel Popkin & Co., June 2003) for R&D estimates and a useful review of manufacturing's national contribution and also for multiplier data. Multiplier data also from unpublished Bureau of Economic Analysis data, available for purchase at www.bea.gov/regional/rims/order.cfm. Latest export and compensation figures, respectively, from TradeStats Express, available at http://tse.export.gov, and Bureau of Economic Analysis, tables 6.2D and 6.5D, available at www.bea.gov.
7. On the high-road versus low-road distinction, originally elaborated in the context of reviving metropolitan areas, see Daniel Luria and Joel Rogers, *Metro Futures: Economic Solutions for Cities and Their Suburbs* (Boston: Beacon Press, 1999). The terms are now common. For recent examples, see Joel Rogers, "Build the High Road Here," *The Nation,* April 17, 2006, pp. 25–26, and Thomas Kochan, "Taking the High Road," *MIT-Sloan Management Review* 47, no. 4 (Summer 2006): 16, 18–19.
8. NAICS and general manufacturing productivity numbers are taken from Susan Houseman, "Outsourcing, Offshoring, and Productivity Measurement in U.S. Manufacturing," Staff Working Paper No. 06-130 (Kalamazoo, Mich.: W. E. Upjohn Institute for Employment Research, April 2007).
9. Ibid.

10. Michael Mandel, "The Real Cost of Offshoring," *Business Week,* June 18, 2007.

11. Marcell Istávo and Saul Lach, *Measuring Temporary Labor Outsourcing in U.S. Manufacturing* (Washington, D.C.: Employment Policies Institute, November 2001); Congressional Budget Office, "What Accounts for the Decline in Manufacturing Employment," p. 4; Matthew Dey, Susan Houseman, and Anne Polivka, "Manufacturers' Outsourcing to Employment Services," Working Paper No. 07-132 (Kalamazoo, Mich.: W. E. Upjohn Institute Staff, December 2006).

12. All data from the Federal Reserve, www.federalreserve.gov/releases/g17/g17tab1.txt.

13. See William Zeile, "U.S. Intrafirm Trade in Goods," *Survey of Current Business* (February 1997), pp. 23–38, and William Zeile, "Trade in Goods within Multinational Companies: Survey-Based Findings for the United States of America," November 2003, available at www.bea.gov/papers/pdf/IFT_OECD_Zeile.pdf.

14. At TradeStats Express at http://tse.export.gov, exports, imports, and balances can be accessed as both maps and tables.

15. Data on manufacturing value-added from Bureau of Economic Analysis, www.bea.gov/industry/xls/GDPbyInd_VA_NAICS_1998–2006/xls; for imports and exports, see Bureau of Economic Analysis, "Exports, Imports, and Balance of Goods by Selected NAICS-Based Product Code," various years, at www.bea.gov/newsreleases/international/trade.

16. Bureau of Labor Statistics data show the employment cost index for manufacturing rising from 87.0 to 100.0 from December 1990 to December 2005; see www.bls.gov/web/ecconst.pdf.

17. On laptops, see James Fallows, "China Makes, the World Takes," *Atlantic Monthly,* July–August 2007; on the iPod, see Greg Linden and others, "Who Captures Value in a Global Innovation System: The Case of Apple's iPod," unpublished paper (University of California, Irvine, Merage School of Business, Personal Computing Industry Center, June 2007).

18. We do not attempt to summarize this vast literature here. See Popkin, "Securing America's Future"; Joseph Cortwright, *Making Sense of Clusters: Regional Competitiveness and Economic Development* (Brookings Institution, Metropolitan Policy Program, March 2006); and the many studies of innovation that have been done by those associated with the Sloan Foundation's Industry Studies Program, available at www.sloan.org/programs/stndrd_industries.shtml.

19. Raymond J. Mataloni, Jr. and Daniel R. Yorgason, "Operations of U.S. Multinational Companies: Preliminary Results from the 2004 Benchmark Survey," prepared for the Bureau of Economic Analysis, available at www.bea.gov/bea/ARTICLES/2006/11Novemberx/1106_mncs.pdf, p. 17.

20. See Mark Weisbrot, Dean Baker, and David Rosnick, *The Scorecard on Development: 25 Years of Diminished Progress* (Washington: Center for Economic and Policy Research, September 2005).

21. We agree strongly with Ann Markusen, "A Consumption Base Theory of Development: An Application to the Rural Cultural Economy," *Agricultural and Resource Economics Review* 36, no. 1 (March 2007), also at www.hhh.umn.edu/img/assets/6158/app_rural_cultural_economy_aug06.pdf, that exporting is not the essential feature of successful regions. Any activity in which a region develops scale, performs efficiently, and is substantially self-supplying can power its own growth and income. We are in less agreement that these conditions apply in a nonurban setting.

22. Inter alia, see Vernon J. Henderson, "Externalities and Industrial Development," *Journal of Urban Economics,* no. 42 (1997): 449–79; Vernon J. Henderson, "Marshal's Scale Economies," *Journal of Urban Economics,* no. 53 (2003): 1–28.

23. Thus we agree with Cortright, "Making Sense of Clusters": "The question about whether it is better, in the abstract, to be diverse or specialized, may actually be of limited policy relevance to states or cities. . . . [E]xisting specializations are a fait accompli, and the relevant policy question is what to do with them. . . . If one has a specialization, it probably is wise to do whatever one can to maximize its prospects for success" (p. 42).

24. We draw here on the findings of the Performance Benchmarking Service, an annual survey of small and medium-size manufacturing plants, drawing heavily but not exclusively from the upper Midwest, which now has detailed information on the performance of more than five thousand firms. See www.performancebenchmarking.org.

25. U.S. Department of Commerce, *Census of Manufactures: 2002* (Government Printing Office, 2004).

26. See Ronald S. Jarmin, "Evaluating the Impact of Manufacturing Extension on Productivity Growth," *Journal of Policy Analysis and Management* 18, no. 1 (1999): 99–119, and Eric Oldsman, *The Pennsylvania Industrial Resource Centers: Assessing the Record and Charting the Future,* unpublished (October 1999), available from www.nexus-associates.com.

27. Even institutionally sophisticated economists often believe, incorrectly, that low-road and high-road firms do not compete, that they serve distinct customer niches. But for reasons suggested in the text, in fact they do compete. The high-road firm, or high-road-wannabe, needs a good deal of routine work to keep its expensive machines running a high proportion of the time. See Daniel Luria, "Why Markets Tolerate Mediocre Manufacturing," *Challenge* 39, no. 4 (July–August 1996): 11–16.

28. See Daniel Luria, "Is Manufacturing in the US Toast?" *ManufactLINE,* September 2007, pp. 10–12.

29. See International Labour Organization, International Labour Office, *Key Indicators of the Labour Market Programme,* 5th ed. (Geneva, September 2, 2007), available for download at http://www.ilo.org/public/english/employment/strat/kilm.

30. See Luria and Rogers, *Metro Futures.*

31. See Economic Research Service, "Rural Industry: What Do Earnings Trends Tell Us about the Rural Economy?" (U.S. Department of Agriculture, December 15, 2003), available at www.ers.usda.gov/Briefing/Industry/earningstrends.

32. Edith Wiarda and Daniel Luria, "Fixing What's Broke Where It Counts: Agglomeration in the Core Industrial Economy," *TechnEcon* 1, no. 2 (1989): 1–13, found a 20 percent productivity and wage advantage for metros in which there were at least 3,500 manufacturing workers and in which manufacturing made up at least 20 percent of economic activity. Globally, bets are being placed on manufacturing-intensive, specialized large cities.

33. Fallows, "China Makes, the World Takes," notes specialization by city in China—in memory cards, disk drives, and other particular laptop components. China is building cities at the rate of several "Manhattans" each year. Global demand has never been higher than it is today for cement, rebar rod, I-beams, elevators, commercial plumbing fixtures, cranes, and many types of equipment that are needed for the construction of cities.

34. Horizon Project, "Report and Recommendations," February 1, 2007, can be downloaded at www.horizonproject.us. This work builds on Ralph E. Gomory and William J. Baumol, *Global Trade and Conflicting National Interest* (MIT Press, 2001), which argued that

higher-wage nations' ideal trading partners have wages of at least 25 percent of their own wages; made the basic point that nations, not just firms or their workers, can sometimes lose from trade; and specified the conditions under which trade moves from "win-win" to "win-lose."

35. For example, engines and automatic transmissions today are instructed by electronic controls. Although the western Great Lakes region has nearly maintained its long-standing share of engine and transmission manufacture, it has lost many of the associated controls components as mechanical and hydraulic controls have been replaced by microprocessor-based controls, which are being manufactured in high-wage facilities outside the region.

36. Richard Freeman and Joel Rogers, "The Promise of Progressive Federalism," in *Remaking America: Democracy and Public Policy in an Age of Inequality,* edited by Joe Soss, Jacob Hacker, and Suzanne Mettler (New York: Russell Sage Foundation, 2007).

37. Midsize cities are an interesting case, because they have often been the most specialized, but lacked the scale to merit a full support infrastructure. States and regions can help some of these weak-market cities. For example, the state of New York could direct heating, ventilation, and air conditioning (HVAC) contracts for super-energy-efficient New York City buildings to metro Syracuse to help maintain that city's longtime specialization in air conditioning (Carrier, Westinghouse). Syracuse, for its part, can get busy substituting New York–made components for components now made "offshore" (in Tennessee). The HVAC units will cost slightly more, but the New York and metro Syracuse economies will be larger and more effective, which will pay dividends that dwarf a modest price premium.

38. George Sterzinger, *Component Manufacturing: Wisconsin's Future in the Renewable Energy Industry* (Washington: Renewable Energy Policy Project, January 2006).

PART THREE

Policy and Practice

10

What Makes a Good Economic Development Deal?

Rachel Weber

After government officials diagnose a municipality with the serious ailment we call "decline," they often prescribe the set of remedies known as "economic development incentives." These incentives, which can take the form of property tax abatements, corporate income tax credits, sales tax rebates, tax increment financing (TIF) allocations, land write-down programs (public land sold below market value), and low-interest loans to businesses and developers, are meant to lure or retain private investment in declining areas and form the basis of the deals that are the backbone of local economic development policy. After several decades of dwindling assistance from the federal government and of state-imposed debt and taxation limitations on municipalities, incentives are perceived to be one of the few tools available to reverse the fates of weak economies.

Although incentives date back to the early years of the country's inception, their use has proliferated, the variety has increased, and subsidy packages are larger than they were a few decades ago.[1] The average state now provides more than thirty different kinds of economic development incentives, many of which are administered by local or regional bodies. Some of the poorest states and cities in the United States offer the most generous incentive packages.

But decline is a multifactor disorder. Even though the deals brokered give the impression that the public sector is doing something important to stem job and population loss, disinvestment, and fiscal insolvency, it is not clear that such deals can affect the root causes of decline. Aside from their ability to fuel vicious inter-jurisdictional competition (and therefore deter regional policy solutions), these deals have come under criticism for not being particularly effective ways of strengthening local economies. The public costs per job are often exorbitant, and businesses often close or leave the area shortly after receiving them. In their more candid moments, businesses admit that incentives have little to do with their location decisions, implying that these public monies could be better utilized elsewhere.

Some critics have called for the elimination of incentives across the board, either through federal suppression of these practices or regional no-poaching pacts. Indeed, they have become the target of expensive litigation. In 2006, for example, *DaimlerChrysler Corp.* v. *Cuno*, in which plaintiffs argued that Ohio's investment tax credit violated the Commerce Clause of the Constitution because the credit favored in-state economic activity at the expense of out-of-state activity, made it all the way to the Supreme Court. The Court narrowly struck down the suit, upholding states' ability to offer these kinds of incentives.

Other critics have realized how, despite their frustration with expensive give-aways that result in few public benefits, incentives offer one of the few tools local governments have in their possession to accelerate and direct, if not cause, new investment, particularly in older industrial cities. If economic development agencies intend to continue the practice of offering incentives, these critics argue, they should just do so in a manner that ensures that deals are necessary, transparent, fair, and accountable to local taxpayers. I share this perspective. Rather than do away with incentives, I argue in this chapter that local governments in weak-market cities need to negotiate better deals. They can do so by being more selective about the businesses and developers they subsidize and by including provisions in the contracts (also known as development, redevelopment, or incentive agreements) that govern performance, disclosure, oversight, and enforcement. These provisions formalize the quid pro quo implicit in economic development assistance and protect local governments from giving away too much for too little in return.

The Essence of the Deal

Many older industrial cities are hard-pressed for private market activity that could provide jobs and pay for basic services and infrastructure.[2] They have experienced rounds of deindustrialization, downsizing, and disinvestment due to the general disappearance of manufacturing employment and previous labor surpluses. Businesses have closed or shifted their primary operations elsewhere. Local workers, often highly skilled, have left the area to pursue employment opportunities elsewhere. Real estate investors have drawn back from further acquisitions and sold their holdings, taking money out of the area and switching it to other regions. The physical signs of decline become evident and may lead to potentially negative social and political consequences, including arson, crime, property tax delinquency, public-service reductions, and health hazards.

It is in the context of such desperate need and the increasing global mobility of business that jurisdictions feel the pressure to craft strategies for attracting and retaining investment. Some advocate for minimalist forms of intervention. Michael Porter, a Harvard management professor, has argued that such places (Porter refers to them as "inner cities") possess hidden but competitive assets that must only be better advertised to the business community in order to be attractive.[3] Struggling municipalities often have the advantages of competitive locations, unmet local demand for goods and services, labor surpluses, and in-expensive land that are innately appealing to business. Aside from supplying the requisite building permits, levying (reasonable) taxes, and implementing stream-lined zoning and environmental regulations, Porter sees little role for the public sector.

In contrast, most government officials and economic development practitioners argue for more activist or entrepreneurial forms of governance. They believe that municipalities, especially those battered by previous job losses and business flight, will not be able to compete for capital unless the public sector steps in to offer something of value that can level the playing field and make their location more appealing. Incentives are the tools they can use that attempt to influence the behavior of private capital because they reduce some of the ordinary costs of doing business that the private firm normally would have to absorb into its own revenue stream. Profit-seeking businesses may be more readily convinced to expand their plants, increase their staff, or relocate to new facilities because of the selective reduction of significant expenses. As older industrial cities present such specific challenges as aging building stock and environmental contamination, it is believed that incentives can reduce the burden of these additional costs and bring profits back up to a rate where the market is comfortable investing.

Indeed, the public sector in the United States has taken this activist stance toward economic development since the country's inception. In the early years of the republic, franchises and charters were offered to businesses, particularly those that could produce desired consumer goods that were in short supply, such as twine and beer. Cities and states established banks, borrowed money in global markets to build large-scale infrastructure, and used their eminent domain power to provide private assistance and settle the vast frontier.[4] They competed fiercely among each other for private investment and often resorted to buying stock in companies and even building their own manufacturing facilities.

After experimenting with public ownership and, during the Progressive Era, public jobs programs, the more indirect form of assistance associated with incentives came back in vogue. States and municipalities in the South took the lead, using municipal bonds to build factories with the intention of recruiting manufacturers from New England and the upper Midwest.[5] Not to be outdone, Rust Belt cities followed in the 1970s with generous subsidy packages of their own.

An incentive-based economic development policy is essentially a privatized one; state and local governments pay private firms to create jobs, generate tax revenues, and provide an economic base for the jurisdiction—activities that the government, acting alone, does not think it can accomplish. With relatively little intervention from higher levels of government, municipalities have been left to their own devices to negotiate deals on an ad hoc basis within the loose legal parameters of fulfilling a "public purpose."[6] They have seized this opportunity to provide a panoply of different incentives and craft a variety of deal structures, none of which—even within the same municipality—ever looks entirely like another.

Types of Incentives

The menu can be overwhelming, but in general incentives fall into several cross-cutting categories. Some are offered "as a right" if a business meets certain preset eligibility requirements, whereas others must be negotiated on a case-by-case basis. Almost every incentive is designed to reduce specific business costs: taxes, capital, land, facility financing, training, or operating (for example, utility) costs. The following four categories classify incentives by the form that they take.

Direct expenditures are budgeted, up-front cash payments granted by governments for specific projects; for example, the city council appropriates a specific dollar amount of its revenues to a local development authority, which provides a grant to a company to install new equipment and machinery. They are perhaps the least accessible to fiscally vulnerable jurisdictions. *Debt financing,* whereby a local government offers subsidized, low-interest loans to desired businesses, is also difficult for such municipalities to access, often because of their low bond ratings and their inability to purchase insurance.

In contrast, other kinds of incentives appeal to even the poorest jurisdictions because they do not always require cash on hand or direct investments of public dollars. More common for places with weak tax bases are *tax expenditures,* which are foregone revenues or uncollected taxes such as those available from property tax abatements, income tax deductions, and sales tax rebates. They are called tax expenditures because the tax system indirectly spends revenues by choosing not to collect them in the first place. In other words, tax expenditures are spending programs implemented through the tax system as opposed to spending directly through appropriations. Municipalities with a surplus of vacant or underutilized land may also rely on *noncash or in-kind assets,* such as land write-downs or changing the zoning. Although both kinds of incentives, tax expenditures and in-kind assets, do come with significant opportunity costs (the difference between the market value of land and the reduced sales price is still a public cost), on the surface they look less painful for cash-strapped municipalities because they do not require difficult budget allocation decisions or the raising of new revenues.

Bargaining Leverage

Deal making typically proceeds from the point of an initial request for one of these kinds of incentives from the private sector—a zoning change, an allocation of future tax increment, or property tax relief. Businesses, even global corporations with multiple locations, are not aware of the smorgasbord that exists, so they regularly hire site-selection consultants to help them learn about their incentive options and craft an initial request.[7]

However, some of these requests are for statutory or as-a-right incentives and can be granted without serious negotiations. For example, if a business is eligible to take a tax credit for hiring employees from a designated location (as is common with state Enterprise Zone and federal Empowerment Zone programs), their accountant will simply reduce their corporate income tax burden by the requisite amount come tax time. No more interaction with local government may be necessary.

In the case of the more high-profile incentive packages, where the dollar amount of the subsidy and other elements of the package are customized to the particular business and context, a request for assistance jump-starts what is often a lengthy period of bargaining. City planners, economic development officials, representatives from business associations and chambers of commerce, site-selection consultants, labor unions, and neighborhood associations may all get involved. Especially at early stages of the game, deal making often lacks transparency. The secrecy, local governments argue, is necessary to keep competing jurisdictions from coming in and undercutting a locality's offer. Local officials also fear that the deals will unravel if debated in public and subjected to media scrutiny. Meanwhile, businesses are free to advertise their offers to other states and cities in hopes of procuring the "best" one (that which involves the greatest public expenditure).

The terms of the actual exchange that takes place between the two parties will ultimately conform to the degree of bargaining leverage that each possesses.[8] Leverage implies some situational advantage—the party who has it has less to lose if the deal falls through. However, bargaining leverage is not fixed in time and space; it moves back and forth as the context changes, new deal elements are added, and time passes.

All local governments start off at a bargaining disadvantage; they are handicapped by the fact that they are embedded in space and not as footloose as the private sector. However, the more assets a particular place possesses, the more leverage and decisional autonomy it is likely to acquire. This is why governments with better market positions relative to their competition as potential business locations are often, although not always, better negotiators. Cities with strong office real estate markets, such as Fort Worth or San Francisco, do not typically offer incentives for office construction. In higher-income locations with strong tax bases, residents may prefer slower growth, choosing less congestion over more development and rejecting ballot measures that would raise taxes to support new large-scale development.[9]

Conversely, weak-market jurisdictions start off at a relative disadvantage—vis-à-vis both their geographic competition and the businesses whose investment they seek. Older industrial cities may have to offer more to induce much-needed development and help private investors overcome perceived and actual development risks.[10] Government officials in such places feel more pressure to reverse the negative perceptions of their jurisdictions. Municipalities in declining regions have been known to "give away the store" to lure branch plants and big-box retailers. In various communities in western New York, for example, national retailers such as Wal-Mart, Target, Price Chopper, Kinney Drugs, and AutoZone have been the recipients of generous property tax and state income tax relief through the state's Empire Zone program.[11]

But any locality that has discretionary powers to grant or deny requests for changes in density, tax burdens, and zoning still has a modicum of bargaining leverage. This is because property development and relocation offer opportunities for the business to profit. The subsidies themselves are also perceived to be a source of leverage, which is one of the reasons why local governments continue to offer them. If jurisdictions had no leverage, businesses would have no need to negotiate with them. Moreover, the more frequently a locality participates in such negotiations, the more skills it acquires to build its bargaining power.[12] Repeat games can improve the capacity of localities with few apparent assets.

The Effects of Economic Development Deal Making

Despite their popularity, it is unclear whether incentive deals have a discernible effect on private location choices and hence job and tax creation and retention. Public officials insist that they work, but incentives have been subject to the scrutiny of countless academic studies, most of which have concluded that they are less effective than these advocates would have taxpayers believe. Targeted inducements, on their own, do not appear to dramatically reverse decline or lead to more favorable economic development outcomes than could have been achieved without the use of these incentives.[13] In some cases, scholars have documented the negative and regressive impact of subsidies, especially tax expenditures, on local finances and the distribution of income.

The Limits of Firm-Specific Incentive Use

Researchers have adopted several standard methodologies for judging the impact of economic development programs. Comparing municipalities that use certain incentives (TIF, Enterprise Zones) to those that do not and developing econometric models to measure changes in employment and tax revenues attributable to the incentives, scholars have generally found no or weak relationships between local incentives and the conventional indicators of economic development.[14] Studies that have modeled a hypothetical firm's profit-maximizing calculations come closer to understanding the relationship between incentives and corporate behavior.[15] They have found that public subsidies generally constitute such a small percentage of total relocation and start-up costs that they are unlikely to drastically influence a firm's locational behavior. Surveys that ask businesses how important these deals were to their investment decisions have provided more upbeat results, but are often discounted because of the bias business has in favor of seeing incentive programs continue.[16]

All of these incentives operate against a backdrop of state and local taxes and general government services that themselves change in response to the same economic pressures that may have played a role in the decline in the first place. Researchers have found that relative differentials in tax burdens and services may have a greater effect on business location than firm-specific incentives.[17]

Academic opinion is always shifting, but when researchers have uncovered positive relationships between economic development programs and outcomes, the magnitude of the effects tends to be marginal.[18] This may be because incentives do not directly affect demand for labor; they merely save recipient businesses money. Once the subsidy enters the firm's accounting stream, it is absorbed into the general operating budget and is subject to management's own distributional calculus and decisionmaking autonomy. Perhaps the cost savings from the subsidy is used to add more jobs or make investments in plant, but it could just as easily be used to enable the business to start scoping out alternative locations or product lines. Local governments are less able to influence the more fundamental determinants of job creation, such as access to markets.

Moreover, the expensive "bidding for business" game in which many American jurisdictions find themselves trapped ends up alienating intended beneficiaries—other members of the business community—because they personally did not benefit or benefit as much from the public largesse. In such circumstances, accusations of favoritism, bias, and arbitrary behavior stymie the entrepreneurial goals of cities. Some businesses would rather avoid municipalities with a reputation for high barriers to entry. In other words, the positive effects of incentives may be undermined by the countertendency to repel additional businesses that do not wish to invest the resources to play the game.

The benefits of incentive use need to be weighed against their costs, and some can be quite expensive. A 1998 study found that federal, state, and local incentives cost "every working man and woman in America the equivalent of two weekly paychecks" each year.[19] The political scientist Kenneth Thomas estimated that state and local corporate subsidies in the United States totaled approximately $48.8 billion in 1995 and 1996.[20]

And these expenditures come with additional (often hidden) public costs that may cancel out some of their expected fiscal benefits. In addition to the dollar amount of the subsidy (often calculated in terms of foregone revenues for tax expenditures, in-kind assets, and low-interest loans), the costs of supporting new development with infrastructure and public services need to be taken into account. Take the case of Willamette Industries, a paper giant that wanted to expand its paper and pulp mill in Hawesville, Kentucky. The state offered the company corporate income tax credits worth over $132.3 million and the company was expected to create 105 new jobs (or $1.26 million per job).[21] Despite the new jobs, residents were angered by the fact that the county's sewer and water rates increased 37 percent because, many argued, the subsidized development had exhausted the capacity of the existing infrastructure.

Even though commercial development can be less of a burden on the municipal fisc when compared to new residential development (due primarily to the fact that education is the most expensive public service), new economic activity may end up attracting new employees to the area, rather than just absorbing unemployed or underemployed residents. And relocated households bring with them additional service demands. Their pressures on the local government may occur simultaneously with a dip in expected revenues, because these same revenues were forgiven or committed as subsidies. Research has begun to examine how municipal economic development incentives influence the finances of overlapping taxing jurisdictions that provide other necessary services to households and businesses.[22] When incentives reduce the tax bill of individual developers and businesses (tax expenditures) or redirect new property tax growth away from overlapping jurisdictions to targeted redevelopment areas (tax increment financing), they deny overlapping jurisdictions such as school districts access to property taxes. This may compel them to make service cuts or raise their tax rates.

These kinds of excesses and hidden costs associated with subsidy programs have incensed taxpayers, and widened the divide between advocates of economic development and ordinary citizens. In the 1980s, many subsidized firms, such as General Motors in Ypsilanti, Michigan, engaged in mass downsizing and closed plants, further fueling public outrage at the footloose recipients of "corporate welfare" and the policies that enabled such behavior. The covert nature of these deals and the off-budget financing instruments only increased public dissatisfaction. Critics on both sides of the political spectrum have called for their elimination. Free-market fundamentalists argue that, lacking market mechanisms, the public sector will always be subjected to pressure from private interest groups seeking to manipulate the system for individual gain and therefore can never be trusted to manage its assets efficiently. On the left, critics warn that the cozy relations between business and the public sector promote favoritism and compromise cities' ability to pursue social welfare. These deals may aid businesses and their bottom lines, but do the benefits really trickle down to households and those most in need?

A middle ground has been charted by labor, "good government," and grassroots activists to limit the use of subsidies to cases of clear need and to increase "fiscal accountability." Organizations such as the Minnesota Alliance for Progressive Action, Kentucky Economic Justice Alliance, Maine Citizens Leadership Fund, Los Angeles Alliance for a New Economy, and the Tax Equity Alliance of Massachusetts have monitored economic development deals, exposing incidents of subsidy abuse. Good Jobs First, a Washington, D.C.–based national clearinghouse on information about subsidy use, provides resources to support this movement, including research that links incentives to suburban sprawl, examines the true cost of stadium subsidies, and exposes the political influence of private prison operators. This movement has evolved to the point where economic development practitioners now must cut deals under more public scrutiny and have fewer excuses for entering into bad deals, where they forfeit much but gain little.

In Which Situations Are Deals Likely to Be More Effective?

Even the staunchest critic of these economic development incentives will admit that there are some situations when deal making is warranted and is more likely to influence the investment decisions of the private market. However, with fewer own-source funds, fewer intergovernmental transfers, and increased community outrage at "corporate welfare," cities have been forced to be more selective about the projects and the project expenses they fund. Ideally, selection criteria for a jurisdiction are related to an assessment of the assets of the area, namely, the skills of its residents, the strengths of existing businesses, and the local real estate market. Selection criteria should flow from the unique and comprehensive vision for the individual jurisdiction.

Some places have institutionalized economic development planning, which provides guidance to city staff about which companies make appropriate negotiation partners. For example, the state of Minnesota requires all state agencies and municipalities to develop explicit benchmarks for awarding subsidies.[23] Planning is "a logical prerequisite for informed public action" and can impart consistency to a process that appears ad hoc and secretive.[24]

The following three selection criteria reflect general thinking on the best use of public resources for economic development:

Overcoming site-specific impediments to development. When businesses are deciding between different regions of the country, proximity to key markets and suppliers, labor and transportation costs, and the whims of corporate executives are much more important than any deal the public sector could offer. Once the business has narrowed its choice of location to a particular region, however, it begins to consider the tax burden and physical characteristics of potential sites. Incentives have been found to exert a stronger locational pull on firms deciding between particular sites within the same region.[25] This is one of the reasons why the competition between central cities and their suburbs is so vicious and can escalate so quickly. Older industrial cities are often located in prosperous regions whose suburbs, with their surfeit of greenfield sites, have become proficient at poaching employers from the declining center.

When they are considering discrete locations within a region, businesses will reject sites that come with some site-specific impediment because it will translate into unusually high market interest rates or high equity requirements. Specific risk factors include potential environmental degradation, historic preservation, oddly shaped lots or noncontiguous parcels, or high demolition costs. The uncertainty of clean-up, site assembly, and renovation costs can preclude developer interest. Older industrial cities are likely to possess more of such challenging properties. Shifts in technology and the nature of their economic base left the physical manifestations of their previous economic glory—the railroad yards and multistory industrial facilities, for example—without much demand or value.

Deals are more likely to provide the right amount of incentive (not too much or too little) and to be more necessary when they are used to eliminate a barrier that is keeping an otherwise profitable location from achieving its highest and best use. Large-scale projects, such as a military base conversion, where it is necessary to consolidate and integrate a massive amount of vacant and deteriorated property into the regional real estate market, are often appropriate projects for public-private investment. Many older industrial cities have found that funding the remediation of brownfield sites or limiting the legal liability of new owners has sped the redevelopment of such sites. Remediated sites with good locational attributes serviced by modern infrastructure can encourage the relocation of existing businesses as well as new business formation.

Investing in durable public goods. One of the persistent critiques of economic development assistance is that it often ends up benefiting the profit margins of individual (often absentee) corporations, but has few of the spillover effects necessary to improve the condition of the local economy. Municipalities often pay for infrastructure for one firm, acquire and assemble parcels for one large project, and amend zoning restrictions for one developer, reneging on their commitment to a master plan.

In contrast, stronger and more durable forms of economic development involve a shift from firm-specific subsidies toward the provision of public goods with more widely dispersed benefits. Cost minimization is not the only motivation for businesses to seek out assistance from the public sector; they also want to maximize revenues. Businesses increase revenues by locating near existing businesses and capable workers, and drawing from the collective infrastructure that builds up as a result of successful agglomerations. Local governments can respond to the collective, as opposed to individual, needs of business with deals that will contribute to the business infrastructure even if the individual firm chooses to leave the area—for example, fixing the infrastructure in an industrial park, investing in transit links to commercial zones, or developing training partnerships in concert with business associations and trade unions. Local governments are slowly learning that it is a better tactic to attract employers and employees with amenities that are linked to improvements in living standards than to blindly bid for business.

Even the most resource-poor municipalities must fight against the tendency to give in to an individual firm's immediate and particular needs in order to seal the deal. Instead, they must look past the present demands of that particular business to future uses and try to extend the useful life and maintain the value of their investments. Real estate brokers refer to this sensibility as an "after-market" view, where property owners minimize the possibility that their investments will become obsolete. Similarly, shrewd economic developers take an after-market approach to public financing. The empty shells of difficult-to-repurpose big-box retailers and customized industrial facilities provide a sad reality check for those who do not consider future uses.

Pursuing high-quality, embedded jobs. When it comes to economic development, weak-market cities often have one-track minds: jobs. However, the gross employment figures quoted in the course of negotiations are often nothing more than wishful thinking; job creation is a function of the underlying market context (demand for an individual firm's product) and work practices adopted by businesses—both of which are constantly changing. Moreover, job quality (wages, benefits, and potential for upward mobility) and the extent to which local residents can fill these jobs have just as important ripple effects on the local economy as the absolute number of jobs created.

If a local government is to enter into a deal with a specific business, it should look for businesses in stable or growing markets for their products that adopt sound labor practices—such businesses have the greatest probability of providing sustained benefits to the locality. The vagaries of the global economy affect local labor markets in ways that preclude businesses from making long-term projections about their employment or location. However, some manufacturers operate in product markets where their business practices are standardized and easily replicated by other producers in lower-cost locations around the world. These companies often deprive themselves of a higher-paid, higher-skilled workforce and then become ill equipped to innovate or grow; they have taken the *low road*.[26] In many retail sectors, particular low-margin and high-volume ones, there is a similar competitive imperative to keep costs as low as possible by providing low wages and few career ladders to employees. In the absence of radical population or income growth, consumer markets, typically, are not growing, and retailers are merely competing for a larger share of the existing retail base. This is one of the reasons why some jurisdictions are beginning to withhold assistance for retail development. For example, the state of Arizona recently passed a statute that restricts cities in Phoenix-area counties from providing subsidies to retail developers.[27]

In contrast, *high-road* businesses are those that dominate their growing markets through long-term investments in technology, facilities, and workforce, rather than through cost cutting. The quality of jobs in such firms is higher, and if local residents can fill them (perhaps with the aid of workforce development programs), the multiplier effects are likely to be greater.[28]

High-road firms are often tightly networked to specialized suppliers and markets, some of which may be local. Deals that support critical nodes in agglomerations of local businesses may result in longer-term payoffs because these relations often work to embed subsidized companies in place and make them less footloose. For example, when the city of Chicago and the state of Illinois negotiated a $115 million incentive package of direct and tax expenditures with Ford Motor Company, the company agreed to develop and own an industrial park whose space is leased to several of its lead suppliers. Ford maintains "just-in-time" relationships with its suppliers, and their close proximity was critical to the company's decision to stay in Chicago despite an attractive offer from the city of Hapeville, Georgia, and subsequent rounds of restructuring at the corporate level. The city of Chicago also agreed to develop more than nine hundred acres of nearby land (much of it contaminated) into an intermodal freight transfer center, which is used by Ford and its suppliers as well as by other area firms. This second element of the deal is an example of a public good where the number of beneficiaries is much greater than just the contracting party.

Structuring the Deal

Local governments are becoming better negotiators—instead of asking for nothing or little in return, they are now more demanding when handing out public assistance. Starting in the mid-1980s, they began placing more strings on aid packages, using more loans instead of direct grants, and requiring job and revenue creation projects as conditions for their largesse. Cities began mandating that real estate developers expend resources for the provision of public facilities or services in exchange for zoning changes or infrastructure.[29] Some even engaged in "profit-sharing"—demanding a specified percentage of a subsidized project's cash flow beyond the expected loan paybacks, job creation projections, and property tax revenues.[30]

But even when a jurisdiction is confident that a prospective business or developer will contribute to its economic development goals and the respective responsibilities appear to be fairly distributed relative to each party's contribution, the formal details of the deal—the contractual and seemingly mundane fine print—can affect its chances for successful implementation. Contract law will govern how an agreement is drafted and how courts will interpret it. Contract law is, however, state law, and state legislation plays a critical role in drafting and enforcing good contracts.[31] In the federal system of the United States, states possess more regulatory powers than municipalities and counties, leading courts to defer to states and their legislatures when enforcing incentive contracts. If the legislature expresses a clear intent to promote specific goals through its economic development programs, even judges who are hostile to these goals will find themselves constrained to a degree to respect that intent. Having state statutes that provide guidance for the quid pro quo of subsidy deals allows for the imposition of conditions that might not be attainable in contract negotiations but must be accepted as a matter of law. Moreover, legislation is uniform throughout the state and establishes identifiable standards that reduce destructive intermunicipal competition. The strongest contracts and redevelopment agreements, therefore, are those whose key provisions are reinforced by similar and strong legislation at the state level.

In addition, certain kinds of contractual designs are more likely to lead to better deal outcomes for the public sector and residents. Specific provisions can protect the public sector's assets while offering the flexibility necessary to negotiate effectively with private businesses. Four elements should be present in any arrangement where public and private resources are combined in the name of economic development: cost-benefit and gap analysis; performance requirements; definition of breach, disclosure, and oversight requirements; and enforcement measures.

Cost-Benefit and Gap Analysis

At a minimum, the marginal benefits of a deal should equal or exceed the marginal costs (including any foregone revenues and additional costs associated with the development) after a reasonable period of time. Cost-benefit analysis allows the local governments to compare the present value of anticipated public costs (foregone revenues and additional expenditures on services, such as schools and infrastructure) to the present value of expected benefits (increased jobs, tax revenues and fees, revenues generated by salaries of new employees, and multiplier effects) ex ante. This kind of analysis can alert public officials to the fact that a deal may provide too small or too uncertain a payback for the expected expenses incurred. In Indianapolis, if analysis shows that it will take more than four years for a particular project to offer a positive return to the city, it is not considered a project that is eligible for incentives.[32] Commonly available spreadsheet programs can help the public sector determine the "tipping point" (perhaps less subsidy, more public benefits) at which the deal makes financial sense.

Ideally the public sector's tipping point should be no more than the *gap* that the targeted business or developer must fill in order to make a reasonable profit. The financial gap is the amount of capital required after all the possible debt and equity have been raised in private markets. Recall that the public sector is willing to provide this "last-resort" assistance because the site or location may have some impediment that makes the desired development look, without assistance, financially unfeasible. It is difficult to get an accurate picture of the size of the gap as the private sector has an incentive to understate its expected revenues and exaggerate the costs, while the public sector may do just the opposite. To assist officials in their analysis, incentive programs should require that applicants share their development and operating pro forma and identify gaps that they are seeking to have filled by public assistance.

Performance Requirements

Local governments need to be clear about the different kinds of public benefits they pursue through these deals. In the absence of clear benchmarks, the recipient business is free to make its own interpretation of its obligations in fulfillment of the agreement and the quid pro quo of public assistance may not be legally binding. If a term is ambiguous, its meaning may have to be interpreted by a judge who could overlook responsibilities that may have seemed obvious to the contracting parties at the time of the negotiations but are not written in the contract itself. Local officials also need to set a *benefits period,* which specifies the length of time that the business has to meet these benchmarks.

More local governments are attaching performance standards that go beyond a simple tabulation of the number of jobs expected to be created by a subsidized business.[33] Performance standards typically make incentives conditional on the factors listed in table 10-1.

Local administrators can also structure deals so that the amount of subsidy is calibrated to the number of jobs or investment actually created. Unlike an outright grant of funds, such programs provide no public benefit to the company until it hires and starts paying workers a designated minimum wage. The private benefits can be phased in as the company meets specified levels of performance. These kinds of incentives may be less popular with the private sector, as businesses typically prefer to receive lump-sum payments to cover development and other start-up costs. However, with proper monitoring, they are easier for the public sector to use and enforce.

Definition of Breach, Disclosure, and Oversight Requirements

Without adequate monitoring, the time and care that go into negotiating the deal are worth little. Local governments typically employ one of two types of monitoring techniques. The first type places the onus of oversight on the public sector but requires that specified documents be available for public inspection and audit. A more effective type of provision creates an affirmative obligation on the part of

Table 10-1. *Performance Standards Common in Subsidy Agreements*

Performance standard	State or city	How it works
Job creation and retention	Michigan	A business taking advantage of the Michigan Economic Growth Act (MEGA) must create 75 new jobs if it is expanding its facility within the state; 150 jobs if it is relocating to the state; and 25 jobs if the facility is relocating to a state Enterprise Zone.
Wages and benefits	Indianapolis	Businesses receiving property tax breaks must pay at least 90 percent of the average county wage level for all new jobs created.
Within-jurisdiction preferences	Idaho	Recipients of Community Development Block Grants must "to the greatest extent possible, provide opportunities for training and employment to lower-income persons residing within the unit of local government or the metropolitan area or nonmetropolitan county in which a project is located."
Environmental and labor protection	North Carolina	Businesses receiving tax credits under the William S. Lee Quality Jobs and Business Expansion Act must certify that they have not violated any programs administered by the state's Department of Environment and Natural Resources.
Capital investment and prohibitions to relocate	Connecticut	A low-interest loan program administered by the Connecticut Development Authority prohibits borrowers "from relocating during the term the loan is outstanding or for ten years after receiving assistance, whichever is longer."

Source: Adapted from Rachel Weber and David Santacroce, *The Ideal Deal: How Local Governments Can Get More for Their Economic Development Dollar* (Good Jobs First and University of Illinois, Chicago, Center for Economic Development, March 2007).

the business to provide necessary information rather than to merely allow local governments to ask for the right of inspection. Kansas City, for example, double-checks self-reported data from firms against information derived from the city's employee earnings tax.[34] Recently, Minnesota, Illinois, North Carolina, North Dakota, Washington, Nebraska, and Maine have passed disclosure laws requiring subsidized companies to provide annual reports on total employment, job creation, and the wages and benefits of existing jobs and job creation. After the first significant audit of New York State's Empire Zone program in its twenty-year history, the state of New York sent out warning letters to more than three thousand companies that had failed to create jobs or make investments in their communities.[35]

If a subsidized business is found not to have complied with the terms and conditions of the deal, it may be considered to have *breached* its contract. In contract law, an immediate remedy is available for almost any breach, although in all but the most extreme cases, the party found to be in breach must be given a reasonable time to "cure" the default. In Indianapolis, for example, companies that have not met the outlined performance standards are put on probation for one year.

Enforcement Measures

If during the probation period the standards are still not met, the Indianapolis Economic Development Corporation has the right to cancel the incentive and require the company to repay the percentage of the incentive already received in proportion to the percentage of their obligation they failed to achieve. Indeed, a breach of contract can trigger a host of remedies and damages, many of which, if they are not laid out in the enabling state statute or local ordinance, must be written into the deal structure.[36] A breach may require recipient businesses to pay back all or part of subsidy costs (*clawback*) or pay a penalty such as the interest accrued on a low-interest loan. It may prompt the local government to terminate the subsidy, adjust the amount, or prohibit the noncompliant business from receiving assistance in the future.

Only in rare circumstances will the courts make an assisted business keep its promises. This kind of relief, referred to as *specific performance,* may take the form of a court order requiring some action, such as compliance with a minimum-wage agreement or an injunction forbidding the company from closing its plant. This remedy is available only when "the remedy at law is inadequate," that is, when monetary damages will not fully compensate the granting authority.

All contracts should contain a waiver provision to protect the public sector from losing its rights under the contract if it delays enforcement. Economic development agencies often hold off enforcing incentive contracts, instead attempting to use other nonlegal means to get the nonperforming business to honor its promises. It is also possible that a new administration may wish to enforce conditions where its predecessor did not.

Unfortunately, local governments often draft contracts too loosely, monitor them too casually, and enforce them too weakly to guarantee a return on the public's investment. They resist the use of these contractual protections and enter into deals where they accept the bulk of project risks for little return. Not only did a review of the state of Kentucky's main cash subsidy program between 1992 and

2001 find that at least 27 percent of recipient businesses did not meet their job-creation requirements, but it also found that 38 percent of the time the state made no effort to try to recover any of the lost funds.[37]

Why the reluctance to enforce? When interviewed for a 2002 study, public officials revealed that they did not wish to develop a reputation for "aggressive" and "anti-business" behavior.[38] They did not want prospective businesses to think that entering a deal with their particular jurisdiction implied future tussles with the law, a lack of flexibility on the part of the public sector, and additional reporting requirements and compliance costs. Moreover, municipalities that place conditions on their financing incentives have occasionally found themselves not just lacking support but being challenged by a legal system devoted to the mobility and free agency of capital.[39] The courts are fickle: they have struck down certain city ordinances and contracts between cities and firms; in other instances, they have not enforced a breach of the contracts when companies reneged on their promises to remain in cities, create jobs and revenues, and provide other public amenities.

Negotiation analysis reveals that fears of a bad business climate may be overstated. If businesses are aware of accountability provisions from the start of bargaining, formalizing the quid pro quo in a contract can actually clarify the expectations of both parties, reducing the uncertainty and potential for arbitrary behavior that plagues incentives. One study notes: "When clawbacks are clearly defined, with pro-rate formulas or timelines that specify all-or-nothing paybacks, the risk of nonperformance is clear and can be calculated. Both parties can leave the negotiation confident that the basics have been articulated and understood."[40]

If accountability mechanisms are clear and reasonable, firms may voluntarily repay the incentive if they renege on their promises, obviating the need for any formal legal enforcement. Moreover, better disclosure allows other nongovernmental actors a role in raising community awareness of the deal terms, which may compel companies into better behavior without sullying the reputation of the local government. For example, after local organizations complained publicly of a deal gone bad, ABB Instrumentation announced that it would give back $1.1 million to the Monroe County (New York) Industrial Development Authority when it failed to create the agreed-upon number of jobs.

Conclusion

Negotiating economic development deals is a complex process in which two primary parties, the business and the public sector, attempt to protect themselves from the hazards associated with uncertainty, often divergent interests, and incomplete information. Deal making is also highly fluid and unstructured, which makes it ripe for capture by powerful politicians and corporations. Rather than capitulate to raw and often erratic power, local government administrators need to adhere to a consistent set of principles that will allow them to pursue public benefits tailored to the priority of needs in their communities.

For municipalities and states that have experienced rounds of deindustrialization and disinvestment, such a strategy is not only shrewd, it is also crucial to their survival. Older industrial cities often have histories of conceding to the demands of large employers. In searching for their replacements or trying to pin down those employers that remain, such cities have increased the size of economic development incentives at a time when their fiscal resources are already stretched to the limit. Although the temptation to accept the first offer certainly exists, weak-market jurisdictions cannot afford to waste scarce resources on expensive deals that have minimal spillover effects and leave ample room for businesses to ignore their reciprocal obligations.

Good economic development deals are those whereby local officials have selected the right partner on the basis of an informed understanding of the kinds of business activity that would match the assets of the locality. For example, a surplus of unemployed skilled workers and small machine shops might point toward a sectoral strategy that favors precision manufacturing. An abundance of vacant land near transportation routes can connote high growth potential, a place for building opportunities. Clearly articulated priorities for local economic development strategies that are consistent throughout different agencies of government send a strong message to potential property developers and businesses about a municipality's commitment to a particular sector.

Selection criteria for subsidies must change in tandem with renewed attention to the form that deals take. Older industrial cities were often company towns, whose larger employers exerted a tremendous amount of influence over local politics and planning, and deals there tended to be firm-specific. But good deals seek not to enrich the coffers of one specific company but to benefit the networks of businesses, employees, and service providers within targeted sectors with infrastructure, training, and property development. These amenities may be enough, on their own, to form the basis for an industrial attraction and retention strategy.

When and if the jurisdiction provides financial or in-kind assistance to a specific business, good deals have contractual safeguards to govern the respective obligations. Up-front analysis provides an estimate of the efficient amount of subsidy, performance standards articulate expectations for public benefits, and monitoring systems can evaluate performance. In the event that a good deal goes bad, the jurisdiction has the capacity and political will to enforce agreed-upon penalties for noncompliance.

Despite the advantages of more stringent selection criteria and more efficient contracting practices, good economic development deals, on their own, can only do so much. They cannot force employers to hire unqualified workers. They cannot keep other municipalities and states from making more attractive offers. They cannot ensure that subsidized businesses will experience expanding markets, growing profits, and future certainty in a volatile, globally integrated economy. But even in a context where public influence over private decisionmaking is severely circumscribed, ignoring these basic precautions for structuring state-market relations at the local level would be imprudent, especially for jurisdictions with much to lose.

Notes

1. KPMG Peat Marwick, "Business Incentives and Tax Credits: A Boon for Business or Corporate Welfare?" (New York, 1995); Susan Clarke and Gary Gaile, *The Work of Cities* (University of Minnesota Press, 1998); Ann Markusen and Katherine Nesse, "Institutional and Political Determinants of Incentive Competition," in *Reining in the Competition for Capital,* edited by Ann Markusen (Kalamazoo, Mich.: W. E. Upjohn Institute, 2007), pp. 1–41.
2. Bruce Katz, "Restoring Prosperity: The State Role in Revitalizing America's Older Industrial Cities," report (Brookings Institution, 2007).
3. Michael Porter, "New Strategies for Inner-City Economic Development," *Economic Development Quarterly* 11, no. 1 (February 1997): 11–27.
4. Alberta Sbragia, *Debt Wish: Entrepreneurial Cities, U.S. Federalism and Economic Development* (University of Pittsburgh Press, 1996).
5. James Cobb, *The Selling of the South: The Southern Crusade for Industrial Development* (University of Chicago Press, 1993).
6. Ferdinand Schoettle, "What Public Finance Measures Do State Constitutions Allow?" in *Financing Economic Development for the 21st Century,* edited by Sammis White, Edward Hill, and Richard Bingham (Armonk, N.Y.: M. E. Sharpe, 2003), pp. 27–50.
7. Greg LeRoy, *The Great American Jobs Scam* (San Francisco: Berrett-Koehler, 2005).
8. Rachel Weber, "Negotiating the Ideal Deal: Which Local Governments Have the Most Bargaining Leverage?" In Markusen, *Reining in the Competition for Capital,* pp. 141–60.
9. Good economic deals closely resemble what I have called "ideal deals" in other research and what other authors have referred to as "type II developmental strategies." Edward Goetz defines a type II strategy as "programs in which local jurisdictions require private developers to provide a service or public benefit in exchange for development rights." See Edward Goetz, "Type II Policy and Mandated Benefits in Economic Development," *Urban Affairs Quarterly* 26, no. 27 (1990): 170–90. See also David Elkins, "Testing Competing Explanations for the Adoption of Type II Policies," *Urban Affairs Review* 30, no. 6 (1995): 809–39.

10. Irene Rubin and Herbert Rubin, "Economic Development Incentives: The Poor (Cities) Pay More," *Urban Affairs Quarterly* 23 (Winter 1987): 37–61.
11. Michelle Breidenbach and Mike McAndrew, "Big Breaks for Big Boxes," *The (Syracuse, N.Y.) Post-Standard,* April 1, 2007.
12. Weber, "Negotiating the Ideal Deal," p. 154.
13. For overviews, see Terry Buss, "The Effect of State Tax Incentives on Economic Growth and Firm Location Decisions: An Overview of the Literature," *Economic Development Quarterly* 15 (Winter 2001): 90–105; John Blair and Richard Premus, "Major Features in Industrial Location: A Review," *Economic Development Quarterly* 1, no. 1 (1987): 72–85.
14. Rachel Weber, Saurav Bhatta, and David Merriman, "Does Tax Increment Financing Raise Urban Industrial Property Values?" *Urban Studies* 40 (September 2003): 2001–21.
15. Alan Peters and Peter Fisher, *State Enterprise Zone Programs: Have They Worked?* (Kalamazoo, Mich.: W. E. Upjohn Institute, 2002); Peter Fisher and Alan Peters, *Industrial Incentives: Competition among American States and Cities* (Kalamazoo, Mich.: W. E. Upjohn Institute, 1998); Michael Luger and Suho Bae, "The Effectiveness of State Business Tax Incentives: The Case of North Carolina," *Economic Development Quarterly,* no. 19 (2005): 327–45.
16. Ernie Goss and Jeff Phillips, "Do Business Tax Incentives Contribute to a Divergence in Economic Growth?" *Economic Development Quarterly* 13, no. 3 (1999): 217–28.
17. Therese McGuire, "Are Local Property Taxes Important in the Intrametropolitan Location Decisions of Firms? An Empirical Analysis of the Minneapolis–St. Paul Metropolitan Area," *Journal of Urban Economics,* no. 18 (1985); Tim Bartik, *Who Benefits from State and Local Economic Development Policies?* (Kalamazoo, Mich.: W. E. Upjohn Institute, 1992).
18. Michael Greenstone and Enrico Moretti, "Bidding for Industrial Plants: Does Winning a 'Million Dollar Plant' Increase Welfare?" MIT Department of Economics Working Paper No. 04-39, November 2004; Michael Wasylenko, "Taxation and Economic Development: The State of the Economic Literature," *New England Economic Review,* March–April 1997, pp. 37–52.
19. Donald Bartlett and James Steele, "Corporate Welfare," *Time,* November 9, 1998.
20. Kenneth Thomas, *Competing for Capital: Europe and North America in a Global Era* (Georgetown University Press, 2000).
21. Greg LeRoy, "The Terrible Ten Corporate Candy Store Deals of 1998—State and Local Corporate Subsidies," *The Progressive,* May 1999.
22. Rachel Weber, "Equity and Entrepreneurialism: The Impact of Tax Increment Financing on School Finance," *Urban Affairs Review* 38 (May 2003): 619–44.
23. *Minnesota Statutes* 116J.994.
24. Charles Simeon, "Public/Private Partnerships and Fundamental Fairness," in *City Deal Making,* edited by Terry Jill Lassar (Washington: Urban Land Institute, 1990), p. 88.
25. Bartik, *Who Benefits from State and Local Economic Development Policies?*
26. Bennett Harrison, *Lean and Mean* (New York: Basic Books, 1994).
27. See Julie Farb Blain and Karla Walter, "Arizona Curbs Phoenix-Area Retail Subsidies" (Washington: Good Jobs First, August 23, 2007), available at their website, www.goodjobsfirst.org/news/article.cfm?id=156.
28. Bartik, *Who Benefits from State and Local Economic Development Policies?*
29. Alan Altschuler and Tony Gomez-Ibañez, *Regulation for Revenue: The Political Economy of Land Use Exactions* (Brookings Institution and Lincoln Institute of Land Policy, 1993).
30. Lynn Sagalyn, "Public Profit Sharing: Symbol or Substance?" in Lassar, *City Deal Making,* pp. 139–53.

31. Rachel Weber and David Santacroce, *The Ideal Deal: How Local Governments Can Get More for Their Economic Development Dollar,* handbook (Good Jobs First and University of Illinois, Chicago, Center for Economic Development, March 2007); available for download at www.goodjobsfirst.org/pdf/idealdeal.pdf. See also Katz, "Restoring Prosperity."

32. Rachel Weber, "Do Better Contracts Make Better Economic Development Incentives?" *Journal of the American Planning Association* 68 (2002), pp. 43–55.

33. Anna Purinton, *The Policy Shift to Good Jobs* (Washington: Good Jobs First, 2003).

34. Weber, "Do Better Contracts," p. 47.

35. Nicholas Confessore and Danny Hakim, "Companies Short of Job and Investment Goals Get Warning on Tax Break" *New York Times,* July 31, 2007, A18.

36. Weber and Santacroce, "Ideal Deal," pp. 21–22.

37. Bill Estep and John Stamper, "Bad Breaks: Places like Harlan County Often Can't Hold Jobs or Plants for Long; Incentives Disappoint Time after Time," *Lexington (Kentucky) Herald-Leader,* November 13, 2005.

38. Weber, "Do Better Contracts," pp. 50–51.

39. See, for example, *Westinghouse Electric Corp.* v. *Tully,* 466 U.S. 388 (1984), holding that a franchise tax credit violated the Commerce Clause because it discriminated against export shipping from other states; *West Lynn Creamery* v. *Healy,* 114 S. Ct. 2205 (1994), overturning a state pricing order because it unduly burdened out-of-state milk producers. In contrast, see *White* v. *Massachusetts Council of Construction Employees,* 406 U.S. 204 (1983), holding that an executive order that all construction projects funded by city funds or funds be performed by a workforce consisting of at least half bona fide residents of Boston did not violate the commerce clause.

40. Karin Richmond, "Clawbacks in Economic Development," *Economic Development America,* Fall 2006, pp. 20–22.

11

The Reality of Economic Development in Older Industrial Cities: The Practitioner's Perspective

Jeffrey A. Finkle, Shari Garmise, and Shari Nourick

The effects of globalization are far-reaching, and American cities are being restructured not only by technological changes but also by geographic shifts that have negatively affected many communities, especially older industrial cities. Restoring these older industrial cities to vibrant places to live and work in the twenty-first century requires the application of mechanisms that not only improve the physical landscape but will also facilitate the transformation to an innovative, knowledge-based economy.

The job of economic development is a hard one. In the twenty-first century, economic development challenges have increased in scope and complexity. Practitioners working in a multidimensional, politically fragmented environment have to coordinate across levels of government, package fragmented resources, and continuously develop new strategies and new tools to help their communities compete in a globalizing, hypercompetitive economy. Sometimes they are successful, sometimes they are not. In this chapter we argue that revitalizing older industrial cities requires a long-term strategic approach in which economic development professionals, working in partnerships with other regional stakeholders, coordinate and leverage investment of their core regional assets—land, businesses, people, and knowledge. These investment strategies need to build and sustain the existing base of the economy by opening up land in cities, strengthening and beautifying neighborhoods, and making regional businesses more competitive while also meeting the long-term needs of the knowledge economy by enhancing the talent pool and strengthening research institutions.

To demonstrate the importance of an assets investment approach, this paper will first outline the history of economic development to illustrate how and why practitioners have gone from supply-side policies based on recruitment, marketing, and incentives to more demand-driven policies that invest in endogenous assets. The broadening and refocus of practice represents a response to the increasing economic development challenges that cities and regions face and thus holds lessons for older cities.

After discussing how economic development practice has evolved, we will identify the core components of effective practice, discuss why they are important, and provide examples of what economic development professionals are doing to strengthen their cities' and regions' core assets and transform older industrial cities.

A Brief History of Economic Development: Adapting to a Complex Environment

One cannot fully examine the reality of economic development in older industrial cities, nor the challenges faced by the practitioner, without discussing economic development history. Economic development is an evolving and increasingly complex field, one in which practitioners continuously strive to manage change. The job of economic developers is to find ways to influence the market to better favor their communities. It is challenging work, as practitioners must cope with inadequate tools in an often hostile marketplace and thus not all approaches bear fruit. As markets change and strategies do not achieve hoped-for results, economic developers look for new methods to use in doing their jobs. Thus mapping the transformations in economic development provides us with an important framework for understanding the challenges that declining regions confront and the potential strategies that exist to address them.

The origins of the field of economic development in the United States can be traced to the period of industrialization that began in the 1860s and continued through the early years of the twentieth century. The expansion of the nation's railroad network, as well as its system of waterways, made mass production in factories economically feasible, and firms needed large groups of unskilled workers in regions and urban centers that were well served by the railroad. By the 1920s, most of this recruitment centered on utilities and railroad companies, and included real estate and industrial site development, location assistance, and regional promotional activities. Cities and regions that could offer low-cost land and labor were believed to have a competitive advantage over other regions. Thus the overall goal of early economic development activities was to lower the costs to business.

Until the 1950s, northeastern and midwestern cities, strategically located on port and rail lines, successfully used these tools to build their business base. By the 1950s, severe congestion, high densities, and dirty manufacturing plants diminished the quality of life in those cities while at the same time the construction of the interstate highway system opened up possibilities to invest in the South. Later, urban riots and increasingly active labor unions in the Northeast and Midwest regions also fueled business relocation decisions, and industrial developers recruited these businesses. Thus the decline of the older American cities began, fueled in part by the tools they had once employed to attract businesses to their borders.

The demise of older cities intersected with the urban riots in the 1960s, leading to the creation of a number of federal initiatives intended to aid the cities in 1965, such as the Department of Housing and Urban Development (HUD), the Economic Development Administration (EDA), and the Appalachian Regional Commission (ARC). The creation of these programs marked a clear financial commitment by the federal government to deal with issues of economic distress. Although the EDA was predominantly a rural-focused agency at its inception, it has been instrumental in empowering urban distressed communities as well. The Housing and Community Development Act of 1974, the emergence of Community Development Block Grants through the 1970s, and the creation of the Urban Development Action Grants in 1978 all led to the designation of newly programmed funds to be used for urban economic development projects. Notably, federal programs targeted development dollars to areas marked by poverty and distress, focusing on projects stressing land development, infrastructure, and site assistance, and urban renewal and revenue sharing. Thus federal programs not only expanded the funding available and the geographic coverage of economic development activities, they also established the parameters of economic development practice, which emphasized land assets as the catalyst for development in this period.

From the late 1970s through the 1980s, the federal government decreased its commitment to cities. By this time many voters now lived in the suburbs, and the urban policy budgets were significantly reduced, leaving a gap in funding for the revitalization of cities. In particular, federal funds from the EDA and HUD declined significantly. Jack Kemp, a congressman during the Reagan administration and HUD secretary under George H. W. Bush, did put forth the concept of urban Enterprise Zones, which followed a model program in the United Kingdom, but it took several years to materialize, which it did in the form of the Clinton Empowerment Zone/Enterprise Community Program. In addition, from the 1980s to the early 1990s, private investment and tax policy were encouraged over direct public sector investment as tools to assist development.

This financial retrenchment of the federal government dovetailed with the multiplying problems emerging from economic restructuring, manufacturing decline, and industrial downsizing. Local governments now had to find ways to manage more complex economic challenges with fewer resources. Consequently, local economic development agencies mushroomed across the nation during these years, which established economic development as an essential public activity. In response to high unemployment, business relocation, and downsizing activities, economic development practice broadened its scope, to retaining and expanding existing businesses and encouraging new local business creation. The number of economic tools to support these new strategies similarly expanded to include small-business finance, workforce development training, incubators, and business retention and expansion (BRE) programs. The use of public-private partnerships also became more prevalent as they helped communities leverage private resources in the absence of federal and state resources.[1] Thus the cumulative impact of the changes of the late twentieth century was the expansion of economic development practice from a narrow focus on business recruitment and tax-based tools to a more comprehensive approach that targeted physical and business assets.

The 1990s and early twenty-first century brought us the information technology (IT) revolution, which accelerated the process of globalization and elevated knowledge and innovation to the economic development driver seat. The knowledge economy puts a premium on knowledge development in the form of a talented workforce, engaged research institutions, and entrepreneurs who can move innovation from the lab to the market; new financing tools such as seed and venture capital to support innovative, fast-growth companies; and new business models that enable innovation, faster product cycles, and global integration. Knowledge and skills represent essential components of a business's competitive advantage; thus the ability of a region to provide these becomes a core element of a community's competitiveness. As the nature of business competitiveness has changed, economic development practice has again responded by refocusing existing tools (from incubators to technology accelerators), expanding tool options (small-business finance must include microenterprise to seed and venture capital availability), and moving into entirely new areas of activity such as education partnerships for increasing science, technology, engineering, and math education to enhance people assets, as well as university partnerships for technology commercialization to build knowledge assets. Also during this period, regional economic development entities and strategies start to emerge to meet these new challenges head-on, many of which, such as developing the labor force, are regional in scope. Working regionally is increasingly deemed necessary, but it presents particular challenges to economic development professionals who are employed by single jurisdictions and may be obliged either through legislation or political expectation to work only within their own borders.

The new economy has also brought heightened competition among localities for businesses and investment, another factor that has fueled the use of economic development incentives. Even though these incentives are more often applied to retain, as opposed to attract, businesses, their continued use tends to create obstacles to regional collaboration. Even in this competitive climate, many economic development organizations (EDOs) have reacted to twenty-first-century demands by acting as entrepreneurs, achieving more with less funding, promoting economic development on a broader scale geographically, and collaborating creatively within and among organizations. Both the practitioners and the organizations they work with have become more global, by market-based necessity, grappling with the issues threatening America's older industrial cities through innovation and creativity, acknowledging that businesses tend to scrutinize regions as a whole today, and not just single municipalities.

In sum, as the world has become more challenging and business models have been changing, the tools and strategies used in economic development practice have widened in reach and scope. Economic development professionals have refocused from a narrow concentration on industrial recruitment to a more holistic view that seeks to leverage partnerships to invest in a region's core assets: land, business, people, and knowledge.

Economic Development in Older Industrial Cities: The Challenges of Transformation

The restructuring from a resource-based to a knowledge-based economy has had a tremendous impact on regions once dependent upon manufacturing and other traditional economic sectors. The older industrial cities are characterized by slow or declining economic growth, higher unemployment rates, and lower per capita income than other U.S. cities.[2]

Between 2001 and 2006, the United States lost 2.9 million manufacturing jobs, nearly 17 percent of the manufacturing workforce.[3] In addition to loss of jobs, these regions grapple with other substantial development challenges, including the following:

—Skill and wage gaps between jobs shed and those created
—Depopulation and sprawl as people and businesses leave for greener pastures
—Brownfields and other abandoned properties that mar the health, aesthetics, and economies of neighborhoods
—Insufficient entrepreneurial capacity
—Aging and deteriorating infrastructure
—A lack of supporting institutions and public and private leadership

As we saw in our brief historical overview, economic vitality today is a function of a very different set of competitive assets and advantages than those that initially enabled the growth of the older industrial cities in their heyday. Older industrial cities face the dual challenge of combating deterioration while fostering a transformation to the knowledge economy. To leverage and manage both public and private investment in order to stimulate economic growth in the older industrial cities, economic developers should follow a long-term strategy of investing in competitive assets: their physical, business, people, and knowledge assets.

Twenty-First-Century Economic Development Practice: Investing in Regional Assets

Strategies to revitalize older urban areas must focus on investing in and strengthening the unique package of competitive regional assets within a strategic framework. It will take developing new collaborative partnerships, embracing new policy tools, recrafting social networks, and thinking about the practice of economic development in bold new ways.

In the following, we outline key approaches for building four core assets: the physical environment, businesses, people, and knowledge. Each section will outline the tools economic developers use to achieve this goal and provide examples of what works. Different cases are highlighted because not every city undertakes all of these strategies well.

Investing in Physical Assets

The quality and value of land and buildings in many neighborhoods dissuade businesses, people, and visitors from returning to the city to work, live, and play. On the positive side, cities have substantial physical assets in the form of historic buildings, cultural anchors, and physical amenities such as parks or waterfronts that could be made into attractive, healthy spaces.

Revitalizing the physical assets of older cities is challenging work. Functionally obsolete lot platting and zoning ordinances coupled with the fragmented ownership of building lots and the high incidence of contaminated properties, known as brownfield sites, discourages, and even prohibits, private investment in many neighborhoods in these cities. Attracting private investment is made even more difficult by the ease of obtaining affordable greenfield sites.

Charlie Bartsch, former director of Brownfield Studies at the Northeast-Midwest Institute in Washington, D.C., eloquently describes the problem:

> On the one hand, a manufacturer can acquire an untouched Greenfield site . . . and build a facility to suit with minimal fuss. . . . Or, that same manufacturer can acquire a previously used site in an old, largely abandoned central city industrial district . . . almost surely contaminated . . . at little or no cost. However, the manufacturer will then spend time and money having it tested . . . spend considerable time and money cleaning it up . . . spend more months pleading with bankers to lend on it . . . spend more time and money to provide additional documentation and monitoring, and then spend the rest of his or her natural life worrying if some as-yet-undetected contamination will surface, undermining the value of the property, and possibly bringing with it potentially costly liability claims.[4]

Economic development professionals initiate investment in urban property assets in two ways. The first is that of facilitating private sector development to achieve a public purpose, whereby the EDO expedites regulatory approval and may provide partial financing, infrastructure, and streetscaping and the private sector does the rest. The second way is by initiating a development or redevelopment project; to do this the EDO assembles the land—often by cobbling together oddly sized lots from multiple owners; ensures the economic, political, and environmental feasibility of the project through research and analysis; obtains regulatory approval and may manage multiple agencies to do so; and engages public participation and selects a developer through a request for proposal (RFP) process. The EDO may also provide partial financing and infrastructure development. When necessary, economic developers may use eminent domain to assemble land into a usable site. Although controversial and often challenged, it remains an important tool for the revitalization of declining neighborhoods. Often redevelopment is initiated through a quasi-public redevelopment agency tasked with managing redevelopment to meet a public purpose. Without economic developers engaging in property redevelopment, many projects, especially in areas unattractive to the market, would not come to fruition.

The practitioner's goal is redevelopment and reuse, which means converting a previously developed property into a higher and more productive use for a public purpose, which includes reducing sprawl, using existing infrastructure, and removing slum and blight. To enable redevelopment, securing finance to move land investment forward is central to economic development practice. In deteriorating neighborhoods, or brownfield sites, the private sector does not have sufficient market incentive to invest, or the costs of remediation or redevelopment are just too high. Thus the public sector helps secure sufficient financing to stimulate redevelopment, which would not happen if things were left to market forces alone. There are quite a few financing tools available, including grants, loans, tax credits, bond financing, and tax increment financing (TIF). The practitioner can also use transfer or purchase of development rights, easement donations, land writedowns, and infrastructure improvements to help developers reduce the cost of the redevelopment project. The economic developer pulls together financing from multiple sources, including the federal government, the state, the city, private sector leverage, and foundations, among others. If the redevelopment project involves environmental contamination, then the economic developer will also work with the state to address environmental liability constraints to the developer. The Baltimore case discussed below illustrates how financing is packaged for redevelopment.

As we have seen, traditional tools evolve to meet more demanding challenges. One of the most promising trends for investing in land assets is the practice of targeted area redevelopment. In this practice, a city identifies a physically and economically blighted or underused area (as opposed to a site) and designates it for comprehensive redevelopment. This includes the preparation of a master development plan for the area with extensive public participation, land assembly, securement of financing—usually through tax increment financing and other sources—and implementation of development.[5]

Targeted area redevelopment offers particular redevelopment benefits for economic developers. It is focused, proactive, and comprehensive; it tries to create synergies among sites, and thus increases the overall market appeal of the area (as opposed to a site). It also gains extensive community support through the planning exercise, and the development of an area master plan is one of the strongest ways to align private investment with the city's and community's vision for the area.

An excellent example of this approach is the revitalization of the east side neighborhood in Baltimore, an area in extreme disrepair with a 25 percent unemployment rate, a 55 percent vacancy rate and a home-owner-occupancy rate of 22 percent. The East Baltimore Development Initiative (EBDI) has been the linchpin organization that has coordinated the $800 million redevelopment of the East Baltimore area around Johns Hopkins Medical Institute, which began in 2003. The project brings residents, urban planners, clergy, business, government, and foundations together with the Johns Hopkins University and the Greater Baltimore committee, a regional development organization, to rebuild East Baltimore. The projected eight-to-ten-year redevelopment plan covers an eighty-acre section of East Baltimore and is expected to offer up to 2 million square feet of space for biotech research. The initiative is expected to create four to six thousand new jobs; over twelve hundred mixed-income homes for buyers and renters, including town homes, duplex homes, apartments, and senior housing; new retail facilities; and a set of supportive services such as job training, family counseling, education programs, substance abuse treatment, and community-building activities. Critically, although the project requires relocating 250 households and thirteen businesses, the city partnered with the Baltimore-based Annie E. Casey Foundation to guarantee fair compensation for these home and business owners. The $105 million the project has raised so far combines funding from all three levels of government, Johns Hopkins University, and the Annie E. Casey Foundation.

For cities wanting to better strategically invest in land resources, the following action steps may help:

—First, identify for targeted redevelopment areas in need of significant attention.
—Do a redevelopment plan for each area.
—If necessary, create a quasi-public redevelopment agency to steward the plans.
—Work with your state government to ensure that legislation governing public involvement in redevelopment is simple to implement and administer. In actual practice, complicated legal frameworks impede successful redevelopment work.
—Put together a package of financial assistance and incentives from various layers of government to enable redevelopment in environmentally and/or economically distressed areas.

Investing in Business Assets

The recession and industrial restructuring of the 1970s and 1980s affected both large and small firms, and as a result business retention and expansion and small business development emerged as an essential economic development focus. Communities affected by business closures and relocations responded with strategies designed to retain and strengthen the companies they had in the region. Increased global sourcing of jobs, compounded with the economic strains on distressed urban areas, has increased the importance of investing in existing business.

Studies demonstrate that 76 percent of new jobs and new capital investment come from business—often small firms already existing in a community.[6] These businesses serve as employers, tax revenue generators, community supporters, property owners and renters, and providers of local economic stability. Business retention and expansion and small business development entail coordinating partnerships among public, private, and nonprofit organizations to assess existing business sectors and the financial, technological, and human-capital needs of individual firms within the community, with the aim of curtailing possible layoffs, closures, or relocations; increasing the competitiveness of regional businesses and helping them grow; and encouraging new business growth.

To develop business assets, economic development professionals can work with downtown development organizations, neighborhood organizations, chambers of commerce, and utility companies; the last have a special interest, since existing companies represent the customer base of their service areas, and they have substantial investments in infrastructure. Small Business Development Centers started by the federal Small Business Administration (SBA), which provide regional technical assistance to small businesses, and the Manufacturing Extension Partnership programs of the National Institute of Standards and Technology, whose brief is to find ways to apply new technologies in order to make small manufacturing firms more competitive, are also important local partners to support local firms.

The core components of BRE and small business development are methods to retain and expand existing businesses, strategies to support new small business development, and ways to provide small-business finance to support the first two.

First, BRE programs are typically partnerships among public, business, and community leaders that continuously monitor the strength of existing businesses and help those businesses access the physical, financial, technological, and human resources they need to survive and thrive. To assist local businesses, economic development practitioners act as advocates for the business community's concerns within local and state governments, as well as brokers between the sources of assistance and the companies needing them, collaborating with various service providers that can help the business.

Leveraging public and private resources is essential to successful BRE programs. A good example of how this works is the Steel Valley Authority, a distinctive development agency founded in 1986 in Pennsylvania that focuses on retaining small manufacturers. Within the agency, a nonprofit contractor, Strategic Early Warning Network (SEWN), was created to prevent job loss and retain business in the region. Launched in 1993, SEWN monitors industries in southwestern Pennsylvania and develops strategies to retain key manufacturers and other businesses when they appear to be at risk of closure or major downsizing. Working with employees, management, and owners to save jobs in Pennsylvania, SEWN also provides a variety of professional and consulting services at no charge, such as dealing with financial restructuring, buyouts, succession transactions, labor relations and workforce strategies, as well as operations management issues that affect firms in distress.

Bridging private market solutions with public resources, SEWN has worked with approximately 450 companies representing over 25,000 full-time employees. The network has contributed to the retention or creation of 12,400 jobs since its founding and has saved the state hundreds of millions of dollars in wages that would otherwise have been lost, plus taxes and required income supports. The network, which got its start in ten counties, eventually became active in twenty-one counties and recently expanded to cover a total of forty-nine.

As another example of leveraging public and private resources, the state of Connecticut took a step in helping the state's smaller manufacturers remain competitive by creating a $1 million Small Manufacturers Competitiveness Fund in 2005 through its Department of Economic and Community Development (DECD). The fund allows DECD to provide firms with technical assistance as well as loans for inventory, working capital, and equipment and machinery. By 2006 DECD-approved loans for small manufacturers had helped these manufacturers create or retain 109 jobs. The popularity of the program among small firms led the governor to add another $1 million in funding in 2006.

Second, fostering new small business growth entails entrepreneurial training: keeping those with an aptitude for self-employment in the region and helping them to foster their entrepreneurial skills and start and maintain their businesses there. Entrepreneurial training programs may be managed by economic development organizations, nonprofit organizations, education institutions, or governmental entities. The programs customarily apply a mix of practical training and assistance in acquiring capital. Economic development professionals can assist small businesses and start-ups by providing technical assistance, education and training, marketing assistance, access to capital and other financial alternatives, and legal assistance and by developing businesses incubators to nurture fledgling entrepreneurs with wide-ranging services (such as management assistance and access to finance) as well as providing an entrepreneurial atmosphere.

The Youngstown Business Incubator, in Youngstown, Ohio, is an example of a successful business incubator in an older industrial city. The incubator, which is funded in part by the Ohio Department of Development, seeks to accelerate the start-up and growth rates of technology-based businesses in the region, with most of the focus on developing B-2-B (business-to-business) software application companies. Of the eleven incubators funded by the Ohio Department of Development's Edison Technology Incubator Program, the Youngstown Business Incubator led the state in sales revenue and outside investment in fiscal year 2005–2006. In the same period, the sales of firms in the incubator increased by $10,300,000 and their payrolls increased by $5,344,000. Furthermore, the incubator, located in the downtown area, was recently awarded $2 million in federal grant money through the city, in order to redevelop vacant buildings downtown to expand its facilities.

Third, economic development professionals use a wide variety of tools to expand the availability of capital to local businesses. Small businesses and start-ups face particular challenges in securing capital from private financing markets. Commercial banks, which are the largest source of financing, do not provide loans for less than $100,000 and are usually short- to medium-term lenders. Because small businesses have a high churn rate, they are seen as higher-risk investments, which makes them unattractive to conventional bank loans. Savings banks and thrift lenders increasingly supply small business loans, but they might have a limited product offering. To expand capital options, economic developers leverage local, federal, and private resources to increase available capital to support small businesses.

The most common tools used for small business financing include direct lending, revolving loan funds, micro loan programs (for very small loans), and minority and female business programs. Revolving loan funds are a widely used economic development finance tool that operate on the basis that loan repayment is recycled into future lending. As loans are repaid, the principal and interest return to a loan pool that can be lent to other businesses. Revolving loan funds can be used to provide direct loans to start-up and growing businesses, with the understanding that the funds will be used to create jobs and combat blight in urban areas. Revolving loan funds usually fill the gap between the amount of capital a business needs and the amount conventional lending sources can provide, and they can be used to leverage private sector funding.

State and federal financing programs, especially the SBA, offer a range of small business financing tools. EDA, HUD, and the Department of the Treasury, through its Community Development Financial Institutions Program, are also important federal sources of small business financing.

Supporting existing businesses is a critical component of a well-developed regional strategic investment plan. For the economic development practitioner in older industrial cities, the following action steps are suggested:

—Survey area businesses to understand who they are, their industry sectors, and what their needs are.

—Identify available business resources and coordinate partnerships among public, private, and nonprofit sectors to ensure that businesses have access to the financial, technological, and human capital resources for stability, competitiveness, and growth.

—Act as an advocate to local and state governments for the business community's concerns, and as a broker between the sources of assistance and the companies that need them.

—Foster an entrepreneurial environment in cooperation with the various stakeholders in the community and region in order to provide an infrastructure including support, training, and capital that will enhance small business success.

Investing in People-Based Assets

Globalization and the nature of competition in the knowledge economy have made investing in people-based assets a critical economic development concern. Older industrial cities in particular face workforce challenges on multiple fronts. They have aging populations, highly mobile youths, and a crop of existing workers who lost their jobs in one industry and are either under- or overskilled for new jobs that have been created—while employers note an inability to find suitably skilled workers. Moreover, inner-city and many inner-ring suburban schools are not preparing youths sufficiently for the jobs of today, let alone for the more demanding jobs based on science, technology, engineering, and math proficiency that government economic forecasts are projecting for the future. To manage these multifaceted, multilayered challenges, economic development practitioners are building strategic partnerships with regional stakeholders to find new ways to invest in their people-based assets to meet current workforce needs, widen the overall pool of talent, and put better workforce systems in place to meet the needs of tomorrow.

These partnerships develop strategic approaches to leverage resources to meet one or more of the following objectives:

—Strengthen the incumbent workforce.

—Increase the pool of knowledge workers, including youths in the education pipeline.

—Enhance the skill sets of low-skilled and other disadvantaged workers.

—Better integrate and align economic and workforce development activities through both systematic and ad hoc attempts at building a workforce system.

In practice, activities practitioners undertake to achieve these goals often address several of them simultaneously.

To begin, economic development professionals have been involved in incumbent training for several decades, as it is viewed as a traditional tool for business attraction, retention, and expansion. Incumbent training provides resources to businesses to train their current workers in new techniques, methods, or technologies to better compete in the economy. Through an economic development lens, training is viewed as critical to augment productivity, which enhances business competitiveness, raises employees' wages, and ultimately increases the community tax base and thus a community's service capabilities. Some of the best programs in the country, such as the Wisconsin Regional Training Partnership (WRTP), an alliance of employees, unions, and public agencies, have focused their efforts on incumbent training attached to modernization efforts because of such training's ability to achieve these three objectives simultaneously. WRTP's program was deemed so valuable by local employers that WRTP was able to leverage its success to add an entry-level training piece for disadvantaged individuals into the industry, with good starting salaries. Most U.S. states have available incumbent training funding streams that localities can tap into. The federal Workforce Investment Act also makes incumbent training funds available, but it is often a struggle for communities to access them.

In addition to improving traditional tools, economic development professionals are reaching into new areas of work to expand the pool of knowledge workers. For example, Philadelphia's Knowledge Industry Partnership (KIP) is a partnership-based effort aimed at attracting and retaining knowledge workers in the city through its One Campus Initiative.[7] This program has three integrated goals:

—To increase the number of students from outside the region attending area colleges and universities

—To engage students in economic and social networks to improve their experience in Philadelphia and plug them into its social and economic life

—To achieve, thereby, higher retention rates of knowledge workers after their graduation.[8]

KIP is a pretty young initiative and benchmarks are not yet available, but it represents cutting-edge activity on the part of practitioners to increase the talent pool. Moreover, other regions are following suit, one such being northeastern Ohio's College 360 program partnership.

Incumbent training and attraction and retention of knowledge workers are only part of a strategy to invest in people assets, however. Economic development professionals also build partnerships to strengthen the skills of low-skilled and disadvantaged workers to meet the demands of area businesses. In Cleveland, WIRE-Net (the Westside Industrial Retention and Expansion Network), a local membership-based EDO serving area manufacturers, combines business retention with workforce development services to strengthen manufacturing firms and the Cleveland region.[9] WIRE-Net has been involved in multiple workforce efforts to accomplish this mission. Through its school-to-career programs, WIRE-Net cultivates the crucial relationship between Cleveland high schools and Cleveland area manufacturers to prepare students in Cleveland city schools for entry-level positions in the machining industry. The program provides students with both occupational training and needed life and employability skills. WIRE-Net also provides adult training, employee screening, and management training.

WIRE-Net's efforts help keep city-based manufacturers competitive, open opportunities for area youth and adults, preserve Cleveland neighborhoods, and allow for further economic growth, thus increasing the attraction of the region. In addition, to sustain a healthy workforce, state and local governments, along with the economic development community, should be assessing both the skills needed today and the skills needed for the future. Gathering, filtering, and disseminating labor-market information is another important role that economic developers play to strengthen a region's people-based assets.

Overall, for economic development professionals, working in the world of workforce development has proved particularly challenging. Obstacles include the following:

—The different operational contexts and cultures of workforce and economic development
—Different funding streams attached to different reporting requirements and performance measures
—A limited understanding of the work the other does
—Political leaders who do not understand the importance of aligning these activities
—Nonaligned service areas
—Limited capacity and resources on each side

But these hurdles are being overcome. Economic development and workforce development are finding ways to work together by participating on each other's boards, cross-training, networking, and advocating for legislative changes (for example, Illinois enacted legislation to enable EDOs to work across jurisdictions). Cities also are making organizational changes to better integrate workforce and economic development to strengthen and expand regional workforce systems. For example, Boston located its Office of Jobs and Community Services, which managed job training, within its economic development agency, the Boston Redevelopment Authority, to achieve such a purpose. Through this alliance, Boston has strategically aligned workforce and economic development investments in a way that enhances both areas and leverages a wide range of financing options.[10] For example, because it receives real-time labor market information, the Office of Jobs and Community Services has been able to negotiate with developers to provide just-in-time training to business locations and expansions, so that it can ensure job access and job training for city residents.

For practitioners facing many of these challenges, there are several action steps that they can take to begin:

—They first need to learn about training and placement resources and initiatives available in their area, including but not limited to federal programs.

—They need to familiarize themselves with types of training and placement issues the business community faces by both talking with employers and reviewing data and reports that communicate both state and national industry needs.

—They need to build relationships with community partners, including education institutions and relevant workforce program administrators, and work to discover areas of common interest. Where possible, they should get involved by joining relevant boards and inviting workforce leaders onto EDO boards or committees.

—Finally, once the particular challenges of their community have been identified and relevant relationships have been established, they can build public-private partnerships based on common needs with community partners and businesses to leverage resources and new financing to meet common goals.

—They can engage in activities that meet both short-term and medium- to long-term challenges.

Investing in Knowledge Assets

Leveraging knowledge competencies is critical to meeting the demands of the new economy, globalization, and the accelerated growth of technology. Competitiveness is determined by the capacity of economies to acquire knowledge capital and the ability to apply this new knowledge in the market. Older industrial regions face many barriers to this transformation: a lack of knowledge workers and educational opportunities; social and political institutions and cultures still embedded in their industrial past; and an insufficient base of entrepreneurs and existing companies that can develop, innovate, and apply technologies in these new competitive conditions. Some industrial regions may have substantial assets in the form of research universities or hospitals, federal laboratories, or private research and development (R&D) efforts, but others do not and these may have to find new approaches to creating and bolstering knowledge assets such as a proactive community college.

Economic development practitioners rely on the following strategies to build knowledge assets:

—Partnerships with governments and universities to build up the R&D and technology-transfer capacities of these institutions to promote new technologies and then move them into the marketplace

—Supporting entrepreneurial efforts, because many innovations represent disruptive technologies (which transform industries and business models) and are more likely to be promoted by entrepreneurs than by existing companies

—Leveraging new types of finance, particularly seed and capital, to enable the rapid growth of new innovations

First, one of the most critical elements in a knowledge-based economy is the strength of its R&D and the ability to transfer technology to the market. The Bayh-Doyle Act of 1980 made it possible for universities, teaching hospitals, and federal laboratories to license inventions that originated from federally funded R&D programs, thus creating incentives for research institutions, government, and business to cooperate on innovative projects and turn R&D results into commercial products and jobs.

Universities and research institutions produce some of the world's most cutting-edge technologies and innovations. Technology transfer fosters economic growth by licensing university research and development to private industries or new entrepreneurs that have the ability to commercialize them, which in turn provides additional sources of research and innovation that can be leveraged by the private sector. Effective economic development plans need to incorporate these institutions into the broader regional economic development strategy. The main advantages to pursuing this approach include the following:

—Universities attract and produce highly trained personnel, who provide the technically educated workforce needed by high-tech companies, further attracting those firms to the region.

—Universities generate research and intellectual property that can lead to new products and processes, as well as the creation of new firms.

By facilitating partnerships between the public and private sector and universities, economic development professionals play a crucial role in fostering innovation and technology transfer and the commercialization process. For example, the regional economic development organization Mohawk Valley Edge (Economic Development Growth Enterprises Corporation), in the center of New York State, is an example of how economic developers contribute to promoting innovation and technology transfer in their community. The agency is marketing Rome, New York, as a site for development into a center for the nano-electronics industry. It is playing a key role in the "NY Loves Nanotech" team to promote nanotechnology research and commercialization in the state. New York State has granted $4 million toward construction of the Marcy NanoCenter, which is located at the campus of the State University of New York Institute of Technology and is close to suppliers and nano-electronics industry R&D at Albany NanoTech and Sematech North. Other participants in the project include the Rochester Institute of Technology, the Empire State Development Corp., the New York State Foundation for Science, Technology and Innovation, the University at Albany's College of Nanoscale Science and Engineering, and a few private firms. The project underscores the importance of a region's building on its knowledge assets in close cooperation with industry and academia, with the expertise of the economic development community.

Universities, federal laboratories, and other formal research institutions are not the only agents that can stimulate R&D, innovation, and entrepreneurship regionally. Recent research on Portland, Oregon, suggests that existing firms can play the role elsewhere played by the university in incubating and encouraging innovative spin-offs in the economy.[11] In some places, community and technical colleges have been be able to step into this role; they have shown themselves to be especially flexible in targeting R&D to support existing regional industries.

Second, economic developers strive to build an enabling culture to support entrepreneurship development, including a well-developed support structure for fledgling entrepreneurs. Support structures include programs for opening new markets, establishing business and supplier networks, and providing access to management resources, start-up capital, technical assistance, research facilities, and physical space. Even traditional incubators are being reinvented as accelerators that consist of a package of services and activities that speed up learning processes for entrepreneurs and increase their potential for capitalization. Accelerators focus on developing entrepreneurship in order to commercialize new science and technology innovations, with an emphasis on fast-growth companies that some define as those capable of reaching sales of $50 million within a five-to-eight-year period.

Third, one of the challenges to knowledge development is the lack of available "patient" capital that can support new, usually noncollateralized ideas for the first few years, the period often needed to develop prototypes and build markets before the ideas, and the firms, can generate revenue. Once launched, these firms have the potential for high rates of return. Debt capital from banks does not support this type of business development trajectory. Supporting this layer of the market means providing access to equity funders such as venture and seed capital firms and angel investors, who are private individuals who provide start-up equity. Venture capital funds seek high rates of return through equity investments in early-stage high-growth firms, meaning that only a small set of companies—those with the potential to provide large investment returns—will be able to profit from access to venture capital.

Generally, venture capital funders are located in regions already marked by dynamic, innovative companies. The lack of available equity capital marks older industrial regions. Finding ways to leverage equity capital is a key concern of the economic development community. Economic development has four main strategies for encouraging the formation of venture and seed capital:

—To educate entrepreneurs and others on the specifics of venture and seed investing to prepare them to access these funds

—To promote regional entrepreneurs to equity investors and to broker relationships between equity investors and entrepreneurs

—To create equity capital targeted to an existing financial gap or specific industrial sector

—To develop equity capital to build a regional or state-based seed and venture capital industry[12]

The Ben Franklin Technology Partnership (BFTP) program in Pennsylvania has been a model for innovation and technology-based development, focusing on providing equity financing for technology-based companies and acceleration services to the entrepreneurial community since its creation in 1982. One practitioner's assessment of the BFTP is that it has been "the most outstanding policy innovation in the last thirty years," a sentiment echoed by many in the economic development community.

BFTP can also be seen as an accelerator because it not only provides equity funding but also embeds its clients in a range of networks and management, consulting, and business services that entrepreneurs need to survive and grow. The BFTP has proved its effectiveness, remaining the most important single source of seed capital for start-up companies in the state of Pennsylvania. With four regional centers serving companies located statewide, they invest risk capital in emerging technology-based enterprises as well as established businesses. From 1989 to 2001, BFTP contributed $8 billion to the state's economy and helped to create 93,105 jobs and also yielded almost $23 per dollar spent in additional state revenues in the same time period.[13]

Detroit Renaissance is another example of a development entity that is leveraging the connection between innovation and entrepreneurship by raising capital through partnerships to improve the city's competitiveness. In 2007, Detroit Renaissance announced the launch of a venture capital fund of at least $100 million to spur innovation and entrepreneurship in the region; the idea was to invest in venture capital firms to support their investments, rather than making direct investments in the companies. The hope is that the fund will help generate an increased volume of funding for tech start-ups and university spin-offs. The initiative will function in synergy with the state's Twenty-First-Century Jobs Fund, which focuses on emerging technology sectors in order to foster economic growth in life sciences, alternative energy, and advanced automotive technologies.

Venture capital is just part of what it takes to launch start-up companies, and studies from the University of New Hampshire's Center for Venture Research demonstrate that early-stage capital, known as *pre-seed, seed,* and *angel funding,* are the drivers in starting and growing the new firms that create future jobs and attract new capital. Angel investing has long been an important source of financial support and mentoring for new and growing businesses, linking the individual and equity investor and providing the larger source of seed capital. Angels prefer to invest in seed and start-up stages of entrepreneurial ventures, usually investing $100,000 to $1 million. Angel investors of a region may at times group together to fill a funding gap for new firms, investing approximately $500,000 to $2 million, sums that are too small for the venture capitalist and too large for the single angel investor.[14]

The role of economic development professionals in fostering the knowledge assets of a region is essential for the transition to the New Economy. By recognizing the importance of these assets and finding the means to capitalize on their potential, the economic development practitioner serves as a catalyst among all stakeholders, contributing to the competitiveness of their cities and regions in the rapidly changing global economy. By strategically placing these goals in an overarching investment framework, knowledge development can synergize, and be synergized by, all other components; the Youngstown incubator—supporting entrepreneurship, knowledge development, and urban revitalization—aims to achieve this.

To effectively apply these strategies in older industrial cities, the economic development practitioner can take the following steps:

—Identify the region's strengths in both industry and the higher education system or other research entities (hospitals, federal laboratories, private firms) and build on the strategic areas that will enhance the existing R&D infrastructure.

—Build relationships and partnerships with university agencies, departments and faculty, research institutions, regional agencies, equity investors, local industry engaged in R&D, and other business support entities and service providers who can assist with relevant economic development endeavors. These relationships need not all be regional. It may be necessary to build relationships with nonlocal venture capital firms specializing in investment in industries relevant to one's economic base.

—Use these relationships and partnerships at the highest levels, bringing together the top people in the region in academia, industry, and local government to establish well founded, long-term plans in the implementation of all strategies, whether it be attracting high-technology firms, fostering R&D, or raising capital.

Challenges and Opportunities for the Twenty-First Century

Economic development in the twenty-first century has become more complex and more challenging than anything that has gone before. As problems compound, economic development professionals have responded by developing new tools, new partnerships, and new approaches to enable their communities to compete more effectively in the global market. In this chapter we argue that for older industrial regions to transform their economies they must develop a strategic approach that aligns and synergizes investment in the region's land, business, people, and knowledge assets. This will not be easy. It may entail taking high risks without guaranteed outcomes.

As well as the economic and structural challenges that we have outlined in this paper, revitalizing urban industrial regions faces many political challenges that stamp each region's portfolio of strategies and establish parameters in which economic developers must work. In this last section, we outline those challenges. Although they pose difficulties, if mastered, they also offer opportunities for change.

First, resources are fragmented among multiple stakeholders across levels of government. This is why a regional strategic approach is so crucial, yet so difficult to achieve. Getting political leaders, the media, the public, businesses, and other stakeholders on the same page can be a significant undertaking. Of course, economic developers typically work in partnerships, and reversing decline means even more partnerships with more stakeholders and the alignment of activities across sectors, partnerships, and geographies. Legislation and political expectation often confine economic developers to work within their jurisdictional boundaries, creating additional obstacles to successful regional collaboration. Moreover, many of these stakeholders, like economic developers, are themselves in a state of transformation. Universities, schools, workforce development professionals, property developers, finance agencies, government agencies, chambers of commerce, community colleges, and many others, too, are adapting to changes wrought by globalization and new technologies. Everyone is in learning, reacting, adapting mode. Although this complicates aligning activities, it also opens the door to evolving together and puts pressure on all stakeholders to do so.

Second, the increasing focus on competitiveness and productivity improvements of enterprises in the twenty-first century may increase community wealth but may not create jobs, at least not in the short term. Economic developers have traditionally been benchmarked by their ability to create quantities of jobs within their jurisdictions in a fairly short time frame. The knowledge economy, however, is marked more by wealth production and job quality than job creation. In other words, in the knowledge economy the most important benchmark for economic development should be regional per capita income, indicating wealth creation and its more equitable distribution. The focus on short-term job creation, entrenched in public policy regulations and political expectations, is not the appropriate benchmark for revitalizing older industrial cities, which, as we have seen, requires long-term investment across a range of assets at a regional level. Economic developers often feel that their need to be accountable to mandated benchmarks prevents them from undertaking the wider-ranging, longer-term actions that could improve the community in light of twenty-first-century changes.

Third, there are insufficient finances to meet many current challenges such as brownfields remediation or literacy, yet emerging challenges such as disaster preparedness and environmental stewardship increasingly need to be factored into a community's resource prioritization and are commanding significant resources. Managing resources and finding innovative financing tools will continue to challenge communities in the twenty-first century.

And finally, obtaining economic development resources is also hindered in some places—including older industrial cities—by a poor media image of the profession as incentive-driven smokestack chasers. Public misunderstanding of the broad, multifaceted activities that make up economic development often inhibits its work in the political sphere.

In sum, through a practitioner's lens, economic development has been transformed from industrial recruitment, which relied on tax incentives and marketing techniques, to managing a multifaceted, complex portfolio of investments across a range of community assets in partnership with a growing number of stakeholders. While this is a daunting task under any circumstances, it is made more difficult by the following circumstances:

—The fragmentation of governments and lack of support at higher governmental levels

—The need to act on a regional scale but deliver project-oriented outcomes within their jurisdiction

—The differing capacities of local and regional institutions to effectively partner to meet common goals

—Local and regional political leadership that does not understand the complexity or the urgency of economic developers' work

—Inadequate tools that were crafted to meet the needs of industrial recruitment and land development, but are limited in their ability to enhance entrepreneurship, the local workforce, and knowledge development

Nevertheless, economic development professionals are learning to work in this new environment and are finding ways to be successful. In many cases, this means taking new types of risks and working in bold new ways. Youngstown, Ohio, a shrinking industrial city devastated by the restructuring of the steel industry, is a good example of this. City leadership and residents committed to revitalizing their community recognized the need for a new approach to meet the realities of the current economy and undertook a forward-thinking strategic planning process. The Youngstown 2010 planning process is a vision that fosters the concept of developing a smaller but more effective city, with a focus on fixing the city's assets and strengthening its knowledge infrastructure. To this end, Youngstown's plan coordinates and targets its investments across a range of assets. Youngstown is landbanking delinquent property while moving to adopt new zoning codes and urban design standards to meet twenty-first-century space and site needs and promote downtown and neighborhood redevelopment. It is creating partnerships with neighboring communities to expand green space and is working through regional initiatives to strengthen education, workforce development, job creation, and infrastructure. The Youngstown Incubator, which supports technology start-ups, located downtown, is expanding into vacant buildings, while a $250 million project is redeveloping the Smokey Hollow neighborhood, which borders the university, thus enhancing this asset. Youngstown has just begun the hard work, but it furnishes a constructive example of how you start and what it takes.

Although older industrial cities face significant challenges, we believe that they can come back. This requires urban economic development strategies that strategically align public-private investments into a region's land, business, people, and knowledge assets, an approach that should comprise the following components:

—Build on the city's physical assets and infrastructure.

—Invest in education and workforce development to meet present and future needs.

—Foster the transition to the knowledge economy with endogenous strategies and economic diversification.

—Develop a regional investment approach adapted to the unique needs of each locality based on public-private-community partnerships.

—Define the roles of all stakeholders to enhance the effectiveness of partnerships and policy implementation.

—Increase funding to the urban cores as part of an overall plan for regional competitiveness.

—Focus on per capita income increases as a central goal and critical benchmark for evaluating success.

Notes

1. Don Iannone, "A Proposal to Advance the Economic Development Field's Professional Status," white paper, *Economic Development Futures Journal,* March 2006.
2. For the methodology used to identify older industrial cities, see Jennifer S. Vey, "Restoring Prosperity: The State Role in Revitalizing America's Older Industrial Cities," report (Brookings Institution, Metropolitan Policy Program, 2007).
3. Paul Craig Roberts, "Nuking the Economy," *Baltimore Chronicle,* February 13, 2006.
4. *On Reclamation and Reuse of Abandoned Industrial Sites,* hearings before the U.S. House of Representatives, Committee on Science, Space, and Technology, Subcommittee on Technology, Environment, and Aviation, testimony of Charlie Bartsch, June 9, 1994, p. 6.
5. This section and the Baltimore case study draw on the work of Alex Iams and Ed Gilliland, *Targeted Area Redevelopment: Area-Wide Improvements for Community Revitalization* (Washington: International Economic Development Council, 2005).

6. International Economic Development Council, *Business Retention and Expansion Training Manual* (Washington, 2006).
7. The Knowledge Industry Partnership comprises eight partners: the Greater Philadelphia Economy League, the Greater Philadelphia Tourism Marketing Corporation, the University of Philadelphia, the Office of the City Representative and Director of Commerce for the City of Philadelphia, the Pennsylvania Department of Community and Economic Development, Campus Visit/Philadelphia, Campus Philly, and Innovation Philadelphia.
8. As outlined at their website, www.kiponline.org.
9. WIRE-Net was created in Cleveland in 1988, during and following a series of plant closings and downsizings to help manufacturing jobs stay in the community.
10. National Center on Education and the Economy, Workforce Development Strategies Group, *Under One Roof: New Governance Structures for Local Economic and Workforce Development*, vol. 2, May 2007.
11. Heike Mayer, "Planting High Technology Seeds: Tectronix's Role in the Creation of Portland's Silicon Forest," *Oregon Historical Quarterly* 106, no. 4 (Winter 2005).
12. Robert G. Heard and John Sibert, *Growing New Businesses with Seed and Venture Capital: State Experiences and Options* (Washington: National Governors Association, 2000).
13. Outlined at the Ben Franklin Technology Partnership website, www.benfranklin.org.
14. "Exploratory Research on Angel Funding and the Funding Gap" (U.S. Department of Commerce, National Institute of Standards and Technology, 2001).

12

Workforce Development Strategies for Older Industrial Cities: Toward a New Approach

Richard Kazis and Marlene Seltzer

In today's knowledge economy, U.S. cities are competing against each other and against cities around the world to attract employers, entrepreneurs, and skilled workers who will drive growth, development, and prosperity.[1] As the authors of the chapters in this volume emphasize, the new terms of competition have resulted in a reshuffling of the prospects of different cities: some have found ways to rise in this new environment, and some, primarily older industrial cities, frequently those with limited human capital-related assets, have fallen further behind. A number are in a spiral of declining population, employment, skills, and earnings, coupled with a deepening concentration of poverty, which is difficult to reverse.

New economic development theorists and practitioners emphasize a range of strategies to help older cities remake and revive their economies. Researchers in the Brookings Institution's Metropolitan Policy Program have argued for five linked priorities that older cities and their leaders should pursue:

—Build on economic strengths that support a "high-road" economy of knowledge, innovation, and entrepreneurship.

—Ensure that essential municipal services are delivered in a transparent, efficient, and effective manner.

—Undertake one or more physical projects that transform the urban landscape and create opportunities for new development and growth.

—Grow the middle class by helping low-wage workers increase incomes and wealth.

—Create neighborhoods that serve families with a broad range of incomes.[2]

The emphasis is on making the most of a city's particular physical, economic, and human assets. The emerging consensus recognizes the dual need to make the city more attractive to quality employers and new good jobs—and to increase the educational and skill attainment of residents so that they can take advantage of new opportunities.

The Brookings framework embeds workforce and education strategies rather than putting them front and center. But the central importance of improving a city's human capital, the productive knowledge and skills of city residents, is clear. Given the steadily growing contribution of skills and educational attainment to economic success and competitiveness for individuals, nations, and economic regions, no city can hope to remake itself without strategies for raising residents' skill and education levels. Cities that want to move from an industrial economy to a knowledge-based entrepreneurial one and pursue development strategies that accelerate that transition need a workforce with stronger academic basics, technical and work-related skills, and the ability to adapt effectively to changing labor-market opportunities.

Another recent Brookings Institution report, "The Vital Center," on strategies for revitalizing the Great Lakes region, makes the implicit more explicit. The authors identify underdeveloped human capital as the first of four challenges to adaptation (the others being lagging entrepreneurship, uncompetitive metropolitan communities, and an outdated social compact).[3] They recommend strategies to "forge a Great Lakes compact for skill and talent" that targets key disciplines and affords better access to postsecondary education and new skills training.

In this chapter we take a hard look at the place of skill development in economic revitalization efforts for older industrial cities. We argue that workforce development, economic development, and education must be aligned and integrated into a more holistic policy framework if the limitations of typical revitalization efforts—and typical workforce programming—are to be overcome. At the same time, we are not persuaded by arguments that all that matters for economic development purposes is attracting or producing more four-year-college graduates. Given national demographic trends—and certainly those in most older struggling cities—upgrading the skills of the workforce more broadly, including the large numbers of adults with only a high school education or less, is also critically important. For this reason, this chapter and its recommendations focus on strategies to help move large numbers of underprepared youths and adults to and through some type of postsecondary credential. We argue that not just four-year institutions but also community colleges should play a central role in urban revitalization strategies that are built upon upgrading human capital.

We recognize that, historically, economic and workforce development strategies have generally proceeded on parallel, nonintersecting tracks. The two systems operate quite differently, with different funding streams, governance structures, performance requirements, and cultures. A National Governors Association paper echoes a fairly common view in the field that "economic developers are from Mars and workforce developers are from Venus."[4]

We also acknowledge that workforce development as typically delivered in America's cities has had at best modest impact on individuals and employers served, particularly in eras and places where employer demand for employees and for higher skills has been weak. Employment and training programs tend to be antiquated, fragmented, poorly funded, and geared to serving the labor-market needs of a prior era, when short-term assistance to find entry-level work was sufficient to start someone on a career that paid a middle-class wage. It is fair to ask whether workforce development providers and agencies have the capacity and the know-how to deliver the services and value that are demanded by knowledge- and innovation-driven economic development.

Despite these challenges, though, we believe the time is right, and the opportunity exists, for a new and more effective alignment of economic development, workforce development, and mainstream educational systems. Educational Testing Service's recent study, *America's Perfect Storm,* documents how the powerful combination of employers' rising skill requirements and expectations, inadequate levels of adult educational attainment and literacy, and a steady increase in the proportion of Americans who are low-income, minority, or immigrants is changing the landscape of economic opportunity and well-being.[5] The report makes a strong case for the increased centrality of skills and educational attainment to any strategy to revive and grow the economy of the nation and of local areas—and for policies that can meet the needs of both adult workers trying to succeed in a more demanding economy and K–12 students who will require a postsecondary credential if they are to easily join the middle class. This and other recent reports detail how the demographic shifts in many states and cities toward less-educated and less-skilled immigrants is likely to lower overall living standards, unless socioeconomic gaps in educational attainment are narrowed significantly.[6]

The new economic reality described by the ETS authors is driving a convergence of economic development and workforce development strategies, to the benefit of both. As one recent report notes, "Now that workforce development focuses more on boosting skills of incumbent workers and economic development focuses more on growth from within, there is considerable overlap between the two missions."[7] We would add a third leg to the stool: as the National Center for Higher Education Management Systems puts it, the "emerging policy triangle" unites workforce development, economic development, and education, because the future belongs to states and cities whose residents have high postsecondary attainment rates.[8]

This chapter emphasizes two broad priorities for strategies and policies that can help older industrial cities transform themselves through upgrading their residents' job-related skills and educational attainment: strategies for linking supply-side training and skill development with demand-side opportunities created by employer need and economic development investments; and strategies for making supply-side education and skill development services to individuals more effective, provided through both education institutions and adult learning systems. We specify some of the most promising approaches within each area and provide illustrative examples from innovative cities and regions. We conclude with suggestions for ways public and private workforce development planning, investment, programming, and policy will need to change if the obstacles to "business as usual" in struggling cities are to be overcome.

There is a third policy priority that we do not discuss in detail, though we believe it is critically important to helping lower-skilled workers succeed economically. These are policies targeted solely to the demand side of the labor market, to affecting the quality of jobs available to these individuals. Examples include raising the minimum wage, revising labor laws, or providing incentives for employers to create jobs that offer better wages and benefits.[9] We omit these strategies because our primary concern here is how skill development policies in particular can be better designed and implemented, and better linked to effective urban economic development strategies.

The intense pressure on cities to compete in the knowledge economy or to fall further behind creates an opening for new programs, policies, and politics. And there are signs of movement. Economic development strategies are beginning to incorporate human capital development. Boundaries between education and workforce development systems and institutions are blurring. New civic partnerships around older city revitalization might help propel the vision, the will, and collaborations for change that can spur skill development institutions to make significant progress toward raising local residents' education and skill attainment. New alliances committed to performance and accountability might generate a virtuous cycle of economic and institutional improvement, even in cities struggling the most to compete in the new economy. Bringing economic development, workforce development, and education into alignment and common purpose could provide a platform for long-term urban change.

Why Older Industrial Cities Need a New Workforce Development Approach

Workforce development activities at the local level have historically been shaped by rules and funding from the federal government, particularly the Department of Labor. For much of the postwar period, this system was geared to helping low-income individuals gain sufficient skills, primarily through short-term training and services, so that they could qualify and obtain an entry-level job in an industry where they could advance to a decent paying career over time. As the MIT economist Paul Osterman characterizes the situation, "It is slightly unfair but not too far off the mark to characterize the old style approach to service delivery as one in which agencies trained people for occupations for which they thought there was demand and then either simply sent people out to look for work or helped them in the process."[10]

Results in this system were generally disappointing; federal rules combined with poor implementation to create programs that tended to serve only minimally the needs of either employers or job seekers.[11] Over the years, the federal government narrowed the reach of the workforce development system—turning away from active labor-market policies such as public employment, narrowing the target population to low-income workers, favoring services to individual workers and employers rather than to industry sectors, and reducing funding for workforce development in real terms about a third from 1985 to 2003.[12] At the same time, the number of small and underfunded training and employment programs created by Congress and various federal departments multiplied. By the mid-1990s, the system was a bewildering, fragmented, and ineffective hodgepodge, typically disconnected from employers and local economic needs and strategies.[13] Perhaps most important, the emphasis was on one-on-one services that targeted individual deficits with little attention to the broader economic context within which people sought opportunity.

The rules and requirements of federal workforce training policy are only one barrier to effective delivery of services to a city or region's employers and workers. Economic development and workforce development agencies frequently operate in isolation from each other, kept apart by culture, bureaucratic traditions, or philosophy. Agencies that manage and oversee, respectively, literacy, adult basic education, workforce development, higher education, and supportive services often have different target populations, eligibility requirements, reporting procedures, performance measures, and funding cycles, making it difficult to combine or align resources for maximum impact. Similar challenges exist at the institutional level. Training and education providers that serve adults with very basic skill needs are often isolated and disconnected from the next step up the education and career ladder, often the community college. Turf battles over shrinking resources, service delivery silos that are resistant to new ways of collaborating, differences in institutional cultures among types of service deliverers, and few compelling incentives to change existing behavior combine to constrain effectiveness and limit the return on public investment.[14]

The deepening disadvantage of many older industrial cities as they try to compete in the knowledge-based innovation economy demonstrates the need for a different approach. Take the case of Holyoke, Massachusetts.

A small city of about 40,000 residents near Springfield, Holyoke is one of eleven older mill towns in Massachusetts that are falling further behind as the state shifts to a knowledge-based economy centered around Boston. Labeled Gateway Cities by the research organization MassINC, these cities have lost population and have seen huge numbers of well-paying manufacturing jobs disappear without being replaced in either quantity or quality.[15] They are effectively shut out from eastern Massachusetts' strong economic comeback.

Between 1970 and 2000, manufacturing in Holyoke shrank from about 40 percent of employment to about 20 percent. Population declined 20 percent: virtually all the population loss was among white residents, while the largely Puerto Rican Latino population grew by 170 percent to reach 41 percent of the total population. Educational attainment lags that of the rest of the state: the city's dropout rate of 30 percent is about twice the state's average. College graduates make up only 17 percent of the population, compared to the state's 33 percent. What manufacturing jobs remain require a higher level of education and skill than jobs in the past. And what new jobs have been created tend to be low-paying, unstable service and retail positions. Not surprisingly, the percentage of families living in poverty more than doubled between 1967 and 2000 and is far above the state average.[16]

In this environment, workforce development services that emphasize job placement and short-term services to address individual employability deficits are not only inadequate but largely irrelevant. As the new economic development strategists emphasize, economic competitiveness requires a significant increase in the stock of human capital. College attainment rates must rise across all economic groups. This is critical if employers with good jobs are to locate and expand in particular areas. For cities that have poor K–12 education systems with high dropout rates, that have low levels of college attainment in their adult population, and whose populations are increasingly made up of immigrants with relatively low education levels, the traditional workforce approach offers too little, too late.

In the 1990s, a more promising model for workforce development began to emerge in reaction to the limits of welfare reform's work-first policies and in response to employers' growing concern for quality and availability of workers in a period of very tight labor markets. Called *sectoral strategies, advancement strategies,* or *career pathways* by different proponents, this model recognized the need to serve "dual customers," employers as well as workers, and to engage employers at every stage of workforce development. Services to clusters of employers and their incumbent or potential employees eclipsed the traditional one-on-one service model. Job retention and career advancement supplanted quick job placement as the ultimate goal. Responding to a growing body of literature that found job quality and employer quality to be important determinants of individual earnings gains, planners and practitioners argued for workforce development services targeted to dynamic industry and occupational sectors in the local economy—a combination of *workforce* and *workplace* development strategies. Building from welfare-to-work program research, the emerging consensus stressed the importance of connecting the mainstream education and second-chance skill development systems more closely—with particular attention to the role of community colleges—so that adults could move along more transparent pathways from training or basic skills programs to postsecondary credentials with significant labor-market payoff.[17] Workforce development needed to be reconceptualized as a vertically linked set of learning opportunities that connect high school graduation, career training, postsecondary education, and skills upgrading.[18]

This approach is gaining some traction. In a number of large and smaller cities, organizations using a mix of public, private, and philanthropic resources have been able to bring local labor-market actors—employers, industry associations, education and training providers, local governmental entities—into stable partnerships to promote career advancement in particular industry sectors. Targeting both employer interests and needs and the employment and advancement hopes of less-skilled workers, these initiatives are redefining how workforce development services might be organized and delivered.

Philanthropic organizations have been seeding experimentation and research to define the emerging paradigm and identify promising practice and policy. An important framing role was played by the American Assembly in 2004, which convened researchers, practitioners, and policymakers to create a public statement on new approaches to workforce development, captured in the book *Workforce Intermediaries for the Twenty-first Century.*[19]

In September 2007, a group of corporate and public foundations and the U.S. Department of Labor launched a National Fund for Workforce Solutions, a $50 million, five-year effort to strengthen and expand effective workforce development partnerships that bring together employers, business associations, educational institutions, unions, community-based organizations, and public workforce agencies. The fund supports regionally targeted, sector-based career advancement efforts for low-skilled workers that are responsive to both workers and employers. A key component of the fund's approach is to support local funder collaboratives that raise flexible funds and leverage other resources to support career advancement. Cities initially involved in this effort included Baltimore, Boston, Chicago, Los Angeles, New York, San Diego, San Francisco, and Washington, D.C., with additional statewide collaboratives in Pennsylvania and Rhode Island. Funders hope to leverage $200 million in local resources from the national investment.[20]

The U.S. Department of Labor has tried to encourage initiatives that meet employer and worker needs and that target important regional industry and occupational niches though several new competitive grants programs, including the Community-Based Job Training Initiative, which awarded $250 million in 2005 and 2006 to 142 community colleges in forty-five states for initiatives that integrate regional economic and workforce strategies for high-growth–high-demand industries, and the Workforce Innovation in Regional Economic Development (WIRED) initiative, which by early 2007 had invested $325 million to support workforce partnerships that are driven by specific regional economic needs and development strategies.[21] State workforce development funds have been tapped to promote a variety of new initiatives. Some states have used incumbent-worker training funds to engage employers in high-growth industries. Others have explicitly funded regional collaboratives and intermediaries to develop career pathway models in industries the state wants to promote.

In the next section we elaborate on the priorities that should drive a workforce strategy aligned to economic development, recognizing the need for a sophisticated long-term approach that breaks down service provision silos and ties workforce development to higher education institutions and to powerful economic development drivers and civic coalitions. We do not underestimate the difficulty that older industrial cities face in moving toward a more coherent, integrated, and ambitious workforce development agenda. The same demographics, market forces, institutional capacities, and policy environments that have contributed to these cities' competitive decline present significant obstacles for business and civic leaders who want to upgrade workforce skills and productivity. There is not a lot of low-hanging fruit to be had. For this reason, we end the chapter with recommendations for ways that policy can and must change if the workforce development system is to contribute significantly to urban economic revitalization—and if the human capital stock of cities such as Holyoke is to rise enough to improve their long-run competitive options.

How Workforce Development Can Support Revitalization of Older Industrial Cities

What would a more relevant, effective, and high-value workforce development system look like in older urban areas? What principles should guide policymakers and practitioners trying to make workforce development more central to efforts to bring their city into the knowledge economy and thereby improve local residents' income and prospects? We highlight two broad areas for strengthening supply-side human capital investments and improving their impact: first, improvements in the coordination and linkages between skill development efforts and the economic opportunities available in a given city; and second, efforts to improve the outcomes of the education and skill development pipeline, for youth and adults.

Strengthen the Links between Supply and Demand Sides of the Urban Labor Market: Align Workforce and Economic Development Strategies

If a key weakness of traditional workforce development is its disconnect from the local economic forces within which both firms and individuals make labor-market decisions, then a better approach must strengthen and deepen the links between economic opportunity and workforce investments. This is consistent with the overall strategy of maximizing the value of a city's existing assets. Innovative practice and policy approaches for older industrial cities stress the following:

—Workforce development activities that target and support industry or occupational sectors important to the local economy

—Workforce services that take advantage of and align with public economic development investments

—Structured forums for convening employers, education and training providers, and others for strategic planning, program design, monitoring of implementation, and assessment of new opportunities

Target sectors that are central to local economic growth. As noted, across the country a large and growing number of initiatives link the supply and demand sides of the labor market by providing training to a cluster of employers in the same industry, with the twin goals of low-wage worker advancement and regional economic growth. These sector-based strategies typically target industries that are important to the local economy in terms of job quality, number of job openings, and connection to other high-wage and high-growth industries. They support economic development strategies that try to "rebuild the middle class from within," as a recent study on Washington, D.C., was titled.[22]

One such initiative is the Building Services Industry Career Path Project, recently funded by the SkillWorks public-private partnership in Boston. This project is a labor-management partnership involving Service Employees International Union Local 615 and seven employers, including business owners and maintenance contractors. The partnership was created to catalyze the development of permanent, sustainable career pathways in the industry, from part-time cleaners to skilled maintenance workers, by improving both English-language and occupational skills and by strengthening human resource practices. The initial effort of the project has been to create a career pathway model of education, training, and career coaching, combining English classes with a building maintenance course and training for cleaning biotech labs. In its first two years, 138 workers enrolled in a course; about 75 percent of those who took an ESL (English as a Second Language) course completed it, and 95 percent of the participants in the first building maintenance class graduated. Project staff work with employers to define job descriptions and competencies needed for better jobs and to change the way one large employer posts weekly lists of job openings. The union hopes to develop a service employees' education and training fund similar to those operating in several other large cities.[23]

As noted, sectoral programs are distinctive for their significant employer involvement in training program design. Employers identify target occupations, provide input on curriculum, and assist in training delivery as appropriate. These initiatives also build upon a rich understanding of the targeted industry and its technology, market, and human resource strategies. Staff use that deep understanding and knowledge to help firms meet particular skill needs and broader growth challenges.[24] They also understand well the landscape of basic skills, technical training, and social-service providers in the region. Most sectoral initiatives attempt to influence industry and firm hiring, training, promotion, and compensation practices, so that the mix of employment opportunities shifts toward better jobs with more opportunity for better-qualified workers. There is, however, great variation in how actively sectoral efforts are geared to changing, rather than working within, employer expectations and practices.

These programs are not easy to launch; they tend to grow slowly; and many, particularly outside health care, remain small. Moreover, they require some form of intermediary organization to bring partners together and keep them at the table. There is some evidence that these programs can raise wages and promote advancement, although formal evaluations are limited.[25]

Massachusetts, Michigan, Pennsylvania, Washington, and other states have created incentives for expansion of these efforts with state funds and assistance. For example, Washington State began in 2001 to create a set of Skill Panels that take a sectoral approach to workforce development, aligned with the state's economic development priorities. These public-private partnerships have involved over three hundred firms in panels that plan workforce investments and system improvements for industries as diverse as health care, construction, IT, manufacturing, marine and industrial safety training, energy, and game software development—industries that the state wants to retain and grow.

Research shows that starting out in a better-quality job—a job with better wages, that provides benefits, and that has opportunities for learning—is associated with higher wages and greater advancement over time.[26] This research provides further impetus to aligning workforce development investments with a city's broader economic interests and targeting higher-wage sectors. Certain industry sectors, such as durables manufacturing and construction, have a higher proportion of good jobs in their employment structures. Moreover, in these two industries the educational barriers to entry are not as high as in other decent-paying sectors.[27] The health occupations provide a number of pathways from lower-skill jobs to better career positions that are clearly defined because of regulatory requirements in the industry. Within other sectors, particularly service industries, the job structure tilts more toward low-paying jobs, and higher-paying jobs tend to require higher educational credentials. A Jobs for the Future analysis of BLS data found sixteen occupations providing 700,000 jobs a year that paid over $25,000 a year and required less than a B.A. degree and no experience in the field. This kind of fine-grained analysis of both local job vacancies and trends and the educational requirements for entry into those jobs is critical for identifying workforce development priorities.[28]

Take advantage of major economic development investments. In older industrial cities, new economic development investments frequently target several areas: infrastructure improvement (removal of old highways, improvement of transportation and communications systems) and housing development. These large public projects create opportunities for cities to align their workforce and economic development efforts. First-source agreements that give preference to local residents, combined with targeted training, can secure apprenticeship slots in the building trades or jobs in infrastructure support jobs such as systems maintenance and engineering.

The Diversity Apprenticeship Program in Philadelphia and the Mayor's Commission on Construction Opportunity in New York City are examples of training pathways that take advantage of economic development efforts to connect disadvantaged urban residents to apprenticeships in the trades. Elements common to both programs include a preapprenticeship program that incorporates soft skill training and case management, assistance with navigating the process of becoming an apprentice, and a mechanism for bringing employers, union officials, government leaders, training organizations, and other stakeholders together to create an integrated set of services that can help less-skilled individuals succeed and advance.[29] Large-scale construction and development opportunities should not replace "grow your own" strategies that make the most of existing assets; but when such opportunities exist, full advantage should be taken to bring less-skilled residents into better-paying jobs and career paths through these projects.

Create ongoing mechanisms for aligning demand and supply sides toward the same goals. Workforce development professionals and employers do not routinely come face to face to identify skill gaps, changing employment trends, and pressing needs. But the kind of sector-based initiatives highlighted here require such interaction and exchange if they are to serve both employer and low-wage worker needs. Most sectoral efforts are managed in some way by an intermediary organization that understands and is able to navigate the needs and constraints of both supply- and demand-side partners. These organizations have the trust of key stakeholders, organize multiple partners and funding streams around common goals and projects, and design services that engage multiple service providers (providing training in, for example, English-language skill development, adult basic skills, technical skills, social supports, and so forth) and meet employers' specific needs.[30] In a growing number of cities, collaboratives of funders have emerged with the goal of guiding local investment efforts that integrate workforce and economic growth strategies. These investor groups can provide a critically important regular venue for strategic planning that engages private, public, and other stakeholders around maximizing the impact of workforce investments.

Workforce intermediary organizations are also important for their ability to generate and test fine-grained labor-market information with employers in particular industry niches; direct, open exchange and feedback from employers can help planners identify promising targets for workforce efforts that more generic national and state-level data miss. For example, a broad analysis of labor-market trends might lead to a recommendation to steer clear of manufacturing, but in a given city, concentrating services for a particular segment of manufacturing firms might make strategic sense. States can help promote this kind of data gathering and exchange and in the process help to cement critical interactions between the demand and supply sides. A few years ago, the Florida Agency for Workforce Innovation made forty grants to regional workforce boards to help them generate a range of valuable labor-market data, including vacancy and hiring needs surveys, analyses of targeted industries and occupations, commuting patterns, and GIS (geographic information system) mapping by education level.

Fix the Pipeline: Increase Overall Educational Attainment in the City

New economic development strategies rightly stress the critical importance of colleges and universities in urban strategies to grow the middle class and maximize the value-added of a city's assets. Higher education institutions—four-year institutions, but also two-year degree-granting colleges—have moved to the center of economic development in two ways: as drivers of innovation and new economic activity and benefits for the community; and as engines of skill development and educational attainment that can attract new knowledge workers and grow a region's own middle-class workforce. These institutions are significant economic assets that are critical to strategies for both attracting and growing a skilled community of knowledge workers.

However, revitalization efforts cannot focus solely on maximizing the value of local colleges and universities in attracting innovators and high-skill talent. Given the basic and technical skill needs of large numbers of their adult residents, older cities need to identify and then fix the leaks across their education pipeline, from preschool to and through postsecondary credentials. K–12 systems need to be overhauled so that they are attractive—and effective—places for the children of new and existing residents to learn. Providers of K–12 education, higher education, and workforce development must work together as partners in a more holistic and long-term effort to raise significantly the skill levels of youths and adults across the city, whereby success is measured in terms of the numbers of people who gain postsecondary credentials and find pathways to career advancement and middle-class livelihoods. This is a significant redefinition of purpose and goals, and it is a daunting challenge. But, as a recent report on career pathways put it, "Given the importance of postsecondary education and training to the economic health of both individuals and regions, maximizing the return on the public's investment in education must be a top priority for policymakers."[31]

To maximize that public investment, cities, given their specific demographics and the educational attainment levels of their residents, will have to focus on three education pipeline priorities in addition to attracting talent through quality colleges and universities:

—Cities cannot afford to let dysfunctional public K–12 systems fail large numbers of their young people if they hope to compete.

—Postsecondary institutions must connect and work with skill development programs for adult workers so that, whatever an adult's basic skill levels upon entering a learning program, postsecondary credentials are the ultimate goal and institutions are aligned toward that goal.

—Poor city dwellers have special needs that go beyond workforce development services and will require collaboration with immigration, social service, and justice agencies.

Raise academic achievement and high school graduation rates in older cities. The need for urban school reform cannot be ignored. Academic achievement in most older industrial cities is extremely uneven and, overall, lags behind that of wealthier districts. Graduates are often ill prepared for college. Moreover, as recent research has made clear, too few urban high school students graduate: nationally, the figure is about 70 percent, but in urban districts the figure can be closer to 50 percent.[32]

Improving outcomes for urban school systems cannot be accomplished without state incentives and sanctions and, in most older cities, more resources. But money is not the only challenge. States need to continue to raise public expectations of what high school graduates need to know and be able to do, so they can advance to and succeed in college and career. The standards-based reform agenda must continue to work its way through districts and deep into schools and classrooms. State standards and expectations should incorporate goals around raising graduation rates at the same time as academic achievement standards are ratcheted up further. State education departments can also support better analysis of student performance data to identify schools and students likely to need more help if they are to succeed.

States will have to help in other ways, too. They must help close down dysfunctional high schools (what Johns Hopkins researchers call "dropout factories") and support improvement in schools that have the capacity and the leadership to improve. Schools that help low-performing urban students become college-ready by graduation are not common, but states can promote, seed, and disseminate results from models that appear to hold promise. This is likely to require states to provide incentives for additional charter or other new schools that target low-performing students and that stress college-going expectations for these students. Schools that target high school students who are overage and undercredited and need more flexible scheduling, such as New York's transfer schools and Young Adult Borough Centers and transition schools, should be considered. States should also target additional funding to low-performing districts to attract better-qualified teachers, expand the school day and year, and provide better academic and career-focused support to students.[33]

At the same time, district leaders must commit to an agenda of high graduation rates and high achievement. Using their power to revamp leadership and professional development, teacher assignment policies, and new school development strategies, district leaders can embrace performance and college readiness and resist excuses that point the finger at students, parents, resource constraints, or other obstacles. New York, Philadelphia, Chicago, and Boston are leading the way in redesigning schools and creating many more and more varied options, particularly for high-school-age youths who are overage and have earned few high school credits and thus are likely to fail to earn a diploma. They are creating offices devoted to supporting new schools, aligning professional development with the challenges facing low-performing students, and moving improvement strategies through the system as a whole. Many of the new smaller schools in these cities are beginning to demonstrate positive results, outperforming other, older schools with higher graduation and lower dropout rates.[34] Smaller cities can learn from and adapt the strategies of these leaders.

Make postsecondary credentials the ultimate goal of workforce development. Perhaps the most powerful shift in the consensus on how the workforce development system must change is the recognition that postsecondary attainment and credentials are now the coin of the realm and that basic skills, short-term training, and other efforts must be better linked to and integrated with institutions and programs that grant postsecondary credentials with value in the labor market. Labor-market participation, employment, and earnings rise with education level and have grown over time. The value of a postsecondary credential for future employment and earnings is also expected to rise. Three out of four of the twenty occupations projected to grow most rapidly in the coming years require some form of post-secondary education; all twenty occupations projected to suffer the greatest decline in job openings by 2014 require only on-the-job training.[35] At the same time, over 60 percent of the U.S. population between the ages of twenty-five and sixty-four in 2004—about 65 million people—had no postsecondary credential.[36] These adults are disproportionately concentrated in struggling industrial cities—and that concentration is unlikely to abate as these cities continue to be magnets for lower-income immigrant workers and families.

The new emphasis on postsecondary credentials means that both workforce development systems and postsecondary institutions need to change and become more closely aligned. Precollegiate skill development has to align more smoothly and transparently with college offerings. Colleges, too, have to be more flexible and accommodating to the needs of adult learners, most of whom are juggling work, family, and school responsibilities.

Cities can no longer afford to treat basic skills programs for workers such as adult basic education and English as a second language as stand-alone programs; rather, these programs need to be expanded and linked more effectively to the next steps in credentialed skill development, both academic and technical.

The community college is often the best place to make these linkages. More flexible than four-year institutions, better resourced than most community-based programs, community colleges have the potential to provide expanded opportunity and to smooth transitions for individuals from basic skill programs into technical skill development programs that lead to credentials. Community colleges enroll more than 2.5 million people age twenty-five and over. Well over 50 percent of community college students are twenty-two years old or older, at least half of whom are in occupational programs. Adult students tend to be even more heavily concentrated in lower-income strata than traditional, younger students who come right out of high school. Perhaps most important, community colleges serve a higher percentage of lower-income students than other postsecondary institutions. These institutions are geographically located to be accessible to almost all Americans, particularly in urban areas. The working poor constitute a large segment of their market. Moreover, they operate at a scale that dwarfs the workforce system funded by the federal Workforce Investment Act (WIA) and that can scale up further when needed. The new No Worker Left Behind initiative in Michigan promises 100,000 dislocated workers in the state two free years of tuition for community college retraining (at a cost to the state and federal governments of $77 million). The state's community colleges can absorb this influx: the WIA-funded system could never do that.

Community colleges often have well-developed relations with key industry sectors and their leaders, through advisory committees and centers that provide customized training and skill development for particular industries. Career pathway models typically center on community colleges for this reason, because they link short-term bridge programs for those who need basic skill remediation and help preparing for a college environment to community college credit and credential programs.

Community colleges are well situated to experiment with models that integrate basic skills and vocational programming more seamlessly. Two examples are the City College of San Francisco's innovative Vocational ESL programs and the Community College of Denver's approach to accelerating developmental learning so that low-skilled adults can enter occupational programs in allied health, public safety, and pre-engineering more quickly.[37] The State Board for Community and Technical Colleges in Washington State launched the Integrating Basic Education and Skills Training (I-BEST) program in 2004 to help students succeed in credit-bearing college courses by pairing adult basic education (ABE) or ESL instructors in the classroom with a professional or technical instructor, pairing basic skills with training in a variety of occupations and using occupational skills content as the context for practicing and mastering English-language skills. This kind of integration is far easier to accomplish in a community college setting than in dispersed settings around a city.

At the same time, it cannot be ignored that higher education institutions, including community colleges, face significant challenges serving adult learners. Adult learners are likely to work and have family responsibilities that compete with the class and semester schedules of colleges, which were designed to serve younger students more likely to attend full-time and work less or not at all. If colleges, particularly community colleges, are to maximize their workforce development value to a city's adults, they need to explore more flexible scheduling options, including modularized curricula and credentials that break a program into smaller units, distance learning, learning located at workplaces, and more flexible entry, exit, and reentry policies. Teaching and learning methods should accommodate adults' scheduling and learning needs by emphasizing teams, practical lessons, and contextual approaches that take advantage of work settings and needs. Efforts to make it easier to move from noncredit to credit programs and to transfer credits earned in other institutions are critical to helping adults advance as quickly and efficiently as possible.[38]

Colleges can make some of these adjustments themselves, but in some areas changes in state policy are also needed. Credit transfer policies can be an important state intervention. So, too, can the design of financing and student aid systems that offer more direct assistance to working adults and accommodate and encourage more flexible delivery mechanisms and methods by institutions catering to adults and their learning constraints.

Address the special needs of residents of older industrial cities. The residents of struggling older industrial cities present particular challenges and opportunities to efforts to help workforce development systems provide greater value to economic development efforts. Two groups that are particularly important in this regard are immigrants and formerly incarcerated low-income males.

In many of these cities, as has been noted, the only significant population and labor-market growth is from immigrant communities. This makes the expansion and strengthening and strategic alignment of English-language skill development critical: language barriers are serious obstacles to both career advancement and success in education and training programs. Urban workforce efforts must tackle this head-on: employers, community-based organizations, and city agencies dealing with immigrants should be important allies. New targeted outreach and support efforts might be needed. In Chicago, a manufacturing firm, Admiral Tool and Manufacturing, developed a skill-upgrading program with the help of partners who understood their business. These included the Business and Industry Services of Truman College, a local community college, and partners who understood the immigrant population, including Instituto Del Progresso Latino, which designed bilingual bridge programs into manufacturing for Spanish- and Polish-speaking workers.[39] In Iowa, the state has created one-stop "New Iowan Centers" that recognize the particular challenges facing the rapidly expanding population of immigrant workers in the state's communities.[40]

A second group that faces particular challenges in career advancement and in taking advantage of training opportunities is the large number of men in older cities who have been in jail and are currently involved in some way with the criminal-justice system. There have been significant declines in the employment rates of the nation's least-skilled male workers. According to the University of California economist Stephen Raphael, on a given day in 2000, only a third of prime age black male high school dropouts were employed, a drop from two-thirds in 1980. During the same period, the percentage who were incarcerated climbed from 8 to 27 percent. Raphael argues that the percentage of unskilled black men with felony convictions and jail time is so large now that it has real impacts on employment, earnings, and neighborhood well-being in communities where these men are concentrated.

Some strategies for eliminating obstacles to economic reintegration of the formerly incarcerated require federal policy changes, such as removing the ban on felons' receiving financial aid for education. Another strategy, though, would be to encourage local workforce partnerships and intermediaries that have long-term credibility and relationships with employers to take on the challenge of prescreening of former inmates, aiding those who are reentering the workforce, and linking former inmates with needed educational and social services that will make them more employable.[41]

How Policy Can Support Workforce Investments That Align with Economic Revitalization Strategies

This chapter has argued for a refocusing of workforce development activities in older urban areas in two directions: toward greater alignment with new economic development strategies that build on local assets and toward closer integration of workforce development with institutions, in particular community colleges, that grant postsecondary credentials of value to both employers and lower-income, less-skilled city residents. These priorities can help workforce investments approach a scale and level of impact and leverage that traditional strategies cannot deliver.

States have an important role to play in any efforts to accelerate alignment of the policy triangle of workforce development, economic development, and education. The federal government can also be a catalyst for change, primarily by creating incentives for state-level innovation and investment. In this final section, we focus on two workforce policy priorities that can help promote urban revitalization: governance and other approaches to aligning goals and investments toward career advancement initiatives tied to local economic need; and strategies for increasing the amount of flexible funding available for localities for designing and delivering programs and services that cut across traditional funding silos.

Structural alignment of workforce, economic, and education policy. Many states and their leadership have turned to structural approaches to aligning workforce and economic development efforts—consolidating agencies, creating job cabinets to coordinate policy implementation, or appointing people to powerful new oversight positions. Examples are many: Minnesota, Michigan, and Kansas are among the states that have merged economic and workforce agencies. Pennsylvania's Governor Ed Rendell appointed a deputy secretary to oversee alignment across five different agencies that affect workforce and economic development. Tennessee created a jobs cabinet led by the Department of Economic and Community Development and chaired by the governor.[42]

Although policy coordination and coherence are desirable, it can be a mistake to spend a lot of political capital on administrative reorganization—and the impact on local practice can be limited. Some states have turned to joint planning and information management, rather than reorganization or consolidation of whole departments, as an alternative. For example, Missouri merged its economic and workforce development research units into a single center that began in 2004 to report on a performance scorecard for the state that includes measures related to workforce development, education, and the economy.

Performance benchmarking that crosses and integrates the policy areas of workforce, economic development, and education is another state strategy—one that resonates well with the goals of the urban revitalization strategies championed in this volume. Oregon Benchmarks, a process that brought leaders from business, labor, education, and government together, resulted in a set of one hundred performance measures (statewide, systemwide, and programmatic) that cut across agencies and funding streams but that focus on the importance of workforce training and academic attainment and achievement to Oregon's economic future. Whether or not these are the right indicators and benchmarks, they provide a provocative way to think about putting performance and accountability front and center to align policy systems that are in different silos.

More flexible funding for workforce development efforts that support urban revitalization. Ultimately, expansion of the kinds of workforce development strategies highlighted throughout this chapter will require expanded and more flexible funding for more training for lower-skilled workers and for funding the various intermediary and partnership activities that are currently outside the funding structure of most publicly funded workforce initiatives. State and federal governments can create incentives for more private-sector and public investment.

Many states have incumbent-training funds that can be used more flexibly than federal workforce dollars. In recent years, a number of states have tried to tie the use of these funds even more explicitly to the priority economic goals and strategies of the state. The Kansas Economic Growth Act in 2004 led to the creation of a Workforce Development Trust Fund that provides resources to the secretary of commerce to offer incentives to community and technical colleges to align their programs with economic development goals. Financed by a diversion from the state's workforce training programs, the fund targets dollars to specific development goals that the traditional training programs did not have to pursue.[43] In Governor Ed Rendell's first year in office in Pennsylvania, he created an Incumbent Worker Training Fund to finance industry-based intermediaries throughout the state. The guidelines for the fund cite workforce development as "a key component of an innovation-focused strategy." Funds are available only to consortia of employers from one of nine industry clusters and seventeen subclusters that, it has been determined, are important to the state's economic future. A $20 million annual appropriation supports regional workforce intermediaries and partnerships and grantees are expected to specify how the workforce services provided will improve industry competitiveness and job quality.[44]

Efforts like these can be expanded to other states. One approach would be for a state to offer matching funds to partnerships and investor collaboratives in cities and regions, spurring local employers, associations, foundations, and institutions to come together to promote new initiatives. The National Fund for Workforce Solutions recently issued a study reporting on existing alternative strategies for financing workforce intermediaries and partnerships that can promote integrated career advancement and economic development strategies. Included are bond financing to fund training; unemployment insurance diversions that fund state training investment funds, being used in almost two dozen states; and federal Food Stamp employment and training funds (available to Food Stamp recipients). The fund plans to pilot and test one or more demonstration projects in alternative funding.[45]

The federal government can also play an important catalytic role. The U.S. Department of Labor can continue to fund and grow its WIRED and Community-Based Job Training Initiatives. Congress could revise the Workforce Investment Act to incorporate some of the principles and funding priorities that guide these demonstrations. A number of researchers have proposed a federal innovation fund designed to provide matching funds to states for promoting more effective and forward-looking workforce development models. In 2007, researchers from Jobs for the Future and FutureWorks recommended a federal-state partnership to promote and test innovative approaches to increasing adult access to and success in higher education and to scale up promising strategies.[46] MIT's Paul Osterman recently proposed creation of a federal "Low-Wage Challenge Fund" that would provide matching funds to encourage states to increase customized training programs oriented toward the low-skilled workforce and encourage community colleges to increase their involvement with firms and the low-wage workforce.

Finally, the federal government could use tax policy to make investments in low-wage worker training more attractive to employers. The Urban Institute's Robert Lerman suggests altering accounting practices so that training investments are treated more like capital investments that are depreciated over time rather than expensed in one year.[47] Paul Osterman advocates a federal tax credit for employers who increase the amount of training they provide lower-skilled workers. Although this approach by itself does not give preference to any particular approach to design and delivery of training, it would be an important spur to further training by employers for their low-skilled workers. With more interest among employers, local partnerships would be able to shape workforce development design and delivery to maximize local assets and opportunities.

Conclusion: Human Capital as Challenge and Opportunity

In a knowledge-based, innovation-driven economy, human capital is the name of the game. Cities that understand this and figure out how to expand residents' educational attainment and productive capacity move up and others fall behind. Struggling older cities face myriad fiscal, cultural, institutional, and political obstacles to maximizing the economic value of their public investments in human capital. We have argued for the obvious, though often elusive, strategy of aligning and integrating economic development, workforce development, and education investments to raise existing residents' skills and attainment while also positioning the city to attract better-educated talent. We have stressed the need to be realistic about the skills and educational levels of existing residents and of the largely immigrant and lower-skilled populations that are the source of population growth in most struggling older cities. Above all, we have stressed the need to take an expansive view of human-capital strategies in urban revitalization initiatives.

The necessary refocusing of workforce development activities to be more strategic, effective, and performance driven is often stymied by long-standing political arrangements, alliances, and priorities and by a weakly organized pro-change coalition. Bringing workforce development into closer alignment with a city's economic development and education strategies holds the potential to change these dynamics by pulling together a different, and perhaps more vibrant, civic coalition of business, government, education, and community around the idea of shaping the city's future in a positive direction by improving its competitive prospects. Breaking down the boundaries between uncoordinated human-capital–oriented policy areas in older cities is not only necessary as a long-term investment and improvement strategy; it may also have the benefit of reinvigorating civic leadership to overcome long-standing barriers to change.

Notes

1. The authors would like to thank our colleagues, Radha Roy Biswas and John Hoops, as well as the editors of this volume, for their assistance and thoughtful comments.
2. Jennifer Vey, "Restoring Prosperity: The State Role in Revitalizing America's Older Industrial Cities," report (Brookings Institution, Metropolitan Policy Program, 2007).
3. John Austin and Brittany Affolder-Caine, "The Vital Center: A Federal-State Compact to Renew the Great Lakes Region," report (Brookings Institution, 2006).

4. Mark Troppe, Stephen Crawford, and Martin Simon, *Aligning State Workforce Development and Economic Development Initiatives* (Washington: National Governors Association, 2005), p. 3.

5. Irwin Kirsch, Henry Braun, Kentaro Yamamoto, and Andre Sum, *America's Perfect Storm: Three Forces Changing Our Nation's Future* (Princeton: ETS, 2006).

6. National Center for Public Policy and Higher Education, *Income of U.S. Workers Projected to Decline If Education Doesn't Improve* (San Jose, 2005).

7. Robert D. Atkinson and Daniel Correa, *The 2007 State New Economy Index* (Washington: Information Technology and Information Foundation, 2007).

8. Dennis Jones and Patrick Kelley, *The Emerging Policy Triangle: Workforce Development, Economic Development, and Education* (Boulder: National Center for Higher Education Management Systems, 2007).

9. For a treatment of demand-side approaches, see Paul Osterman, "Improving Job Quality: Policies Aimed at the Demand Side of the Low Wage Labor Market," paper prepared for the W. E. Upjohn Institute on Employment Policy Conference, A Future of Good Jobs? America's Challenge in the Global Economy (Kalamazoo, Mich., June 22, 2007), and Elizabeth Lower-Basch, *Opportunity at Work: Improving Job Quality* (Washington: Center for Law and Social Policy, 2007).

10. Osterman, "Improving Job Quality."

11. W. Norton Grubb, *Learning to Work: The Case for Reintegrating Job Training and Education* (New York: Russell Sage Foundation, 1996).

12. Robin Spence and Brendan Kiel, *Skilling the American Workforce "On the Cheap"* (Washington: Workforce Alliance, 2003).

13. Robert P. Giloth, ed., *Workforce Development Politics* (Philadelphia: Temple University Press, 2004), chapter 1.

14. Annie E. Casey Foundation, *Strengthening Workforce Policy: Applying the Lessons of the Jobs Initiative to Five Key Challenges* (Baltimore, 2007), p. 3.

15. Benjamin Forman, David Warren, Eric McLean-Shinaman, John Schneider, Mark Muro, and Rebecca Sohmer, "Reconnecting Massachusetts' Gateway Cities: Lessons Learned and an Agenda for Renewal," research report (Boston: MassINC and Brookings Institution, Metropolitan Policy Program, 2007).

16. Northeastern University, Center for Urban and Regional Policy, *The Third-Tier Cities Project: Final Report* (Boston, 2002), chapter 3; Beth Siegel and Andy Waxman, *Third-Tier Cities: Adjusting to the New Economy* (Washington: U.S. Economic Development Administration, 2001).

17. See Nan Poppe and others, "Whose Job Is It? Creating Opportunities for Advancement," in *Workforce Intermediaries for the Twenty-First Century,* edited by Robert P. Giloth (Philadelphia: Temple University Press, 2004).

18. Giloth, *Workforce Development Politics,* p. 10.

19. Giloth, *Workforce Intermediaries for the Twenty-First Century.*

20. For more information on the National Fund for Workforce Solutions, see www.nfw solutions.org.

21. Latest information on the WIRED initiative can be found on the U.S. Department of Labor website at www.doleta.gov/wired.

22. Martha Ross and Brooke DeRenzis, "Reducing Poverty in Washington, D.C., and Rebuilding the Middle Class from Within," report (Brookings Institution, Greater Washington Research Program, 2007).

23. SkillWorks, *Building Opportunity and Good Jobs: A Profile of the Building Services Industry Career Path Project* (Boston: SkillWorks and the Boston Foundation, 2007).
24. Karin Martinson and Pamela Holcomb, *Innovative Employment Approaches and Programs for Low-Income Families* (Washington: Urban Institute, 2007), pp. 22–24.
25. Osterman, "Improving Job Quality," p. 27.
26. Poppe and others, "Whose Job Is It?," pp. 35–37.
27. Laura Dresser, *Stronger Ladders, Stronger Floors* (Madison: Center on Wisconsin Strategy, 2007).
28. Susan Goldberger, Newell Lessell, and Radha Roy Biswas, *The Right Jobs: Identifying Career Advancement Opportunities for Low-Skilled Workers—A Guide for Public and Private Sector Workforce Development Practitioners* (Boston: Jobs for the Future, 2005).
29. Ross and DeRenzis, *Reducing Poverty in Washington, D.C.*
30. Richard Kazis, "What Do Intermediaries Do?," in Giloth, *Workforce Intermediaries for the Twenty-First Century,* chapter 3.
31. Davis Jenkins, *Career Pathways: Aligning Public Resources to Support Individual and Regional Economic Advancement in the Knowledge Economy* (New York: Workforce Strategy Center, 2006), p. 4.
32. Adria Steinberg, Cassius Johnson, and Hilary Pennington, *Addressing America's Dropout Challenge* (Washington: Center for America's Progress, 2006).
33. Nancy Hoffman, Joel Vargas, Andrea Venezia, and Marc S. Miller, eds., *Minding the Gap: Why Integrating High School with College Makes Sense and How to Do It* (Harvard Education Press, 2007).
34. Robin Jacobowitz, Cindy Maguire, and Norm Fruchter, "The Effectiveness of Small High Schools, 1994–95 to 2003–04," report (New York University, Institute for Education and Social Policy, 2007).
35. Daniel Hecker, "Occupational Employment Projections to 2014," *Monthly Labor Review Online* 128, no. 11 (2005): 70–101.
36. U.S. Census Bureau, *American Community Survey* (2004), available at www.census.gov/acs.
37. Brian Bosworth, Abigail Callahan, Vickie Choitz, Chris Davidson, John Hoops, Richard Kazis, and Annie McLeod, *Adult Learners in Higher Education: Barriers to Success and Strategies to Improve Results,* Employment and Training Administration Occasional Paper 2007-3, prepared by Jobs for the Future, EduVentures, and FutureWorks for U.S. Department of Labor, Employment and Training Administration, 2007, pp. 4–11, available for download at http://www.jff.org/Documents/adultlearners.dol.pdf.
38. Ibid., section 2.
39. Manufacturing Institute and Center for Workforce Success and Jobs for the Future, *Improving Workplace Opportunities for Limited English-Speaking Workers* (Washington: National Association of Manufacturers, 2006), pp. 19–20.
40. Muro and others, *Reconnecting Massachusetts' Gateway Cities,* p. 45.
41. Steven Raphael, "Boosting the Earnings and Employment of Low-Skilled Workers in the United States: Making Work Pay and Removing Barriers to Employment and Social Mobility," paper prepared for the W. E. Upjohn Institute on Employment Policy conference, A Future of Good Jobs? America's Challenge in the Global Economy (Kalamazoo, Mich., June 22, 2007).
42. Troppe, *Aligning State Workforce Development and Economic Development Initiatives.*
43. Radha Biswas, Jack Mills, and Heath Prince, *Building Skills, Increasing Economic Vitality* (Boston: Jobs for the Future, 2005), pp. 9–10.

44. Ibid., pp. 13–14; Osterman, *Improving Job Quality,* p. 22.
45. Heath Prince, ed., *Strategies for Financing Workforce Intermediaries: Working Papers* (Boston: Jobs for the Future, 2007).
46. Kazis and others, "Adult Learners in Higher Education," pp. 50–51.
47. Robert Lerman, "Are Skills the Problem? Reforming the Education and Training System in the United States," paper prepared for the W. E. Upjohn Institute on Employment Policy Conference, A Future of Good Jobs? America's Challenge in the Global Economy (Kalamazoo, June 22, 2007).

13

Promoting Inclusive Economic Renewal in Older Industrial Cities

Angela Glover Blackwell and Radhika Fox

This is a moment of optimism for older industrial cities. Once iconic engines of productivity and manufacturing, then forgotten casualties of deindustrialization, these places are now poised to benefit from the renewed interest in urban America that has finally reached their borders after years of focus on "hot" cities such as San Francisco and Washington, D.C.[1]

But the renaissance of older industrial cities and their regions will prove shallow and unsustainable unless it is economically inclusive. Traditionally disadvantaged populations—low-income residents and people of color—must be brought into the economic mainstream so that they may contribute to and share equitably in market recovery.

Inclusion is especially crucial in our changed and changing economy. Over the past several decades, the economic base of the nation has shifted away from basic industry and toward what is often called the new economy. Success in this new technology- and knowledge-driven economy requires a set of ingredients different from the industrial economy, including, among other things, a skilled workforce and an emphasis on quality-of-life factors over the natural resource advantages of manufacturing-age cities.

In the new economy, inequity hampers economic growth largely because it prevents the development and optimal utilization of a city's most valuable asset—

its people. If large and growing classes of people are being left behind, the long-term economic viability of cities and regions is compromised because not all residents are productively contributing to growth and prosperity.

This is a particular danger in older industrial cities, which face the dual challenges of economic distress and entrenched economic, racial, and social inequity. Poverty rates are 23 percent in older industrial cities as compared to 15 percent in other cities (see chapter 6 of this volume, by Harold Wolman, Edward W. Hill, Pamela Blumenthal, and Kimberly Furdell). Older industrial cities are also among the most racially segregated in the nation, and regional income disparities between city and suburbs in these areas have grown, even as they have shrunk nationwide.[2]

Many of these cities have spent decades seeking the silver bullet that will restore them to their former glory, what Mayor Jay Williams of Youngstown, Ohio, has called the "infomercial" approach to economic development. These approaches typically focus on lowering costs and regulations and offering incentive packages sometimes worth hundreds of thousands of dollars per promised job and expecting very little in return.[3] These "growth-at-all-costs" approaches often produce dead-end, low-wage, hard-to-access jobs, compounding the economic isolation of low-income and minority residents.

At the same time, community development strategies that have sought to improve the life prospects of lower-income people have often focused on subsidized housing developments. These approaches can improve housing options for the poor, but have often furthered the deep socioeconomic divide by concentrating affordable housing in already low-income, disinvested neighborhoods.

In this chapter we make the case for why economic inclusion must be a central component of any long-term agenda for the economic transformation of older industrial cities and their regions. We also lift up several promising examples of how public, private, community, and foundation leaders are undertaking creative approaches to economic renewal that integrate the goals of shared prosperity and economic recovery. These innovations point the way toward a truly sustainable economy for cities and regions that have been left behind.

The Links between Economic Inclusion and Economic Competitiveness

There is a growing body of evidence that supports the premise that fully integrating the goal of economic inclusion enhances, not distracts from, broader efforts aimed at transforming the economic base of older industrial cities.

In chapter 4 in this volume, Manuel Pastor and Chris Benner present a statistical model that illustrates that high levels of inequality have a negative impact on growth and that this impact is generally stronger in metropolitan regions that house older industrial cities than in other regions. Other research suggests that U.S. metropolitan areas with higher poverty levels experience slower economic growth than those with lower poverty rates.[4] Numerous indicators also show that urban distress undermines regional competitiveness, whereas, conversely, improving incomes and decreasing poverty in cities can boost metropolitan economic performance.[5] In almost all regions in the United States, between 1970 and 1990, income gains in central cities corresponded with growth in suburban incomes, population, and home values.[6] And an earlier study by Pastor and others incorporating data from seventy-four regions found a positive relationship between the reduction of poverty in central cities and overall metropolitan growth.[7]

A recent analysis of factors contributing to regional economic progress prepared by scholars at the W. E. Upjohn Institute for Employment Research found that racial inclusion and income equality were also associated with regional economic growth.[8] Researchers examined a wide range of variables for correlation with economic growth measures in 118 metropolitan regions and condensed that list into just eight indicators (among them racial inclusion and income equity), each encompassing a few key variables. They found that the less segregated the region, the stronger the economy. Racial inclusion, as measured by a combination of the percentage of the population that was African American and segregation levels (as measured by dissimilarity and isolation indexes), had a strong positive correlation with economic health.[9] In fact, racial inclusion had the third strongest effect of all eight indicators on three of the four economic measures used: employment growth, productivity, and change in real output.[10]

Income equality, too, had a significant positive correlation with three of the four economic measures, in this case employment growth, output, and per capita income. There has been much debate about the relationship between income equality and growth, with some researchers asserting that higher levels of *inequality* (which often indicate high levels of affluence) are positively associated with growth.[11] In the Upjohn research, the "income equality" indicator encompassed two variables: the percentage of children in census tracts with poverty rates of 20 percent or higher and an income equality index based on the difference between the income at the 90th and 10th percentiles of the regional income distribution, divided by the income at the 10th percentile.[12] The incorporation of a concentrated poverty variable in the indicator makes it more of a measure of economic inclusion than simple measures of income distribution.

A correlation between social goods and economic progress doesn't necessarily make clear which comes first. These numbers may mean that racial inclusion and income equality encourage economic growth in the first place or that the most economically successful regions are the ones where the benefits of initial growth were carefully shared and used to reduce racial and income gaps. The implication for economic development practice is the same—economic inclusion is part of a virtuous cycle that enhances competitiveness.

Elements and Examples of an Economic Inclusion Framework

Although most economic development initiatives generally provide some trickle-down benefits to lower-income and minority residents in terms of an increased number of jobs, improved services, and revitalized physical landscapes, too often cities that begin to experience a renaissance find that unless a conscious, up-front effort is made to create deliberate linkages, benefits primarily accrue to new residents, businesses, or commuters, while poverty rates, racial income gaps, and neighborhoods of concentrated poverty persist.

Newark, New Jersey, is a good example. While the city is currently enjoying renewed investment based on its proximity to New York City (including housing development, corporate and university investment, and new public amenities), this infusion of resources has thus far had little effect on the city's 45 percent poverty rate, high unemployment, and low homeownership rate. In fact, many longtime residents have seen their housing cost burden rise as the market tightens, but no corresponding improvement in their job prospects. Alan Mallach describes a phenomenon of "parallel commuting," where large numbers of commuters travel both into and out of Newark and other New Jersey cities each day as a result of a "mismatch between a city's job base and its workforce."[13]

Numerous barriers prevent economic growth from automatically leading to improved life prospects for disadvantaged residents. Older industrial cities are deeply segregated, with poor and minority residents isolated in neighborhoods that are deteriorating physically, rife with toxic sites, lacking in business activity, and poorly connected to distant job centers. Rates of educational attainment in these cities are far behind those of their wider regions, while physical and social isolation leaves residents disconnected from the social networks that others rely upon to find jobs and advance careers. The retail and service-sector job market that filled the vacuum left by manufacturing in older cities is also bifurcated, with limited functioning career ladders from low-wage entry-level jobs to family-supporting professional positions.

Less concretely, but no less importantly, stereotypes about the urban workforce—often rooted in racial prejudice and discrimination—fuel the misconception that only new residents can "save" a city. This attitude discourages businesses and government from tapping the creativity and productivity of existing residents.

The good news is that many of the barriers faced by lower-income and minority residents of older industrial cities are not intrinsic, but rather are the legacies of decades of inequitable practices, policies, and attitudes. Charting a more inclusive and prosperous future can be supported by developing a framework that guides economic development planning, investments, and strategies in a manner that prioritizes fair and equitable outcomes. Such a framework can help public, private, business, foundation, and community leadership think comprehensively about the barriers to and opportunities for inclusion, assess the range of mechanisms available, establish priorities for action and investment, and measure progress. The framework should be holistic, encompassing strategies aimed at helping people connect to the economy, improving the places where they live, and building the markets that affect them.

People-based inclusion strategies build the skills and capacity of individual residents so that they can take full advantage of existing and emerging economic opportunities. People-focused strategies include small business development and sector-specific job training, as well as efforts to support resident participation in policy and planning processes.

Placed-based inclusion strategies shape the planning and implementation of physical revitalization efforts so that local residents can reap tangible benefits. They include ensuring that the locations of new developments are accessible to residents, making new jobs generated by place-based investments widely available, better integrating downtown development and neighborhood revitalization, and stabilizing residents at risk of displacement as a result of physical revitalization.

Market-based inclusion strategies, finally, grow particular industry sectors in ways that are equitable and sustainable: targeting resources to growth sectors of the economy that provide family-wage jobs, aligning workforce and economic development systems, and growing unique local markets that draw on the talents and creative assets of residents.

Leaders in older industrial cities can maximize limited resources and expand economic opportunity by integrating all three types of strategies into their economic development efforts. For example, a major downtown development not only promotes physical revitalization and job creation over the long haul in the central business district, but can also create meaningful shorter-term job opportunities for lower-income residents if there are explicit efforts made to connect people to the construction jobs generated by the development project. Similarly, the "inclusion effects" of a market-based approach to growing a particular industry cluster can be maximized if simultaneous investments are made in workforce training so that there is a ready stream of workers in the pipeline trained to compete in the targeted industry.

In the following sections we describe an array of promising initiatives with proven track records in older industrial cities. Although this is far from an exhaustive inventory of ways to foster economic inclusion, taken together, the examples illustrate a range of people-, place-, and market-based approaches to economic development that can promote equity and growth at the same time.

Aligning Workforce Systems to Growth Sectors of the Economy

Too often, economic development initiatives and workforce development systems operate like ships passing in the night. Economic development initiatives may focus on growing particular industry sectors, or cultivating companies or developers with the potential to generate large numbers of jobs. When the workforce development system is disconnected from (or sometimes even unaware of) these opportunities, however, both sides miss an opportunity to leverage new economic activity to benefit the region's lower-income workers. Workforce systems that train workers with little regard for the changing job market and little feedback from employers will ultimately struggle with placement and retention.

With the right coordination, however, these two systems can work together to forge a win-win scenario for new businesses and for workers: economic growth *and* inclusion. Sectoral employment initiatives exemplify such an integrated approach. These initiatives train low-skilled workers for good but previously inaccessible occupations (such as machinist, nurse, computer technician, construction worker) or improve the quality—in terms of wages, benefits, or career advancement opportunities—of low-wage jobs typically held by lower-income people (for example, home health aide, child-care worker, contingent, or temporary, worker).[14] The Aspen Institute characterizes sectoral strategies as those that

—target a particular industry or occupation,
—create a strategic partnership within the industry and leverage extensive industry knowledge and understanding of workforce issues,
—are able to channel employment opportunities to low-income job-seekers,
—are set up to work with relevant stakeholders to create systemic change within the industry's labor market.[15]

Program evaluations—and the testimonies of individual program participants—indicate that sectoral initiatives can improve employment outcomes for the poor, sometimes dramatically. One longitudinal study, which tracked the labor-market progress of 732 participants in a sectoral initiative over three years, found that participants had increased wages, income, and benefits. A year after completing their training programs, participants were earning over one and a half times their previous incomes; two years later, they were making twice their original salaries.[16]

Of course, building a skilled local workforce requires building a strong K–12 education system; hence, investing in the development of high-quality public schools must be one of the pillars of revitalization efforts in older industrial cities. Sectoral training programs, community colleges, and vocational schools cannot succeed over the long haul if they are required to spend the bulk of their resources teaching remedial reading and math. Improving city school systems is a long-term investment that strengthens a metro area's overall attractiveness to business and also levels the playing field for city residents in a regional labor market. In the meantime, sectoral workforce programs that meet residents where they live, work with school systems, and incorporate market-based growth strategies can make crucial connections that both reduce economic isolation in the cities and improve the attractiveness of a region's workforce.

Example: Newark/Essex Construction Careers Consortium. In 1999, when the New Jersey Supreme Court's 1999 *Abbott* v. *Burke* decision directed the state to renovate or replace crumbling schools in the state's poorest school districts, the New Jersey Institute for Social Justice (NJISJ) saw more than just an opportunity for children to finally have adequate school facilities. They recognized that the $12 billion construction project would generate living-wage, union construction jobs—just at a time when New Jersey's building trade unions were already facing a shortage of skilled workers as longtime members retired. Historically, however, there was little contact between the unions and poor minority communities. Would those most in need of jobs be able to access employment opportunities created by the school construction boom?

To bridge this gap, NJISJ launched a preapprenticeship program, now called the Newark/Essex Construction Careers Consortium (N/ECCC), in the summer of 2001. The six- to ten-week program, targeted to graduating seniors in the four Essex County school districts covered by the Abbott decision, focuses on sharpening math and life skills and introduces participants to the building trades through tours and presentations. The goal is to prepare students to meet the qualifications for a formal union apprenticeship. Since its inception, the preapprenticeship initiative has placed 230 African American and Latino men and women in apprenticeships with seventeen of the nineteen unions in the Essex County Building Trades Council. Over forty others have gone on to work for independent contractors.

Close working partnerships have been central to the program's success. Knowing that the Building Trades Council's cooperation was essential, NJISJ worked to understand and meet the standards for apprentices. In return, the unions committed significant time and effort to the training program. The county's vocational high schools and community colleges provide the course content, and NJISJ has developed recruiting partnerships with the high schools in Newark, Orange, East Orange, and Irvington, as well as with parole offices, halfway houses, and churches.

The trades were a good fit for a sectoral employment program in Essex County because construction is a growth industry and the jobs offer living wages with opportunities for advancement. Unlike some high-tech industries, where there are few jobs available to workers without a college or graduate degree, construction offers jobs that are both family-supporting and accessible to those with a basic level of education.

Rebecca Doggett, senior fellow at NJISJ, notes, however, that participants still face numerous barriers to success that often require additional intervention. "Most of what we learned is less about how to run a program" and more about "the life barriers put on people's shoulders," she says. For example, suspended driver's licenses were a major obstacle for many low-income participants. Unions require a valid driver's license for membership, but in New Jersey, licenses are often suspended for non-safety-related reasons such as lapsed insurance coverage or child support delinquency. NJISJ instituted a license reinstatement program that works with the state to reduce fines and surcharges, consolidate bills, and offer payment plans for license reinstatement charges.

Despite the success of N/ECCC, there are still never enough apprentice slots for all of the preapprenticeship program's graduates. Doggett says she'd like to see the building trades commit to giving a larger percentage of apprenticeships to minorities and women. "We're trying to open the door wider now that we're sure we can find and prepare people to be competitive."

Leveraging the Procurement and Hiring Roles of Anchor Institutions

Older industrial cities are home to dense concentrations of higher education institutions and medical facilities, often referred to as "eds and meds." These institutions are major employers and leaders in producing innovations and skilled workers—both essential to growth in a knowledge-based economy. Anchor institutions are also important fixed assets in urban centers: they cannot easily relocate their offices and operations, and their identities are tied to the cities and communities in which they are located. For example, Yale University's assessment of its impact on New Haven found that "Yale's strength and the health of the city, fiscally and socially, are inextricably linked."[17]

One important way that anchor institutions can play a leadership role in promoting economic inclusion is by prioritizing local- or minority-owned firms in their procurement and contracting practices. Urban educational institutions purchase $69 billion worth of goods and services every year (not including the purchases of faculty and students).[18] Leveraging these existing spending streams for revitalization can create sustainable local economic growth and connect local residents to social and career networks within these institutions.

Of course, targeted purchasing and hiring are not as easy as it might seem. Given the level of long-standing economic distress of their home neighborhoods and cities, anchor institutions are not likely to find an existing bevy of employees and suppliers that are prepared to meet all their needs. Anchor institutions can grow nascent local potential by offering business development support, educating firms about procurement requirements, and providing preapprenticeship programs and other workforce supports. To achieve this, anchor institutions will need to tap into community networks for recruitment, and partner with existing workforce development programs, labor unions, business organizations, and community institutions.

Example: West Philadelphia Initiatives. Could a prestigious Ivy League university continue to prosper while its surrounding neighborhood suffered from severe physical distress, economic decline, and high poverty? This was the fundamental question facing Judith Rodin when she assumed the presidency of the University of Pennsylvania in 1994.

Once a vibrant neighborhood with quaint homes and thriving businesses, West Philadelphia began to decline in the 1950s. By 1994, the neighborhood's crime rate had risen 10 percent in ten years, three of the area's elementary schools were ranked among the worst in the state, housing was deteriorating, and area commercial corridors were failing. In 1996, the murder of a graduate student near campus prompted the university to take quick and decisive action, and in 1997 it launched its West Philadelphia Initiatives, a comprehensive effort that includes a specific focus on economic inclusion.

To leverage its purchasing and hiring power in support of local businesses and residents, Penn (with the assistance of the Greater Philadelphia Urban Affairs Coalition) formulated an Economic Opportunity Plan that stipulates university-wide policies for minority and community contracting, purchasing, and employment.

Technical assistance that introduces minority and community contractors and suppliers to the technicalities of working for the university and helps them to scale up to meet the university's needs was a key element of the plan. Penn only purchases electronically, so assistance was provided to businesses to help them develop e-catalogues and work with electronic purchasing systems.

The university also required some of its longtime corporate suppliers to establish local offices, branches, or warehouses and hire local residents. Any contractors on university construction projects over $5 million must meet specific goals for participation of minority and community firms and residents; the mandate has been so successful that Penn plans to lower the $5 million threshold to increase the program's impact.

Over the decade since the initiative was founded, Penn's efforts have led to 170 construction jobs and 200 new permanent jobs for residents, $134 million in construction contracts for minority- and women-owned businesses, and $344 million in Penn purchases from local vendors between 1997 and 2003.[19]

This successful program was not the first attempt by Penn to formally increase its purchasing from West Philadelphia businesses, but previous attempts had lackluster results. Penn learned from its early failures that changing procurement and hiring practices throughout such a large and decentralized organization requires both leadership from the top and broad organizational buy-in. Strong leadership by Rodin, the involvement of relevant department heads who served on the Advisory Committee on Economic Inclusion, and systematic, institution-wide policies and results monitoring moved Penn's program from a nice sentiment to a local economic driver.

Understanding local firms' challenges in accessing procurement opportunities was also key to the initiative's success. Penn designated four purchasing specialists to be the first point of contact for new suppliers, and also launched a Supplier Mentoring Program "to help current and prospective Penn suppliers develop the expertise and business skills needed to succeed in the University's purchasing environment."[20] Framing these types of initiatives as business-savvy strategies that stimulate the local economy—not as charity for local residents and merchants—is key, notes one researcher who studied Penn's program: "The institution's approach must limit support to the level needed to enable targeted businesses and workers to compete for jobs or contracts, then allow them to do so without the need for additional support. Such an approach provides the best assurance of integrating local businesses and residents into the mainstream economy and positioning them for long-term success."[21]

Programs like Penn's can have a deeper impact if several anchor institutions and the local government coordinate similar efforts. By working together, institution leaders and local officials can not only prevent duplication of work but also identify and qualify more local businesses, introduce suppliers to several prospective purchasers at once, and provide a wider range of employment options to residents in targeted training programs.

Supporting Minority-Owned Businesses

Businesses owned by people of color, often called minority business enterprises (MBEs), have tremendous, often untapped, potential to foster economic inclusion of low-income and minority city residents. MBEs are more likely than white-owned businesses to hire people of color, locate in urban and first-ring suburban neighborhoods that are experiencing high job losses, and serve minority residents as customers, making them both an important economic force in underserved urban communities and a potential link between those communities and the larger mainstream economy.[22]

MBEs face a number of challenges, however, including many of the same problems that plague low-income urban job seekers. MBEs are often disconnected from the long-standing social networks that offer white-owned businesses opportunities for relationships, mentoring, partnerships, and sales.[23] Lack of connections (which are especially critical in generating sales and accessing public contracts) can exacerbate, and sometimes also mask, continuing discriminatory behavior. Lack of credit history or persistent redlining practices also sometimes prevent MBEs from accessing capital. Furthermore, in many places there has been a backlash against public policies that set targets for a percentage of procurement from minority and women-owned businesses, and this has slowed progress and created an unsupportive political climate for MBE assistance initiatives.

Example: Cleveland regional model for minority business advancement. In 2005, when the Cleveland Foundation funded a report on minority business development in the Cleveland region, the outlook for MBEs was both hopeful and a source of concern. MBEs made up 19 percent of all Cleveland firms, but accounted for only 1.7 percent of sales and receipts.[24] Although MBEs had been growing, tripling their business in the 1990s, they were growing more slowly than white-owned businesses, taking seven years to reach the five- to nine-employee level and eleven years to reach ten to nineteen employees (compared to five and six and a half years, respectively, for all firms).[25] In 1998 and 2000, courts struck down two public set-aside programs, a blow that likely contributed to an 8 percent decrease in sales and receipts experienced by MBEs across Ohio from 1997 to 2002.[26]

Despite these challenges, the Cleveland region's MBE businesses are poised for growth and advancement now that several regional collaboration agendas have prioritized economic inclusion and minority business success.

In 2004, the Greater Cleveland Growth Association (the regional chamber of commerce), Cleveland Tomorrow (a group of CEOs from the largest corporations in northeastern Ohio who were committed to improving the long-term economic vitality of the region), and the Greater Cleveland Roundtable (a group aiming to improve race relations and economic inclusion) merged to form the Greater Cleveland Partnership (GCP), one of the largest regional chambers of commerce in the country. GCP provides a prominent home for the Commission on Economic Inclusion, a coalition of "100 Northeast Ohio employers who are committed to making the region's diversity a source of economic strength."[27]

Around the same time, over eighty of the region's leading foundations and philanthropists established the Fund for Our Economic Future to coordinate regional economic development grant making, research, and civic engagement for greater impact. In 2007, the fund worked with the region's public and private sector leaders to develop Advance Northeast Ohio, a regional economic action plan. One of the plan's four pillars is "Growth through Racial and Economic Inclusion Initiatives."

A report commissioned by the Presidents' Council—a group of African American CEOs, funded by the Cleveland Foundation, whose focus is on ways regionalism could affect the area's African American community—also raised regional awareness of equity issues.

The result of this groundwork, says Deborah Bridwell, senior director for inclusion initiatives at the Commission on Economic Inclusion, is that "minorities will not be an afterthought" in the region's economic development planning.

The increased attention to economic health and inclusion is fueling a growing and ambitious regionwide movement. In 2005 and 2006, the fund underwrote a research and planning process that brought together over twenty organizations from across a fifteen-county region for four facilitated work sessions. Trust and unity were not automatic, admits Bridwell: "It is natural to feel a bit territorial. It raises difficult questions: If you and I both do it, who does it better?" But periodic meetings in a facilitated environment allowed the organizations to form partnerships, establish distinct roles for each group, and ultimately generate a comprehensive model for regional MBE advancement.

Effective MBE development requires both supply- and demand-side work. "We don't want to be just another organization that says, 'We developed the capacity of x number of businesses, but they don't have any more sales,' " explains Bridwell. Historically, in Cleveland and around the country, MBE initiatives were geared toward increasing public procurement opportunities—but, notes Bridwell, those set-asides are frequently challenged in court. Moreover, the private sector often has far more flexibility than public agencies to leverage MBE opportunities in innovative ways. For example, Case Western Reserve University shifted their contracting rules so that companies could perform larger amounts of work with lower bonding requirements. A subsequent university evaluation found that easing contractor restrictions allowed Case Western to greatly increase their hiring of MBEs without negative consequences or defaults on projects.

Cleveland leaders were eager to implement the MBE model that grew out of the meetings of the participants in the Fund for Our Economic Future. The Presidents' Council submitted a proposal on behalf of a consortium of partners, and in March 2007, the fund provided a $1 million grant for the first year of operations for a minority business accelerator that will work with large and midsize minority-owned businesses to improve their access to capital, technical assistance, and markets. The accelerator aims to increase participating companies' sales by 20 percent and double their number of employees (see figure 13-1).

Figure 13-1. *Greater Cleveland Minority Business Enterprise (MBE) Model: Regional Economic Inclusion*

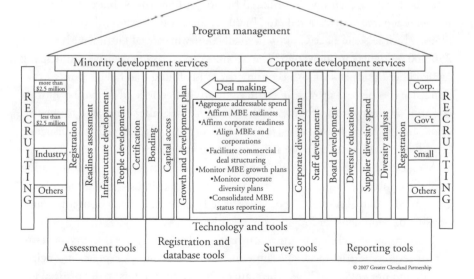

© 2007 Greater Cleveland Partnership

Source: Greater Cleveland Partnership.

Note: This diagram represents a collaborative economic development model that leverages the existing resources in the region to provide the best services to the constituents. The primary goal is to facilitate the growth of MBE and corporate business.

The Cleveland experience, although still in its early stage, illustrates that taking a regional view, strategically applying the power of regional business organizations and funders, and developing both the capacities of MBEs themselves and the supplier diversity of majority-owned firms can take MBE development to a larger scale.

Promoting Digital Inclusion

In today's world, access to broadband infrastructure is necessary to attract economic development and connect people to the economic mainstream. Computer literacy is becoming essential not just to qualifying for a job, but even finding job openings, as employment listings and recruitment increasingly gravitate to the Internet.

Despite the Internet's apparent ubiquity, a digital divide remains. Although basic broadband service is now generally available in most urban areas, few low-income residents are connected. Families with incomes under $30,000 per year have only a 30 percent rate of broadband adoption, compared to 76 percent for those with incomes over $75,000 per year.[28] African American and Hispanic broadband adoption rates also still trail those of whites, though African Americans are rapidly closing what had been a much wider gap. As of 2007, they were only about 8 percent, or one year's worth of growth, behind.[29]

Cities and states are taking action to close the high-speed Internet access gap, often by creating their own municipal broadband networks that are offered to residents at a free or discounted rate. In 2001, the city of Leesburg, Florida, began offering businesses in Lake County (a small county in central Florida with around 250,000 residents spread over 953 square miles) access to an extensive municipally owned fiber optic network. An econometric study found that Lake County experienced a 100 percent growth in economic activity (compared to similar Florida counties) in the two years following the network availability compared to the two years prior. (The study controlled for other factors that might explain the disparate economic growth rates between Lake and other counties.)[30]

Municipal broadband programs can foster economic inclusion by incorporating affordable Internet connections for residents into a business-focused plan. Local governments can also establish or encourage broadband networks in affordable housing developments or low-income neighborhoods.

Unfortunately, telecommunications companies have lobbied many states to ban or severely restrict local governments from deploying widespread municipal broadband networks. In 2004, the state of Pennsylvania drastically limited the ability of local governments to establish and administer their own broadband networks (Philadelphia was granted an exemption).[31] The legislature is considering a bill—HB327 in the 2007 session—that would reverse these restrictions. Michigan has also curbed local governments' broadband rights.[32]

Communities can also lobby the private sector to increase broadband access at more affordable rates. Cable companies are often granted exclusive contracts in an area in exchange for providing community benefit, typically in the form of public-access television stations. Community and municipal leaders could lobby to include affordable broadband in cable service negotiations.

A successful initiative in Kentucky illustrates how public-private partnerships with broadband providers can also increase coverage and affordability as providers realize that there are gaps in service and market demand for lower-cost packages.

Example: ConnectKentucky. Kentucky's broadband problem was somewhat different from that of older industrial cities: in 2004, 40 percent of the heavily rural state had no broadband Internet access whatsoever—a problem that is very rare in even the most distressed cities. But the solution nonetheless serves as a promising model for increasing broadband in low-income urban areas.

ConnectKentucky is a nonprofit public-private partnership that joins state and local leaders with broadband providers and private industry to find collaborative solutions for technology expansion across the state. To increase broadband adoption and reach the eventual goal of universal deployment, ConnectKentucky first needed detailed statistics about the current availability and rates of adoption—but existing data coded an entire zip code as served by broadband even if only one address had access. ConnectKentucky partnered with major corporate broadband providers and local entrepreneurs to map broadband access down to the household level. Providers that may have been wary about releasing proprietary customer and service data were reassured that since ConnectKentucky was not a government agency, their data would remain confidential.

The maps showed the size and density of markets that none of the companies were serving, and spurred increases in deployment to 94 percent coverage as of mid-2007. The maps gave the companies market intelligence they didn't have. "We found that broadband providers themselves did not know which areas of the state were not being served, so it was impossible for them to attempt to create a business case for deployment in those areas," explains Brent Legg, director of state and local initiatives at Connected Nation, an organization formed to take ConnectKentucky's approach national.

Next, ConnectKentucky created "eCommunity leadership teams" in each county to improve county use of technology, verify map accuracy, and conduct surveys about why people were not using broadband. Survey results showed providers that because cost was one of the primary obstacles to broadband adoption, there was tremendous untapped market potential for more affordable broadband.

Interestingly, the eCommunity surveys also showed that the number one barrier to adoption was not affordability but lack of understanding about how broadband can benefit businesses and citizens. "If we can find a way to make technology relevant to people, they will usually shift resources and find a way to adopt it," says Laura Taylor, vice president of research for Connected Nation. The eCommunity teams are raising broadband awareness through strategic technology plans for each community; two-year goals for increased use; and step-by-step plans for creating targeted applications, making smart technology investments, developing awareness campaigns, and driving demand for broadband and computer use.

ConnectKentucky has also helped municipalities set up wireless networks in their downtowns. Legg says providers have realized that municipal networks function more often as demand generators than direct competitors: after experiencing high-speed Internet at a downtown park or café, suburban or rural commuters and visitors are more likely to sign up with a private provider for home broadband access.

From 2005 to 2006, broadband adoption in Kentucky increased 58 percent, compared to 40 percent nationwide.[33] Rural states are eager to replicate ConnectKentucky's success, but the approach is also relevant to help bring broadband equity to older industrial cities. Even though older industrial cities are likely to be covered with some kind of broadband, some areas may be lagging in the deployment of higher-speed infrastructure. Detailed data on this are limited, and the kind of mapping done in Kentucky could also be relevant in states that are home to older industrial cities. Mapping could also be used to track adoption rates and home in on neighborhoods that the market is not serving, despite the technical availability of broadband access. This might include discounted access rates or programs that help residents and businesses understand broadband and make it relevant, which was a critical program component in Kentucky.

Fostering Accountable Development

The public sector has a complex and powerful arsenal of tools at its disposal to foster and steer economic growth: grant programs; bonding authority; dollars for site preparation and assembly; new equipment, feasibility studies, and infrastructure upgrades; and a multitude of funding streams. Beyond direct spending, governments can also subsidize new industries or businesses with tax breaks or abatements, loan guarantees, or relaxed regulations.

Understanding the way these public dollars flow—and maximizing the public benefits that these public dollars deliver—are critical to advancing sustainable and inclusive economic growth in older industrial cities. An important mechanism for promoting economic inclusion through major development projects that receive public money is community benefits agreements. Community benefits agreements are legally enforceable contracts, signed by community groups and by a developer, setting forth a range of community benefits that the developer agrees to provide as part of a development project. Community benefits agreements are often the result of a negotiation process between the developer and organized representatives of affected communities, in which the developer agrees to shape the development in a certain way or to provide specified community benefits. In exchange, the community groups promise to support the proposed project before government bodies that provide the necessary permits and subsidies.[34]

Community benefits agreements advance economic inclusion through local hiring programs for neighborhood residents, livable wage employment opportunities, training or educational opportunities, increased transit access and services, health-care and child-care services, increased access to technology, and opportunities for ownership and profit sharing for community residents. On the project side, community benefits agreements can also require developers to contract with locally owned, minority-owned, and women-owned businesses for project design, construction, and ongoing operations, and incorporate nonprofit or community partners as owners, developers, organizers, providers, or property managers.

State policy also has tremendous influence on economic development accountability. Local governments often need state-level *clawback* provisions (which require companies that renege on subsidy-related promises to repay incentive monies they received) to enforce even the most basic community benefits agreements. Clawbacks vary widely in strength; some take effect only if a company flagrantly violates a key subsidy condition (for example, if the business leaves the state entirely). Minnesota's clawback policy (the strongest in the nation) directs all state and local subsidy agreements to require total or partial recapture of subsidies, with interest, if companies fail to meet agreement terms.

Example: Milwaukee Park East Freeway Redevelopment. In 1999, Milwaukee decided to demolish the Milwaukee Park East Freeway to open up sixty-seven acres of land, including a twenty-four-acre downtown parcel, for redevelopment. Recognizing the potential of such a large-scale project, a twenty-seven-member coalition of labor, faith, environmental, and community groups, called the Good Jobs and Livable Neighborhoods Coalition (GJLN), began working to ensure that the surrounding community benefited from redevelopment of the downtown parcel.

In December 2004, the Milwaukee County Board of Supervisors voted 15–4 to include GJLN's community benefits provision, the Park East Redevelopment Compact (PERC), as a formal requirement for any developers interested in purchasing some of the sixteen acres owned by the county.[35] The PERC includes consideration of job quality standards, establishes local hiring and prevailing wage requirements, requires affordable housing construction and minority business contracting, encourages the use of environmentally friendly materials, establishes a public process for evaluating development proposals, and calls for data collection on job creation in the Park East corridor.[36]

To date, the Milwaukee County Board has approved several projects for the former freeway corridor and several parcels of land have been sold.[37] Despite concern that the community benefits requirements would dampen real estate and business interest in the area, the development teams have met all of the mandatory community benefits provisions—and voluntarily added more community benefits, including higher targets for some of the original agreement's goals and green building elements.[38] The citizen advisory committee that works on the requests for proposals (RFPs) and in forming the agreements has been emboldened by their successes to push for more ambitious benefits in later projects.

It is crucial to have a strong, active, and alert coalition supporting community benefits measures, which usually encounter opposition from developers or government officials who are afraid they will deter economic activity. For example, the county executive initially vetoed PERC, but community benefits agreement supporters turned out in great numbers to successfully lobby county supervisors to override the veto.[39]

Expanding on the Park East work, GJLN has succeeded in raising the profile of accountable development on a citywide level, and has brought hundreds of people to public meetings to discuss ways to standardize economic development provisions such as living-wage jobs, local hiring, affordable housing, and environmental standards so that future deals will not be crafted in isolation from these issues and goals. John Goldstein, former co-chair of GJLN, notes that just learning how the subsidy process operates builds incredible community power. GJLN plans to raise accountable development as an issue in the 2008 elections.

Conclusion

These examples illustrate how older industrial cities and their regions can simultaneously promote economic growth and inclusion through people-, place-, and market-based revitalization strategies. Indeed, many of the examples reveal that fully integrating economic inclusion into economic development initiatives does not distract from but rather enhances and supports the goal of market recovery. There are several cross-cutting lessons that undergird the successful implementation of the strategies discussed:

—*Treat inclusion as an economic driver, not just a charitable goal.* Leaders will hesitate to invest the time and energy in economic inclusion unless it is viewed as an essential engine of economic development, and not simply a charitable side benefit.

—*Find synergies between existing needs and opportunities and unite the interests of disparate groups.* The New Jersey Institute for Social Justice capitalized on the opportunity presented by a legal decision, connecting a court-mandated increase in school construction projects with growing union retirement rates and city residents' need for family-supporting jobs.

—*Cultivate close working partnerships, motivated by enlightened self-interest.* Given its importance to economic progress, economic inclusion should be a goal of a wide range of institutions and leaders. Rather than leave it to the same few antipoverty and racial-justice advocates to champion inclusion initiatives, build broad coalitions (as was done in Cleveland and Philadelphia) that appeal to the enlightened self-interest of educational and arts organizations, anchor institutions, and business and union leaders.

—*Develop creative solutions to individuals' real-world barriers.* In the low-income neighborhoods of already-struggling older industrial cities, economic inclusion efforts will falter unless they address nitty-gritty real-world barriers such as driver's license suspension (faced by the students in the Newark trades program) or bonding requirements (which prevented Cleveland minority-owned businesses from winning contracts).

—*Change the culture of key institutions, both public and private.* Recognizing the overlap between economic inclusion and economic development will require a culture shift in both government agencies, and major public and private institutions. Top leaders, such as Judith Rodin at the University of Pennsylvania, can model this change, but it must be broadly infused into the practices of an institution.

—*Deal with issues of supply and demand in tandem.* The most basic characteristic of markets is that they function through a balance of supply and demand. Successful economic inclusion efforts should always recognize both sides of the equation.

—*Work regionally.* Labor and housing markets are regional. To successfully address economic inclusion—whether of minorities, low-income people, or city residents—economic development efforts need to look regionally at spatial mismatches, exclusionary housing, and policies that contribute to divestment from the urban core.

Older industrial cities are poised to shed the legacy of their industrial decline and make great strides toward a promising future. To reach their full potential, however, these cities must ensure that the economic benefits of revitalization are widely shared. As they work to retool their economies, now is the time to establish the attitudes and approaches that will make these communities linchpins of globally competitive regions, and leaders in an inclusive, equitable style of twenty-first-century economic development.

Notes

1. The authors wish to thank Miriam Axel-Lute for her assistance in the development of this chapter.
2. Radhika K. Fox and Sarah Treuhaft, "Shared Prosperity, Stronger Regions: An Agenda for Rebuilding America's Older Core Cities" (Oakland, Calif.: PolicyLink and Community Development Partnerships' Network, 2006), pp. 34–35.
3. Bill Schweke, "A Progressive Economic Development Agenda for Shared Prosperity: Taking the High Road and Closing the Low" (Washington: Corporation for Enterprise Development, 2006), p. 2.
4. Saurav Dev Bhatta, "Are Inequality and Poverty Harmful for Economic Growth: Evidence from the Metropolitan Areas of the United States," *Journal of Urban Affairs* 23, no. 2-4 (2001): 335–59.
5. Mark Muro and Robert Puentes, "Investing in a Better Future: A Review of the Fiscal and Competitive Advantages of Smart Growth and Development Patterns," discussion paper (Brookings Institution, 2004).
6. Richard Voith, "Do Suburbs Need Cities?" *Journal of Regional Science* 29, no. 3 (1998): 445–64.
7. Manuel Pastor, Jr., Peter Dreier, J. Eugene Grigsby III, and Marta Lopez-Garcia, *Regions That Work: How Cities and Suburbs Can Grow Together* (University of Minnesota Press, 2000).
8. Randall Eberts, George Erickcek, and Jack Kleinhez, "Dashboard Indicators for the Northeast Ohio Economy," Working Paper 06-05 (Federal Reserve Bank of Cleveland, 2006).
9. Ibid., p. 12.
10. Ibid., p. 20.
11. Bhatta, "Inequality and Poverty," p. 337.
12. Eberts, Erickcek, and Kleinhez, "Dashboard Indicators," p. 13.
13. Alan Mallach, "Cities in Transition: New Jersey's Urban Paradox" (Trenton: Housing and Community Development Network of New Jersey, 2006), p. 6.
14. Mark Elliot and Elisabeth King, "Labor Market Leverage: Sectoral Employment Field Report" (Philadelphia: Public/Private Ventures, 1999).
15. Peggy Clark and others, "Jobs and the Urban Poor: Privately Initiated Sectoral Strategies" (Washington: Aspen Institute, 1995); see also S. L. Dawson, Maureen Conway, and I. Rademacher, "Industry-Specific Workforce Development: Key Research Findings and Implications for the Workforce Investment Act" (Washington: Aspen Institute, 2004).
16. Aspen Institute, "Working with Value: Industry-Specific Approaches to Workforce Development" (Washington, 2002), p. 11. The average incomes were $12,295 in the baseline year, $17,363 in year one, and $21,216 in year two.

17. Yale University, "Economic Impact: Yale and New Haven" (Yale University, 1993), cited in Ira Harkavy and Harmon Zuckerman, "Eds and Meds: Cities' Hidden Assets" (Brookings Institution, 1999), p. 3.

18. CEOs for Cities and Initiative for a Competitive Inner City, "Leveraging Colleges and Universities for Urban Revitalization: An Action Agenda" (Chicago: CEOs for Cities, 2002).

19. John Kromer and Lucy Kerman, "West Philadelphia Initiatives: A Case Study in Urban Revitalization" (University of Pennsylvania, 2004).

20. Ibid., p. 42.

21. Ibid., "West Philadelphia," p. 39.

22. john a. powell, Julie Nielsen, Jason Reece, Roger A. Clay, Jr., and Tim Lohrentz, "The Business of Color: Strengthening the Regional Economy," *Focus* (Joint Center for Political and Economic Studies), March–April 2007, p. 16; and john a. powell, Julie Nielsen, Jason Reece, Roger A. Clay, Jr., and Tim Lohrentz, "A Minority Business Development Framework for the Cleveland Foundation" (Cleveland: Kirwan Institute for the Study of Race and Ethnicity and the National Economic Development and Law Center, 2005) p. 10.

23. powell and others, "Minority Business Development Framework," p. 17.

24. Ibid., p. 4.

25. Ibid., p. 9.

26. Ibid., pp. 13–14.

27. Greater Cleveland Partnership, "Commission on Economic Inclusion," at www.gcpartner ship.com/Commission.aspx (access to site for members).

28. John B. Horrigan and Aaron Smith, "Home Broadband Adoption 2007," report prepared for Pew Internet and American Life Project, June 2007, p. 4, available at www.pewinternet. org/PPF/r/217/report_display.asp.

29. Horrigan and Smith, "Home Broadband," pp. 4–5.

30. George S. Ford and Thomas M. Koutsky, "Broadband and Economic Development: A Municipal Case Study from Florida," *Applied Economic Studies*, April 2005.

31. An Act Amending Title 66 (November 30, 2004), *Pennsylvania Consolidated Statutes,* sec. 3011–3019.

32. Michigan Telecommunications Act, Public Act 235 (November 22, 2005), *Michigan Compiled Laws,* amending Public Act 179 of 1991, sec. 484.2101–2701.

33. Horrigan and Smith, "Home Broadband," p. 4; Laura Taylor, memo to PolicyLink re "Connected Nation," August 24, 2007.

34. Julian Gross, Greg LeRoy, and Madeline Janis-Aparacio, "Community Benefits Agreements: Making Development Projects Accountable" (Washington: Good Jobs First and Partnership for Working Families, 2005).

35. Dave Umhoefer, "Board OKs Rules for Park East Developers," *Milwaukee Journal Sentinel,* December 17, 2004, available at www.jsonline.com/story/index.aspx?id=284823.

36. Institute for Wisconsin's Future, "A Resolution" (Park East Redevelopment Compact), at www.wisconsinsfuture.org/workingfamilies/econdev/PERC_Compact.pdf.

37. Joe Rice, Milwaukee supervisor, memo to PolicyLink, "Question re: Park East Development," July 8, 2005.

38. Craig C. Dillman, Real Estate Services, Milwaukee County, memo to PolicyLink, July 11, 2005, "Park East Development"; see also Sean Ryan, "Condo, Retail OK'd for Milwaukee's Park East Property," *Daily Reporter,* June 15, 2005.

39. Dave Umhoefer, "Board Overrides Park East Veto," *Milwaukee Journal Sentinel,* February 4, 2005, available at www.jsonline.com/story/index.aspx?id=298740.

14

The Market-Building Potential of Development Finance in Older Industrial Cities

Jeremy Nowak

There is a significant literature on capital investment in older industrial cities, including studies of mortgage investment, small business finance, microenterprise, and private equity. This literature discusses the challenge of capital access in those communities, public policy incentives designed to drive capital flows (particularly tax-based incentives), and the nonmarket constraints to development.

This chapter explores the market-building role of development finance in older industrial cities. By *development finance* I mean market-oriented capital that requires a return on investment but is willing to take nonmarket positions and risks due to its public purpose. It is capital that must be profitable but does not have to be profit-maximizing. By *market-building* I mean creating conditions through which capital investment, entrepreneurship, and consumer demand flourish in competitive and self-organizing ways.

Development finance may be originated through public economic development institutions, housing finance agencies, privately organized community development financial institutions, or any of a variety of public-private partnerships or authorities. Although the target of specific development finance portfolios may vary—job creation, wealth building, place-based revitalization, home ownership, business start-ups, environmental remediation—the notion of combining market disciplines with social outcomes to restore market vitality remains constant.

I explore four roles of development finance: as a provider of liquidity to housing developers; as a facilitator of public innovation through capitalizing public revenue; as a force for old-economy industrial transformation; and as an investor in
the food retail business. I note the role of capital investment in each area and the
nonmarket tools or conditions that facilitate or constrain successful investments.
I argue that development finance's market-building capacity is based, in part, on
its ability to align capital investments with nonmarket inputs for which it cannot
directly price through its loans or investments.

Throughout the paper, I refer to my experience at The Reinvestment Fund
(TRF), a community development financial institution that has provided more than
$650 million in financing in support of urban businesses, community facilities,
commercial real estate, and residential real estate. I draw on our portfolio in older
industrial cities in the mid-Atlantic region (particularly the Philadelphia region),
rather than a scientific sample or comparative assessment of cities or portfolios.

Capital Availability and Project Incubation

Capital investment from the private sector is a key driver of development and economic opportunity. It can bring retail amenities, jobs, community facilities, and
housing to previously underserved communities. In addition, through bond
financing the capital markets provide investments into basic infrastructure, as well
as the expansion of major urban institutional anchors such as hospitals, universities, and cultural centers.

There is a long history in the United States of trying to ensure that capital access
is based on the merits of a project or borrower and not the inherent characteristics
of race, gender, or place. Much of the recent research and analysis on this issue has
revolved around race and mortgage lending, but there have been many other concerns as well. For many years, for example, the role of credit in the rural sector was
a political issue; the creation of a broad-based mortgage industry to serve low- and
middle-income borrowers also occupied decades of public policy discussion.

A large number of American institutions, such as the various government-
sponsored enterprises (such as Fannie Mae), were created to stabilize capital markets and help increase—some would even say democratize—access to credit,
including home mortgage credit, farm credit, and education loans. The passage
of the Community Reinvestment Act (CRA) in 1977 represented a place-based
mandate for regulated banks, and was designed to increase the flow of private capital into underserved areas. The influence of the CRA with respect to urban community and economic development has been substantial.

Although discrimination has not been eliminated, changes in information technology, communications, and global capital exchange have created a wide array of financial instruments that tie together Main Street and Wall Street in unprecedented ways. Banks and nonbank financial institutions move capital without being impeded by the friction of geography as they were only decades ago. Households and businesses can be researched and underwritten through technology that should obviate historical patterns of discrimination.

Indeed, delinking capital and place should create an opportunity for older urban centers. Urban projects that make market sense can get capital in more efficient ways than ever, despite historical issues of disinvestment and social policies that encouraged nonurban economic growth.[1] The problem is that historical disadvantage is sticky; it has its own momentum, its own institutions and political culture, and its own recovery costs that are not easily removed by the newly available capital technology.

Historical legacy and contemporary policies affect project incubation and the consequent demand for capital. The lack of project and firm incubation in many urban areas is rooted in environmental costs, regulatory inefficiencies, and other public infrastructure issues that create barriers to development and therefore limit the usefulness of new capital sources. In addition, the costs of concentrated poverty and a history of inefficient tax policy often play havoc on bond ratings and budgets in older industrial cities, driving up operating costs and limiting public borrowing capacity. Specifically, poor tax policies create higher costs for businesses and residents without correspondingly high service quality, making these cities noncompetitive compared to nearby jurisdictions. High operating costs and low borrowing capacity make it difficult to lay the public and even the civic groundwork for private-sector housing and business investment.

Consider small business credit scoring, which ought to be place-agnostic. Indeed, studies have shown that credit scoring has increased the availability of credit to businesses in low-incomes areas.[2] However, the rates of business development in low-income urban areas, as measured by the number of new start-ups, the absorption of venture capital, commercial real estate vacancies, and other indicators, are not comparable to suburban districts. This limits the aggregate number of urban credit-scored projects and contributes to credit-scoring marketing strategies that are not as urban focused as they might be otherwise.

Moreover, development happens through a context of reinforcing activities. Development is both an end product of a process and the initiating component of additional investments, developments, and consumer decisions. Think of development as a virtuous circle of decisions. While the technology of capital can potentially drive investment into areas that have lacked historical access, this does not mean that an *ecosystem* of incubation will exist to capture and use the capital. There will be limited effective demand for financial products in the absence of a promising investment environment.

The role of development finance is in part to foster demand by using both capital and nonmarket tools to construct or support a virtuous circle of development decisions on the part of investors, consumers, and others. Four examples of development finance activity within the context of older industrial cities that capture the complexity of the processes and issues are discussed in the next section.

Four Examples from The Reinvestment Fund

To illustrate the role of development finance in older industrial cities, I turn to four portfolio examples: housing developer liquidity, public-sector innovation, old-economy transitions, and retail investments in the food industry.

Housing Developer Liquidity

The most important feature of capital investment in older cities is the existence of predictable liquidity for housing development. *Liquidity* refers to the ability of investments to be converted into salable assets that others will buy. Liquidity in a housing market requires the availability of capital for developers who acquire land and buildings and rehabilitate them for sale or rent, and the ability of home owners to access the mortgage market and other investments for upgrading. The absence of liquidity at either end of the development cycle limits the potential of the market by limiting both supply and demand, ultimately constraining the growth in housing values. A market without liquidity cannot grow and change over time.

Mortgage markets (and now home-equity financing) comprise well-developed financial instruments in terms of availability, the diversity of structures, and the institutions that originate, insure, fund, and sell them as securities. Historically, mortgage markets have been the market innovator for transforming long-term fixed assets into shorter-duration securities bundled together for sale to third-party investors. Along with the revolution in information technology, securitization has created extraordinary efficiencies in market access. Information technology has made loan origination less expensive and the capacity to obtain liquidity has made it less risky for the originator.

The other side of the liquidity equation has to do with developer liquidity provided to households, businesses, contractors, nonprofit organizations, and entrepreneurs who use capital to buy, build, and rehabilitate property. In older industrial cities, this kind of capital, particularly at the acquisition stage, has been the hardest capital to obtain; yet it is the availability of this financing to property owners and developers that drives market change.

Acquisition and early-stage development capital can be hard to obtain for several reasons:

—The uncertainty of the market in terms of financial value and consumer demand

—The lack of financial capacity of small, niche developers that work in those communities

—The inability to understand the market as a result of limited experience or institutional presence

—The lack of standardized products that can reduce transaction costs for lenders and make liquidity more certain

Any of these four factors make it difficult to evaluate risk and price capital. This is particularly true for an early entrant to a market. The early-entrant investor takes on more risk and incurs higher costs to organize the market through information, product development, and the creation of demand. A market organizer ordinarily expects to be rewarded for this risk through pricing or a temporary monopoly position on the initial pipeline of projects. Early entrants want to extract value from the new market prior to subsequent entrants' free-riding on their market-building investments.[3]

Inner-city markets that have been relatively stagnant require early-entrant capital. This is a typical development finance role. In East Camden, New Jersey, for example, TRF provided financing to a nonprofit church-based community development organization called St. Joseph's Carpenter Society. Over a ten-year period St. Joe's Carpenter Society used our capital to acquire, rehabilitate, and sell 650 units of housing, most of which were sold to home buyers who received a mixture of prime and subprime mortgages. Their earliest units had sales prices of $20,000 and their 650th unit sold several years ago for $120,000. The community saw an average increase in value of 40 percent during the 1990s, when almost all other Camden neighborhoods saw price declines.

One of the key issues that determined this value change, according to St. Joe's Carpenter Society's executive director at the time, was the predictability of development capital. Curbside activity of houses being rehabilitated led to a belief among residents that if they invested in their homes they could get the value back, plus a potential increase in equity over time. This led to a general impression that the area was improving. It became one of the best choices among Camden's low-wealth areas. Each time a vacant unit on the block was rehabilitated, the other housing units gained value. The expectation in the neighborhood was that the rate of reinvestment would surpass the rate of disinvestment, eventually eliminating all vacant units. The increases in value eventually resulted in a greater income mix of families, which in turn had a stabilizing effect.

Although other factors played important roles in the community stabilization of East Camden—the redevelopment of a major public housing project, the role of a strong Catholic high school, an unusually strong job market in the region—they were supported by St. Joe's willingness and ability to buy vacant units and reintroduce them onto the market, ultimately helping to increase the amount of product, the amount and nature of demand, and overall housing values.

Building the quality and quantity of demand was a significant part of the St. Joe's strategy. As part of their community development program, St. Joe's recruited and trained potential home buyers by establishing a Homeowner Academy. This program provided potential new buyers with credit counseling and household budgeting assistance. Only individuals who completed the program could buy a St. Joe's home, creating a hurdle that measured participants' willingness to commit, sacrifice, and own. In this way St. Joe's was creating both a pipeline of housing units and a pipeline of housing buyers. They were making a market in the most basic sense.

St. Joe's was willing to act as an early-entrant developer because of its mission, and it was able to function as such because of the availability of predictable capital. Both the developer and lender were able to manage risk, in part through the existence of market information regarding the neighborhood, the housing product, and the pipeline of home buyers. The mission result was that new home owners who used mortgage debt wisely derived considerable wealth impact in a relatively short period of time; they bought a house and they bought into a housing investment strategy.

We have repeated the St. Joe's story in a variety of other older urban communities with previously declining values and moderate levels of vacancy. While the St. Joe's example is largely a home ownership story, we have also done similar interventions with low-income rental units, including those occupied through the support of Section 8 (of the U.S. Housing Act) rental income vouchers. For example, our investments with Neighborhood Restorations, a private developer in West Philadelphia, created one thousand new rental units during a similar period of time as the St. Joe's development.

For Neighborhood Restorations we again provided predictable acquisition and construction financing. The developer focused on rebuilding a market it knew well, concentrating largely on a two-square-mile area and eliminating the vacancies on those blocks. The developer used no public subsidy (outside of the low-income housing tax credit), and demonstrated a capacity to maintain development and management costs significantly below expectations, while management quality remained strong and unit vacancies were kept to a minimum.

Our study of the Neighborhood Restorations developments showed positive correlations between property values and crime reduction on their target blocks as compared to similar West Philadelphia streets; this was despite the fact that residents of the Neighborhood Restorations blocks often had lower median incomes than residents of the comparison blocks.[4] High-quality management, the visible sign of rehabilitation, and the elimination of vacancies appear to have had the desired impact.

The impact of the East Camden and West Philadelphia investments was dependent on at least three things:

—The capacity to deliver predictable front-end capital
—The existence of entrepreneurs and investors who know the local market and stake it out as a place of business over a period of time
—The position of the community in terms of existing urban assets and proximate real estate markets

The third point needs additional explanation. Although East Camden is a low-income area, it is far from the most disadvantaged area of the city of Camden. It is proximate to stronger inner-ring suburban areas and has areas of market strength to build out from and toward. Investments in this community can be productive because of their links to these stronger markets. Similarly, while the West Philadelphia investments supported very moderate-income households, they bordered an expanding university district that provided a major proximate asset. The approach taken in these communities, which depended on proximity to strength, is not possible everywhere; the assets placed back onto the market may not have an adequate impact in a market whose liabilities are too dramatic.

Both St. Joe's and The Reinvestment Fund made significant investments in information and other market-building costs (such as home-owner training) in order to succeed. There were tipping points during the decade of initial development when some of those costs no longer had to be incurred or they could be covered by the value of the transaction itself. As the dynamics of supply and demand became increasingly self-organized, small private entrepreneurs entered the market.

There are, of course, often limitations to housing development success in older industrial cities because of public infrastructure qualities, public management, and public costs that developers and investors can influence but not always control. Camden demonstrates those limitations. St. Joe's can build housing units, but they do not have the delegated authority to redevelop or manage public infrastructure critical to housing development, from street repairs to the installation of water and sewer systems to the assembly and sale of publicly owned land. Moreover, the irrationality of high real estate taxes in Camden in comparison to those in its neighboring suburbs places a cap on St. Joe's housing values. The combination of higher tax and insurance costs in Camden often makes buying a unit across the city line more rational; in addition to higher values and lower costs, the suburban units usually include higher-quality public goods such as public safety, public education, and other basic municipal services.

Financing Public Revenue Streams

An important area of TRF financing in older cities involves facilities finance and working-capital loans in support of education, health, and social service providers. The devolution of services traditionally provided by centralized public agencies has opened up new opportunities for nonprofit organizations and businesses to manage these services. The distribution of workforce training funds to dozens of small- and large-scale nonprofit agencies is just one example of this transfer of responsibility. To some extent, we have become a banker of new forms of decentralized urban reform.

The most important TRF portfolio in this regard is our charter school portfolio, which has originated more than $100 million of debt to forty schools in Pennsylvania, Washington, D.C., and New Jersey. These loans now provide school opportunities for 20,000 children. In general, our analysis of TRF-financed charter schools demonstrates that they perform better than their district competition and have lower rates of crime. We were drawn into charter school financing by the residents of the communities in which we work who demanded alternatives to local district schools, particularly given the poor public safety records of many schools.

From the perspective of capital markets, the significance of this portfolio is related to its quick transition from a high-risk idiosyncratic product to something that functions like a predictable commodity. This shift demonstrates the way in which capital markets can support the creation of organizational and business scale from an initial point of boutique incubation.

The first charter school transactions that TRF underwrote were difficult to understand and manage. The schools were start-up businesses that functioned in an uncertain school district policy context. Their charters required recertification after the first five years and could be revoked at any time. Moreover, because TRF was largely financing acquisition, construction debt, and mortgage debt for their facilities, we were working with the schools in an area that few of them understood: real estate. In the first years of charter school financing it was clear that there would be no external source of liquidity—that is, no other lenders were going to purchase our loans. Finally, in the most distressed areas of a city such as Philadelphia, facilities options were limited and it was often difficult to make the loan-to-value ratios satisfy even the most flexible lenders.

After five years of making high-risk loans that were difficult to underwrite, we developed a solid underwriting model that recognized the key factors in both financial and educational program viability. That underwriting capacity and our experience enabled us to structure large debt syndications dedicated to long-term charter school finance supported by major bank investors, although we and other partners did have to take a subordinate position in the pools. The structured debt vehicles were signals of market acceptance, including recognition of our ability to leverage our early experience into an agreed-upon set of underwriting standards. Thus charter school lending moved from boutique transactions to an identifiable commodity. This represented a major point of change rooted in agreement on the viability of a product and the legitimacy of a market originator.

As we were working with large banks to syndicate debt for charter schools, other lenders were also financing projects directly. In some cases they began to purchase parts of or entire loans we had previously originated; ad hoc forms of liquidity became available. Charter school risk was now being activity priced and there was even competition for the best schools—usually those that had proved their operational longevity through recertification, had expanded into larger schools or multischool charters, or had significant third-party guarantees, which naturally mitigated credit risk.

Several years later, we were facing competition for the best loans not only from bank portfolios but from banks and others (such as public authorities) offering tax-exempt bond rates. This meant that the credits were being viewed through an organizational underwriting lens no different from nursing homes or health-care facilities, common recipients of bond financing. This marked a broader recognition of the industry and of a new generation of projects that were large enough to be profitable for bond financing. In this new environment, TRF was able to use its underwriting and capital investment capacity to participate in some bond financing transactions as both a consultant and an investor; we also continued to finance schools that were unable to get more price-advantageous debt from either banks or bond conduits.

This progression from a boutique high-risk transaction to a standardized debt syndication and then to a tax-exempt bond market demonstrates the scaling capacity of capital. At each stage of market acceptance, new financial instruments could be used to provide increased levels of competition, standardization, and liquidity to the market. But again, an early-entrant form of risk capital had to help make the market.

Let's look at the capitalization of public revenue through a more conventional entrepreneurial example. The child-care industry for low-income children in Philadelphia and other older cities is fragmented in terms of the nature and size of participating institutions. The industry comprises established public-sector providers, large nonprofit institutions, small nonprofits, small family-run enterprises, and informal (largely unregulated) household-based providers. With the entry of welfare reform in the 1990s and a stronger demand for low-income service workers, the demand for child care increased significantly.

Although the child-care sector has national and regional chains in middle-class neighborhoods, there were no examples of successful inner-city chains in Philadelphia. To help meet this need, TRF provided a private equity investment to a for-profit company looking to build such a chain, driven largely by third-party public-sector payments. The company had initial success with several facilities in Pittsburgh and wanted to expand to Philadelphia. We decided to invest subordinated debt with equity-like features that gave the entrepreneurs patient capital to build the company and grow the number of centers very quickly, something which appeared disruptive in the existing fragmented market.

We were interested in this company's business model for several reasons. We had experience in financing small nonprofit and for-profit operators, as well as in making micro loans to household child-care businesses that agreed to become regulated as a condition of our loans. Given the extraordinary inefficiencies and cost delays linked to third-party subsidies, we believed that the company had the capacity to build operating efficiencies across multiple sites; they understood the costs of child-care operations in ways that many small nonprofits did not. The company planned to build a competitive advantage by locating near transportation lines, which would help working families that had to commute to work as well as drop off and pick up children. They also planned to provide nighttime assistance for service and manufacturing workers who had late working hours or overnight shifts. Moreover, the company's business strategy and TRF's social mission complemented each other.

This investment has had significant peaks and valleys. When the original entrepreneur failed, we and other investors had to take the company through bankruptcy. It was eventually recapitalized with stronger management and a major infusion of equity from a large conventional private equity fund with more experience in building a successful chain than we had. Since that point, Brightside Academy has become a profitable investment. Today, Brightside Academy serves 5,500 children in forty facilities and employs more than six hundred workers. Despite the difficulties the company experienced, it has since established a track record of high-quality service as recognized by Commonwealth of Pennsylvania regulators. If the original estimates of child-care demand were accurate, this chain has accounted for as much as 20 percent of the number of slots needed in Philadelphia.

As we became involved in this venture, TRF realized the importance of investing both financial and human capital. In fact, the role we played for Brightside Academy in workforce capacity is very much analogous to St. Joe's approach to making a market by building a high-quality pipeline of home buyers. We helped structure employee recruitment, training, and support programs for the low-income women the company employs, as well as design aspects of Brightside's compensation and benefits program. Our human resource assistance has ranged from compliance consultation to training and accreditation classes, to helping employees learn about and receive social benefits—including the earned-income tax credit and state-subsidized child health care. We understood that a business with high employee turnover and low compensation would benefit from a career training program and extra compensation through social benefits, and the investment has been more successful as a result.

Old-Economy Transitions

TRF's equity fund and debt portfolio has provided financing for a number of urban manufacturing companies in the older cities of our market, including, for example, Philadelphia, Chester, Norristown, and Pottstown. Although these cities still have many manufacturing firms, the role of manufacturing in the nation and in those cities has diminished significantly as a percentage of overall jobs.

Small manufacturing firms that assemble products less reliant on labor costs and more reliant on advanced technology and proximity to appropriate design solutions can still thrive locally. Many of these companies are what are often termed *lifestyle companies,* owned by small partnerships or families and not accustomed to having equity investors (as opposed to lenders for physical plant and inventory). Their owners often want to sell the company but have limited capacity to achieve liquidity while maintaining operations in the area.

We invest in these companies if we think that their product is competitive and we can use our investor leverage to shape the business strategy, management team, and technology investments that need to be made. These are difficult companies to invest in, given the global competition in manufacturing and the complexity of retooling even seemingly profitable companies. To grow, these manufacturing companies need capital that is more patient than debt but is still willing to take returns lower than those offered by the companies most equity investors seek.

Ricochet Manufacturing is an example of such a company. Located in an industrial park in Philadelphia, it builds off of the city's largely extinct textile tradition. However, this textile firm is different from the older generation of cut-and-sew shops. It manufactures emergency first-response clothing that is lightweight and protects wearers from chemical and biological contaminants and fire. Using technology that it developed in collaboration with Philadelphia University (formerly the Philadelphia College of Textiles and Science), Ricochet integrates old-economy "cut-and-sew" operations with new-economy computer-aided design and machinist technology. Because unit production costs are largely for materials and technology, there is no cost benefit to manufacture the clothing overseas; the trade-off between labor and transportation costs is negligible.

Any company competing within a new and dynamic market needs investment in people, technology, and customer relationships. This requires the kind of capital that will allow a business to build product, enter into contracts, and conduct research and development. As with Brightside, TRF also invested in the capacity of Ricochet labor, helping workers use new equipment and helping supervisors manage the complexity of a culturally and linguistically diverse shop floor.

I could name other companies like Ricochet in our portfolio. They have to be retooled in terms of managers, technology, and market positioning. Retooling requires the right combination of capital, labor quality, and strategic advice. Some companies succeed and grow and others do not. In general, however, these companies do not attract large private equity funds. They do not have a special new technology with a promise to shake up the market; they are often in cities for historical reasons that seem illogical from today's perspective; and their owners have limited experience promoting the company's potential to equity investors. The question is whether these companies can be repositioned to be flexible, technology-smart, manufacturing firms that make twenty-first-century sense.

The Retail Food Industry

During the past several years, TRF has become a provider of financial support to high-quality food retailers that are locating or expanding their operations in many of Pennsylvania's oldest industrial cities. We have done so through a partnership with the Commonwealth of Pennsylvania and a coalition of civic organizations.

The interest in building such an initiative came from a variety of sources: economic development organizations that saw a market failure regarding supermarket location; civic and consumer groups that complained about the higher cost of food in the inner city; and public health advocates who viewed limited inner-city food options as contributing to higher rates of certain diseases among urban populations, particularly low-income minority populations.

Financing fresh-food retail outlets that charge competitive prices, particularly in the inner city, has been a controversial issue for many years. Estimates show that our nation's low-income areas have about 30 percent fewer grocery stores per capita than do higher-income neighborhoods.[5] Store size, an important factor in determining product cost, varies between these two types of areas as well. As a result, lower-income residents have to rely on more expensive stores or travel long distances to shop for affordable food. Since these residents tend to have low car ownership rates, the scarcity of supermarkets limits these people's potential for competitive choices.[6]

Assembling sites with the specific characteristics that supermarket developers seek is more challenging in low-income urban environments than in higher-income areas. Part of this is related to suburban chain managers' perspectives on store size and parking lot requirements, among other issues. Most inner-city neighborhoods have lower median incomes than suburban areas, which dissuades some market analysts from investing. There are urban areas that demonstrate that low disposable income can be offset by high population density.[7] However, this does not deal with the problem of higher operating costs, which are passed on to urban consumers in the form of higher-priced goods. Food retail is a particularly complex sector in which to manage these higher operating costs because even in successful stores, profit margins are thin.

The issue of higher development and operating costs became clear to us not only from available industry literature but from the focus groups we ran with supermarket and food retail entrepreneurs. We organized these meetings as part of our research in designing the Fresh Food Financing Initiative with the Commonwealth of Pennsylvania. We heard from existing urban operators of large-scale markets, operators of smaller markets who wanted to expand, and entrepreneurs who had considered the urban market but chose not to enter. The Philadelphia-area focus groups all pointed to three cost problems over and above the high cost of business and wage taxes in the city: the cost of site assembly and lack of predictability in site assembly and development; the cost of labor recruitment, training, and turnover; and the cost of public safety and crime. The third issue was reflected in physical infrastructure costs, insurance premiums, more limited business hours, and higher levels of actual theft.

The extent of these costs depended on contextual issues such as store size and location, union presence, and the experience and capacity of smaller versus larger operators (those with multiple stores connected to chains or cooperative whole-salers of various types). The most successful operators, certainly those with mul-tiple sites, did not locate in urban areas because of the cost issues described above. With the best managers going to the most opportune locations, urban store man-agers with more limited options lacked the scale and industry muscle to solve the problem of higher costs and limited inventory. We considered this a major prob-lem for inner-city stores. Given the limited profit opportunities in urban locations, competition for urban market share among store operators was minimal.

In response to these issues we designed a program with the Commonwealth of Pennsylvania that provides both direct subsidies for certain costs—site assembly, safety, and workforce development—as well as debt and equity financing from TRF for store expansion and development. Now an $80 million program, it has provided financing to thirty stores in its first three years of operation, through tar-geted grants, loans, and the allocation of new market tax credits.

Labor recruitment issues from our first store illustrate the issues of higher costs. This supermarket, located near the Philadelphia airport, had to process more than four thousand applications in order to determine two hundred qualified workers, and most of these applicants required significantly more training than workers in suburban stores owned by the same entrepreneur. The owner estimated that first-year labor recruitment, training, and turnover costs in his urban store would be four times the cost in similar suburban stores. As a result of our experience with this store, we have established a statewide project for retail service workers that recruits new employees, trains incumbent workers, and provides owners and man-agers with strategic guidance.

Development Finance and Market Building

In the beginning of this chapter I described development finance as investments that are market oriented but have a public purpose that allows them to be profit-making without having to be profit-maximizing. This mission can be traced through a variety of public and private agencies, authorities, and partnerships, in contrast to the expectations of conventional capital markets. Furthermore, I noted that the historical legacy of many older industrial cities manifests in low levels of project and firm incubation. Some of this involves macro-demographic and macro-economic trends, but much of it is related to costs and capacities embed-ded in the present governance and infrastructure of those places.

The function of development finance in older industrial cities is to reverse the legacy of low incubation levels through mission-oriented capital allocation and by means of its capacity to provide or influence the allocation of nonmarket investments. Reflecting on the previous four examples from The Reinvestment Fund's portfolio, I would divide the market-building functions of development finance into three categories: providing direct, early-stage financing; substituting or influencing public infrastructure investments; and organizing broader capital market access.

The direct financing role involves deployment of capital at a price for which development-financing institutions cannot be easily compensated, given the risk of its early stage, the quality of collateral, or the predictability of liquidity. We can see this in the discussion of land-acquisition financing in Camden, subordinated debt investments into Ricochet, or high-transaction-cost loans to early charter schools. Each exhibits some mismatch between risk and price. In all cases there was the assumption that capital could be preserved and pay a return; in fact, it might lead to substantial returns in certain situations. But regardless of the ultimate level of compensation, it was assumed that the extra costs of market entry as defined by this mismatch had an important development consequence that warranted pursuing the project.

The compensation for the risks may come about as a result of the growth of a company with significant value and liquidity, additional flows of projects related to the initial investments, and the eventual standardization of the early projects. But this outcome, though common, still does not, in pure economic terms, justify the choice of making those investments. Economic logic would dictate the pursuit of less risky investments with greater upside potential.

Moreover, even at the point of success there is a potential paradox. In general, if a financial institution is successful in seeding a housing market, a viable company, or a new industry sector, then its information monopoly and temporary control over some aspect of the market give it the advantages that ought to compensate it for any early market-building costs. However, it can take advantage of this only if it has the capital capacity to do so. The value we helped to create in East Camden created construction loan opportunities that we could not fulfill because of their size. The success of Ricochet will also eventually require levels of investment that we cannot provide ourselves. No matter how successful the company is, we will eventually lose our ability to control it and get all the available upside. Unfortunately, we do retain the ability to suffer the full downside.

Most development finance institutions do not have the capital to take full advantage of an emerging market or a company that is growing at a significant level. They are therefore reliant, by capital constraint and perhaps also by mission, on leveraging other capital providers into the market. The paradox of success comes down to this: How does development finance extract value from the value that it helps create, especially given the early costs of market building? If TRF is pushed out of the charter school lending field by cheaper bond financing conduits and left only with the highest-risk, highest-cost projects, then the very industry it helped to create cannot produce longer-lasting financial value for the institution. We try to solve that paradox by adapting to different capital facilities in the market by selling our experience and information as well as our capital. But the paradox remains native to the development finance enterprise.

The second market-building role of development finance relates to public infrastructure investment, which includes human capital capacity, land assembly, and basic public services such as safety and information. These are costs that investors, developers, and entrepreneurs may pay for themselves in situations where the cost can be justified by the projected revenue or longer-term asset value of the project or property. The supermarket operators mentioned above saw these as deal-breaking constraints because the initial outlay or ongoing operating costs would inhibit profitability, especially if there was a social expectation that urban and suburban consumer prices would remain the same.

To catalyze an enterprise that is constrained by public qualities such as these, a development-financing institution can provide short-term, transaction-based compensation for poor infrastructure or influence public investment in order to facilitate greater market viability for everyone. In fact, many transactions that we work on have some combination of the two approaches embedded within the project. In many of the examples cited—from worker training programs to niche market information to public safety costs to the ubiquitous problems of land assembly and environmental remediation—a deficit of public infrastructure forms a substantial barrier to development.

The Reinvestment Fund uses transaction-based models that combine public subsidy with our financing as a way to demonstrate the importance of quality public services and to facilitate a more aggressive posture on the part of the public sector toward development. It can be argued that these are answers only to specific transactions and not to general city deficits that have more structural impediments, of which these are symptoms. It is logical to argue, for example, that resources from The Reinvestment Fund and the Commonwealth of Pennsylvania that are helping entrepreneurs with public safety costs should never exist. Rather, those issues should be dealt with by local government and civil society if markets are expected to function. Similarly, one could argue that the transaction cost of land assembly in many cities is a problem of public reform and should not be paid for through concessionary financing rates or added public subsidy. Doing so gets the transaction done, but to some extent it enables the very inefficiencies for which it is paying. Similarly, if it takes four times the amount of resources to hire inner-city workers for a supermarket as it takes to hire suburban workers, what does that tell us about the limits of public investments in schools and other institutions?

These transaction-based infrastructure investments are actually at the heart of a great deal of economic development policy. For example, there are many strong arguments against tax incentives according to which such incentives are little more than inefficient surrogates for fixing the basic qualities and costs of public goods.[8] To some extent, this is not the whole story; some added infrastructure costs are a result of a radically deteriorated environment. Building something new in Philadelphia means engaging with one hundred and fifty years of industrial history and a chronically underfunded school system. The cost of retooling land and human capital is a legitimate public cost central to development opportunities, one that may require compensatory levels of support—though this should only be done in the expectation of high-quality outcomes.

The challenge for development finance is to influence the market orientation of public investments that must be made. This is where the transactional quality of development finance can be useful. The integration of private and public capital as part of a process of market building within discrete transactions can lead to broader reform if its assumptions become part of the public sector's organizing code. Our supermarket project can be used as a way to rethink more bureaucratic approaches to public economic development investment. The realization that East Camden's values are capped and the city is losing a potential middle class ought to demonstrate, on the basis of good transactional experience, the necessity of changing the cost and quality of public goods. Through these examples I am posing the possibility that development finance organizations have the potential to contribute to public change through the experience and credibility of their portfolios.

The third market-building category involves facilitating conventional capital flows, which has always been a signature function of development finance. New capital providers come to markets, products, and places as a result of information that emerges from the evidence of other portfolios as well as evidence of effective demand. They use their own competitive advantages—pricing, technology, the ability to cross-sell other financial products to new borrowers, scalability, and access to secondary markets—to position themselves in the new market.

Facilitating conventional investments is largely a matter of lowering initial barriers and reducing transaction costs. This occurs through evidence of performance, information transparency about the market, and the standardization of underwriting. All three of these cut costs for the second wave of lenders or investors, who can now price the risk more easily, buy product that is already underwritten without having to be the primary underwriter, and use their existing institutional capacities to align their interests with the new market.

Moving Forward

These three market-building roles provide an important structural positioning for development finance institutions. In a society where capital has lost much of its traditional place connections and the public sector has limited capacity to function in an efficient manner, public purpose institutions able to organize and invest capital become critical to restoring older cities.

Surprisingly, there is limited research and analysis regarding how the integration of markets and public investments can work most efficiently. Rather, we still seem to believe in the polarity of public purpose and market-based approaches and solutions. Any analysis of the processes of rebuilding urban markets has to start with a rejection of this polarity. It must embrace a complex alignment between new market tools and public purpose.

Notes

1. For an overview of federal policies that encouraged nonurban growth, see Kenneth Jackson, *Crabgrass Frontier: The Suburbanization of the United States* (Oxford University Press, 1985).
2. See, for example, W. Scott Frame, Michael Padhi, and Lynn W. Woosley, "Credit Scoring and the Availability of Small Business Credit in Low- and Moderate-Income Areas," *Financial Review* 39 (2004): 35–54.
3. See Gary L. Lilien and Eunsang Yoon, "Timing of Competitive Market Entry," *Management Science* 36, no. 5 (May 1990): 568–85.
4. "Neighborhood Restorations: Assessing Impact," report (Philadelphia: The Reinvestment Fund, 2006).
5. See "The Need for More Supermarkets in Philadelphia," report (Philadelphia: The Food Trust, 2001).
6. See "Stimulating Supermarket Development: A New Day for Philadelphia" (Philadelphia: The Food Trust, 2004).
7. See, for example, Robert Weissbourd and Christopher Berry, "The Market Potential of Inner-City Neighborhoods: Filling the Information Gap," discussion paper (Brookings Institution, 1999).
8. See Michael Porter, "The Competitive Advantage of the Inner City," *Harvard Business Review*, May–June 1995.

Report of the 106th American Assembly

Preface

On November 8, 2007, fifty-six men and women representing business, labor, academia, government, nonprofit organizations, and the media gathered at The Hotel Hershey in Hershey, PA for the 106th American Assembly entitled "Retooling for Growth: Building A 21st Century Economy in America's Older Industrial Areas." For three days, participants examined policies, approaches, and development strategies aimed at meeting the needs of older industrial metropolitan areas seeking to find their place in a changing global economy.

This project was conceived and directed by Paul C. Brophy, President, Brophy and Reilly LLC. Pennsylvania Governor Edward G. Rendell and Chairman and CEO of Bank of America Kenneth D. Lewis served as co-chairs and jointly wrote the foreword to the commissioned volume described in the appendix of this report. The project was also ably assisted by a steering committee of distinguished leaders from around the country, whose names and affiliations are also listed in the appendix.

Background papers were prepared for the participants by twenty-eight of the nation's leading thought and policy leaders under the editorial supervision of Richard M. McGahey, Program Officer, Ford Foundation and Jennifer S. Vey, Fellow, Metropolitan Policy Program, The Brookings Institution and will appear as chapters in a book entitled *Retooling for Growth: Building a 21st Century*

Economy in America's Older Industrial Areas, to be published by Brookings Institution Press in early 2008. The chapters are listed in the appendix along with information about how to obtain a copy of the volume.

During the Assembly, participants heard formal addresses by Robert E. Litan, Senior Fellow, Economic Studies, Global Economy and Development, Brookings Institution and Vice President for Research and Policy, Ewing Marion Kauffman Foundation; Bruce Katz, Director and Founder of the Metropolitan Policy Program, Brookings Institution; and Henry Cisneros, Executive Chairman, CityView and former U.S. Secretary of Housing and Urban Development. The participants also heard a panel discussion with Daniel Gunderson, Co-Chair, Empire State Development Corporation, and Commissioner, New York State Department of Economic Development and John Blake, Executive Deputy Secretary, Pennsylvania Department of Community and Economic Development, moderated by Jeffrey A. Finkle, President and CEO, International Economic Development Council. Mark Willis, Executive Vice President, JP Morgan Chase, moderated a panel discussion on anchor institutions among Eugenie L. Birch, Lawrence C. Nussdorf Professor of Urban Research and Education and Chair, Department of City and Regional Planning, School of Design, University of Pennsylvania; Nancy Cantor, Chancellor and President, Syracuse University; and Henry S. Webber, Vice President and Senior Lecturer, The University of Chicago. All of these addresses and panel discussions are available on The American Assembly's web site, americanassembly.org.

Following their discussions, participants issued this report on November 11, 2007. It contains both their findings and recommendations. The text of this report is also available on The American Assembly's web site.

We gratefully acknowledge the generous support of Bank of America, the Ford Foundation, The Rockefeller Foundation, the William Penn Foundation, the Kresge Foundation, the Surdna Foundation, and JPMorgan Chase & Co.

The American Assembly takes no positions on any subjects presented here for public discussion. In addition, it should be noted that participants took part in this meeting as individuals and spoke for themselves rather than for their affiliated organizations and institutions.

We would like to express special appreciation for the fine work of the discussion leaders, rapporteurs, and advisors in helping to prepare the final draft of this report: Kim Burnett, Don Chen, Raymond Christman, Anika Goss-Foster, Richard M. McGahey, Manuel Pastor, Vickie B. Tassan, and Jennifer S. Vey.

David H. Mortimer
The American Assembly

Retooling for Growth: Building a 21st Century Economy in America's Older Industrial Areas

At the close of their discussions, the participants in the 106th American Assembly, "Retooling for Growth: Building a 21st Century Economy in America's Older Industrial Areas" at the Hotel Hershey in Hershey, Pennsylvania, November 8–11, 2007, reviewed as a group the following statement. This statement represents general agreement, however, no one was asked to sign it. Furthermore, it should be understood that not everyone necessarily agreed with all of it.

The Global Context

Once the world's unchallenged economic leader, the United States is now one competitor of many in a global economy. Although the U.S. economy continues to be the strongest in the world, there are clear indications that the United States needs to contend with both the challenges and opportunities in the new globalized economy.

Fifty years ago, the United States was not primarily an urban nation. Our population now predominantly lives in metropolitan areas, and our economic future is dependent on their health. The largest 100 metropolitan areas contain 65% of America's population and generate 75% of gross domestic product. In meeting the global economic challenge, our metropolitan areas will be increasingly important.

The economies in most of these metropolitan areas and the cities in them are thriving—job growth is strong, and their labor force is increasing. Many of the central cities in these metropolitan areas are the core location for shifts to knowledge-based jobs, a key economic driver in the 21st century.

However, as the Brookings Institution has reported, some of these metropolitan areas—particularly the older industrial areas in the nation—are having difficulty finding their niche in today's global marketplace. Those metro areas that host older industrial struggling cities are home to nearly 30% of America's metropolitan population and are clustered in the Northeast and Midwest.

These are places that thrived through the post-war period, but began their decline in the 1960s. This economic stagnation has many complex causes, including a decline in manufacturing as a share of national employment that rendered older plants obsolete, a movement of people and jobs to low-labor-cost areas, residential shifts to other regions, social and racial segregation, and inappropriate government policies.

Increasing economic health in these areas will add to the nation's prosperity; but if large numbers of these places decline, the economy as a whole will be damaged. Moreover, they have many significant assets—including land, infrastructure, business opportunities, underutilized labor, and many of the nation's major medical, educational, and research institutions—all critical building blocks for our nation's future competitiveness. Restoring competitiveness to these places also conserves our environment, as new growth can occur within them rather than endangering our country's open spaces. Finally, because nearly two-thirds of all Americans live in our top 100 metropolitan areas—of which the older industrial areas are an important component—increased prosperity serves to engage the labor force more productively, especially the large number of low-income minorities residing in these metropolitan areas.

However, there are serious impediments to a more prosperous future. These include:

—*The economics of doing business in these places is impaired.* The business conditions in these metropolitan areas sometimes drive businesses to move elsewhere. Helping these places grow means improving public safety, reducing local government red tape, educating the labor force, and cleaning up environmental liabilities.

—*There is insufficient civic collaboration.* Fresh networks that engage people of all walks of life and the younger generation in new and exciting ways are needed to help these metropolitan areas overcome dysfunctional competition among local governments, missed opportunities for regional growth, and exclusionary practices that inhibit shared vision and strategy.

—*These places have difficulty holding their populations and attracting newcomers.* The quality of these places needs to be improved—better schools, safer streets, and improved amenities to make living in these places more competitive with other locations.

—*The problems of concentrated poverty are intensified in these areas.* These metropolitan areas house a disproportionate percentage of low-income people, many of whom are minorities, who do not have the skills, education, and opportunities needed to compete successfully in the job market. Building an opportunity-based economy is critical.

Yet, even with these challenges, these metropolitan areas are poised to benefit from the growing knowledge economy, since the factors driving prosperity are changing. Human capital is ascendant. More open, flexible, adaptive, organic networks of occupations, functions, and firms are driving innovation and growth. These changes favor cities, whose density enhances knowledge-based innovation and creates opportunities to align prosperity, equity, and sustainability.

This American Assembly report presents a broad framework of actions that, if implemented, can help these older industrial areas create 21st century economies with robust growth and shared prosperity. Change must start with metropolitan leaders taking dramatic steps to improve their economies, in partnership with others at the state and national levels. But this will only happen if it is part of a new national compact. America needs to invest in its older industrial areas, but it is also right to demand accountability in the places where investments flow.

In a new cooperative federalism, responsibilities of the federal and state governments should be consistent with their competence and the current realities of dynamic markets and regional and local innovation. The federal government should be setting floors, not ceilings, on local achievement of national goals of shared sustainable prosperity; it should provide the information, technical assistance, and other infrastructure needed to support these areas and share its results; and it should again take responsibility for some degree of fiscal federalism—providing those places that, through no fault of their own, have extraordinary legacy costs, with the opportunity to relieve them. As discussed later, this Assembly proposes the creation of a National Infrastructure Bank to finance needed infrastructure in these places, with deployment of capital based on strategies that advance their economic competitiveness.

Assistance from the federal government should be directed toward the consensus national goal of shared and sustainable prosperity, but it should also require specific strategies to advance that goal in metropolitan areas. All capital investments should be competitive and peer reviewed. Continued funding should be both presumptively adequate and conditional on progress.

In cooperation with the federal government, states should move from simply transferring federal monies in categorical streams to consolidated funds to underwrite area-wide strategic plans for improvement. Metropolitan areas should compete for such funds.

These metropolitan areas must change their business and civic culture to be more entrepreneurial, inclusive, innovative, and capable of attracting and leveraging investment, while being attentive to business, market, and financial realities. Local, state, and federal governments, foundations, unions, and business organizations need to become better partners by eliminating obsolete practices, cultivating approaches that work, and innovating through new techniques and ideas that assist local leadership create improved performance and opportunity.

The approach to economic restructuring needs to be twofold. These areas must create a robust environment for economic growth, and promote a more inclusive economy, one that produces opportunity for those on the margins.

There are three key strategic elements to creating successful 21st century economies in these areas: business creation and growth, human capital development, and improving the quality of place. In addition, achieving universal digital competence and participation is critical to all three of these areas, as economic access, exchange, innovation, and value creation increasingly occur through digital technologies. In each of these approaches metropolitan areas need to innovate for a new future, cultivate what is working, and reform or eliminate what does not work. Innovation must include an emphasis on the opportunities presented by the emerging green economy and the technological changes required by the need to conserve energy, reduce greenhouse emissions, and create a more sustainable economy and global environment.

An overarching principle is that metropolitan areas need to treat businesses as customers and continuously seek out and listen to those customers (both current and prospective) and use that feedback to help set priorities for infrastructure investment, workforce development, and public services. This feedback should be communicated to the residents of the area to help build public understanding and support for the actions needed to make the economies of these metropolitan areas more successful.

Business Creation and Growth

Economic growth depends on business creating products of value. Jobs are derived from the demand for these valued products. The capital to create, grow, and sustain jobs and firms needs to be supported by strategic public investments in infrastructure and human capital.

Each metropolitan area has to determine how to organize its priorities and structure its organizational capacity to support its own particular economic development goals. Moreover, the rapidly changing nature of the global economy also suggests that local and regional responses need to be flexible and modified periodically.

To stimulate business creation and growth, metropolitan areas should:

—*Create an entrepreneurial culture.* Most job growth occurs through the retention and expansion of existing businesses and the creation of new ones, not by luring existing companies across jurisdictional lines. Developing an entrepreneurial economy also broadens participation in the workforce, especially among minority, low-income, and immigrant residents. Recent immigrants to metropolitan areas tend to be oriented toward starting and operating their own businesses. Encouraging and supporting self-employment can be one positive strategy for creating a more inclusionary regional economy.

As such, older industrial regions must create an economy where entrepreneurship at multiple levels can thrive—from the small neighborhood micro-business to the rapidly growing firms. To accomplish this goal metropolitan areas need access to capital, transparent and efficient government processes, and a local culture that recognizes and rewards the value of risk-taking activity.

The development of a favorable entrepreneurial culture is in part intangible and subjective. The leadership of these metropolitan areas—public and private— needs to celebrate, reward, and incentivize entrepreneurial behavior as a key pathway to economic growth. Examples exist of technology trade associations and technology development organizations—like the Ben Franklin Partnership in Pennsylvania—developing innovative efforts to build an entrepreneurial culture.

Entrepreneurs also need early-stage capital—the initial money that can support an idea in its early formation and development into a business. While venture capital is generally more available in these metropolitan areas today than ten to twenty years ago, it is still in too short a supply, particularly for start-up firms. Major research universities, which are anchor institutions in many of these regions, can be particularly critical in spawning entrepreneurial businesses and facilitating capital flow to them.

Local governments must be more innovative in their approach to helping companies conduct their business. This means revamping outmoded rules, regulations, and processes to create an environment that is hospitable to the formation, attraction, and growth of businesses. Fort Wayne, Indiana, for example, has streamlined its permitting procedures, drastically cutting the time and uncertainty involved in getting required approvals. Investing in these process innovations can be difficult for areas with weak economies. Therefore, new philanthropic, federal, and state resources and technical assistance must be provided to struggling cities and metropolitan areas that seek to reform their rules, regulations, and policies concerning permitting, zoning, building codes, tax scale processes, and more. But areas receiving assistance must be held accountable for delivering reform.

Public sector unions need to re-examine their approach to work rules, making governments themselves more innovative and effective. Unions must be part of the movement to create a culture of entrepreneurship.

States must continue to strive to ensure that their economic development policies and programs are responsive to the shifting needs of the new economy. This means incentivizing new partnerships among businesses, anchor institutions, and workforce development organizations that can help drive local and regional economic development. It also means finding ways to restructure and better coordinate existing programs, whether economic development or not, that would impact business decisions, so that they are delivered in a more transparent and effective manner.

Foundations have a unique role to play by investing in projects that can catalyze the market where it is weak or under-performing. By leading the way, like the Annie E. Casey Foundation has done in creating a neighborhood environment conducive to biotech research in East Baltimore, foundations have the ability to lower the risk profile in recovering neighborhoods to a point where other investors can follow.

Finally, the federal government needs to be more innovative in how it helps states and metropolitan areas grow the businesses and jobs that the country needs to compete in the global marketplace. This might include creating a modern version of the Urban Development Action Grant program of the 1970s, establishing a secondary market for economic development loans, and chartering a new national center for regional innovation.

Economic development in these metropolitan areas should exploit the opportunities offered by foreign governments, which are facilitating the expansion of foreign firms into the United States. Innovative programs should be initiated to attract foreign investment into U.S. urban and regional development.

—*Focus on clusters.* Economic activity tends to agglomerate in clusters of a similar or complementary nature: metalworking, textiles, plastics, software design, and the like. This may take the form of firms in a similar industry or companies engaged at different levels of the supply chain doing business with one another. Building supply chain networks within a metropolitan area can also create new opportunities for minority firms to broaden their markets and become more successful. As importantly, in the knowledge economy, innovation and productivity flow from an agglomeration of occupations and functions.

While trying to artificially create or attract clusters can present the same disadvantages for a region as "smokestack chasing," a well-researched and defined cluster approach can be a key economic strategy. Focusing on clusters means understanding economic strengths and an area's economic base and responding appropriately.

For example, older industrial regions should look at opportunities where the growth in new industries may align with an area's strengths in existing business activity or university research. Examples may include biotechnology, environmental technology, alternative energy technologies, new forms of chip design, or precision manufacturing. Often, new industry clusters and research concentrations can emerge from older specializations: Akron, Ohio, for example, has developed a specialization in polymers stemming from its historic role as a rubber and tire manufacturing center.

—*Grow export-oriented firms.* In every metropolitan economy, there are companies producing goods and services for sale outside of the area, producing particular economic benefits for the area. These firms need to be identified and supported as key elements in the region's economic development strategy. In older industrial communities, many of these firms are manufacturing companies. Despite recent job losses, manufacturing typically remains the single most important contributor to these regions' economic output. High value manufacturing can be a critical element of an economic strategy for many older industrial regions. Focus needs to be placed on product innovation and productivity growth.

Capital is much more available today for companies with strong growth potential than it was even a decade ago due to the globalization of capital markets and low, stable interest rates. But today, capital access can still be an issue in older markets. Metropolitan areas need to explore creative use of development finance techniques to achieve their economic objectives.

—*Strengthen federal and state support needed for business development.* The programs and tools of the federal and state governments to finance and support business development and competitiveness should be strengthened and innovative initiatives introduced and tested.

—*Make business attraction efforts highly selective.* Regions should carefully scrutinize the extensive use of firm-specific subsidies as the centerpiece of metropolitan area economic development strategies. Opportunities for attracting an investment from outside the area—whether a manufacturing, distribution, research and development or another kind of business—occur from time to time. Every metropolitan area should have the capability to respond selectively to these opportunities. But the new global economy provides relatively few opportunities in older industrial regions for this kind of "big game hunting." Attracting major manufacturing plants, new corporate headquarters, and the like, is a more competitive activity with fewer prizes available than in the past. States should not allow local governments to use subsidies to bid against each other, especially for in-state firms.

—*Hold providers and receivers of subsidies mutually accountable.* The use of subsidies can be particularly problematic. The cost/benefit relationship of many of these subsidies has proven questionable, and more reasonable guidelines and judgments need to be applied to their use. For example, major economic development incentive programs—whether local or state—should adopt clear and enforceable contracts, such as Michigan's job creation and retention standards, or Connecticut's prohibition on relocation for ten years. Many states, including Minnesota, Illinois, and Maine, now require companies to produce annual performance reports so that compliance can be monitored.

States and local governments spend more than $50 billion per year in economic development programs, and there is a trend toward greater accountability. Twenty-three states now disclose company-specific data about development incentives. Almost as many states and dozens of cities use "clawbacks"—safeguards to recapture monies if a company fails to deliver on job creation or capital investment. And forty-three states and many local governments attach job quality standards—wage and/or healthcare requirements—upon companies receiving job subsidies.

—*Reform economic development subsidies.* The practice of firms shifting locations within a metropolitan area and using that decision to leverage significant subsidies (including infrastructure) from a local government can be counterproductive from a regional competitiveness standpoint. Moreover, older central cities are more often the losers in this process. Governments within metropolitan areas should work together to discourage this process and not provide intrametropolitan area subsidies. While there may be occasional exceptions where a firm will otherwise leave the metropolitan area or cannot find an acceptable site in its existing jurisdiction, metropolitan area economic development organizations should always give priority to retaining the businesses in their existing jurisdictions.

The practice of site location consultants receiving commissions based on the size of a client's abatement packages is both obnoxious and potentially unethical. It encourages consultants to focus on the abatement package rather than the impact of the location or their client's income statements. It also needlessly adds fuel to the fires of the abatement wars.

Develop Human Capital

Economies grow by adding inputs, and by increasing productivity, so each worker produces a greater share of output. In the growing knowledge economy, human capital is increasingly important as the drivers of economic growth are knowledge embedded in people and technology requiring smarter human capital.

As the baby boom generation retires in the next twenty years, the labor force is expected to grow more slowly, with virtually all new workers coming from two groups: African-Americans, especially younger workers who have not been attached to the labor market; and Hispanics, many of them either new immigrants or the children of immigrants. For the economy to succeed, these workers will need higher levels of education, job readiness, and sector-based training to expand their potential for permanent employment and economic sustainability.

For industrial metropolitan areas, this demographic challenge is heightened because they have older populations, and their emerging workforce has lower rates of high school completion and post-high school education and training, including occupational certificates, community college degrees, and four-year college diplomas. The retirement of baby boomers creates a demographic opportunity for these younger workers in older areas, but only with increased investment in human capital to overcome years of poverty, neglect, and inadequate resources. Investment in human capital reduces inequality and can help turn around these communities and economies. This will only happen if metropolitan area leaders make smart investments in education and sector-based training programs that have demonstrated results and stop wasting resources on ineffective or outdated programs.

The workforce in older cities and regions too often faces inadequate schools, fragmented and ineffective workforce training programs, and a lack of clear and effective pathways to two and four-year colleges with real skills and career opportunities.

In order to succeed at developing human capital, metropolitan areas should:

—*Sharply improve public education.* Older metropolitan areas need a radically better level of performance from urban educational systems, increasing high school graduation rates, college completion rates, and technical training. This will require a concerted effort to align all human capital investment vehicles—including early education providers, public schools, civic leaders, training providers, teachers' unions, community colleges, and four-year colleges—to significantly raise the skill levels of youth and adults, measured in meaningful postsecondary credentials, pathways to careers, and middle-class livelihoods. There is a need for more innovation in public education encouraging the development of well-designed and well-executed district, charter, magnet, and contract schools.

—*Advocate for a National Innovation Bank for K–12 education.* Creating an effective K–12 education system is one of the greatest challenges, and one of the greatest potential investments, for an older metropolitan area. But many would-be reformers do not have access to new, effective approaches. The federal government should create a National Innovation Bank for K–12 education that would provide concrete examples of effective reform strategies for urban schools, and help finance new experiments and innovations.

—*Create new workforce partnerships to reform training.* Many metropolitan areas have been frustrated in their efforts to make their fragmented job training resources effective. But others are making substantial progress through focusing on their "dual customers"—workers and businesses. Major foundations and the U.S. Department of Labor are now helping to spread these innovations through the new National Fund for Workforce Solutions, which provides assistance to those setting up new partnerships to implement effective training programs tied to growing sectors, such as health care, construction, and "green" jobs and to advocate for the necessary system changes required to transform workforce development.

—*Elevate the role of community colleges.* Two-year colleges are emerging as critical institutions to provide workers with skills valued by businesses that can lead to careers, and also provide a more effective way for students to continue and complete four-year college degrees. There are many examples of good institutions, such as LaGuardia Community College in New York. Some of LaGuardia's strategies include First Year Academies for incoming students organized around curricular themes, learning communities linked to developmental or English as a Second Language (ESL) and credit-level courses, and pedagogies designed to engage and challenge its extremely diverse student body. As a result of such practices, LaGuardia was among the top twenty-five community colleges for degrees granted to minorities in 2004.

In addition to developing innovative approaches, human capital strategies need to cultivate better programs, building on and improving promising practices. These include:

—*Provide entrepreneurial training and assistance.* Older industrial metropolitan areas need new businesses and entrepreneurs. While some argue that entrepreneurs are born, not made, the Ewing Marion Kauffman Foundation reports promising results with its Fast Trac program, which provides budding entrepreneurs with business insights, leadership skills, and professional networking connections so they are prepared to create a new business or expand an existing enterprise. The Kauffman Foundation is also launching new efforts to close the entrepreneurial gap for minorities and women. These metropolitan areas should build from this successful model by making it easier for new businesses to grow, and by focusing assistance on entrepreneurs in new immigrant communities.

—*Partner with unions.* Unions have historically provided an essential pathway to skills and improved wages. With a projected boom in construction over the next generation, there is a need to recruit and train new construction workers. Unions should follow examples like the BIG STEP program in Milwaukee, coordinated by the Wisconsin Regional Training Partnership (WRTP), which improves the access of minorities and women to construction trades, helping them to develop the skills necessary to pass apprenticeship tests and get high-paying jobs. In growing service sectors like hospitality, older cities should look to the successful efforts of UNITE HERE, the Hotel Employees and Restaurant Employees Union in Las Vegas, where training, organizing, and negotiating with employers to eliminate unnecessary work rules and improve pay and benefits have helped make that area's diverse workforce among the highest paid hospitality workers in the country, narrowing racial income gaps and providing higher-level training for careers through the Culinary Training Academy.

—*Retain younger, college-educated workers.* Older areas also need to find ways to retain younger college-educated workers to help businesses and communities grow. In Philadelphia, the city-wide "Campus Philly" project markets the city to prospective students, but also arranges for internships with local companies, striving to link students to careers in the city and region, and reversing the "brain drain" by using the area's colleges and universities as anchors.

—*End the fragmentation of workforce development programs and align them with industries and jobs.* Although more funding is needed, workforce development programs are scattered across agencies and departments. In 2002, the Reinvestment Fund, a Philadelphia-based finance organization, identified more than $1.2 billion in Pennsylvania for workforce development, which was scattered in forty-nine separate funding streams, administered by literally hundreds of entities, without common performance standards or links to regional economic development and jobs. A similar fragmentation could be found in many states.

When he took office, Pennsylvania Governor Edward G. Rendell made reform of this broken system a top priority, and Pennsylvania has made great progress in streamlining programs and making them more accountable. Pennsylvania also has linked workforce more closely with regional economic growth, through a groundbreaking program supported by more than $20 million of new funds for regional workforce partnerships, awarded on a competitive basis to joint proposals from regional business, community, and training partners.

In particular need of change at the state and federal level is the system of local Workforce Investment Boards (WIBs). They are often too bureaucratic, disconnected from current business needs and projected workforce-based needs, and insufficiently supportive of incumbent worker retraining. As a result they frequently lose the support of businesses that are creating the jobs WIBs seek to fill.

Reform of the system to ensure that it better meets the needs of employees and potential employees is needed.

—Stop wasting valuable human resources. The demographic challenge of the retiring baby boomers means that any working-aged adults cannot be spared. There are many workers, disproportionately minority, who already are in the workforce but do not have good jobs, due to a combination of factors, including discrimination, transportation barriers, and inadequate education and training. Additional attention will be required for new entrants, including new immigrant workers. These metropolitan areas need more effective programs for immigrant workers tied to jobs. Admiral Tool and Manufacturing in Chicago works with a local community college to upgrade skills for immigrant workers, including instruction in ESL tied to on-the-job training for Spanish and Polish-speaking workers.

Additionally, these metropolitan areas must implement effective programs for young people, especially men, at-risk and adjudicated within the criminal justice system, where this experience not only reduces their earnings and employment, but also harms the communities where they live. These areas need to create programs modeled after those in Baltimore operated by Living Classrooms and Catholic Charities' Maryland Re-Entry Partnership (REP), which provide a mix of behind-the-fence education, transitional jobs and work crews to ease these transitions.

Improve the Quality of Place

Older industrial cities have a magnificent history—they were once the centers of culture, engines of industry, meccas for education and innovation, magnets for investment, and beacons of prosperity. They were the places where people wanted to be.

In today's high-tech economy, the workforce includes many knowledge workers who have unprecedented mobility and locational choice. With globalization, the same type of freedom is being exercised by many companies that can take part or all of their operations offshore and have their pick of American metropolitan areas for their business locations. Firms and workers increasingly look to quality of place as an important factor in deciding where to locate.

Metropolitan areas that offer quality places will thrive and grow. Those that cannot offer an attractive quality of place will stagnate or continue to decline. Experience has shown that there are four critical issues that older industrial areas must address in order to improve their quality of place.

First, these metropolitan areas must fix the basics including reducing crime, improving schools, streamlining development permitting, and better utilizing physical resources (e.g., land, buildings, infrastructure, and historic resources). Second, they must focus resources on making older neighborhoods more attractive for new private sector investment, so that those neighborhoods can compete successfully with locations on the sprawling fringes of their metropolitan areas. Third, they must create distinctive places by leveraging historic and cultural amenities, eliminating blight, designing beautiful public spaces, and boosting community livability. Finally, older industrial areas must develop infrastructure strategies to manage legacy costs, leverage the value of older systems, and invest in future improvements.

In pursuing all these priorities, it is important to combine the attraction of new residents with serious efforts to engage, retain, and benefit those who have made their lives in these metropolitan areas. The historical role of the central cities in these metropolitan areas is to create, not just attract, a middle class. These metropolitan areas need to adopt an inclusive approach that enables local people to take maximum advantage of changes that improve the quality of place.

These older industrial metropolitan areas should take the following steps to improve their quality of place:

—*Invest more in infrastructure.* Federal and state infrastructure spending needs to be dramatically overhauled, such as with the creation of a National Infrastructure Bank, identified earlier. Funding for many infrastructure programs is inordinately fragmented, uncoordinated, and driven by earmarks and formula grants. To maximize the value of public infrastructure dollars, programs should be consolidated or coordinated, and funding should be allocated based on performance and competition. One way to achieve this would be the creation of infrastructure banks that coordinate investments for transportation, water, and sewer systems, site preparation, etc. and that pick investments based on competitive, performance-based criteria, much like the way that the National Institutes of Health determines its research grant making. These banks should invest more money than current spending levels, because of the enormous infrastructure needs of America's older industrial communities. The use of performance criteria, and blending investments with private capital, would ensure that investments would boost competitiveness and contribute to the revitalization of central cities. Such an approach would reward metropolitan areas that are "growth-ready," i.e., ones that have streamlined the redevelopment process, stimulated entrepreneurial opportunities, sparked regional cooperation, and embraced transparency and accountability in their decision-making.

—*Increase connectivity through transit.* The great cities of the world have successful mass transit. Rather than continuing to allow billions of dollars to pay for inefficient sprawl-inducing highways, older industrial areas should advocate for the redirection of portions of transportation funds to support reinvestment, enhance livability, and facilitate accessibility to major employment centers. For example, many metropolitan areas have invested heavily in public transportation in recent years, and have altered local zoning rules to allow for higher concentrations of commercial and residential development at stations and along corridors to maximize the utility of such transit systems. Such "transit-oriented development" (TOD) strategies also ensure greater ridership levels, which further increase the viability of service.

—*Reform the development process.* Rewriting the rules governing development is perhaps the most important challenge to metropolitan areas seeking to transform the physical landscape to better suit their ambitions. Building codes must work for rehabilitation and redevelopment, particularly those that lead to more efficient energy and water usage. New Jersey and Maryland have created special "rehab codes" to provide developers with the flexibility to refurbish buildings at lower costs. Many communities are seeking to concentrate development where it makes sense—along transit corridors and in downtown areas—while lowering densities in places where the housing stock may be too small or where vacant lots might be converted to parks or side yards. Development processes must be transparent and predictable, with clear time limits and decisions.

—*Mobilize vacant property for economically and socially productive uses.* Many older metropolitan areas are searching for better ways to manage vacant and abandoned properties. Many local governments have thousands of vacant properties, and yet existing tax foreclosure processes in most places are not designed to handle widespread abandonment. The local governments in older industrial areas need to take direct action here.

Governments need to focus on land assembly and land recycling. Site assembly and clean-up can be a key strategy to attract private investments. To accomplish this, eminent domain is an important and necessary tool for redevelopment, but it must be used in a sparing and prudent way with full transparency. As Flint, Michigan, has demonstrated there are opportunities to change tax foreclosure and property management strategies so that such properties can be used as community development assets. Flint has also demonstrated the positive impact of a land bank authority to oversee the procurement, treatment, and future marketing of acquired parcels. Like Michigan, New Jersey has also reformed its tax foreclosure laws.

—*Reduce local fragmentation.* The widespread hyper-fragmentation of local governments makes it difficult for localities within metropolitan areas to coordinate on big investments in infrastructure, large-scale attractions and amenities, and environmental improvements, all of which have a vital role in determining community livability across a metropolitan area. Some areas have taken steps to overcome this fragmentation. Leaders in Denver have worked with their suburban counterparts to successfully advocate for a metropolitan rail network called FasTracks, which is now the focus of an ambitious regional transit-oriented development initiative.

—*Reform local tax systems.* The over-reliance on local taxes, especially property taxes, for services such as schools has produced the worst of all worlds: high local taxes, low amenities, significant inequalities, as well as intense competition between neighboring jurisdictions for tax "ratables" and an unwelcoming attitude towards children. Also, many central cities provide support for regional services and amenities without fiscal support from their suburbs or the state. Ineffective or inequitable local taxes should be replaced with regional or state-level revenue systems. Some states like New Jersey, Connecticut, and others have sought to reduce property taxes and replace education funding with sales taxes or income taxes.

—*Encourage brownfields redevelopment.* During the past fifteen years, many older cities have cleaned up and redeveloped thousands of acres of contaminated industrial properties. These projects have benefited from a combination of federal, state, local, and private funding sources, and they have been overwhelmingly successful, not only from an economic standpoint, but also in terms of civic pride and quality of life. A continuation and expansion of these efforts have overall benefits to metropolitan areas.

—*Redevelop urban waterways and waterfronts.* Many urban water features were regarded as industrial sewers and eyesores for many decades. They are now regarded as anchors for tourism, employment, recreation, parks, and commercial and residential development. Many cities have "day lighted" their formerly covered urban rivers. Others have cleaned up and redeveloped their urban waterfronts to make them environmentally and economically viable. In many cities, such areas, like the Flats in Cleveland, the Inner Harbor in Baltimore, and the RiverWalk project in Detroit, have become catalysts for additional investment.

—*Build from the strengths of anchor institutions.* Anchor institutions are also a tremendous asset in older industrial areas. Universities, hospitals, foundations, sports and entertainment complexes, arts and cultural centers, and other large employers are a major presence in older cities, and many have been catalyzing reinvestment, real estate investments, and quality of place. The University of Pennsylvania has transformed its surrounding neighborhood; the University of Chicago is dramatically improving public schools; Syracuse University has stimulated downtown revitalization. The Verizon Center in Washington DC's Chinatown has caused enough critical mass to create a lower-risk environment for further investment in that area. There is great opportunity in other older industrial areas given the concentration of anchor institutions in these places.

—*Improve the Community Development Block Grant (CDBG) program.* All of these examples—brownfields, waterfronts, anchor-sponsored redevelopment—have benefited from Community Development Block Grants (CDBG). The CDBG program is the only source of federal funds that have some degree of flexibility for economic development, and it has contributed to enormous success in challenging settings. Unfortunately, funds have been dramatically cut, and because in recent years funds are apportioned based on population, current policies actually penalize older industrial locations that have lost population even though they need flexible funds the most.

Federal housing policies should also aim at financing homes that are affordable and are in close proximity to job locations outside of central cities. Congress should allocate a dramatically increased level of funding for mixed-use, mixed-income affordable housing to accommodate the needs of working families.

Moving Forward

This Assembly has offered a menu of strategic ideas, some based on emerging best practices, many incorporating innovative ideas for the future, and all reflecting the best thinking of experts and practitioners that have long cared about cities and metropolitan areas.

Implementing this vision will require that metropolitan areas know where they have been and where they are going. New data systems, perhaps developed with regional partners like foundations and universities, can help to uncover competitive advantages, identify key labor market trends, and point to possibilities in the changing economy. Such systems—essentially regional scorecards like that developed by the Fund for Our Future in northeast Ohio—can also help track progress on achieving growth, spreading opportunity, and restoring neighborhoods, and can thus serve to both motivate action and promote accountability.

But while putting together the policy package, measuring progress, and naming specific objectives is crucial, the nation needs much more than these planning elements. A nation cannot be great, if it squanders its legacy cities. This Assembly calls for a strategic vision that includes these older industrial metropolitan areas and their businesses, workers, and residents as a central component to a strategy for the United States to enhance its competitiveness in the world economy in the 21st century.

Getting America to renew its investment and its commitment to its older industrial cities is central. This Assembly asserts that using the underutilized assets in the nation's older industrial metropolitan areas is important to our national well-being. To accomplish this goal requires a shift in the current economic calculus through changes in behavior by all stakeholders. Creating open, flexible, adaptive systems applies to government and development institutions as well as the business community. In addition to enabling more organic, self-organizing networks of individuals and firms, government and development institutions themselves need to become much more open, inclusive, and customer driven.

This realignment can only succeed if it is part of a new national compact. America needs to invest in its older industrial areas, but it is also right to demand accountability in the places where investments flow. Measurement is part of that but so is seeking to reward those who have begun the hard work of recovery. For, ultimately, revitalization cannot be driven from outside—while outside resources can and must help, it is local leadership that needs to be nurtured, to step up, and to lead.

Who leads may vary. In some cases, a major political figure will lead; in some cases, business representatives will point the way; in other cases, community-based organizations or local foundations will take the first step. But there are general principles that the best of each of these share—a love of place, a commitment to inclusion, and a willingness to take risks. Full engagement of all sectors is key to revived prosperity.

Fortunately, a new type of leadership—one which grasps the possibilities and not just the downsides of the global economy, which can organize multiple constituencies for multiple purposes, and which sees inclusion as central to success—is emerging. This leadership knows that government will have to play a role but also realizes that reinvention is demanded of business, labor, and other sectors. This leadership understands the responsibilities of representation and redistribution but tends to focus on problem-solving, productivity, and performance. And these leaders deserve support and cooperation from the citizens in the region and from state and federal officials in order to create a nimble, entrepreneurial, regional culture.

In 1993, The American Assembly produced a report entitled "Interwoven Destinies: Cities and the Nation" that helped launch a wave of new thinking and a slew of new metropolitan organizing activities, much of it noting that suburbs were only as strong as the cities with which they were linked.

It is now nearly a decade and a half later and this Assembly intends to continue and reinvigorate the conversation. The nation must take to heart that cities and suburbs are linked in their various regions but also that our destinies are inter-woven across our nation's metropolitan landscape. This Assembly believes that America will be strengthened economically and socially by the agenda proposed here—more ready to cohere, more ready to compete, and more ready to connect. For while America's cities may have different legacies and different challenges, the nation faces a common set of global challenges and shares a common national future.

Participants: The 106th American Assembly

Project Director
Paul C. Brophy
President
Brophy and Reilly LLC
Columbia, MD

Robert D. Ansin
President, CEO, and Founder
MassInnovation LLC
Lawrence, MA

Timothy D. Armbruster
President & CEO
Goldseker Foundation
Baltimore, MD

Eric Avner
Associate Director
Cincinnati Business Committee
Cincinnati, OH

Chris Benner
Associate Professor
Department of Human and
    Community Development
University of California, Davis
Davis, CA

♦ **Eugenie L. Birch**
Lawrence C. Nussdorf Professor of
    Urban Research and Education
Chair, Dept. of City and Regional
    Planning
School of Design
University of Pennsylvania
Philadelphia, PA

♦ **John Blake**
Executive Deputy Secretary
Pennsylvania Department of
    Community and Economic
    Development
Harrisburg, PA

Garry Bliss
Director of Policy &
    Intergovernmental Affairs
City of Providence
Providence, RI

Barry Bluestone
Dean, School of Social Science,
    Urban Affairs, and Public
    Policy
Director, Center for Urban and
    Regional Policy (CURP)
Northeastern University
Boston, MA

Brian J. Boyle
Co-Founder/Group Publisher
Issue Media Group, LLC
Pittsburgh, PA

Lavea Brachman
Co-Director
Greater Ohio
Columbus, OH

Austin Burke
President
Greater Scranton Chamber of
    Commerce
Scranton, PA

Kim Burnett
Program Officer
Surdna Foundation
New York, NY

♦ **Nancy Cantor**
Chancellor and President
Syracuse University
Syracuse, NY

** **Don Chen**
Founder and Executive Director
Smart Growth America
Washington, DC

▲ **Raymond Christman**
Chairman
Peachtree Corridor Partnership
Atlanta, GA

* **The Hon. Henry G. Cisneros**
Executive Chairman
CityView
San Antonio, TX

Carol Coletta
President and CEO
CEOs for Cities
Chicago, IL

John P. Colm
President
WIRE-Net
Cleveland, OH

Stephen Crawford
Director
Social, Economic & Workforce
    Programs Division
National Governors Association
    Washington, DC

Joanne Denworth
Senior Policy Manager
Governor's Office of Policy
Harrisburg, PA

The Hon. Chris Doherty
Mayor
City of Scranton
Scranton, PA

Michael Ettlinger
Director, Economic Analysis and
    Research Network
Economic Policy Institute
Washington, DC

♦ **Jeffrey A. Finkle**
President & CEO
International Economic
    Development Council
Washington, DC

** **Anika Goss-Foster**
Director of Philanthropic Affairs
City of Detroit
Detroit, MI

♦ **Daniel C. Gundersen**
Co-Chair, Empire State
    Development Corporation
Commissioner, NYS Department
    of Economic Development
Buffalo, NY

Victor A. Hausner
Managing Partner
Keystone Global LLC
Chevy Chase, MD

Edward W. Hill
Vice President for Economic
    Development
The Maxine Goodman Levin
    College of Urban Affairs
Cleveland State University
Cleveland, OH

Feather O. Houstoun
President
William Penn Foundation
Philadelphia, PA

Ted L. Howard
Executive Director,
The Democracy Collaborative
University of Maryland
College Park, MD

● Charlotte Howard
Midwest Correspondent
The Economist
Chicago, IL

* Bruce Katz
Vice President
Director, Metropolitan Policy
  Program
The Brookings Institution
Washington, DC

Greg LeRoy
Executive Director
Good Jobs First
Washington, DC

* Robert E. Litan
Senior Fellow, Economic Studies,
Global Economy and
  Development
The Brookings Institution,
Vice President for Research
  and Policy
Ewing Marion Kauffman
  Foundation
Kansas City, MO

Shana F. Marbury
General Counsel & Manager
Inclusion Initiatives
Greater Cleveland Patnership
Cleveland, OH

Bryce Maretzki
Policy Director, Pennsylvania
  Department of Community
  and Economic Development
Harrisburg, PA

Rudolph E. Marshall
Director of Centers of Excellence
Delaware Economic Development
  Office
Dover, DE

** Richard M. McGahey
Program Officer
Ford Foundation
New York, NY

Chris Mead
Senior Vice President
American Chamber of Commerce
  Executives
Alexandria, VA

Harold D. Miller
President
Future Strategies, LLC
Pittsburgh, PA

Leslie Moody
Executive Director
The Partnership for Working
  Families
Denver, CO

Ioanna T. Morfessis
President
IO.INC
Phoenix, AZ

Dede Myers
Vice President and Community
  Affairs Officer
Federal Reserve Bank
  of Philadelphia
Philadelphia, PA

Jeremy Nowak
President and CEO
The Reinvestment Fund
Philadelphia, PA

Paul Oyaski
Director
Department of Development
Cuyahoga County
Cleveland, OH

▲ Manuel Pastor
Professor
Department of Geography
University of Southern California
Los Angeles, CA

Christopher Perez
Program Officer
F.B. Heron Foundation
New York, NY

● Anne Power
Deputy Director, Centre for
   Analysis of
   Social Exclusion (CASE)
Professor of Social Policy
London School of Economics
London, UK

● Kevin Quinn
Vice President for Public Affairs
Syracuse University
Syracuse, NY

Joel Rogers
Professor of Law, Political Science,
   and Sociology
University of Wisconsin-Madison
Madison, WI

Victor Rubin
Vice President for Research
PolicyLink
Oakland, CA

Andrew J. Rudnick
President and CEO
Buffalo Niagara Partnership
Buffalo, NY

Marlene B. Seltzer
President and CEO
Jobs for the Future
Boston, MA

● Matt Stroud
Editor in Chief
The Next American City
Philadelphia, PA

Vickie B. Tassan
Senior Vice President
Bank of America
Washington, DC

Laura Trudeau
Senior Program Officer
The Kresge Foundation
Troy, MI

Mark D. Turner
President & CEO
Optimal Solutions Group LLC
Hyattsville, MD

▲ Jennifer S. Vey
Fellow, Metropolitan Policy
   Program
The Brookings Institution
Washington, DC

Orson Watson
Advisor, Community
    Revitalization Program
The Garfield Foundation
Boston, MA

♦ **Henry S. Webber**
Vice President and Senior Lecturer
The University of Chicago
Chicago, IL

Rachel Weber
Associate Professor,
Urban Planning and Policy
    Program
University of Illinois at Chicago
Chicago, IL

Robert Weissbourd
President
RW Ventures, LLC
Chicago, IL

♦ **Mark A. Willis**
Executive Vice President
JP Morgan Chase
New York, NY

Hal Wolman
Director
George Washington Institute of
    Public Policy
George Washington University
Washington, DC

♦ Panelist
* Speakers
** Discussion Leader
▲ Rapporteur
● Observer

Steering Committee

Director
Paul C. Brophy
President
Brophy and Reilly LLC
Columbia, MD

Book Editors
Richard M. McGahey
Program Officer
Ford Foundation
New York, NY

Jennifer Vey
Fellow
Metropolitan Policy Program
The Brookings Institution
Washington, DC

Members
Eugenie L. Birch
Chair, Department of City and
    Regional Planning
University of Pennsylvania
School of Design
Philadelphia, PA

Angela Glover Blackwell
Founder and Chief Executive Officer
PolicyLink
Oakland, CA

Kim Burnett
Program Officer for Community
    Revitalization
Surdna Foundation
New York, NY

Nancy Cantor
Chancellor & President
Syracuse University
Syracuse, NY

Henry G. Cisneros
Executive Chairman
City View
San Antonio, TX

Carol Coletta
President and CEO
CEOs for Cities
Chicago, IL

Michael Ettlinger
Director, Economic Analysis and
    Research Network
Economic Policy Institute
Washington, DC

Jeffrey A. Finkle
President & CEO
International Economic Development
    Council
Washington, DC

Mick Fleming
President & CEO
The American Chamber of
    Commerce Executives (ACCE)
Alexandria, VA

William W. Ginsberg
President & CEO
Community Foundation for
    Greater New Haven
New Haven, CT

Anika Goss-Foster
Director of Philanthropic Affairs
City of Detroit
Detroit, MI

Daniel C. Gundersen
Co-Chair, Empire State Development
   Corporation; Commissioner, NYS
   Department of Economic
   Development
Buffalo, NY

Carlton Jenkins
Partner
Yucaipa Corporate Initiatives Fund
Los Angeles, CA

William A. Johnson, Jr.
Distinguished Professor
   of Public Policy
Rochester Institute of Technology
Rochester, NY

Matt Kane
Senior Policy Analyst
Northeast Midwest Institute
Washington, DC

Greg LeRoy
Executive Director
Good Jobs First
Washington, DC

Harold Miller
President
Future Strategies, LLC
Pittsburgh, PA

Dede Myers
Vice President and Community
   Affairs Officer
Federal Reserve Bank of Philadelphia
Philadelphia, PA

Jeremy Nowak
President and CEO
The Reinvestment Fund
Philadelphia, PA

Manuel Pastor
Professor
Department of Geography
University of Southern California
Los Angeles, CA

Rip Rapson
President and CEO
The Kresge Foundation
Troy, MI

Michael Schewel
Partner
McGuireWoods LLP
Richmond, VA

Marlene B. Seltzer
President and CEO
Jobs for the Future
Boston, MA

William Traynor
Executive Director
Lawrence Community Works
Lawrence, MA

Robert Weissbourd
President
RW Ventures, LLC
Chicago, IL

Nancy L. Zimpher
President
University of Cincinnati
Cincinnati, OH

About The American Assembly

The American Assembly, founded by Dwight D. Eisenhower in 1950, is affiliated with Columbia University. The Assembly is a national, non-partisan public affairs forum that illuminates issues of public policy through commissioning research and publications, sponsoring meetings, and issuing reports, books, and other literature. Its projects bring together leading authorities representing a broad spectrum of views and interests. Assembly reports and other publications are used by government, community, and civic leaders, and public officials. American Assembly topics concern not only domestic and foreign policy, but also issues that include arts and culture, philanthropy, health, business, economy, education, law, race, religion and security.

Contributors

Chris Benner
University of California, Davis

Angela Glover Blackwell
PolicyLink

Pamela Blumenthal
George Washington University

Andres Cruz
Optimal Solutions Group

Laurel Davis
Optimal Solutions Group

Jeffrey A. Finkle
*International Economic
    Development Council*

Mick Fleming
*American Chamber of Commerce
    Executives*

Radhika Fox
PolicyLink

Kimberly Furdell
George Washington University

Shari Garmise
*International Economic
    Development Council*

Edward W. Hill
Cleveland State University

Pauline O. Hovey

Richard Kazis
Jobs for the Future

Randall Kempner
Council on Competitiveness

Daniel Luria
*Michigan Manufacturing
    Technology Center*

Ann Markusen
University of Minnesota

Richard M. McGahey
Ford Foundation

Stephen Moret
*Baton Rouge Area
    Chamber of Commerce*

Shari Nourick
Nourick & Associates

Jeremy Nowak
The Reinvestment Fund

Manuel Pastor
University of Southern California

Joel Rogers
University of Wisconsin

Greg Schrock
University of Illinois at Chicago

Marlene Seltzer
Jobs for the Future

Mark Turner
Optimal Solutions Group

Jennifer S. Vey
Brookings Institution

Rachel Weber
University of Illinois at Chicago

Harold L. Wolman
*George Washington University
    and Brookings Institution*

Index